Arthur Badley Hayes, Samuel D Cox

History of the City of Lincoln, Nebraska

Arthur Badley Hayes, Samuel D Cox

History of the City of Lincoln, Nebraska

ISBN/EAN: 9783744734561

Printed in Europe, USA, Canada, Australia, Japan

Cover: Foto ©ninafisch / pixelio.de

More available books at **www.hansebooks.com**

OF THE

CITY OF LINCOLN

NEBRASKA

WITH BRIEF HISTORICAL SKETCHES OF THE
STATE AND OF LANCASTER COUNTY.

AN ACCURATE COMPILATION OF FACTS AND HISTORICAL DATES, TOGETHER
WITH MANY INTERESTING REMINISCENCES OF THE EARLY
DAYS OF LINCOLN.

*THE LINCOLN OF TO-DAY AND THE TERRITORY OVER WHICH
SHE HOLDS COMMERCIAL SUPREMACY.*

BY

A. B. HAYES AND SAM. D. COX.

LINCOLN, NEB.:
STATE JOURNAL COMPANY, PRINTERS.
1889.

PREFACE.

The authors of this work have undertaken the task of recording the history of Lincoln at this time, because they felt that it was a work that should be performed while it was still possible to get the facts from those who are personally cognizant of them. Even at this time, only twenty-two years away from the founding of the city, much difficulty has been experienced in getting the absolute facts of the early days; and while great care has been taken to secure strict accuracy in all the features of this work, the authors cannot hope to have been entirely successful in their endeavor. But the volume is given to the public with the request that such credit be given to it as is due to work conscientiously and honestly performed. History is made rapidly in this representative city of a wonderfully developing State, and the authors of this work expect to continue in the future the work they have begun in the following pages. They therefore request all who read this volume to notify them of any inaccuracies that may be discovered in its pages, and to communicate to them any facts omitted herein and which would be of interest and value to the people of Lincoln and of the State as a part of the city's history. The authors desire to express their thanks to those persons who have generously assisted in the preparation of these pages, among whom may be mentioned Hon. C. H. Gere, Hon. John Gillespie, Col. Simon Benadom, Hon. Thomas Hyde, Hon. John S. Gregory, Major Bohanan, and others.

CONTENTS.

		PAGE
CHAPTER I.	The Lincoln of To-day	9
II.	Coronado's Discovery of Nebraska	15
III.	Nebraska from Territorial Times	25
IV.	Nebraska's Resources	57
V.	Early Settlement of Lancaster County	67
VI.	Lancaster County Politically	82
VII.	The Salt Basins	90
VIII.	Removal of the Capital to Lincoln	100
IX.	Incidents of the Capital Removal	114
X.	An Interesting Document — The Original Report of the Capital Commissioners	124
XI.	The Village of Lancaster from its Founding to 1867 — Reminiscences of the Early Days	136
XII.	Lincoln from 1867 to 1869	147
XIII.	Lincoln for Twenty Years — The Wonderful Growth into a City	164
XIV.	Lincoln Politically	177
XV.	The Railroads which Enter the City — The great Territory which they lay Tributary to Her	200
XVI.	The State Institutions — The Penitentiary Revolt	213
XVII.	Lincoln as an Educational Center	226
XVIII.	The Churches of the City	247
XIX.	Secret Orders	277
XX.	Irish National League — Sketches of its Prominent Leaders	299
XXI.	Financial Institutions of the city	313
XXII.	The Press of Lincoln	325
XXIII.	Incarceration of the City Council	335
XXIV.	The Tartarrax Pageant	339
XXV.	Formation of the Old Settlers' Association — Its list of members	346
XXVI.	Lincoln's Remarkable growth — Sketches of Some of her Prominent Citizens	357

HISTORY OF THE CITY OF LINCOLN.

CHAPTER I.

The Lincoln of To-day—Why the City has Grown so Rapidly, and why Expectations of Future Growth are Reasonable—The Country Tributary to Lincoln—What Lincoln Really is and has.

A city is builded upon a great water way, where the commerce of half a hundred states may float to its wharves; near the waters of a rapid stream that frets its banks with the impatient power which might turn the busy wheels of a hundred mills; where the generous earth needs but to be asked, to give up for man's uses unlimited stores of baser metals and the fuel with which they may be converted into things of utility and beauty; at the foot of mountains filled with gold and silver that attract thousands of fortune seekers, wild with dreams of sudden wealth, and yield to Fortune's favored few the incomes of princes and kings.

Another city is builded where no vessels float, no water power roars and foams, no coal nor iron nor gold nor silver rewards the delver in the earth; where nature offers no bonus to the favored few, nor cheats the many with the baseless fabric of dreams never to be fulfilled, but with even-handed justice holds out to all the promise of an adequate return for labor faithfully performed.

Capital flows to the first city to take the bonus held out by nature's hand, and builds with the accumulations of other times and other fields, in the hope of an ultimate return. Men to whose imaginations the extraordinary advantages of the place appeal, flock to it in the hope that there they may obtain the reward of labor without the unpleasant necessity of its exercise. It is built from without. Its future is mortgaged to the capitalist — it has borrowed his money instead of making it. Its continuing present is menaced by its poorer citizens, who have come to find wealth, not to produce it. But its growth is rapid, for it holds out the gambler's hope of enormous gains, and appeals to the imagination of the restless emigrant.

The second city attracts little capital from the outside; it has no extraordinary inducements to appeal to capital. The eyes of the country are not turned upon it; it has nothing within it to excite the imagination of the emigrant or fortune hunter. The capital within it is that only which it has itself produced. The residents are only those who have come because of the employment which they have been enabled to find in the ordinary avenues of life.

If these two cities grow side by side, and the second shows the same percentage of growth as the first, which is the more remarkable? the one which has displayed lavish natural advantages to attract capital and excite the imagination of the world, or the one which could only hold out as an incentive the hope of moderate returns for energy and industry?

If these two cities grow at an even pace, which has the more substantial prosperity and the more solid basis for future growth? the one which has been built up from the outside, which has attracted population by vague and extraordinary promises; or the one which has grown out of its own resources, and whose people have come to it because they saw work awaiting them which they were willing to do?

An extraordinary effect ceases to be extraordinary when it is found to follow an extraordinary cause. An extraordinary effect for which no extraordinary cause can be discovered, becomes a phenomenon.

The growth of Lincoln has been more remarkable than that of any other city in the West. It has no fuel, no mines, no water power, no remarkable natural advantages; and yet, on the spot where twenty-one years ago the emigrant, in his lonely covered wagon, scared the timid antelope from its grassy couch, and scanned the horizon with anxious eye to see if he might discover the form of some Indian brave cutting its even line, fifty thousand busy people throng the streets of a great city; a city which reaches 200,000 square miles of territory, and 2,000,000 people, by ten radiating lines of railroad which do a business of nearly a million tons per year, and give employment to 1,350 men; a city which is traversed by thirty-five miles of street railway, and has seven miles of paving, with as much more provided for; twenty miles of sewerage, twenty miles of water mains; a hundred jobbing houses and as many factories; four great State institutions, besides the Capitol; three universities; a million dollars invested in church property; and hundreds of the finest residences in the State.

The growth of Lincoln has not excited widespread interest over the country because there has been nothing sensational connected with it; and yet there is no visitor to the city who does not express the amazement which he feels when he learns its size and importance. Indeed, half the residents of Lincoln are themselves amazed when they drive about the city and see the growth and improvements which have been going on while they slept. The reason of this is that the growth has been due not to extraordinary causes, but to the steady though rapid development of the country of which Lincoln has become the most convenient point to supply. An agricultural region is the richest in the world; but its development is steady and commonplace. Lincoln is the railroad center of as magnificent an agricultural empire as exists in the world; and the whole secret of her great and rapid growth lies in this fact. This growth has been so quiet as hardly to excite comment; but it is as substantial, and certain of continuance, as is that natural and irresistable development in which its roots are driven deep.

The explanation of the growth to greatness, of a city which could boast of no water power, mines, fuel, nor other so-called "natural advantages," lies in the fact that it is commerce, and not manufactures, that builds great cities. Natural advantages may afford the foundation for a limited number of factories; cheap coal may give birth to a few industries in the operation of which fuel is the most expensive item; abundant raw material may attract a few of the factories which use the material; and these factories may support a hundred or a thousand families; if they support five thousand families the limit of population may be little beyond this number. Some of the largest manufacturing institutions in the United States are in small towns. They present no attractions to anybody except to a man who wants to buy a bill of goods and get away, or to the sight seer whose curiosity is of a limited and special character. But commerce knows no natural limitations. Given the means of reaching a great and populous territory, and a commercial city lays under tribute the factories of the world, and turns to its own profit the special advantages that have given rise to a thousand manufacturing towns. It becomes the center to which tradesmen of every kind collect to purchase their wares; to which the members of all professions gather to procure those things which they use in the practice of their vocations; to which the sight seer and the politician gravitate to see the most of things or persons in the shortest time. In the commercial center supply and demand meet in every avenue of life,— mercantile, professional, physical, intellectual, æsthetic, moral. The diversity of interests in such a city becomes its greatest power of attraction; every source of supply seeks there a demand; every demand seeks there a source of supply. There are no waterways west of the Mississippi river which are of service to commerce, and it is at the great railway center, wherever that may by man be placed, that she sets her throne.

It is by virtue of being such a railway center that Lincoln has grown so marvelously; grown in spite of the lack of "natural advantages;" grown in the face of the repeated predictions of her own citizens that no further growth could be looked for. And that growth will continue until the development of the country which her railroads make tributary to her shall cease. The railroad system of most importance to Lincoln is the Burlington & Missouri River Railroad, which has nearly 2,500 miles of track in the State, and almost as much as all the other roads. There is no city in the country so preeminently the center of any railroad as Lincoln is of the B. & M. The road has six lines radiating from Lincoln to every part of the State. It handles all its transferring and reshipping here, as it has no yardage at any other place in the State. Here it has forty-two miles of side track, on which 800 men handle from 1,000 to 2,000 cars a day. Over these radiating roads there run out from Lincoln every week-day thirteen passenger trains and from fifty to seventy-five freight trains. The system girds the entire southern half of the State, and reaches out into northwestern Nebraska by three parallel lines which will occupy three-fourths of the northern half of the State and extend into the mining regions of Wyoming and Idaho, and the cattle ranches of Dakota and Montana. Every pound of merchandise that passes into all this vast territory from eastern points of supply, and every pound of grain, and every hog and steer that goes out of the State over the B. & M. system, passes through Lincoln.

Besides this system, the Elkhorn operates over 960 miles of road in the State, giving Lincoln connection with all the northwestern part of the State to the line; the Union Pacific operates over 875 miles of track, giving Lincoln connection with the Pacific coast and with the southern systems in Kansas; the Missouri Pacific has 400 miles of track in the State, and gives Lincoln a short line to Kansas City, St. Louis, and the Atlantic seaboard, and places the city in direct communication with the southern markets.

In an elaborate review of Lincoln's railroad situation, published March 12, 1888, in a special edition of the *State Democrat*, prepared by one of the authors of this history, it was shown that the population reached *directly* by Lincoln's railroads was 989,591. This was an accurate estimate, made up from the censuses and votes of the counties reached by the roads in Nebraska, Kansas, and Colorado, and did not include any of that vast territory in Colorado, New Mexico, and Wyoming, which is reached by lines connecting with Lincoln's roads, and in which Lincoln jobbers are doing a large and rapidly-increasing business.

There is a philosophy of history; and this brief discussion of the territory tributary to Lincoln, and the city's facilities for reaching it, has been given in recognition of the fact that it is a part of the historian's duty to explain the causes of events, as well as to chronicle events themselves. The value of such historical study is in enabling the student to make the past foreshadow the future; and the following summary of the possibilities of Lincoln's growth, taken from the article referred to above, is deduced from the study made therein:

"But it may be asked what grounds there are on which to expect that the country tributary to Lincoln will increase so steadily and rapidly in population as to build up a great commercial center here. The reply is that nearly all this territory is the very best kind of agricultural land, and that such land is too valuable to be idle. This, we take pains to say again, is not mere assertion. The settlement of the western counties of Nebraska has been and is marvelous. A few examples are given below, with authentic figures showing the population in 1880, in 1885, and in 1887, together with the population that the same territory would have at thirty-five per square mile:

COUNTIES.	Population in 1880.	Population in 1885.	Population in 1887.	Pop. at thirty-five per sq. mile.
Blaine (unorganized in 1880)		275	1521	25200
Brown (unorganized in 1880)		6689	16971	80640
Chase	70	170	5196	30240
Cheyenne	1558	1653	13800	275625
Cherry (unorganized in 1880)		2619	8500	195300
Custer	2211	12399	21600	90720
Dawes (unorganized in 1880)		2516	10000	47880
Sheridan (unorganized in 1880)		2919	10000	86310
Total	3839	29240	87591	831915

"These figures are accurate, although one who is unacquainted with the development of the great West might well imagine that they were the creation of some statistical romancer. Here is a region, nearly all of which was so sparsely settled as to be unorganized in 1880, now supporting a population of 87,591; an empire which would easily support 800,000 people. The estimate of thirty-five per square mile is not an extravagant one. Kentucky has forty people per square mile; Indiana and Illinois have each fifty-four; Ohio has seventy-seven; New York has 103; Connecticut has 124; and Rhode Island has 243. If Cheyenne county had as many people per square mile as Rhode Island, her population would be 1,918,620.

"Is it any wonder that Nebraska villages have grown into cities in a few years? Is there any reason to doubt that this growth is but the substantial and inevitable result of the development of the State? Is there any reason to doubt that Lincoln will become a great city when the 1,000,000 people now directly tributary may be swelled to 5,000,000 without making the population more dense than that now supported by Indiana and Illinois?"

CHAPTER II.

EARLY NEBRASKA—ITS DISCOVERY IN 1540—THE EARLY LEGENDS OF THE LAND OF QUIVERA—CORONADO'S VISIT—THE EXPLORATIONS OF PENALOSA—THE POINTS REACHED BY THESE FIRST VISITORS TO NEBRASKA.

Nebraska as a State is comparatively new. As a country its history dates back centuries, covered partly by the records of the priests, the old-time chroniclers, and partly by the legends which have come down to us through generations from the old Spanish settlers in Mexico, and the Indians who inhabited the land. The early history of Nebraska is a part of the history of all this western country, extending from the Missouri river to the Rocky mountains, and from the Platte river to the Rio Grande, and westward into Mexico. Around and over all this region is thrown the glamour and halo of the early days of chivalry in America, and the tales the legends tell are vague and weird enough to form the climax of any tale of chivalry, romance, or discovery. Away back three centuries and a half ago begins the legendary history of Nebraska. At that time the Land of the Sun, Mexico, had been taken possession of by the Spaniards, and from the City of Mexico exploring parties were wont to take their trips of discovery and exploration, led hither and thither by the frequent stories of wealth and splendor told the people by Indians who had strayed into that southern capital, or had been captured by the Spaniards in some of their frequent raids into the adjacent territories. Legend has it that years before the first recorded date, troops of Spanish cavaliers, traveling northward, entered a vast territory of grassy plains, crossed by broad rivers, which was said to be the home of a wonderfully wealthy people, whose cities, rich beyond compare, numbered seven. Later research has shown that some of these expeditions undoubtedly crossed what is now the northern boundary line of Kansas, and camped and traveled within the territory now known as Nebraska.

As early as 1536, legendary history tells us, the Spaniards in Mexico had heard fairy tales of a land far to the northward, called Quivera — a land of unlimited wealth, of populous cities with lofty dwellings and stores fairly glittering with gold and silver and precious gems, whose people lived in a style of grandeur unknown in this country, and who were highly civilized, and acquainted with the arts. In the year 1536 four men, half starved and worn with toil, heat, cold, shipwrecks, and battles with the natives, reached the City of Mexico from the mountains and plains of the north. These four men were all that were left of a band of four hundred Spaniards that eight years before had landed on the coast of Florida, for the purpose of exploring that unknown country. That company of troops had traveled to the northwestward many weary years, but hunger, toil, and conflicts with the hostile tribes of Indians they met, had reduced the ranks to the four, whose coming into the City of Mexico, and the marvelous tales they told, excited the curiosity of the people. This band of four hundred had evidently traversed the country from the southeast as far north as Kansas, and west through Colorado. The stories of these four men confirmed the legends that had been handed down among the Mexicans for many generations, and if they had been doubted before, none now dared to dispute the existence to the northward of a country such as had been pictured to them.

From this time forward we have not to depend upon legends only, for the events following this date were recorded, possibly inaccurately, by the priests, who were the historians of the time. Immediately following the arrival of these toil-worn explorers at the City of Mexico, an expedition was fitted out under the leadership of Marcos de Niza, a Franciscan monk, and sent to discover and report upon these mysterious cities and pave the way for Spanish colonization. Friar Marcos, the commander, soon became discouraged and disheartened by the cruelty practiced upon his band of soldiers by the natives, who slew many of them, and turned back, but not wanting his comrades at home to think him the coward that he was, he instructed his soldiers, who were ready for any scheme that would end their marching, to say that they had really seen the seven cities of Cibola from afar, and that they were more populous and far more wealthy than had ever been told. These tales again excited Spanish curiosity and cupidity and at once a larger and more powerful expedition was fitted out under the command of the Viceroy of Mexico, Francisco Vasquez de

Coronado. This expedition marks the time when Nebraska was really discovered — the discovery which history records.

Judge Savage, of Omaha, has spent much time and labor in collecting the scattered information to be had upon this early discovery, and from his account many of the facts and incidents of this expedition, and also his conclusions as to the points visited by Coronado and other explorers, are used. According to the authorities upon this subject, Coronado's expedition, composed of three hundred Spaniards and eight hundred natives, set out from the City of Mexico early in the spring of 1540, with bright anticipations and sanguine hopes. These were somewhat dampened by the hardships of the way, for the country traversed was rough, mountainous, and a desert; and now and then, notwithstanding the marvels of the seven cities which they expected to find at the end of their journey, distrust and homesickness overmastered their curiosity, and they longed to return home. It was only the stern resolution of their commander which prevented the expedition being a failure almost at the very start. But at last, after a tedious and toilsome march, what were thought to be the seven cities of Cibola were reached, and here the disappointment was so great that a mutiny was almost successful. And the soldiers were really not to blame, for the highly-colored tales had all proved false. The seven cities were seven hamlets; the houses were small; gold was not found; the minerals were of little value; and farms there were in Mexico far better and richer than all of Cibola.

But the fitting out of the expedition had cost too much money to thus come to an ignoble end, and Coronado began to inquire if there were not other cities, richer and more populous, which it would be profitable to visit. The natives, eager to get rid of their Spanish visitors, answered in the affirmative. Two hundred and fifty miles to the eastward, they said, was a rich, peaceful, and populous province, where their desire for wealth and ambition for power might be gratified. Following the directions given, Coronado led his little army to this new locality, a point which is identified to-day by its natural characteristics and by its ruins, as being the country which is now the eastern part of the Territory of New Mexico, and not far south of the present site of Santa Fé. Here the natives gave the Spaniards a cordial and sincere welcome, they being of a gentle and kindly nature, in return for which the Spaniards treated them with the utmost cru-city. Having been instructed by the Spanish viceroy to let these people (meaning the inhabitants of the cities of Cibola) know that there was "a God in Heaven," Coronado proceeded to instruct the natives, first by stealing everything they had, then by imprisoning the chiefs of the leading tribes, and lastly, by burning their villages. Not satisfied with these outrages, Coronado's soldiers made inroads upon the families of their entertainers, debauching their wives and children. Notwithstanding these acts of "Christian charity," the natives still treated the Spanish troopers with what kindness they could, but naturally schemed for some way by which they could rid themselves of their unwelcome and unbidden guests, in which they were finally successful.

One of these natives, willing to sacrifice his life for the salvation of the rest, and with a self-sacrificing spirit wonderful for a savage, took upon himself the task of carrying the scheme agreed upon into operation. Early one morning he suddenly appeared before Coronado, with much mystery in his movements, and great pretended hostility to the natives. He described a far-off country with such eloquence of language that the country pictured surpassed all previous imaginings of the Spaniards. The man came, he said, from a land far to the northeast, where there was a river seven miles in width. "Within its depths were huge fishes as large as horses, and upon its broad bosom floated canoes which carried twenty oarsmen on a side; huge vessels with sails which bore upon their prow a golden eagle, and upon the poop a sumptuous dias, whereon their lords were wont to sit beneath a canopy of cloth of gold. That every day the monarch of this favored region, named Tartarrax, long bearded, gray haired, and rich, took his noontide sleep in a garden of roses under a huge spreading tree, to the branches of which were suspended innumerable golden bells, which sounded in exquisite harmony when shaken by the wind; that this king prayed by means of a string of beads, and worshiped a cross of gold and the image of a woman, the queen of Heaven; that throughout the land the commonest utensils were of wrought silver, and the bowls, plates, and porringers, of beaten gold. This land of plenty, he said, was

THE KINGDOM OF QUIVERA,

And thither he waited to conduct his friends whenever they should be pleased to accompany him."

The tale was well concocted, and told with consummate skill. The king being pictured as a man who worshiped after the fashion of the men to whom the tale was told, naturally made them more ready to believe, and the stories of such magnificent wealth, pictured with every appearance of honesty, made them eager to conquer the land. Coronado, while a brave, intrepid, and ambitious man, was superstitious, and had a wonderful belief in signs and omens. In his youthful days he had made the acquaintance of an Arabian sage, who, after long study and travel in the East, where he had collected the knowledge and skill in necromancy supposed to be native there, had taken up his residence in the city of Salamanca, Coronado's birthplace. To this sage Coronado intrusted the duty of looking into the future and telling him what was in store for him in the years to come. After consulting his sacred parchments and communing with the supernatural beings who had imparted to him their wisdom, the necromancer received Coronado, and gave to him what the gods said was in store for him. The mystic forces which reveal future events to mortals he said foretold that the then young Salamancan student should one day become the lord of a great and distant country; but the portents thenceforward were gloomy and sinister; they foretold that a fall from his horse would end his life.

This made a strong impression on Coronado's mind, which grew as the years passed, and as he stood in the midst of the vast prairie which stretched beyond the vision of the eye on every side, surrounded by only a handful of dissatisfied, jealous, restless men, and listened to the marvelous tale of the Indian, who had volunteered to guide him to the fabled realm where wealth was piled mountain high, no wonder that the fate predicted by the sage of Salamanca came to his remembrance. The first prophecy had come true—he was the lord of a great and distant land;—and how soon would the second one prove true? But the story of the Indian was so straightforward, and he stood the rude cross-examination of the Spaniards so well, that Coronado threw his fears to the wind, and determined to make this last attempt to find the kingdom of Quivera and the seven cities of Cibola. So on the 5th day of May, 1541, Coronado and his army quitted the valleys which they had terrorized and "Christianized" so thoroughly, crossed the Pecos river from Santa Fé, and soon entered upon the treeless prairies of what is now Indian Territory and the State of Kansas. Across mighty plains so bare and treeless that the adventurers had to make large piles of buffalo chips to guide them on their return, they made their way for 800 miles northeasterly, to the banks of a considerable river, which is admitted by all who have studied the route and the distance traveled to have been the Arkansas.

At this point of the march a soldier named Castaneda, ignorant and credulous, but pious, became the historian, and he records the story of this weary march. Its weariness may be imagined by thinking of this band of soldiers, clad in the heavy armor of the times, plodding its way through the long summer days over the burning plains of Kansas, grim and silent, each one counting his steps, the more accurately to compute the distance passed. And the picture has a tinge of sadness hanging over it — a pathetic tint coloring both the foreground and the perspective.

But the adventurous knights seem to have had some little amusement to beguile the weary hours — their regular amusement of robbery. On one occasion it is related of them that finding a village with an enormous quantity of skins, they cleaned it out so thoroughly and expeditiously that within fifteen minutes there was not a skin left. The Indians tried to save their precious possessions by force of arms, and the entreating tears of the squaws, but neither availed.

Coronado at first, it will be remembered, had been suspicious of his guide, but had conquered his fears and suspicions. Now again these same suspicions became aroused in Coronado's mind, and they quickly spread among his troops. It was noticed that when they met with the wandering nomads of the plains, if the Turk, as they called the guide, was the first to meet and converse with them, they confirmed his stories, and pointed to the eastward as the true course, whereas if communication was prevented, the tribes knew nothing of the riches and splendor of the land of Quivera, and insisted that the country lay to the north instead of to the east.

Coronado, therefore, seeing that the guide had deceived him, and that with the exception of the meat of the buffalo provisions were growing scarce, called a council of war to consider with his captains and lieutenants the best plans to adopt for the future. It was there decided that the general, with thirty of his bravest and best mounted men and six foot soldiers, should proceed northward in search of the land of Quivera, while the main body of the army should return to the vicinity of the Pecos river. So, with the Turk securely bound, and with guides selected from the Indian tribes, Coronado recommenced his march.

Northward from the Arkansas river for many weary hours the little band pursued its way over the Kansas plains. July had come; the days were long and hot, and the nights sultry. But dogged perseverance and good horses brought them at last to the southern boundary of Nebraska. And near there, along the Platte river, they again found the long-sought kingdom of Quivera, with Tartarrax the hoary-headed ruler of the realm. But alas for their expectations! Their dreams of glory and conquest had a most rude awakening. The only precious metal that they saw was a copper plate hanging from the old chief's breast, by which he set great store, and which he seemingly regarded as a god. There were no musical bells, no golden eagle, no silver dishes, no indications of a religious worship—the light of truth had dispelled the dreams of magnificence. Coronado hung his guide, but the guide met death bravely, and with his last breath declared that he knew of no gold, of no cities, of no realm of magnificent riches, and that he had led the Spaniards away from his people that they might be free from persecution and spoliation. In August, Coronado, after erecting a cross which bore the inscription,

"Francisco Vasquez de Coronado, general of an expedition, reached this place,"

set his face southward and passed out of the land of Quivera; but Nebraska had been discovered.

THE NEXT EXPEDITION.

For one hundred and twenty-one years the great plains of Nebraska were untrodden by the feet of any save the Indian tribes that for centuries had roamed from the Missouri to the Rockies. Their buffalo-skin tents formed the only cities, and the battles of the various tribes the only excitement on the prairies, except the chase of the buffalo and deer, and the festive pranks of the storm-king. For a century and nearly a quarter, the copper-colored wild man of the prairie held sway undisputed in his possession of the land. In the year 1662 another visit was made to Quivera, which has been recorded by the Spanish historians, and is the second visit of which record is made, the latter visit and the points reached being more easily determinable than of the first in 1541.

The second civilized man to set his foot upon the soil of Nebraska whose visit has been recorded in authentic history, was a soldier, a knight of Spain, Don Diego, Count of Penalosa. This knight, who belonged to that period marked by all the glitter, romance and adventure which throw such a charm over the sixteenth and seventeenth centuries, was not a Spaniard, but a Creole; that is, one of American birth but Spanish descent. He was born at Lima, South America, in 1624, and after a career of wonderful vicissitudes, finally left his native continent and drifted northward to Mexico. Here he came into high favor with the Viceroy of the country, who made him, at the age of thirty-six, Governor and Captain-General of New Mexico. This was a most responsible position; but once settled in it, Penalosa became again restive, and sought to perform some feat which would bring him everlasting glory and renown. Quivera was then the same goal of bright prospects that it had been to Coronado, and to that fabled country this knight resolved to force his way. So on the 6th of March, 1662, while the colonists in New England and Virginia were laying the foundations of an empire that has since taken in Quivera, and not only that but thousands of square miles beyond, this Spanish knight set out from Santa Fé to explore the regions to the north and east, to accumulate precious stones and metals, to annex a vast territory to his domains, to conquer the fabled opulent cities, and to win for himself renown and added power and influence at the Spanish court.

He set out with a great company of soldiers, Indians, and retainers, two score of baggage wagons carrying his trappings and provisions, and six cannon with which to batter down the walls of the cities of Cibola when he should reach them. A friar, Nicholas de Freytas, was the historian of this expedition, and gives with much elaborateness and detail the events of the march northward, the disappointment, disaster, and return of Penalosa. After proceeding for several weeks along the route laid out, the little Spanish army found itself confronted by a mighty river, along which dwelt an Indian nation who were called the Escanzaquas, the residence of this nation being near the fortieth parallel of latitude. This nation was at war with the Indians of Quivera, and when Penalosa arrived were just on the point of starting northward to give their enemies battle. The force of the Escanzaquas numbered about 3,000, and immediately upon his arrival Penalosa joined this force and accompanied the Indians on their journey. For a day this army marched westwardly along the right bank of a mighty, rushing river, until it made a bend so that its current came from the north. For another day the march was continued to the northward, until toward evening the soldiers perceived across the river, now flowing eastward again, a high ridge whose sides were covered with signal fires, which showed that the natives were aware of their approach. Still marching forward, following the curves of the river, the little army came to a spot where, on the opposite side, another river, flowing from the ridge, entered the stream previously followed. Here was found a very populous city — one of the cities of Quivera — of vast extent. The chiefs of Quivera came over the river to welcome the Spaniards, and showed them every mark of esteem; but on that same night the Escanzaquas crossed the river, burned the city, and put thousands of the Quiverans to death. The next day the Spaniards spent some time in extinguishing the flames, admiring the vast number of dwellings and the great fertility of the soil, and in hunting for the fabled wealth of Quivera. After spending some time in this search and finding nothing, Penalosa, on the 11th of June, 1662, turned his troops southward and departed for his Mexican home.

To what points these expeditions penetrated has been the subject of much contention and of much difference of opinion. But none claim that Coronado failed to enter this State some distance, and none dispute that Penalosa reached the Platte. At just what point the Platte was touched, or at what point Nebraska was penetrated, is the dispute.

As to the visit of Coronado: The most generally accepted opinion, based upon the description of the country, its grasses, animals, and general topography, is that Coronado entered the State somewhere between Gage county on the east and Furnas county on the west, probably east of the present location of Superior, Nuckolls county. Authorities differ as to the distance and direction traveled by Coronado; but the opinion of Gen. Simpson and of Mr. Gallatin is that the Republican river was crossed and the march taken in a northeasterly direction, and that the northern point reached was somewhere west of and on nearly the same parallel with the present site of Lincoln. The Spanish cavalier evidently did not reach the salt basin, or his chronicler would have noted the peculiar appearance of the country, and the presence of the salt. Coronado himself states that his expedition reached beyond the fortieth degree of north latitude, but how much further can only be judged by the description of the country traversed, the streams crossed, and the direction of the line of march. The recent finding of Spanish stirrups, bridle-bits, and other horse trappings of Moorish pattern, near the Republican, buried deep in the ground, while it does not prove that so early a visit was made to Nebraska, does indicate that the Spaniards, hundreds of years ago, traversed the region now embraced in the State, and left traces of their presence.

The point reached by Penalosa has not so much to do with the present treatise; but without entering upon any discussion of the reasons for the location, it seems to be the most generally accepted theory that Penalosa reached the Platte at or near the spot now occupied by the city of Columbus.

It will be noticed that the land of Quivera was located by these early explorers in a half dozen different places, each spot being discarded on fresh reports of wealthy regions "just beyond," and the Quivera of tradition never was discovered. But the legends spurred on those early explorers mile after mile, league after league, northward from their southern home, until they had crossed the line that brought them within the confines of the State of Nebraska. The realm of Quivera is now a reality, and the seven cities of Cibola are legion. The dreams of the Spaniards have come true, and in this land, visited by them centuries ago, are found the gold and silver, the populous cities, the magnificent houses, the wealth and civilization, of the fabled kingdom of Tartarrax.

CHAPTER III.

NEBRASKA FROM TERRITORIAL TIMES—THE FIRST OFFICERS UNDER THE TERRITORIAL ORGANIZATION, AND A LIST OF STATE OFFICERS FROM THE BEGINNING TO THE PRESENT TIME—THE PRESENT STATE OFFICIALS.

In 1673 the domain of modern Nebraska was claimed by Spain. It was a part of the great Northwest Territory, then but dimly known or appreciated. In 1683 LaSalle claimed this region in the name of the king of France. In 1762 the French formally relinquished Louisiana to Spain; but it was receded to France in 1800, and Napoleon Bonaparte sold it to the United States, a master stroke of good policy on the part of the great Frenchman, and an act which alone would serve as a foundation for the fame of Thomas Jefferson. The sale was ratified by the United States October 31, 1803. The formal transfer was made December 20, 1803. On the 26th of March, 1804, Congress divided the territory into two sections, the southern portion being named "The Territory of Orleans," and the northern, "The District of Louisiana." Nebraska was included in the District of Louisiana, as was the domain lying west of the Mississippi, north of Louisiana, as far west as claimed by the United States, including Minnesota. This magnificent territory, of 1,122,975 square miles, was organized as the "Territory of Louisiana," under an act of Congress passed March 3, 1805. St. Louis was made the capital, and President Jefferson promptly selected General James Wilkinson for Governor, and Frederick Bates for Secretary. These two officials, together with Judges R. J. Meigs and John B. C. Lucas, of the Supreme Court, were given legislative control of the great Territory.

Great Britain looked with resentful eye upon the success of the United States in getting possession of the splendid Louisiana domain. She had expected to wrest it from Napoleon, but by a swift stroke of diplomacy he placed it beyond her reach. But it was not her intention to give up the great advantages offered by the possession of at least a portion of Louisiana, and she only awaited the time when relief from continental war should enable her to recover the lost advantage. Thomas Jefferson knew this, and with masterly decision and genius he proceeded to do all that lay in his power to seize upon the fullest possible interpretation of the stipulations with Bonaparte. To that end he set up a government under General Wilkinson, as related. He at once organized an expedition under the command of Captains Merriweather Lewis and William Clarke, known as the Lewis and Clarke Expedition, to go into this unexplored region by way of the Missouri and Columbia rivers, in order to claim portions of the territory by virtue of discovery, to estimate its resources, and find a short and practicable route to the Pacific ocean. This party of forty-three men left the Mississippi one mile below the mouth of the Missouri river on Monday, May 14, 1804. On the 21st of July the expedition camped at the mouth of the Platte river, and the next day stopped near Bellevue. On the 2d of August, a council with chiefs of the Otoe and Missouri Indians of the Platte country was held, on the site of Fort Calhoun, in Washington county.

The party proceeded northward, stopping near the mouth of the Niobrara river, on Nebraska soil for the last time until its return, in 1806, after having made its way through a trackless wilderness for over four thousand miles, in going and returning.

The first permanent settlement upon the present territory of Nebraska was made by the American Fur Company, at Bellevue, in 1810, under the leadership of Col. Peter A. Sarpy, a shrewd, bold, and enterprising Frenchman. In 1842 John C. Fremont made a path across the Territory, up the Platte valley, and in 1847 the Mormons widened the trail in finding their way to the "promised land." About 1850 the great rush to the California gold fields opened the great highway across Nebraska never to be discontinued, and exhibited the splendid possibilities of the "Platte country" to a class of men who did not fail to let the light of Nebraska's great natural resources, which they had seen, shine before the Eastern States in after years, when the craze for the golden West had subsided. In 1847 the Presbyterian church established a mission at Bellevue. In 1848 Fort Kearney was planted by the Government, on the present site of Nebraska City, but was afterward removed to Kearney county, taking the name of Fort Childs, but later the name of Fort Kearney.

Congress made an effort to organize a Territory west of Iowa and

Missouri in 1851-2, which failed, owing to the clash of party zeal for and against the spread of slavery.

In 1852-3 a bill was introduced to create "Platte Territory," comprising all of the present domain of Kansas and all of Nebraska south of the Platte River. This bill went to the House Committee on Territories, which reported a bill creating the same domain into Nebraska Territory. The people of Iowa were anxious to have the new Territory directly west of their border, and to that end such of them as were interested in having a good field for schemes of emigration, sent Hadley D. Johnson, of Council Bluffs, to Washington to induce Congress to readjust the boundaries of the proposed Territory. Through his zealous activity two Territories were recommended by the committee instead of one, in the famous Kansas-Nebraska Bill, which developed such a bitter war between the slavery and anti-slavery parties, in Congress and out.

Finally, Nebraska was organized as a Territory on May 30, 1854, with an area of 351,558 square miles. It reached from the 40th parallel of north latitude to the present boundary of the British possessions, and from the Missouri river westward to the summit of the Rocky mountains. On February 28, 1861, 16,035 square miles were cut off to be attached to Colorado, and on March 2, 1861, 228,907 square miles were set apart for Dakota. Finally, on March 3, 1863, another slice was taken off to form Idaho Territory. This was the final change in the area of Nebraska Territory, and consisted of 45,999 square miles.

President Franklin Pierce appointed as officers for the new Territory, the following: For Governor, Francis Burt, of South Carolina; for Secretary, Thomas B. Cuming, of Iowa; for Chief Justice, Fenner Furguson, of Michigan; and for Associate Justices, James Bradley, of Indiana, and Edward R. Harden, of Georgia; for Marshal, Mark W. Izard, of Arkansas; and for Attorney, Experience Estabrook, of Wisconsin.

Governor Burt reached Bellevue, the Territorial capital, October 7, 1854. He took the oath of office on October 16th, and died there October 18, 1854. Secretary Cuming became the acting Governor.

The Territory was divided into the eight counties of Burt, Washington, Dodge, Douglas, Cass, Pierce, Forney, and Richardson. One or more voting precincts were established in each of these counties.

An enumeration of the Territorial inhabitants was made in October, 1854, for Legislative representation. According to this, each county was entitled to one Councilman, except Douglas, which was entitled to four, and Pierce, which had three. Burt, Washington, Dodge, Forney, and Richardson, each had two Representatives. Douglas had eight, Cass three, and Pierce five. The first general election took place on December 12, 1854, and the first Legislature met at Omaha, whence the capital had been removed, on January 16, 1855. This pioneer body was composed of the following-named gentlemen:

THE FIRST COUNCIL.

RICHARDSON COUNTY—J. L. Sharp, *President*.

BURT COUNTY—B. R. Folsom.

WASHINGTON COUNTY—J. C. Mitchell.

DODGE COUNTY—M. H. Clark.

DOUGLAS COUNTY—T. G. Goodwill, A. D. Jones, O. D. Richardson, S. E. Rogers.

CASS COUNTY—Luke Nuckolls.

PIERCE COUNTY—A. H. Bradford, H. P. Bennett, C. H. Cowles.

FORNEY COUNTY—Richard Brown.

OFFICERS OF THE COUNCIL.—Dr. G. L. Miller, of Omaha, Chief Clerk; O. F. Lake, of Brownville, Assistant Clerk; S. A. Lewis, of Omaha, Sergeant-at-Arms; N. R. Folsom, Tekamah, Doorkeeper.

HOUSE OF REPRESENTATIVES.

DOUGLAS COUNTY—A. J. Hanscom, *Speaker*; W. N. Byers, William Clancy, F. Davidson, Thomas Davis, A. D. Goyer, A. J. Poppleton, and Robert Whitted.

BURT COUNTY—J. B. Robertson, A. C. Purple.

WASHINGTON COUNTY—A. Archer, A. J. Smith.

DODGE COUNTY—E. R. Doyle, J. W. Richardson.

CASS COUNTY—J. M. Latham, William Kempton, J. D. H. Thompson.

PIERCE COUNTY—G. Bennet, J. H. Cowles, J. H. Decker, W. H. Hail, and William Maddox.

FORNEY COUNTY—W. A. Finney, J. M. Wood.

RICHARDSON COUNTY—D. M. Johnston, J. A. Singleton.

OFFICERS OF THE HOUSE.—J. W. Paddock, Chief Clerk; G. L.

Eayre, Assistant Clerk; J. L. Gibbs, Sergeant-at-Arms; B. B. Thompson, Doorkeeper.

Napoleon B. Gidding was elected delegate to Congress at the same election that the Legislature was chosen.

The several counties were divided into three Judicial Districts.

A capitol building was completed in Omaha in January, 1858.

Mark W. Izard was appointed Governor in February, 1855, and William A. Richardson in April, 1857, who resigned in 1858. J. Sterling Morton was then Secretary, and became the acting Governor until the appointment of Samuel Black, in 1859. He closed the line of Democratic Governors for Nebraska, and was succeeded by Alvin Saunders, of Mt. Pleasant, Iowa, who was appointed by Abraham Lincoln, in 1861. Governor Saunders was succeeded by David Butler, in 1867, when Nebraska became a State.

The question of organizing a State government was voted on in March, 1860, and the people rejected the proposition to erect a State, by a vote of 1,987 to 1,877. Congress passed the enabling act in 1864 for the admission of Nebraska. The Territorial Legislature framed a constitution in 1866, which was ratified at an election held on June 21st of the same year. Congress passed an admission act July 28th, which was vetoed by Andrew Johnson, who vetoed a similar bill in January, 1867; but it was passed over his veto on February 8th and 9th. There was one condition to this act: Nebraska must assent to "no denial of the elective franchise, or any other right, to any person by reason of race or color." The Legislature promptly ratified this condition, on February 20th, and President Johnson proclaimed this compliance on March 1, 1867.

As soon as the State was admitted, the Legislature decided to remove the capital from Omaha, which was accomplished by commissioners, in October, 1867. A small hamlet named Lancaster, in Lancaster county, was chosen by the commissioners and approved by the Legislature. The new capital was named Lincoln, after Abraham Lincoln.

NEBRASKA AS A STATE.

David Butler had been elected Governor of the proposed new State in 1866, and now entered upon his duties as the first Governor of the State. He was reëlected October 8, 1868, and October 13, 1870, but was impeached and removed from office on June 2, 1871, and Secreretary William H. James acted as Governor until after the regular election of 1872. Robert W. Furnas was then elected Governor, and installed on January 13, 1873. He was succeeded in 1875 by Silas Garber, who was re-elected, and served until January 9, 1879, when Albinus Nance was inducted into the office, and held it until January 4, 1883. James W. Dawes was the State's Chief Executive thence until succeeded by John M. Thayer, January 6, 1887, who is now serving his second term. Gov. Thayer is one of Nebraska's citizens most distinguished for long and honorable service. He was born in Bellingham, Massachusetts, and is the son of Elias and Ruth (Staples) Thayer. He graduated from Brown University, in 1847, having studied law. He removed to Nebraska in 1854, and settled at Omaha, near where he farmed for several years. He entered politics in 1855, becoming a candidate for Congress, but was beaten by Fenner Ferguson, perhaps the most successful politician of Territorial times in Nebraska. He was defeated for the same office in 1860 by Samuel G. Daily, but was elected to the Territorial Legislature in 1860, and served during the term of 1860–1.

In 1855 he was elected Brigadier-General of the Territorial militia by the Legislature, and that year led a company of 150 men against the troublesome Pawnee Indians, and again in 1859 led 194 men, with a piece of artillery, against the same Indians, capturing an entire camp. He was also employed in peace negotiations with the Indians. This gave him quite a military experience.

In 1861 he was instrumental in raising and organizing the First Regiment of Nebraska Volunteer Infantry, of which he was commissioned Colonel. After seeing some service in Missouri, he was sent with a brigade to help Gen. Grant at Fort Donelson, commanding the Second Brigade of Wallace's Division in that battle, and also at the battle of Shiloh. For able and gallant conduct in these two memorable actions he was promoted to the rank of Brigadier-General. At the time Sherman stormed Chickasaw bayou, in his attempt to approach Vicksburg from the north, General Thayer led one of the most important of the storming columns, having a horse shot under him. He participated in the Vicksburg Campaign, helped Sherman to capture Jackson, and then assisted to reduce Pemberton at Vicksburg. Here he was appointed Major-General of Volunteers for gallant conduct. Subsequently he was engaged in a campaign with

GOV. JOHN M. THAYER.

General Steele in Arkansas, and near the close of the war he was placed in command of the Army of the Frontier, to subdue the Indians, who had been terrorizing the West with their barbarities.

He was elected United States Senator for Nebraska by the Legislature of 1866, when it was thought the Territory would be at once admitted as a State; but it not being admitted until the following year, he did not take his seat until March, 1867. He drew the four-year term, and Thomas W. Tipton the six-year term. In 1875 he was appointed Territorial Governor of Wyoming, and served one term.

In 1886 he was elected Governor of Nebraska by about 25,000 majority, and was reëlected in 1888, making about thirty-four years since he began to distinguish himself in the public service of the Territory of Nebraska. He is the most distinguished military man of this State, and is Nebraska's oldest living United States Senator. His military service alone has given him a national reputation.

He was married to Miss Mary T. Allen, a lady of ability and refinement, who was the daughter of the Rev. John Allen, a minister of the Baptist church in Massachusetts. Mr. John M. Thayer jr. is the Governor's private secretary.

The growth of Nebraska has been steady and rapid, as the development of population will indicate. In 1855 the census returns gave the Territory a population of 4,494. In 1856 the inhabitants were set down at 10,716. In 1860 the number had grown to 28,841. By 1870 there were 122,993. In 1875 the population had advanced to 246,280, and by the census of 1880, Nebraska had 452,542 people. In 1885 the enumeration showed an aggregate of 740,645, and the election returns of 1888 indicated a population of about 1,200,000. In other words, the increase from 1870 to 1880 was nearly 300 per centum, and that from 1880 to 1890 will approximate close to 200 per centum. By the year 1900, Nebraska will doubtless have quite 2,000,000 population, and her wealth will have increased accordingly.

In fact, the development of the resources of the State has fully kept pace with the growth of population, and in some features has outrun the rate of settlement.

In 1871 a constitutional convention assembled at the capitol, on June 5th, and adjourned August 19th. The people refused to adopt the constitution framed, on the 19th of the following September. In the summer of 1875, a second convention framed another constitution, which was adopted by the people at the October election following. This constitution provided that there should be eighty-four Representatives and thirty Senators, until 1880, when the number should be regulated by law; but the Senate should not exceed thirty-three and the House should not exceed one hundred. The first Legislature under this constitution assembled on the first Monday in January, 1877. John M. Thayer and Thomas W. Tipton were chosen United States Senators in 1867, the former to serve until 1871, and the latter until 1875. The roster of United States Senators elected since the State was admitted is as follows:

UNITED STATES SENATORS.

John M. Thayer, 1867-71.
Thomas W. Tipton, 1867-75.
Phineas W. Hitchcock, 1871-77.
Algernon S. Paddock, 1875-81.
Alvin Saunders, 1877-83.

C. H. Van Wyck, 1881-87.
Charles F. Manderson, 1883-89.
Algernon S. Paddock, 1887-93.
Charles F. Manderson, 1889-95.

TERRITORIAL DELEGATES IN CONGRESS.

Napoleon B. Gidding, December 12, 1854.
Bird B. Chapman, November 6, 1855.
Fenner Ferguson, August 3, 1857.

Experience Estabrook, October 11, 1859.
Samuel G. Dailey, October 9, 1860.
Phineas W. Hitchcock, October 11, 1864.

NEBRASKA STATE REPRESENTATIVES IN CONGRESS.

T. M. Marquett, 1865-67; the 39th Congress.
John Taffe, 1867-69; the 40th Congress.
John Taffe, 1869-71; the 41st Congress.
John Taffe, 1871-73; the 42d Congress.
Lorenzo Crounse, 1873-75; the 43rd Congress.
Lorenzo Crounse, 1875-77; the 44th Congress.

Frank Welch, 1877. Died in office.
Thomas J. Majors, 1878-9. To fill vacancy.
E. K. Valentine, 1879-81; the 16th Congress.
E. K. Valentine, 1881-83; the 17th Congress.

For the 18th Congress, 1883-85, there were elected:

A. J. Weaver, for the First District.
James Laird, for the Second District.

E. K. Valentine, for the Third District.

For the 19th Congress, 1885-87, there were elected:

A. J. Weaver, for the First District.
James Laird, for the Second District.

George W. E. Dorsey, for the Third District.

For the 50th Congress, 1887-89, there were elected:

John A. McShane, for the first District.
James Laird, for the Second District.

George W. E. Dorsey, for the Third District.

For the 51st Congress, 1889-91, there were elected:

W. J. Connell, for the First District.
James Laird, for the Second District.
George W. E. Dorsey, for the Third District.

Nebraska is in the eighth United States Court Circuit, composed of Minnesota, Iowa, Missouri, Kansas, Nebraska, Arkansas, and Colorado. The court officers for both the United States District and Circuit Courts are as subjoined:

David J. Brewer, Circuit Judge.
Elmer S. Dundy, District Judge.
George E. Pritchell, District Attorney.
Brad D. Slaughter, Marshal.
Elmer D. Frank, Clerk Circuit Court.
Elmer S. Dundy jr., Clerk Dist. Court.

Hon. Brad D. Slaughter, who is now the United States Marshal for the District of Nebraska, was commissioned on the 19th of March, 1889. He is one of the best known public men of this State, and his administrative ability in a position of this kind is hardly excelled by any man in the State.

His father was the Rev. W. B. Slaughter, D. D., and his mother was a daughter of Rev. E. Buck, both ministers being members of the Geneseo Conference of the M. E. Church of New York.

Brad D. Slaughter was born in Wayne county, New York, on November 12, 1844. His father removed to Chicago, where Master Brad was educated in the city public schools, and where he learned the printers' trade and graduated as a newspaper correspondent. For this reason he is always most accommodating to correspondents, as any newspaper man knows who has reported the House during recent Legislative sessions.

He enlisted in the Union army with his father, who was captain of Company G, 39th Illinois Volunteer Infantry, which rendezvoused at Chicago. Afterward he enlisted in Company K, of the 67th Illinois Volunteer Infantry, and gave faithful service to the cause of the Union throughout the war.

At the close of the great conflict he removed to Nebraska City, where he married in 1866. He made his residence in Omaha for a time, and later removed to Lincoln, where he lived until 1879. At the close of the Legislative session of that year he took up his residence in Fullerton, Nance county, which county he had been instrumental in bringing into existence.

He was first elected Chief Clerk of the House of Representatives of the Nebraska Legislature in 1877, and he has held this position at every succeeding term except that of 1885. In this office he distinguished himself for the exceedingly able and thorough management he gave to its intricate affairs. He was also recognized as a very skillful parliamentarian, and many a time he has rescued the House and Speaker from a complication in the proceedings, the run of which he never seemed to lose. The House of the Twenty-first Legislature presented him with a beautiful silver tea service, as a token of the esteem of the members for his careful work as recording officer and the general esteem that body entertained for him personally. He is not a man of many words, and accepted the gift in a brief and pertinent speech, in which he used a sentence substantially like the following: "In all duties I have been called upon to attend to, I have made it a rule to do the work just exactly as near right as I knew how." This sentence contains the explanation of his success and that of all men who sustain themselves in responsible positions.

In 1880 he was appointed Supervisor of the United States census, his district including the entire South Platte section of Nebraska. It fell to his province to appoint, supply, instruct, and obtain reports from 363 enumerators, but his management of this responsible and difficult office was as prudent and efficient as could be possible under the circumstances. Few supervisors performed better service, and of the sixty-one United States Marshals in the United States it may safely be doubted whether one will prove more faithful, able and successful than Marshal Brad D. Slaughter, of Nebraska.

Nebraska as a Territory and a State has had eleven Governors and four acting Governors. The Territorial Governors were as follows:

Francis Burt,[1] October 16, 1854.
Mark W. Izard, February 20, 1855.
W. A. Richardson,[2] January 12, 1858.

Samuel W. Black, May 2, 1858.
Alvin Saunders, May 15, 1861.

The State Governors have been six in number, as follows:

David Butler, February 21, 1867.
Robert W. Furnas, January 13, 1873.
Silas Garber, January 11, 1875.

Albinus Nance, January 9, 1879.
James W. Dawes, January 4, 1883.
John M. Thayer, January 6, 1887.

[1] Died in office, October 18, 1854. Office filled by Secretary Thomas B. Cuming until appointment of Governor Izard.

[2] Resigned, the office being filled by Secretary J. Sterling Morton until arrival of Governor Black.

Elected in 1866, but did not become Governor until February 21, 1867, owing to the delay in admitting Nebraska into the Union. Secretary W. H. James acted as Governor from June 2, 1871, until installation of Governor Furnas, January 13, 1873.

Nebraska has had but five Lieutenant-Governors since she became a State, as follows:

Othman A. Abbott, 1877–79.
Edmund C. Carns, 1879–83.
A. W. Agee, 1883–85.

H. H. Shedd, 1885–89.
Geo. D. Meiklejohn, 1889–91.

The Territorial Secretaries were four in number, three of whom, Cuming, Morton, and Paddock, became acting Governors. They were:

Thomas B. Cuming,[1] August 13, 1854.
John B. Motley,[2] March 23, 1858.

J. Sterling Morton,[3] July 12, 1858.
Alg. S. Paddock,[4] May 6, 1861.

The Secretaries, since Nebraska became a State, have been as noted in the subjoined list:

Thomas P. Kennard, February 21, 1867.
Wm. H. James,[5] January 10, 1871.
John J. Gosper, January 13, 1873.
Bruno Tzschuck, January 11, 1875.

S. J. Alexander, January 9, 1879.
Edward P. Roggen, January 4, 1883.
Gilbert L. Laws, January 6, 1887.

Gilbert L. Laws, now Secretary of State for Nebraska, was the sixth of a family of eleven children, and was born on a farm in Richland county, Illinois, March 11, 1838.

His father, James Laws, was born near Wilmington, North Carolina, in 1801, of Scotch-Irish parentage, his father being a Scotchman and his mother an Irish woman. He removed with his parents to Southern Illinois, and in time, by industry and economy, became a large farmer and stock raiser, supplying in part the Indian Agency at Chicago with beef cattle. The corn from his own and neighboring farms was by him shipped in flat-boats down the Wabash and so on to New Orleans for a market. Opening farms and planting orchards, building houses and bridges, constructing roads and operating mills, taxed not only his own energies, but kept at work a number of men settled about him, who were constantly in his employ.

In religious faith he was a Campbellite, uniting with that church in early manhood.

Politically, he was an ardent Whig, and a great admirer of Henry Clay, becoming in later years a radical Republican, and so intolerant

---

[1] Was Acting Governor from October 18, 1854, to February 20, 1855, and from October 25, 1857, to January 12, 1858. Died March 12, 1858.

[2] Acting Secretary until the arrival of J. Sterling Morton.

[3] Acting Governor from December 5, 1858, to May 2, 1859, and from February 24, 1860, to 1861.

[4] Acting Governor from May, 1861, and so continued during most of the term of Gov. Saunders, or until 1867.

[5] Was Acting Governor from June 2, 1871, to January 13, 1873.

in his views during the war that he regarded every Democrat as a public enemy, and would not exchange the common courtesies of neighbors with any member of that party.

The mother of G. L. Laws was Lucinda Calhoun, a second cousin to the statesman of that name. She was born in Abbeyville, South Carolina, in 1806. She, too, was a Campbellite, and her whole life was sacredly dedicated to the discharge of motherly cares and Christian duties.

G. L. Laws spent the first seven years of his life on his father's farm in Richland county, attending school a few weeks in winter when old enough, dropping corn and helping "shear sheep" in the spring, carrying water and other drinks to "the hands" in summer, and "shucking the down row" in the fall. In school he became somewhat noted as a speller, and was a fair reader, these being the only branches taught boys under ten years of age in those days in that country.

In 1845 the family removed to Iowa county, Wisconsin, bought a tract of land, and opened a farm. Here were no schools, and over five years elapsed before an opportunity offered to attend school again. In 1847 he worked a lead mine on the halves. In 1850 his father traded his farm for a tract of land on the Wisconsin river, where he opened a ferry, now known as "Laws's Ferry," and where he kept a lumber yard, the subject of this tale being obliged to make himself useful as ferryman and salesman in the yard.

In the winter of 1851 and 1852 he chopped cord wood and split rails. Here, in the summer of 1853, he crossed the river and walked three miles morning and evening to attend a district school. In the winter of 1854 he "did chores for his board" and attended the same school. In June, 1855, he left home without consulting the family, for the sole purpose of making it possible to attend better schools for a longer term each year. During June and July he put in a number of weeks of very hard work for a good deacon of a church, for which he received no pay, and this fact may have affected his whole religious life.

During the years 1856 and 1857 he worked a short time on a farm, rafted railroad ties, helped build the Illinois Central with barrow and spade, "rolled sugar" on a steam-boat, cooked for a crew of men in a logging camp, chopped saw-logs, drove saw-logs, and run a saw-mill, rafted and run lumber, landing in St. Louis in August of 1857, with a large "fleet" of lumber, which he could not sell, and was obliged to start a lumber yard in that city, which he did on Ninth street and Cass avenue. His experience as a ferryman, with something of an aptitude for such work, made him an expert riverman, and brought him from $3.00 to $10.00 per day during spring and summer months, rafting lumber down the Wisconsin river to Mississippi towns. After the first winter, during which he was a cook, studying meantime, and receiving much valuable assistance from the "boss," who was a graduate of Yale, he attended school winters and such parts of fall and spring terms as he could until twenty years old, when, after paying yearly some small debts for those in a measure dependent upon him, he found himself the possessor of $300.00 in cash. This fund enabled him to quit the more lucrative but less desirable lines of labor, and turn his attention to teaching school, reversing the order of former years, now working winters and attending school summers. He enjoyed, for longer and shorter terms, the advantages afforded by Hascall University, at Mazo Manie; at Silsby Academy, at Richland City; and at Milton College, all in Wisconsin; but, except the latter, all very poor and without libraries or apparatus. At one of the academies he finished a course in trigonometry and surveying where the only instrument for use was an old surveyor's compass with a broken needle. The teachers were all educated gentlemen, and some of them able men, earnest, honest, and patriotic in their efforts to establish "seats of learning" in the West.

The winter of 1860–61 he was employed as principal of the schools at Richland Center, where he was accredited a very successful teacher.

This was at the opening of the Civil War. "Men and steel" were wanted for national defense. In March, 1861, Mr. Laws signed his name to a paper, pledging his services provided the company was called into service before he became located in the University at Madison, Wisconsin, where he had arranged to complete his education. His school closed on Friday, the 2d of May, and the next morning a dispatch was received calling the company into service.

On such little threads of time and circumstance hang the destinies of men!

Mr. Laws went to the front with his company as its Fourth Sergeant, and with a military life comprising the usual routine, he drifted into the Army of the Potomac, and his regiment was assigned to General Hancock's corps, and with McClellan's great army entered upon the Peninsular Campaign. Almost on the anniversary of his call to the front, May 15, 1862, Mr. Laws was in the field, engaged in the Battle of Williamsburg. He was twice wounded in that action, once in the left arm and again in the left ankle. With 1,200 other wounded men, of both armies and several nationalities, Mr. Laws was taken on board the steamer "Vanderbilt," which was moored above Yorktown, and all were conveyed to Baltimore, Maryland, for hospital care and surgical treatment. On the voyage those twelve hundred men had no aid or care except that given by four Sisters of Charity, who labored for the comfort of the suffering soldiers with an impartial fidelity that was the perfection of heroic Christian fortitude. No man was neglected; all were treated precisely alike. Those faithful women stayed at their posts as long as they could stand up, and the men almost forgot the agonies of their own wounds in grateful admiration of those most noble attendants. Mr. Laws to this day regards their grand devotion to duty as one of the most genuine and splendid exhibitions of human excellence that he has ever known. For eight days Mr. Laws's wounds went without surgical attention. The bones of his ankle being shattered to pieces, the flesh had begun to decompose when treatment was at last begun, and his leg above the ankle had to be amputated. Even with this severe remedy the battle for life was a terrible one, and his friends hardly expected to see him rise from his bed again. He lay on his back in the hot hospital until the processes of his spine protruded, and his flesh wasted away until he weighed but little over seventy pounds.

The ladies of Baltimore carried on the most perfect hospital service organized anywhere in the Nation. Fifteen thousand of them were banded together, and every day they visited every sick and wounded soldier, administering comforts and delicacies until they, in matters of diet, actually killed some of the men with kindness. This they did without regard to which army the soldier fought in. But amongst themselves they enjoyed a partisan hate that was not excelled anywhere in the United States. Under their gracious care Mr. Laws continued from the 13th day of May until the 29th of July, part of the time hovering in the very shadow of the Dark Valley; but his strong constitution enabled him to pass the crisis safely.

On the 29th of July his brother came from Wisconsin and easily took him in his arms to the train which conveyed them back to his home county. In September he was able to get out on crutches, for the first time in over four months. On that day he went to the county seat to attend the Republican county convention, at the earnest solicitation of the loyal people. The moment the convention was organized a resolution was passed, unanimously and amid much enthusiasm, providing that G. L. Laws could take his choice of the county offices, and his selection would be ratified by the people.

Mr. Laws agreed to accept the office of County Clerk, and the nomination was given him by the unanimous voice of the convention. He was elected on November 4, 1862, by a majority of 843, when the average Republican majority of the county was about 300. He was reëlected in 1864, and again in 1866, and served six years in that office. At the expiration of his term he was appointed postmaster of Richland Center, which position he filled with ability until April, 1876, when he resigned for the purpose of removing to Nebraska.

Mr. Laws has enjoyed enough newspaper experience to fully entitle him to wear the badge of the craft. In November, 1863, in company with Samuel C. Hyatt and William J. Waggoner, he bought the Richland County *Observer*. Although this was the first experience of these gentlemen in newspaper work, they made a live and successful paper of it. All were soldiers and fast friends. On May 12, 1864, he sold his interest in the paper to a brother of William J. Waggoner — James H. Waggoner. On August 8, 1867, the *Observer* and *The Live Republican* were consolidated under the name of the Richland County *Republican*, of which Mr. G. L. Laws owned a one-fourth interest, in company with James H. Waggoner, who owned one-half and managed the paper, and C. H. Smith. In a few months Messrs. Laws and Smith sold their interest in the *Republican* to George D. Stevens. On September 1, 1874, Mr. Laws again bought a half interest in the *Republican* from Mr. Waggoner, and he continued a joint proprietor of the paper with W. M. Fogo for two years, and finally sold his interest to O. G. Munson, and so ended his newspaper work until he became a citizen of Nebraska.

Incidentally it may be said that Mr. Laws was ever a very busy man. If he ever had any months of idleness from the age of six years to the present time, the records do not reveal when it was. Besides the evidences of his industry already related, we find him president of the board of town trustees of Richland Center in 1869. About the same time he had a business connection with a real estate firm. During this busy period of his life, if one period could be much more busy than another, he was one of a board of five trustees who gave personal attention to the erection of the First Baptist Church of Richland Center. This structure was of brick, on a high stone basement, and cost $6,000, a very large sum for the pioneers of that locality to raise at that date. The work was delayed from time to time because of a lack of funds, but the trustees held on tenaciously and finally completed the building, which was the finest church structure in the county as late as 1884. The name of G. L. Laws also appears on the roll of Masters of Richland Lodge No. 66, A. F. and A. M., of Richland Center, which was organized in 1856.

In April, 1876, Mr. Laws resigned the office of postmaster of Richland Center, and removed to Nebraska. He located at Orleans, in Harlan county, at which point he purchased the Republican Valley *Sentinel*, and took up the editorial pen for a fourth time. He soon became secretary of the Republican Valley Land Association, which position he held until about 1880, when he was succeeded by J. D. Macfarland, of Lincoln. In 1881 he sold the *Sentinel* to Wenn & Knight. From 1881 he was engaged as a clerk in the land office at Bloomington, and also assisted in a bank at Orleans during a part of this period.

He was appointed and confirmed registrar of the Federal land office at McCook on March 3, 1883, and took possession of that office on June 15th following. He administered the affairs of this responsible post with unquestioned efficiency until he was removed by Grover Cleveland, on November 2, 1886. He had already been nominated by the Republican party of the State for the office of Secretary of State, and on the next day after he left the land office he was elected Secretary of State over Richard Thompson, Democrat, (who ran ahead of his ticket,) by 21,450 votes, the total vote cast being less than 139,-000. Mr. Laws administered the affairs of this very important office with fidelity and success, combining, as it does, responsible relations to nearly all the State institutions, the State Board of Transportation, and other State executive boards, these complex relations calling for large executive ability and sound judgment. He performed the work of his first term so well, however, that he was renominated for a second term by acclamation by the Republican State Convention of 1888, and was re-elected by nearly 28,000 majority. The present administration of Secretary Laws has been able in an eminent degree, and he ranks as one of the very safest and best officials that Nebraska possesses to-day.

Though somewhat out of chronological order, yet, on the principle of reserving the best things for the conclusion, we will here refer to the marriage of Mr. Laws. This took place at the former residence of the bride's father, Mr. Isaac Lawrence, in Bear creek valley, in Richland county, Wisconsin, October 25, 1868. The bride was Miss Josephine Lawrence, and, as Mrs. G. L. Laws, is too well known to Lincoln society to require an introduction. Mr. Laws was one of eleven children. His own children are three in number, all daughters. Their names are Gertrude H., Theodosia C., and Helen Lucile Laws.

The Territorial Auditors were six in number, as follows:

Charles B. Smith, March 16, 1855.
Samuel L. Campbell, August 3, 1857.
William E. Moore, June 1, 1858.
Robert C. Jordan, August 2, 1858.
Wm. E. Harvey, October 8, 1861.
John Gillespie, October 10, 1865.

The State Auditors have been six, Mr. Gillespie continuing from Territorial times into the State administration about six years. The list of State Auditors is as shown below:

John Gillespie, February, 1867.
Jefferson B. Weston, January 13, 1873.
F. W. Liedtke, January 9, 1879.
John Wallichs,[1] November 12, 1880.
H. A. Babcock, January 8, 1885.
Thomas H. Benton, January 3, 1889.

Hon. Thomas H. Benton, the present State Auditor of Nebraska, was installed in the very responsible position he now occupies on the third day of January, 1889. He was then but a little over thirty years of age, the youngest man who ever held such an important office in this State, and one of the few who have been elevated to so high a place of trust in the United States at so early an age. And in making him their choice for Auditor his fellow citizens exhibited a confidence in his ability to discharge the difficult duties of the place that was remarkable, as he received the highest vote of any state officer, notwithstanding the fact that a number of able men and tried officials were associated with him as candidates.

---

[1] Appointed to fill vacancy.

Mr. Benton was born in the city of New Haven, Connecticut, October 17, 1858. His father, William I. Benton, was engaged in the practice of law when a young man, but later in life followed agricultural pursuits. He was a plain, sturdy citizen, and with his wife, Mrs. Emaline Benton, believed in the good old customs and principles for which the descendants of the New England Puritans are distinguished. Both his parents were Americans, possessing the staunch virtues of the people who founded the civilization of the Western world, along the shore of the Atlantic.

The State Auditor spent his boyhood on a farm until he reached the age of ten years, attending to the usual duties of farm life, and at the same time cultivating the advantages afforded by the common schools of the locality where he lived. At the age of ten, and in 1868, his father removed to Nebraska, and located in Fremont, becoming one of the pioneers of the State, and thus initiating his son, the future State Auditor, into the severe school of practical western farm life in the early days of Nebraska. He worked on a farm in summer time, and attended school during winters, at Fremont, until he reached his thirteenth year, when he spent a year, that of 1872-3, at Doane College, at Crete, Nebraska.

In the summer of 1873 young Benton entered a telegraph office at Fremont, where he spent nearly a year, and became a practical operator. The following spring he became recorder in the county clerk's office at Fremont, then in his sixteenth year, and, perhaps, the youngest recorder of important public instruments who ever performed such work in Nebraska. But young Benton always made it a point to do his work well, and filled the position with credit to himself until January 1, 1877, when he secured the position of clerk in the office of State Auditor J. B. Weston. This he filled acceptably until the summer of 1877, when he accepted a place as salesman in the book store of Arthur Gibson, of Fremont. Here he remained until the spring of 1878, when he was given the post of book-keeper for a foundry at Fremont, and discharged the duties of that position until December of that year.

On the first day of January, 1879, at the age of twenty-one years, he was elected second assistant clerk of the House, and discharged the duties of that office with marked ability until the close of February, when he was given the position of book-keeper by State Auditor F. W. Liedtke.

HON. E. H. BENTON, AUDITOR OF STATE.

HON. J. E. HILL, STATE TREASURER.

In this situation Mr. Benton was at home, his ability and skill as an accountant being even at this time beyond question. He continued to occupy this responsible post during the entire term of Auditor Liedtke, and that of his successor, John Wallichs.

On January 7, 1885, H. A. Babcock, then State Auditor, selected Mr. Benton for the position of Deputy State Auditor. In this important trust Mr. Benton acquitted himself with all that thoroughness, prudence and tact which the duties of an efficient administration of the duties of the place required, and to such a degree of success that when he became a candidate for the office of State Auditor, in the summer of 1888, the most searching criticisms of his opponents could not reveal a blemish in his integrity, nor a shortcoming in the execution of the work that had been assigned him. He was nominated against such strong competitors as John Peters, of Albion, and Henry Groshans, of Sutton. His election was accomplished by the highest aggregate vote received by any State officer on the ticket, a circumstance which affords Mr. Benton occasion for a large degree of just pride.

On the third day of January, 1889, Mr. Benton was duly installed in the office of State Auditor of Nebraska, and he has discharged the complex responsibilities of this important position, since that date, with conspicuous fidelity to duty and the high manifestation of esteem expressed for him by the people of the State at the polls.

Hon. Thos. H. Benton is a relative of the famous Senator Thomas H. Benton, of Missouri, who so ably and honorably represented the people of his State in eminent positions of trust for a third of a century.

Mr. Benton was married to Miss Fanny McManigal, of Lincoln, on the 8th of August, 1881, and is a brother-in-law of Hon. G. W. E. Dorsey, Member of Congress from the Third District. He esteems his honors highly; but his little daughter, Hazel M. Benton, born August 24, 1886, is regarded by Mr. Benton, next to Mrs. Benton, as the best of all his treasures.

The three Territorial Treasurers are noted in the annexed list:

B. P. Rankin, March 16, 1855.   Augustus Kountze, October 8, 1861.
Wm. W. Wyman, November 6, 1855.

Mr. Kountze was continued in office by the State. The list of State Treasurers is here shown:

Augustus Kountze, February, 1867.
James Sweet, January 11, 1869.
Henry A. Koenig, January 10, 1871.
J. C. McBride, January 11, 1875.

George M. Bartlett, January 9, 1879.
Phelps D. Sturdevant, January 4, 1883.
Charles H. Willard, January 8, 1885.
John E. Hill, January 3, 1889.

Hon. John E. Hill, the Treasurer for the State of Nebraska, is by virtue of his office a member of the State Board of Transportation, the State Board of Educational Lands and Funds, the State Board of Public Lands and Buildings, the State Board of Purchases and Supplies, the State Board of Equalization, the State Board of Pharmacy, the State Board of Printing, the State Board of Banking, and the State Normal Board. In other words, he is a member of the main executive boards of the State.

As biography is the foundation of history, a brief sketch of Mr. Hill's life is very appropriate to a history of Lincoln, in which he is now a prominent figure.

His father's name was Samuel Hill, who was born in Washington county, Pennsylvania. He was descended on his father's side probably from the Scotch. His mother, a grandmother of the State Treasurer, was named Van Ordestrand. She was probably a native of Holland. Samuel Hill was apprenticed, when young, to learn the hatter's trade, and spent four years "bound out" at this occupation. Then he followed the life of a farmer, in Ohio, and later in life became a merchant. He was a prudent, cautious, business man. He spent his closing years at Heyworth, Illinois, where he died, in 1882. During his life he held several important public positions.

The mother of the Treasurer was, before marriage, Miss Pamela Edgar. She was a woman of high spirit and energy, courageous, persistent, devoted to duty and success. She was born at Berlin, Holmes county, Ohio. On her mother's side she was descended from the Scotch. Her father was of Irish nativity. His ancestors made a name in the military history of Ireland, Col. Edgar and others of the name being brave defenders of the cause of Ireland's independence. Her father was a prominent Whig politician of Ohio, and was a member of the early Legislature of that State. Her death occurred at Heyworth, Illinois, in 1871.

The Treasurer, John E. Hill, was born in Berlin, Ohio. He spent his boyhood on a farm, working in summer, and going to school in winter, like most farmer boys had to do, from 1840 to 1865. When seventeen years of age he removed, with his father's family, to Defiance county, Ohio, near Farmer's Center, where he continued to follow agricultural pursuits in summer, but taught district school in the winter. This was the routine of his life until 1861, with the exception of one year, which he spent at West Unity Academy, near his home.

In 1861 he enlisted in the 14th Ohio Infantry, but was soon afterward prostrated with typhoid fever, and did not recover his health for nearly a year. The perilous condition of the Union in 1862 stirred the blood of the men of his home region, and early in August they assembled and formed a company by general agreement. The work of its organization required only four days, and at the close of the fourth the company chose John E. Hill its captain, unanimously. On the fifth day the company reported for duty at Toledo, Ohio, and was assigned to Company F, of the 111th Ohio Volunteer Infantry, commanded by Col. J. R. Bond. The regiment soon began duty under Gen. Buel, at Louisville, Kentucky. After moving to Frankfort and thence to Bowling Green, Company F and one other company, under the command of Capt. J. E. Hill, were assigned to Fort Baker, Kentucky, of which Capt. Hill had charge during the winter of 1862 and 1863. Here he was attacked by typhoid-pneumonia, and his life was despaired of for several days; but he was able to take command of his company in the spring. The company next was engaged in the campaign in East Tennessee, and was with the first troops that entered Knoxville. This was the active contest to oppose the advance of Longstreet, after Chickamauga. During the campaign in Tennessee, Capt. Hill was designated as Provost-Marshal by General Schofield, and had command of the captured towns of that State.

The winter of 1863–64 was spent in East Tennessee, and then Captain Hill's command joined Sherman in his grand campaign of battles from Chattanooga to Atlanta, one of the longest periods of continued fighting in the history of the world. The guns of the two armies were not silent a day from the 9th of May until some time in September. On the first date named Captain Hill's company engaged the enemy at Buzzard's Roost, and he led his command into every important action from that point to Atlanta. It seemed to be the fortune of his company to be in the hottest of nearly all the great battles of this memorable campaign, such as Resaca, Peach Tree, Kenesaw, and Atlanta. When Atlanta fell Captain Hill's company was sent back with General George H. Thomas to meet Hood's desperate attempt to cut Sherman's communications, and here again Company F was frequently in the hottest of the fight, and suffered severely, especially at Nashville and Franklin. In fact it was reduced to a mere skeleton of its former self.

When Hood was overthrown the 111th Ohio was ordered to North Carolina to help Sherman crush Joseph E. Johnston, but the many months of constant exposure, nervous strain, privation, loss of rest, and long, hurried marches, had utterly broken the health of Captain Hill, and he was compelled to remain at Louisville and enter the hospital. It seemed that he was a physical wreck. After remaining in the hospital for some time, the board of physicians, without his knowledge, recommended his honorable discharge on account of physical disability. This recommendation was complied with near the close of hostilities.

When able to do so, he returned to Ohio, and soon afterward removed to Heyworth, Illinois, with his father's family. There he and his father entered into the mercantile business, under the firm name of Hill & Son.

In 1866 he was married to Miss Laura Stewart, an estimable lady of Fairmont, West Virginia. He continued in business, with reasonable success, until 1871, when he felt that he could do better in a new and expanding country, and removed to Beatrice, Nebraska.

He there engaged in the nursery and stock-raising business for four years. When Beatrice was organized under the law as a city of the first class, in 1872, Captain Hill became a member of the first city council. In 1875 he was elected County Clerk of Gage county, and was twice afterward reëlected. After concluding his third term, he engaged in the grocery business for three years, and then devoted his time to growing fine stock. During this period he was a member of the Board of Supervisors of the county for two years, and of the Board of Education of Beatrice for six years, his last term closing in the spring of 1889.

On February 1, 1887, Governor Thayer selected Captain Hill for his private secretary without giving the Captain any previous intimation of his intention. This position Captain Hill filled with efficiency until August 1, 1888, when he resigned to become a candidate for

State Treasurer. He was nominated over twelve strong competitors, and was elected by nearly 28,000 majority, receiving the highest net majority of any candidate. He is now discharging the duties of this very responsible office with the same fidelity and ability which he has manifested in guarding the many duties that have been confided to his hands during the past twenty-seven years.

He recently removed his family to Lincoln. It consists of his wife and six children, three of whom are now young ladies. Their names are Gertrude, Carolina, Anna, Herbert Stewart, Hannah, Winifred, and John E. He has one brother younger than himself, Mr. Fred H. Hill, who resides at the old homestead at Hayworth, Illinois. He also has a sister, likewise younger than himself, who resides at Stuttgart, Arkansas. Her name is Mrs. Anna M. Lowe, and her son, Mr. Sam Lowe, is now an efficient clerk in the Governor's office.

The Justices of the Supreme Court of the Territory, Federal Judges, were as follows:

Fenner Ferguson, October 12, 1854.
Augustus Hall, March 15, 1858.
William Pitt Kellogg, May 27, 1861.
William Kellogg, May 8, 1865.
William A. Little,[1] 1866.
Oliver P. Mason,[2] 1866.

The Justices of the Supreme Court of the State have been as follows:

Oliver P. Mason, February, 1867.
George B. Lake, January 16, 1873.
Daniel Gantt,[1] January 3, 1878.
Samuel Maxwell, May 29, 1878.
George B. Lake, January 5, 1882.
Amasa Cobb, January 3, 1884.
Samuel Maxwell, January 1, 1886.
M. B. Reese, January 3, 1888.

Following are the names of the Associate Justices and Judges of the Territorial Supreme Court:

Edward R. Harden, December 4, 1854.
James Bradley, October 25, 1854.
Samuel W. Black.
Eleazer Wakeley, April 22, 1857.
Joseph Miller, April 9, 1859.
William F. Lockwood, May 16, 1861.
Joseph E. Streeter.[1]
Elmer S. Dundy,[2] June 22, 1863.

The Associate Justices and Judges of the State Supreme Court have been:

George B. Lake, February 21, 1867.
Lorenzo Crounse, February 21, 1867.
Daniel Gantt, January 16, 1873.
Samuel Maxwell, January 16, 1873.
Amasa Cobb, May 29, 1878.
M. B. Reese, January 3, 1884.

[1] Died in office.
[2] Appointed to fill vacancy.

The Clerks of the Supreme Court have been seven in number, as subjoined:

H. C. Anderson, 1856.
Charles L. Salisbury, 1858.
E. B. Chandler, 1859.
John H. Kellom, 1861.

William Kellogg jr., 1865.
George Armstrong, 1867.
Guy A. Brown, August 8, 1868.

SUPREME COURT REPORTERS.

James M. Woolworth, 1870.
Lorenzo Crounse, 1873.

Guy A. Brown, 1875.

The eight Attorney Generals of the State are named below:

Champion S. Chase, 1867.
Seth Robinson, 1860.
Geo. H. Roberts, January 10, 1871.
J. R. Webster, January 13, 1873.

Geo. H. Roberts, January 11, 1875.
C. J. Dilworth, January 9, 1879.
Isaac Powers jr., January 1, 1883.
William Leese, January 8, 1885.

The five State Superintendents of Public Instruction have been as follows:

Seth W. Beals, 1869.
J. M. McKenzie, January 10, 1871.
S. R. Thompson, January 4, 1877.

W. W. W. Jones, January 6, 1881.
George B. Lane, January 6, 1887.

There have been but four Commissioners of Public Lands and Buildings, namely:

F. M. Davis, January 4, 1877.
A. G. Kendall, January 6, 1881.

Joseph Scott, January 8, 1885.
John Steen, January 3, 1889.

Hon. John Steen, State Commissioner of Public Lands and Buildings for Nebraska, was installed in that office on January 3, 1889. By virtue of his office he is a member of the State Board of Transportation, which possesses, to some extent, judicial authority, as well as administrative and executive powers, in the adjustment of the relations of the railroad interests of the State, amicably and equitably, with those of the people. He is also a member of the State Board of Educational Lands and Funds. He is Chairman of the State Board of Public Lands and Buildings. He is, in addition, one of the State Board of Purchases and Supplies, and he is also a member of the State Board of Pharmacy. These boards are all composed of the principal State officers, and Mr. Steen's work as a State official is of a difficult and highly responsible character. He is regarded as a most efficient and prudent officer, well worthy the high trust confided to his charge by the people.

Mr. Steen has earned his present distinguished position by a life of hard work, patriotism, courage, and fidelity to duty and principle. A brief sketch of his personal history cannot fail to be of interest in a story of the history of Nebraska's capital, in which he is now a conspicuous figure.

He is a native of Norway. His father was Tron A. Steen, who was born near Christiana, Norway, January 17, 1804. His occupation was farming and manufacturing. Large importations of leaf tobacco were shipped into Christiana, and the father of Nebraska's Commissioner was engaged, in part, in making caddies in which to pack the manufactured tobacco. His father was always an anti-monarchist in political sentiment, and his sons inherited republican opinions from him.

Mr. Steen's mother was Miss Ingeborg H. Torsdag before her marriage, and was born near Lillehammed, Norway, on January 31, 1804. Her marriage with Tron A. Steen took place near Christiana, on December 25, 1827. She was a woman of great energy and industry, and never tired in making home pleasant for her children and in aiding to develop in them the spirit of manly character. She was a woman of strong and noble characteristics, one of the women who are naturally the mothers of heroes.

John Steen was born on his father's farm, near Christiana, Norway, on October 21, 1841, and was the sixth of a family of eight sons. He spent his boyhood, while in Norway, in going to school, though he was taught industrious habits between terms.

In 1853 his father's family emigrated to the United States, and settled on a farm near Decorah, in Winneshiek county, Iowa. Here Master Steen continued to go to school in winter, but applied himself to hard farm work in summer until 1861, taking the main control of affairs, as his father was getting old. The heavier part of the work fell to his lot, and thus it happened that he cut most of the grain on the farm with the old-fashioned cradle, which, in the hands of a powerful man, had a good deal of the "poetry of motion" about it, if some other man had to swing it. Mr. Steen's muscles became compact, and his body well knit by the years of hard work he put in on the old home farm.

On October 21, 1861, the day after he was twenty years old, Mr. Steen enlisted in Company G of the 12th Iowa Infantry, under Captain C. C. Tupper, a West Point graduate. His regimental commander was Col. J. J. Woods, who had also had some training at West Point. Two of his brothers, Theodore and Henry, joined the same company, and they served through the war together. But all six of these patriotic brothers were in the Union Army. The three brothers in the 12th Iowa were in their country's service until January, 1866. The regiment went into a camp of instruction at Dubuque, Iowa, until November 28th, and thence proceeded to Benton Barracks, Missouri. It left there January 29, 1862, and proceeded to Smithland, Kentucky, and from that point joined General Grant's expedition against Forts Henry and Donelson. The 12th Iowa assisted to take Fort Henry, which surrendered February 6, 1862. Then it proceeded to Fort Donelson, which it reached February 12th, and participated in the storming and capture of that stronghold as a part of Col. Cook's Brigade, of Gen. C. F. Smith's Division. Here it will be recalled that the 12th and 2d Iowa were on the extreme left, and that the 2d Iowa made a very gallant charge, and gained the first lodgment, and was immediately supported on its right by the 12th Iowa, which made almost as brilliant a dash as the 2d. This was on the 15th of February. Gen. Buckner surrendered the fort the next day, and the country was proud of Grant and the Iowa and Illinois troops, that had accomplished this brilliant achievement.

Then the gallant 12th went to Pittsburg Landing, and assisted all through that terrible 6th of April, 1862, to hold the center of the line, in company with the famous Iowa Brigade, composed of the 2d, 7th, 12th, and 14th, Iowa regiments, under the command of General J. M. Tuttle, and in the division of General W. H. L. Wallace. After this brigade had held the spot now historically illustrious as the "Hornets' Nest," and after the rebel force had broken away the Union line both to the right and left, and had surrounded the 12th and 14th and attacked them from all sides, they surrendered, and became prisoners of war. General Tuttle had ordered the brigade to fall back, but the order failed to reach the 12th and 14th. Just at the moment of capture Mr. Steen received a wound on his right side, under the right arm. The surrender took place between five and six o'clock in the evening. The prisoners were taken to Corinth, and for three days were without food. Of course the pangs of hunger became very keen with such a fast, after such a struggle as that of April 6th.

From Corinth the prisoners were taken to Memphis, Tennessee, where they remained a few days, and were thence forwarded to Mobile, Alabama. From that place they were removed to Cahaba, Alabama, where they were huddled together in an old tobacco warehouse, and there suffered their first severe trial of rebel prison life. Here the starving process was begun. After two weeks of this pen, the prisoners, of whom Mr. Steen was one, were taken to Macon, Georgia, where he endured the infamous mistreatment for which that pen is historical, for two or three months. Then he was paroled, and was taken to Benton Barracks, Missouri, where he did garrison duty, until exchanged in January, 1863. Then the men of his regiment were reorganized in time to join in Gen. Grant's magnificent campaign, whereby he swung below Vicksburg, and with a masterly movement, as brilliant as any executed by Napoleon, in sixty days whipped an army of over sixty thousand, in detail, with a force of but forty-five thousand. Mr. Steen made the quick march to Jackson, Miss., where Sherman and McPherson splendidly defeated Joseph E. Johnston, on the 14th of May, 1863. The 12th Iowa did not get to Champion Hill soon enough to help whip Pemberton, but, with Sherman, participated in the two gallant charges on the works at Vicksburg, on the 18th and 22d of May. Mr. Steen's regiment was with Sherman's 15th corps, on the right. This regiment, with others, was assigned to watch Johnston at Black River Bridge, during part of the siege. When the surrender took place, on July 4, 1863, the 12th Iowa was of the troops which made a dash after Johnston, and beat him at Jackson and Brandon, and sent him whirling for safety beyond the Pearl river.

The term of enlistment of the gallant Twelfth expired in January, 1864, and the men promptly enlisted for a second three years, and were then allowed to visit home on a veteran furlough. During the summer of 1864 the regiment was attached to the Sixteenth Army Corps, commanded by Major General A. J. Smith, and was engaged in movements against Forrest, in Tennessee and Mississippi. At the battle of Tupelo, where there was terrific fighting for a short time, he lost the best friend he ever had, Lieut. Augustus A. Burdick, who had been as faithful to him as a brother. This was the saddest event of his army life.

Mr. Steen's regiment pursued Price through Arkansas and Missouri, and assisted to fight the battle of Pleasant Hill. Then his command hurried to Nashville, and arrived just in time to help General Thomas fight the magnificent battle of Nashville, whereby Hood's army was annihilated and Thomas's soldiers were covered with glory.

In the spring of 1865 the 12th Iowa was sent to Mobile, Alabama, where it aided to capture Spanish Fort, after a hot fight, on the day Lee surrendered at Appomattox. This ended the gallant battle career of John Steen and his company; but his regiment was held at Selma and Talladiga, Alabama, guarding the freedmen from the keen resentment of the Southern people until January, 1866.

Mr. Steen returned home after the war, and the Steen family was justly honored because of its six gallant veterans. He was engaged in mercantile pursuits for a few months, and then was appointed deputy sheriff of Winneshiek county, Iowa, and held that position with credit until he removed to Nebraska, in 1869.

On coming to this State he settled in Omaha, and was soon afterward appointed registry and money-order clerk in the Omaha post-office. From that position he was promoted to postal clerk on the Union Pacific railroad, through the influence of Senator William B. Allison, of Iowa. He continued in this service until the spring of 1871, when he was elected City Treasurer of Omaha. He served two terms of one year each with his usual faithfulness and skill.

He then was appointed Clerk to the Chief Paymaster of the Military Department of the Platte. This post he resigned in 1874, and he then removed to Fremont to engage in the lumber and agricultural implement business, in which he was wholly successful. In 1877 he took up his residence at Wahoo and entered the hardware trade. When the State militia was organized he became the first captain of a company at Wahoo belonging to the First Regiment. He was appointed postmaster of that place in 1875, and Postoffice Inspector in 1883, his division comprising Nebraska and Wyoming. In this position he was very efficient, having been educated for the work while Deputy Sheriff and by his previous experience in the postal service. He was removed from this office as an "offensive partisan," by the Democratic Postmaster General, in 1885, and then reëngaged in the hardware trade at Wahoo until elected to his present office, by about 28,000 majority, in 1888.

Mr. Steen was married on September 10, 1870, to Miss Marie

HON. JOHN STEEN, COMMISSIONER OF PUBLIC LANDS AND BUILDINGS.

HON. JOHN JENKINS, COMMISSIONER OF LABOR.

Louise Hough, an excellent and accomplished lady of El Dorado, Fayette county, Iowa. They had four children born to them, and all are living. Their names are Nora Cecelia, Theron Hough, Clarence Guido, and Mona Lillian. The family resides at Wahoo at present, where it possesses the highest respect of the people.

There have been eight Librarians, Mr. Kennard being the first State Librarian, as follows:

James S. Izard, March 16, 1855.	Robert S. Knox, 1861.
H. C. Anderson, November 6, 1855.	Thomas P. Kennard, June 22, 1867.
John H. Kellum, August 3, 1857.	William H. Jones, January 10, 1871.
Alonzo D. Luce, November 7, 1859.	Guy A. Brown, March 3, 1871.

Among the most important of the offices of the State is that of Commissioner of Labor, created by act of the Legislature of 1887. By this act the Governor is the named Commissioner, (this being to avoid the constitutional prohibition against creating any new office,) with power to appoint a Deputy, to whose care the whole work of the department is consigned, and who is recognized as the real head of the department, the *de facto* Commissioner of Labor. And in selecting the Hon. John Jenkins to be the head of the State Bureau of Labor, Governor Thayer showed excellent judgment.

Mr. Jenkins is descended from distinguished ancestors. His grandfather was John Jenkins, whose residence was Hengoed, Wales. He was a minister of distinction in the Baptist church, and a college in Pennsylvania conferred upon him the title of D. D., about 1850, on account of his learned works on the Bible. He was the author of a commentary on the Bible which required sixteen years of labor to produce. The great work of his life was a religious allegory entitled the "Silver Palace," a work somewhat resembling Bunyan's "Pilgrim's Progress." It was this which won him his theological title. He was also distinguished as an orator. There is no record of Mr. Jenkin's grandmother.

Mr. Jenkins's father was also John Jenkins. He was also a minister of distinction on account of learning and intellectual energy. He was sent by the Welsh Society to Morlaix, France, in 1832, to establish a Baptist Mission. He was the author of various works of a literary and scientific character, and on account of their high merit he was elected a member of the French Academy of Sciences. He died in France in 1873. Mr. Jenkins's mother was an excellent woman, and the mother of twelve children, eleven of whom were born in France. Of these, Mr. Jenkins, the Commissioner, was the fourth child and the third John Jenkins in direct succession. He was born at the Mission at Morlaix, France, May 25, 1838. He spent his boyhood there in educational and industrial pursuits, and was sent to Wales in 1853, articled to become a mechanical engineer, under the tutelage of T. W. Kennard, Chief Engineer of the Atlantic & Great Western railway. In this position Mr. Jenkins became a skillful engineer and mechanic — in fact, a master workman.

In 1861, owing to the fact that the United States Mail Steamship, Arago, running from New York to Havre, of which he was engineer, was stopped in New York harbor because the rebel privateer Sumpter was on the seas, he enlisted in the Seventy-first New York Infantry, in 1862, to meet the rebel invasion at the time Banks was driven out of the Shenandoah Valley. The regiment reported to Secretary of War Edwin M. Stanton for a three months' term. The regiment was engaged in detailed service in Maryland, to prevent rebel recruits from passing from Maryland into Virginia. Soon after the term of enlistment, and subsequent to the second battle of Bull Run, Mr. Jenkins returned to his old work, mechanical engineering. In 1863, during Lee's raid into Pennsylvania, Mr. Jenkins again enlisted, this time in the Forty-fourth Pennsylvania Infantry. His regiment was mainly employed in defending Harrisburg against the advance of the rebel General Jenkins, until he left to join Lee at Gettysburg. Then the Forty-fourth pressed on to Gettysburg, but arrived just in time to see the battle won by the Union forces. His regiment was mustered out after three months' service, and Mr. Jenkins returned to New York and resumed his occupation as a mechanical engineer, being mainly employed in the construction of Federal monitors. He helped to build the monitors, Tonwanda, Susquehanna, Lehigh, and others.

After the war his efficiency as a mechanical engineer called Mr. Jenkins to the oil regions of Pennsylvania, where he was employed for a time on the John Steele oil farm. By his skill he was enabled to make a fortune in eighteen months' time, but lost it all in an equal period, owing to the shrinkage of values which followed the first advance. He left there penniless and in ill health, and his physician recommended a trip on the western plains. He made a journey over the western trail in 1867, and had the exhilaration of fighting Indians frequently added to that of the fresh prairie air. During this trip he made the acquaintance of Col. W. F. Cody, (Buffalo Bill,) who was scouting for General Custer. He also met Generals Custer and Hancock during the trip, they being west looking after the Indian warfare then in progress. On one occasion one wagon was captured by the Indians which contained everything of value possessed by Mr. Jenkins. So he arrived in Denver in better health but with a low state of finances. He worked in Denver, then a mere village, for a while, and during the same year returned to Omaha, where he had the pleasure of assisting to build the first stationary engine ever manufactured in Nebraska, in the shop of Hall Brothers. From Omaha he went to work at his trade on the Erie & Susquehanna Railroad, and a few months later became connected with the Panama Company, on the Isthmus of Panama; this was in 1869. He spent two and one-half years on the Isthmus, two of which he was foreman of the shops there. At the end of that period he was called to Peru to assist in the mechanical department of the railroad Henry Meigs was constructing in that country. From 1872 to 1875 he was connected with this road, and assisted to construct water works at Iquique, and salt petre works at Pampanegoro. He concluded his work in Peru by driving a tunnel for Mr. Meigs, on the Oroya railroad, at a height of 13,000 feet above the level of the sea, during which he invented a new way of boring with diamond drills.

From Peru he returned to the United States and went to the mining regions of Nevada to introduce his diamond drill, but received such illiberal inducements that he abandoned the project, and entered the office of the chief engineer of the Union Mills and Mining Company, of Virginia City, Nevada, where he remained until, by the death of Mr. Ralston, the company was found to be intimately connected with the Bank of California, which, being deeply involved, caused the mines to change hands.

Mr. Jenkins then came east and engaged with the C. B. & Q. railroad company, in 1877, expecting to return to South America; but the course of his life was changed by meeting the lady in Council Bluffs who became his wife. This was Miss Alice M. Canning, to whom he was married in June of 1878. Mr. Jenkins worked for the C. B.

& Q. in various capacities, being employed at one time as draughtsman, at Aurora, Illinois, under G. M. Stone, now general manager of the road. Owing to rheumatism, he had to resign a position in the service of the Atlantic & Pacific railroad company, and coming west entered the employ of the Union Pacific railroad in the fall of 1882. He worked three months at the bench, and then entered their offices as one of their mechanical engineers, where he remained until appointed by James E. Boyd, though a Republican, to the position of boiler inspector for the city of Omaha. This was in 1886. This position he held, with credit to himself, until appointed Commissioner of the Bureau of Labor by Governor Thayer, in 1887.

Through his eventful career Mr. Jenkins has come to understand very thoroughly the relations that should govern employers and employes. He is a prominent representative of the labor organizations of the day, and is a worthy man in the place, for he teaches just principles, intended to be thoroughly fair to employer and employed. He urges workingmen to be fair to employers, so that they can insist upon just treatment themselves. He favors patriotism, peace, and obedience to law. When anarchism was flauntingly and menacingly rampant in 1877, at the suggestion of Julius Meyers Mr. Jenkins led in the preparation of a grand labor demonstration on the 4th of July, in the city of Omaha, with the purpose of showing that labor organizations are loyal to the flag, and are not in sympathy with anarchy, and allow no ensign to be carried in their processions but the flag of the United States. This demonstration had 8,000 men in line, and was conducted in perfect good order.

Mr. Jenkins distinguished himself in Omaha as an advocate of free education and free text books; and so effectively did he lead the workingmen in the contest with the school board that the board was compelled to adopt the free-text-book system in the Omaha schools, which the city now enjoys, to the great advantage of the general education of the masses.

As Commissioner of Labor Mr. Jenkins is making a marked success. The last Legislature was highly pleased with his report, and commissioned him to inquire into the feasibility of beet-sugar culture in Nebraska, which he is now giving a thorough investigation.

His family consists of Mrs. Jenkins, a daughter, Millie Maud, and a son, John Benjamin. He has a comfortable property at Omaha.

CHAPTER IV.

NEBRASKA'S RESOURCES—HER DEVELOPMENT FROM THE "GREAT AMERICAN DESERT"—TOPOGRAPHY, CLIMATE, SOIL, ETC.—COMPARISONS WITH OTHER STATES—THE FIELD LINCOLN POSSESSES.

Less than thirty years ago the words, "Great American Desert," were printed in large capitals on nearly all maps representing the western half of Nebraska and adjacent territory. Less than ten years ago a really wise editor of Iowa gravely announced in his paper that farming, west of the one hundredth meridian, could not be carried on successfully in Nebraska and Kansas. These opinions are part of the candid belief of their time, and are standard humor in Nebraska at this time. The hundredth meridian passes through Keya Paha, Brown, Blaine, Custer, Dawson, Gosper, and Furnas counties; and millions of bushels of corn, wheat, oats, potatoes, and other farm products, are annually produced in Box Butte, Cheyenne, Arthur, Keith, Lincoln, Frontier, Red Willow, Chase, Hayes, Dundy, Hitchcock, and other counties west of that ancient geographical dead line. Hundreds of thousands of farm animals are supported in that region. Many bright cities and towns are building up there, and railways have penetrated nearly every part of that much-libeled territory. The development of Western Nebraska has only fairly set in, and it is not beyond the power of any ordinary citizen of the State to certainly predict that within ten years the western half of Nebraska will be a populous, rich, and thriving empire, nearly five times the area of Massachusetts, and more than thirty times as productive of King corn.

The growth of Nebraska in population, wealth, schools, churches, and general improvements, has not been surpassed, probably not equaled, by any equivalent area on the globe, in the past ten years, and she now ranks as one of the great States of the Union. Her real merits will not be appreciated by the country at large until after the next census is reported, when it will be admitted that she is swiftly moving to a position beside the richest agricultural and commercial States of the Nation.

The State of Nebraska is situated between 40° and 43° north latitude, and long. 95° 25' and 104° west from Greenwich. The length of the State is about four hundred and twenty miles east and west, the width about two hundred and eight miles, north and south. The area is 76,855 square miles, or 49,187,200 acres. It is the eighth State in the Union in size, not considering Montana, not yet fully admitted. The topography of the State is made up of rolling prairie, table land, and valleys, with a small percentage of bluff land, or high rolling surface. The State is devoid of mountains, possesses few lakes, and is practically without swamps. The prairie is as beautiful as any in the world, and comprises about fifty per cent of the whole area; the table lands are really high prairies, terraced, and make about twenty per cent of the area. The valleys are generally low, level prairies, and, perhaps, make up nearly twenty per cent of the surface, while the high, rolling and bluff portion may be estimated at about ten per cent. There is a gradual slope from the west end of the State to the Missouri river, causing the three principal rivers, the Niobrara, Platte, and Republican, to take nearly an easterly course. The principal tributaries of the Niobrara, which is on the northern side of the State, flow northward; those of the Platte, which occupies the lower central portion of the State, flow to the southeast, and the branches of the Republican, which has its course along the south side of the State until it passes into Kansas, in Nuckolls county, also run in a southeasterly direction. A glance at the river system of Nebraska will give an idea of the general topography of the State. The Loup river is a tributary of the Platte, on the north side, and, with its branches, drains and waters nearly all of the north center of the State. The Elkhorn river is also a considerable stream, flowing southeasterly across the northeast corner of the State, and meeting the Platte about thirty-five miles from its confluence with the Missouri river. The Blue river takes its rise within five miles of the Platte, and flows in a southeasterly course through the southeast corner of the State, and empties into the Republican river, in Eastern Kansas. This is one of the most picturesque streams in the State. All three streams were fringed with timber in the earlier years of the State's history, and much of this yet remains. Along the Niobrara the trees were pine, cedar, ash, oak, walnut, and such varieties as grow with these. In the western cañons there was and is yet fine cedar timber. Along the easterly and southerly streams there were cottonwood, oak, hickory, elm, maple, ash, locust, willow, box elder, linn, hackberry, sycamore, mulberry, coffee-bean, and ironwood. There are fifty species of forest trees in Nebraska. Blackberry, gooseberry and other shrubs grow luxuriantly, and nearly all kinds of ordinary fruit trees are found in the orchards of the State. Almost every farmer has a grove of maples, cottonwood, walnut, or other trees which he planted, and in a few years fuel enough for use can be grown in almost any part of the State. The cultivation of groves of forest trees has been greatly encouraged by the establishment of "Arbor Day," a holiday conceived by Hon. J. Sterling Morton, of Nebraska City, and devoted by the people to planting trees. This day is now made the subject of a general proclamation by the Governor every year.

The planting of trees and cultivation of the soil has made Nebraska a State of very equable climate. Drouth very seldom visits the State. Rains come with almost perfect timeliness in the State generally, and tornadoes are scarcely ever known. This seems strange, and is, in fact, a phenomenon of nature; but it is true that while the face of Kansas is raked from end to end by the most terrific storms, and while Missouri, Iowa, Minnesota, and Dakota, are frequently devastated in places, Nebraska has scarcely ever known a genuine tornado. The atmosphere is dry and invigorating, and such diseases as consumption are little known. The mean average temperature during 1888 was 49° Fahrenheit. The winters are not severely cold, and the summers are not oppressively hot. The climate is both favorable to human health, the growth of farm animals, and agricultural products of all kinds. This is shown by the fact that Nebraska has had excellent crops for three years past, while States and Territories on all sides have suffered from drouth during the same period. The reason for this favorable condition of climate is owing, probably, to permanent natural causes, based on the topography of the Missouri Valley, and the location of the State with reference to the meeting of the hot and cold currents of air from south and north.

But the soil of Nebraska is peculiarly adapted to stand drouth or heavy rainfall. This is true of every part of the State. To show the remarkable homogenity of the soil of various sections of Nebraska, we will quote the figures of an analysis of soil taken from the counties of Douglas, Buffalo, Loup, Clay, and Harlan, representing the eastern, central, northern, and southern parts of the State. The columns represent the counties in the order named:

COMPOSITION OF SOIL.	1.	2.	3.	4.	5.
Insoluble (silicious) matter	81.28	81.32	81.35	81.30	81.32
Ferric oxide	3.86	3.87	3.83	3.85	3.86
Alumina	.75	.75	.74	.73	.74
Lime, carbonate	6.07	6.06	6.03	6.05	6.09
Lime, phosphate	3.58	3.59	3.58	3.57	3.59
Magnesia, carbonate	1.29	1.28	1.31	1.31	1.29
Potassa	.27	.29	.35	.34	.33
Soda	.15	.16	.14	.16	.16
Organic matter	1.07	1.06	1.05	1.06	1.06
Moisture	1.09	1.08	1.09	1.08	1.09
Lost in analysis	.59	.54	.53	.55	.47
Totals	100.00	100.00	100.00	100.00	100.00

This analysis was made by Prof. Samuel Aughey, of the Nebraska State University, and is of soil taken from the high prairies and table lands. It is of the lacustrine or loess deposit, and is unsurpassed for agricultural purposes. Speaking of the foregoing analysis Prof. Aughey says: " From the above it is seen that over eighty per cent of this formation is silicious matter, and so finely comminuted is it that the grains can only be seen under a good microscope. So abundant are the carbonates and phosphates of lime, that in many places they form peculiar rounded and oval concretions. Vast numbers of these concretions, from the size of a shot to a walnut, are found almost everywhere by turning over the sod and in excavations. The analysis shows the presence of a comparatively large amount of iron, besides alumina, soda, and potash.

"As would be expected from its elements, it forms one of the richest and most tillable soils in the world. In fact, in its chemical and physical properties, and the mode of its origin, it comes nearest to the loess of the Rhine and the Valley of Egypt. It can never be exhausted until every hill and valley which composes it is entirely worn away. Owing to the wonderfully finely comminuted silica, of which the bulk of the deposit consists, it possesses natural drainage in the highest degree. However great the floods of water that fall, it soon percolates through this soil, which, in its lowest depths, retains it like a sponge. When drouths come, by capillary attraction the moisture comes up from below, supplying the needs of vegetation in the dryest season. This is the reason why, all over this region where this deposit prevails, the native vegetation and cultivated crops are seldom either dried or drowned out. This is especially the case on old breaking and where deep plowing is practiced. This deposit is a paradise for all the fruits of the temperate zone. They luxuriate in a soil like this, which has perfect natural drainage, and is composed of such materials."

About seventy-five per cent of the soil of Nebraska is of this wonderfully perfect kind for the production of grains, fruits, vegetables, and other vegetation. This soil ranges in thickness from five to two hundred feet.

The river valleys generally possess a soil of alluvium deposits, which is rich, like the upland or lacustrine soil, and differs from it in possessing less silica and a greater percentage of organic matter and alumina. This soil varies from two to twenty feet in depth, often has an understratum of sand, and is generally dry and warm, though it at times and in places becomes cold and wet, and is not always good for farming purposes. These valleys produce almost unrivaled crops of vegetables and corn, and, perhaps, not as good wheat, oats, and fruits, as the high rolling lands. Both soils are valued very highly by farmers, and are scarcely surpassed in the world for reliability and abundance of yield.

There are a few alkaline spots in the central portions of the State, and somewhat larger areas in the western part. But all told, there is not enough to merit any special mention.

With such a splendid wealth of soil, it might be expected that Nebraska's farms would prosper, her population increase rapidly; that railroad mileage would multiply with great activity, and manufactories come swiftly into existence.

The facts will justify all these deductions; and a swiftly-growing State always attracts the best people; and so schools, newspapers, and churches, have multiplied in Nebraska. Located in the center of the temperate region of this continent, it becomes the theater for the highways and cross-roads of the "Belt of Empire" of the world. The city of Lincoln is nearly in the geographical center of the United

States, and the growth of the State and her capital have both been the marvel of the past two decades.

The growth of population shows that Nebraska has genuine merits. There were 122,993 people in the State in 1870. In less than nineteen years 1,100,000 more have been added, an average annual growth of 61,000 for the entire time. Texas, with nearly three and one-half times the area of Nebraska, and twenty-one years the start as a State, only gained at the rate of 98,000 population annually, or but a little over 28,000 per year for the same territory that Nebraska possesses. Minnesota, with nearly nine years the start as a State, and nearly seven thousand more square miles of area, has only made about even figures with Nebraska since 1870. It is probably fair to say that but two States have made such splendid progress in population since 1870 as Nebraska. One is Iowa, probably without an equal in the Union, area and age considered, but with twenty-two years the start of Nebraska as a State; and Kansas, with much the same natural advantages as Nebraska, and with over five thousand more square miles of area, and six years the lead in admission as a State. So Nebraska has made a very creditable race with the best States in the Union in attracting home-seekers.

Now, how has the soil of Nebraska supported the high opinion of scientific analysis and the confidence of the armies of people who annually cast their lot within the State's borders? In 1880 Illinois produced 326,000,000 bushels of corn. (Round numbers are used in all these illustrations.) Iowa produced 275,000,000 the same year; Kansas, 105,000,000; Nebraska, 65,000,000. In 1888 Illinois harvested 278,000,000 bushels of corn; Iowa, 278,000,000 bushels; Kansas, 158,000,000; and Nebraska, 144,000,000. Here it will be seen that Illinois did not maintain her record, Iowa gained a very small percentage, Kansas improved her record by a little over fifty per cent, and Nebraska leaped forward at the rate of one hundred and twenty-one per cent. Here Nebraska soil meets and overmatches the giants in her rate of progress. It will be found that the percentage of successes of the corn crop in Nebraska will be equally as favorable as her growth in number of bushels.

The year 1888 was not generally favorable to a wheat crop in the States named above, but the remarkable power of Nebraska soil to endure unfavorable seasons was manifested, though there was really nothing approaching a drouth here, as known in other States. The striking superiority of Nebraska soil and climate is shown in the subjoined table comparing the wheat crops of 1880 and 1888 in Illinois, Iowa, Kansas, and Nebraska. Nebraska was the only one of these cereal-producing States that made progress on the record of 1880. Here is the exhibit of that fact, taken from the tenth census and report of the Washington Bureau of Agriculture for 1888:

STATES.	1880, Bushels.	1888, Bushels.	Per cent of gain or loss.
Illinois	51,000,000	34,000,000	Loss, 33⅓.
Iowa	31,000,000	24,000,000	Loss, 22½.
Kansas	17,325,000	16,000,000	Loss, 7½.
Nebraska	13,850,000	14,500,000	Gain, 4 3-5.

In a similar way it can be shown that Nebraska is in the front rank of the world's most progressive States in the production of oats, hay, potatoes, and other farm grains and vegetables. It can also be demonstrated that the numbers, grade, and value of her horses, hogs, and cattle, are going forward with the very best States of the Union. In fact, the climate of this State is very favorable to the health and growth of domestic animals.

And it will be found by the census of 1880 that the manufacturing interests of Nebraska have increased several hundred per cent in magnitude; in fact, are moving forward with her other and diversified interests.

On the first of January, 1865, there was not a mile of railroad in Nebraska. At this time, July, 1889, twenty-three and one-half years later, there are about 5,000 miles in operation in the State. There has been an increase in mileage of over eighty-one per cent in four years. The gross earnings of Nebraska roads in 1887 were $23,-446,343, and the net earnings were $10,571,858.

Popular intelligence and enlightenment generally follow rich soil combined with favorable climate. Hence the many schools and numerous fine churches of Nebraska are one proof of her great natural resources. By the census of 1880 Nebraska had the lowest percentage of illiteracy of any State in the Union, and Wyoming Territory alone had a better record in all the United States. The following table will show this, the States and Territories there exhibited having the lowest rate of illiteracy in this Nation, and being, probably, unequaled in the world:

STATES, ETC.	Per cent unable to read.	Per cent unable to write.	Average illiteracy.
Wyoming Territory	2.6	3.4	3.00
Nebraska	2.5	3.6	3.05
Iowa	2.4	3.9	3.15
Dakota	3.4	4.8	3.95
Kansas	3.6	5.6	4.60

We believe that leading educators of this State now calculate that Nebraska has improved her record since 1880, and stands at the very head of all States in the world in freedom from illiteracy.

At the close of 1888 there were 5,187 school houses in Nebraska, or sixty-five (nearly) to each of the eighty organized counties. These were attended by 215,889 children during the year, and this army of children were instructed by 9,886 teachers. The wages paid teachers for the school year ending in 1888 amounted to $1,699,784, or a sum equal (nearly) to all money paid out for educational purposes in Alabama, Florida, and Georgia, put together, for 1886-7. Besides the wages of teachers, the State spent enough on her common schools, for the year ending in the summer of 1888, to make a total cost of $3,238,442, an amount not exceeded by over fourteen States in the Union. The total value of public-school property in the State for the same date was $5,123,180. Besides these public schools, there are now probably ten colleges in Nebraska, two having been added to Lincoln alone since the last report of the United States Commissioner of Education. In these higher schools there were, it is fair to estimate, fully 1,500 students during the year which closed in June, 1889, taught by about 100 instructors, and possessing libraries aggregating probably 25,000 volumes. These institutions possess buildings and grounds worth, together, about $1,000,000. Such are some of the evidences of educational growth in a State which did not possess an academy in 1870, and employed but 536 teachers at that date in her public schools. The churches have grown as rapidly as the schools.

We have given these statistics and estimates to suggest the real wealth and greatness of Nebraska as it is to be in a few years. It has been such a few years since the buffalo and antelope roamed over the ground where the State Capitol stands, that even our own people have not come to realize the swift progress our State is making in gathering population, wealth, and facilities for mental culture; and States east of the Mississippi are positively incredulous that such almost miraculous results can be realities. But they are, as we have shown, and it is but just that the merits of this noble State shall be properly appreciated now.

When we see how the State of Nebraska has moved forward, it is easy to explain the wonderful growth of her capital, Lincoln, which is declared a marvel by intelligent people even within the State, and is incomprehensible to men of the Eastern States. The city is merely moving with the farms, the railroads, and the factories. The multiplication of farms explains it. The wealth of grain, stock, and other products within her trade limits shows why the city grows. Her railroad system comprises twelve roads, radiating like the spokes of a wheel to every section of Nebraska's noble domain, and also piercing Dakota, Wyoming, Montana, Colorado, New Mexico, and Kansas, and, with their connections, supplying Lincoln with a direct territorial patronage fully double the area of Nebraska, or 154,000 square miles, equal to nearly 100,000,000 acres, or over 600,000 farms of 160 acres each. Here is a trade of 1,000 towns, representing now fully 2,000,000 people, and the same area will, within ten years, possess 4,000,000 people, or more.

The corn and wheat alone of this territory were worth $44,000,000 last year. The oats, hay, potatoes, horses, cattle, and hogs, were worth twice as much more. So that the buying power of the territory in review was more than $125,000,000 last year, without counting the products of wool, butter, cheese, fruit, timber, vegetables, minerals, and manufactures. Here is a magnificent jobbing trade that must be attended to. Lincoln divides Northeast Nebraska with Omaha, but is on shorter lines to Central Nebraska and all the South Platte country than Omaha. Lincoln divides with St. Joseph and Kansas City in Southeastern Nebraska, and is on shorter lines to South-central Nebraska, Northern Kansas, and Eastern Colorado, than either. Omaha is cut off on the north by Sioux City, on the south by St. Joseph, and on the southwest and west by Lincoln, which has actually the same in-tariff as Omaha, St. Joseph, and Kansas City. Hence, for jobbing and distributing manufactures, the future of Lincoln is fully equal to that of Omaha, and it is a possibility that may yet be realized, that Lincoln will out-strip Omaha, on account of commercial superiority. This is a possibility of the next twenty-five years. To supply this commercial empire, there is a perfectly legitimate reason why Lincoln's jobbing trade should grow; and it has grown, there being sixty-eight wholesale houses in the city now, and four hundred traveling men make Lincoln their home. Lincoln's jobbing trade will require her to grow for fifty years to come, at least. For the same reason, Lincoln's manufacturing interests require her to grow. There is call for vast supplies of all ordinary manufactures, and this city must grow to keep up with this demand. In keeping with this demand, seventy factories are now operated in Lincoln. On this account alone there will be a call for a city larger than Lincoln at the hub of the main railroad system of this splendid territory. Then, the railroad interests of Lincoln require a city at this place, and those who think Lincoln will stop growing should remember one fact, namely: the railway system of Nebraska is cast for all time in favor of Lincoln; and instead of the city failing, there is reason to believe that on this account alone reliance may be placed for long-continued advancement. The roads have reason to push the city, and they will do so. Here are three great universities, calling in many who desire to educate, and who spend large sums, in the aggregate, to the inspiration of trade. Here is the capitol and three State institutions, amalgamating the interests of the State with those of this city. Here is a center for beef and pork packing, and we find two large packing houses with growing businesses, and a town springing up on their account alone. In brief, there are all the diversified commercial demands for a supply and distributing metropolis here that the swift development of a territory of almost unlimited resources could require. With her intelligent, enterprising, and persistently energetic people, the wonder is not that Lincoln grows with phenomenal momentum, but whether the city could stop growing if it so desired. It must grow; it will grow. The buildings erected during 1888, with permanent improvements, amounted to $3,287,418. From raw prairie in 1867, the progress of Lincoln for twenty-two years has been about 2,500 population on an average for every year of that period. Last year her growth was 7,000 people. At the rate the city is now advancing, and has gone forward for several years, it will contain 125,000 inhabitants before the close of the next decade.

CHAPTER V.

LANCASTER COUNTY—ITS EARLIEST SETTLEMENT AND GROWTH—INCIDENTS OF THE EARLY TIMES—THE PROMINENT MEN WHO BRAVED THE DANGERS OF THE WILDERNESS.

To write the history of Lincoln comprehensively, Lancaster county, of which Lincoln is the seat of government, must be touched upon more or less extensively. It is a fundamental, a preparatory step, absolutely necessary to be taken. Hence the preceding pages, touching briefly upon the history of the whole State of Nebraska, are logically followed by a *résumé* of the history of the county, to be followed in turn by the history of the city proper.

It is agreed by all that the first white man to take up his residence in Lancaster county came here in the spring of 1856—thirty-three years ago. John Dee, who lives near Waverly, disputes with John W. Prey, of Lincoln, the honor of being the first white settler in the county. These two men arrived at nearly the same time, and settled in different parts of the county, Mr. Prey settling on Salt creek. The authors of this work held a long and very interesting talk with Mr. Prey, one evening during the early part of June, 1889, and from him gained many of the points given hereafter.

Being one of the earliest, if not the earliest settler, to make his permanent home in Lancaster county, a few words regarding Mr. Prey will be of interest to the readers of this book. John W. Prey was born in New York City, May 11, 1828, his father, John D. Prey, being in business in the city at that time. When John W. was only four or five years of age his father moved from New York City to the western part of the State, where he resided until John jr. was fourteen years of age. In the year 1842 the Prey family left New York for the West, stopping one winter in Illinois, and from there going to Wisconsin, where they resided until the spring of 1856, the family residence being a farm seventeen miles north of Milwaukee. During the residence of the Preys in Western New York and in Wisconsin, John W., with his brothers, worked at farming, and built up a constitution which enabled him to pass through the hardships of pioneer life in two States, and still retain almost the vigor and strength of youth.

In the spring of 1856, John D. Prey and his son John W., left the homestead in Wisconsin intending to take up a new home in Iowa, but on reaching that State decided to push on and see what Nebraska had in store for them. They crossed the Missouri at Council Bluffs, on the ferry, and found Omaha a little hamlet of probably twenty or twenty-five houses. Continuing their journey, they reached Plattsmouth, and learning of the fine country on the "salt basins," determined to see for themselves what it looked like. So pushing on, they reached Salt creek on June 15, 1856. Here they determined to settle, and while John W. remained in the State and county, his father went back to Wisconsin to dispose of his property, and to bring the rest of the family to the new land of promise. While coming across the country from Plattsmouth, and when nearly to the Salt Basin, the Preys met three men who were returning from Salt creek, where they had staked out claims for speculation, not intending to settle on them. These men were from Plattsmouth, and their names were Whitmore, Cardwell, and Thorpe. These three men were, in all probability, the first to take up claims in Lancaster county, so that the history of the county really dates from the latter part of May or the early days of June, 1856.

At that time the land in this county was not surveyed, nor was there a land office established until 1857, at Nebraska city. In that year Lancaster county, or at least a part of it, was surveyed, and settlers could know just where their land was located. The Prey family took up five claims, John W. Prey's claim being on Salt creek, in Centerville, section 24, town 8, range 6, on which land he made continuous residence until December, 1888, when he moved with his family to Lincoln.

The Prey family was quite numerous, the names of the boys being John W., Thomas R., James, William, David, and George, some of whom still live in the county. Those were days of hardships, times that tried men's souls, and the pioneers who braved the dangers of storm and cold and starvation and Indian depredations are to be honored. Soon after the Preys located in Lancaster county the salt basins began to attract people from everywhere, and the present site of Lincoln was the Mecca for many a settler who came to get the salt wherewith his daily food should be savored, and his horses and cattle salted. From Plattsmouth and Nebraska City, and later from Beatrice, from near and from far, came the people, with ox-teams and on foot, to get the product of the basin. Some of these visitors would remain a few hours, some several days; some would boil down the water of the basin, and thus get the salt, while others would scrape up the thin deposit and clean it from the dust, and use that. Of the salt basins further will be said in a succeeding chapter.

For some time the Preys were the only people living any where near the salt basins, the Plattsmouth men merely staking off their claims, and coming out semi-occasionally to look after their interests. During the first summer the early settlers could do nothing except break land, they having arrived too late to put in any crops.

The winter of 1856-7 was very severe; the cold was intense, and the snow averaged on the level three to four feet deep. It was about the hardest winter that has been seen in Nebraska, and while it lasted the people were much discouraged, and thought of returning to their Wisconsin home. But the bright, warm, bracing days of early spring-time dispelled this feeling, and the Preys set out to break more land and put in their spring crops. Only a little corn was planted this year — 1857 — but in 1858, the third year, a large crop was raised, and prosperity began to dawn upon them.

Soon after the Preys settled here, and before the early settlers numbered more than eight or ten, occurred the first Indian scare. From the beginning the Indians had been a source of uneasiness to the settlers, but not until early corn planting time in 1857 did any outbreak occur. At that time settlers began to drop in and take up land in Saltillo, and among them was a man named Davis. This man had a great desire to add to his experiences that of killing an Indian, and it was not long until he found an opportunity of gratifying this desire. He shot his Indian; but the consequences were worse than he anticipated. The Indians were numerous, the Pawnees, Otoes, and Omahas, taking precedence in point of numbers; so when they found that one of their number had been the victim of a white man's bullet, they went on the war path immediately. The settlers became alarmed, and taking with them only those things which to them were the most valuable, they started as rapidly as possible, and under cover of the darkness, toward Weeping Water falls, where there was quite a settlement of whites. The Lancaster settlers remained at Weeping Water about two weeks, but during that time several reconnoitering parties were sent out to view the country and report upon the feasibility of returning. During that time, also, a company of about one hundred men was formed at Nebraska City to quell the Indian uprising, and it marched toward the scene of supposed devastation. This trip resulted in the capture of one Indian, a Pawnee, who was brought into camp with a great flourish of trumpets, and consigned to the care of three men — one of whom was John W. Prey — to guard through the night. Early in the night the Indian asked to be allowed to step out of doors, which was granted, but no sooner had he stepped across the door sill than he bounded away into the darkness, leaving his moccasins, leggings, and cloak, and was never seen again by the guards. John Prey shot at him as he speeded into the darkness, and he afterward learned that the bullet from his gun grazed Mr. Lo's head, leaving a little furrow through the hair. It was a narrow escape, for Mr. Prey prided himself upon the accuracy of his aim. However, the reconnoitering parties found that the Indians had quieted down, and in about two weeks the settlers returned to their homes. Most of the settlers found their houses either destroyed or raided, but the Prey house was untouched. This ended the scare of 1857, but it came at such a time that the planting of crops was seriously interfered with, and the harvest that fall was consequently light.

Within two weeks after the return of the settlers after this scare, the Government surveyors came and laid off the land so that it could be properly entered.

Everything was then quiet until in 1859, when bands of Cheyennes and Arapahoes came to the salt basins bent on mischief of some sort. Their coming was unannounced and unexpected, and when they reached the Prey homestead the men folks were all away, leaving only the mother, a young daughter aged twelve years, named Rebecca, and two boys, aged eight and fifteen years. This young girl was some little distance from the house when the Indians appeared, and she was immediately seized upon, with the evident intention on the part of the Indians of stealing her. Their plans were, however, frustrated by the courage of the mother and the timely arrival of the male members of the family. But little damage was done to the Salt creek settlements by these Indians, who soon passed on to the north. With the exception of a false alarm in 1864, these were the only troubles of any note that the Lancaster county settlers had with the Indians, but at the time they furnished considerable interest to the little handful of men, who were braving these western wilds.

Mr. Prey is blessed with a splendid memory, and tells many interesting happenings, including the above, of these times of excitement. The nearest trading point, for some time, was Nebraska City, but during the first winter, a severe one, the Prey family were very fortunate in having laid in an ample stock of provisions from St. Louis, which doubtless saved them much suffering. Mr. Prey was treasurer of the old county of Clay, before it was divided, and has been one of Lancaster county's commissioners a number of terms.

During the Indian scare of 1864, when it was thought that the bloodthirsty Sioux would continue their marauding movements eastward from the Big Blue river, nearly all the people left the settlement in the region of Lincoln, then Lancaster. Several men decided to take chances and remain until they saw or heard something of the savages. Not being attacked for two or three days, they decided to go westward, toward the Blue river, until they should learn something of the movements of the Sioux. They were well mounted and armed with rifles and revolvers, the party consisting of Capt. W. T. Donovan, John S. Gregory, E. W. Warnes, Richard Wallingford, James Morgan, John P. Loder, Aaron Wood, and one other, eight in all. They saw no signs of redskins until they came in sight of the Blue river. Then while looking around for the wily Sioux warriors, they saw a single Indian peeping over a hill some distance to their rear, and decided to ride back, lest this incident might bode mischief. They had only began the movement of retreat, when suddenly there rose up from the low grounds, in response to signals, several hundred mounted Indians, right across their pathway, and the savages began to bear down upon the little company of whites, and to hem them in. The pale faces were paler than usual then, for it looked as though they were going to see more of the Indians than they had expected, and that death was not many minutes ahead. Having strapped their rifles to their shoulders and drawn their revolvers, they made a start, to attempt the desperate feat of forcing their way through the line of savages, or die in the endeavor. They had only begun this movement, when the Indians put up a white flag, and one warrior rode down upon them, throwing away his gun to show his friendly intentions. The Indian hunters halted. The Indian came up, and said: "How. Me no Sioux, me Pawnee; me no fight white man."

To the great relief of the whites, this proved to be true. This was a band of Pawnee warriors, who were also out after the Sioux, and supposed they had caught a party of Sioux stragglers. When they saw their mistake they raised the white flag.

After this explanation the Pawnees rode right on after the Sioux, while the Salt creek soldiers returned to their homes, having lost a large part of their interest in the Sioux.

For some years everything moved along quietly, the number of settlers gradually increasing. Among the earliest settlers who came into the county subsequent to the arrival of the Prey family and John Dee, can be mentioned, L. N. Haskin, of New York, who came in 1863; Geo. A. Mayer, Germany, 1863; W. E. Keys, Ohio, 1863; E. G. Keys, Canada, 1863; J. S. Gregory, Vermont, 1862; John Michael, Pennsylvania, 1856; J. F. Cadman, Illinois, 1859; J. P. Loder, Ohio, 1857; Maurice Dee, a native of Nebraska, born in 1860; M. Spay, Ireland, 1859; J. A. Snyder, Indiana, 1862; C. F. Retzlaff, Germany, 1858; E. Warnes, England, 1863; R. Wallingford, Ohio, 1859; J. A. Wallingford, Ohio, 1858; W. A. Cadman, Illinois, 1859; W. E. Stewart, Indiana, 1860; Oren Snyder, Wisconsin, 1862; Solomon Kirk, Tennessee, 1857; and Dr. W. Queen, in 1860; all of whom still reside in the county.

Chris Roche, brother of Lancaster county's present efficient Treasurer, Hon. Jacob Roche, has the distinction of being born in mid ocean, on board the ship that brought his parents to this country, but there is no record that the passage money for the young man was ever paid. However, he is a staunch, loyal American citizen, even if his birth was on the "rolling deep."

Lancaster county furnished but one soldier to the Union army during the late unpleasantness — that is, but one was enlisted from the county — and that one, who bears the distinguished honor, is Dr. Wesley Queen, who enlisted in the Second Nebraska Cavalry, at Nebraska

City, having then been a resident of this county but two years. He was postmaster of Saltillo when he enlisted, and left John Cadman to perform the duties of his office while he was away.

On the second day of July, 1861, W. W. Cox, the historian of Seward county, came to the present site of Lincoln, on the invitation of Wm. T. Donovan, from Nebraska City, and engaged in the manufacture of salt. In his "History of Seward County" Mr. Cox gives a number of incidents of early life in Lancaster county, and especially in connection with the salt basins. In company with Darwin Peckham, Mr. Cox began the manufacture of salt on the 20th of August, 1861, and continued the business for some years. At that time the nearest settlers to the salt basins were W. T. Donovan, who lived on the old Cardwell place, on Salt creek, about five miles up the creek; Joel Mason, who lived a mile further up; Richard Wallingford, who lived just across the creek; John Cadman, whose place was just across the line in old Clay county, near where the hamlet of Saltillo now stands; Dr. Maxwell, who lived near Wallingford; Festus Reed, who lived in the same neighborhood; and J. L. Davison and the Prey family, who had located above Roca. To the east lived William Shirely, on Stevens creek, while a little further up lived Charles Retzlaff and John Wedencamp. Aaron Wood was located near the head of Stevens creek, while John and Louis Loder lived down Salt creek, near Waverly. Michael Shea and James Moran were also neighbors, as the term then applied.

Late in the fall of 1861 the first frame building in Lancaster county was commenced, and it was finished in the spring of 1862. Richard Wallingford was the owner, and the work was done by W. W. Cox, he being a carpenter. Mr. Wallingford was evidently desirous of making a very fine house, for the doors were of black walnut, which timber was also worked into other parts of the structure.

The most of that little band of patriots that opened the way for civilization in Lancaster county, sleep. Jacob Dawson lived long enough to see Lincoln well established, while Elder Young lived long enough to see the city grow strong and vigorous, and well on the road to commercial supremacy. Elder J. M. Young was closely identified with the early history of Lancaster county, the town of Lancaster, of which he was the founder, and later with the city of Lincoln. He died on

Saturday, February 23, 1884, and a subsequent issue of the *State Journal* says of him:

It is seldom that the *Journal* is called upon to chronicle the death of a man who, living, had so many claims to the love and respect of his fellow men, and who, dead, leaves so great a lesson of faith and works behind him, or is so sincerely mourned, as Elder J. M. Young, who has at last, after seventy-eight years of labor in his Master's vineyard, gone to receive the reward of his faithful toil.

Up to within a year Elder Young had been quite vigorous and active, notwithstanding his burden of years. For the last year he had been suffering from bronchial affections, and for about two months was confined to his bed.

Elder J. M. Young was born in Genesee county, N. Y., near Batavia, on the old Holland purchase, November 25, 1806. In 1829 he married Alice Watson, at that time eighteen years of age, who now survives him at the age of seventy-four. The following year he moved to Ohio, and from Ohio he went to Page county, Iowa, in 1859. In 1860 he came to Nebraska, and settled at Nebraska City. In 1863, near the end of the year, he came to Salt creek, and selected as a site for a town, and what he predicted would be the capital of Nebraska, the present site of Lincoln.

The following-named persons located here at the same time: Thomas Hudson, Edwin Warnes, Dr. McKesson, T. S. Shamp, Uncle Jonathan Ball, Luke Lavender, Jacob Dawson, and John Giles. It was the original intention to make the settlement a church colony, but the idea was never utilized as projected.

On eighty acres owned by him Elder Young laid out the town of Lancaster, which was made the county seat. He gave the lots in the city away, half to the county and school district, and half to the Lancaster Seminary, a school which he hoped to see established here for the promulgation of his faith. He built from the proceeds of the sale of some of the lots a building, which was called the seminary, and which was occupied by the district school and church. It was burned in 1867, and was never rebuilt.

A church was organized here, and Mr. Schamp was its first pastor. Elder Young was then President of the Iowa and Nebraska Conference. The next year after the capital was located, the stone church was built. Elder Young's dream was to build up a strong church in the capital city. He worked assiduously for the object, and put into the work some eight or ten thousand dollars of his private means. When the church went down, and he saw that his dream, in so far, had been in vain—that his dream could never be realized—he was almost broken hearted; and this was the chief cause of his departure from Lincoln, which took place in 1882, when he went to London, Nemaha county, the scene of his closing days.

Elder Young began his labors as a minister soon after he moved to Ohio, in 1829. He was President of the Ohio Annual Conference for several years, and was President of the Nebraska and Iowa Conference for about twenty years. He was a man of rare vigor and fine attainments.

Elder Young left four sons: John M. Young, of Lincoln; James O. Young, of London; Levi Young, Lancaster county; and Geo. W. Young, of Taos City, New Mexico. He was buried in Wynka Cemetery, on February 26, 1884. Elder Hudson conducted the funeral services, by request of the deceased, assisted by Rev. D. Kinney and W. T. Horn.

Reminiscences of those early days are yet plentiful. Elk and antelope were abundant, and the settlers brought down many of these prairie animals to eke out their provisions. No buffalo were here at that time, having early — before 1856 — taken their departure for the west. Besides the four-footed animals, water fowl used to congregate around the basin, such as geese, brant, swan, ducks, and pelicans.

As the Union armies gained a foothold in Missouri, large numbers of rebels found it convenient to find homes elsewhere, and many of them came to the Lancaster salt basins, thinking, probably, that salt, being a great antiseptic, might save their somewhat unsavory reputations. Great hordes would congregate at the basins, and they would frequently show their spirit by acts that were hard for Union men to endure. Once they became so insolent and insulting that the loyal men of Lancaster found it necessary to organize for self-defense, but the rebels did not care for any real demonstration of their loyalty, and hence made themselves scarce.

The first sermon preached in Lancaster county, at least near the salt basins, was by Elder Young, on the Sabbath following the fourth of July, 1863, at the house of W. W. Cox, a fair-sized congregation being present. A Sabbath-school was organized soon after, it being the first one between the Missouri river and the Rocky mountains.

It seems to be pretty well settled that the honor of being the first white child born in the county belongs to F. Morton Donovan, son of Capt. W. T. Donovan, who was born March 12, 1859. Mr. Morton Donovan is still living, or was a few months ago, and in 1867 had the honor of breaking the ground for the capitol building in this city. On March 18th, of the same year, the wife of Michael Shea, on Camp creek, gave birth to a son, and soon afterward a child was born to William Shirley.

In 1862 the homestead law was passed, and the first homestead in Lancaster county entered under this law was by Capt. Donovan, on January 2, 1863, he choosing a place just east of the present location of the insane hospital. It was in the summer of 1863 that Elder J. M. Young and his associates, representing a colony of Methodist Protestants, settled on the site of the old town of Lancaster, (now Lincoln,) which land then belonged to the Government. Jacob Dawson and John Giles took homesteads adjoining the site, and in 1864 the colony was increased by the location on or near the site of a halt dozen more settlers. Up to that time Dr. J. McKesson, Luke Lavender, E. W. Warnes, J. M. Riddle, J. and D. Bennet, Philip Humerick, E. T. Hudson, C. Aiken, Robert Monteith and his two sons, John and William, William and John Grey, O. F. Bridges, Cyrus Carter, P. Billows, W. Porter, Milton Langdon, and three or four others, were the settlers on and near the site of the old town of Lancaster. In 1864, Silas Pratt, the Crawfords, Mrs. White and daughters, C. C. White, and John Moore, settled on Oak creek, about twelve miles northeast of the Lancaster settlement.

During the Indian scare of September, 1864, the great majority of the settlers abandoned their claims and sought refuge in the towns along the Missouri. A few, however, stuck to their claims, among whom were Capt. Donovan, J. S. Gregory, and E. W. Warnes, in the vicinity of Lincoln; Richard Wallingford at Saltillo; James Moran and John P. Loder on "Lower Salt," Aaron Woods on Stevens creek, and the Prey family on the Salt, south of Lincoln. The scare was of no great account, the Indians coming no further east than the Big Blue.

In the early days there were many lively and ludicrous scenes in the courts at the basin. Hon. J. S. Gregory and Milton Langdon were the principal local attorneys, and in nearly all causes were arrayed against each other. They were both keen and tricky, ever on the alert to catch the other napping, and their legal contests were sometimes very lively. Occasionally a case would arise that would put the lawyers, court, and officers, on their mettle, and such a case was one which came off along about 1864. A rough customer, who, it is said had been a member of the rebel army, came into the county and squatted for a few days in the little settlement which was afterward Lancaster. This individual having made some dangerous threats, and having stated rather publicly and offensively that he intended to kill certain men of the settlement, an information was filed and a warrant issued and placed in the hands of the Sheriff. All was then excitement, and while the court (W. W. Cox) was giving some directions to the citizens about assisting the Sheriff, who should appear but the alleged criminal, who came stalking into the court room, carrying his rifle in convenient position for immediate use, the Sheriff following him at a respectful distance of ten or fifteen feet. Judge Cox, with his native politeness, invited the gentleman to take a seat, but the criminal promptly declined. He then took a careful survey of the court, all the surroundings, and with his rifle cocked and finger on the trigger, began a retreat, requesting all hands to stand out of the way, which they seemed much inclined to do. The Judge remarked to the Sheriff and posse: "You will be justified in taking that man if you have to kill him to do it," but they did not take him. He backed out with his drawn weapon, and no one seemed willing to risk his capture. But the culprit was bent on vengeance, and had seemingly no intention of leaving until he had wreaked it on somebody. He had become angry at the Judge for telling the officers to take him dead or alive, and so the next morning, while Mr. Cox was busy at the salt furnace, the scoundrel came sneaking up a small ravine in the rear, with a view of getting a sure shot at the man who had advised his capture. But the Judge saw the rascal before he could get a good shot, and the latter started off rapidly across the basin, followed by the Judge, who soon halted him. The villain cocked his rifle, but Mr. Cox did not seem to care for that, and marched straight up to the fellow, who curled down like a whipped cur. He received a court blessing in the open air, after which he left for parts unknown, and was never seen again.

The first term of district court was held in November, 1864, in Jacob Dawson's log cabin, and was presided over by Judge Elmer S. Dundy with the same rude dignity which he preserves to-day as Judge of the federal court.

Dawson's cabin stood where the St. Charles hotel now stands, and during the term of court Uncle Jacob was reduced to great straits to properly entertain the judge and attorneys. The term is all the more memorable because of a regular blizzard of whirling, drifting, driving snow, which came down almost the whole week. Judge Dundy appointed Judge Pottinger, of Plattsmouth, as prosecuting attorney, and as Hon. T. M. Marquett was the only other representative of the legal profession then present, he appeared on the other side in almost all the cases.

Soon after the first term of district court was held in the county, the legal talent was increased by the coming in of Ezra Tuttle, who located on Oak creek in 1865, and S. B. Galey and Hon. S. B. Pound, who settled in Lancaster in 1866. When it became certain that the war would result in the preservation of the Union, and that there would be ample security here as elsewhere for life and property, great numbers of settlers began to arrive; and a further stimulus to settlement was the certainty of the building of the Union Pacific railroad. Its eastern terminus had been fixed in the fall of 1864, and the first ground broken at that time, and this may be said to commence the era of a new and vigorous life for Nebraska and for Lancaster county.

In 1866 the Hardenburghs and Lindermans took possession of the salt works at the big basin, and erected a portable saw-mill, which was of great use to the settlement. They also erected that year a frame house, which was used for a hotel, and a frame building, in which they opened a general merchandise store. In 1867 John Monteith and sons erected a building, in which they kept a boot and shoe store. Dr. McKesson built a residence in the north part of town, and Jacob Dawson commenced the erection of an elegant stone mansion, in which he afterward resided and kept the post-office.

At the old settlers' picnic, held at Cushman park on June 19, 1889, Mr. John S. Gregory was one of the speakers, and delivered an address full of interesting reminiscences, from which the following is taken:

The early summer of 1862 found me residing in Eastern Michigan, possessed of a comfortable bank account, with the ambition for adventure usual to adolescent youth and a Government commission as United States mail agent, a position which enabled me to pass free over the mail routes of the United States, including stage lines. About this time a relative who had passed by the salt basins on his return from California, called upon us, and advised me to take advantage of my opportunities and visit them, which I immediately proceeded to do.

The only railroad line then in operation west of the Mississippi was the Hannibal & St. Joe through Northern Missouri, and I took that route. The road was then in possession of the Missouri "rebs," their pickets guarding most of the stations; but the United States mails were permitted to pass freely, and although I wore the livery of Uncle Sam, I was not molested.

From St. Joseph to Plattsmouth I went by stage. At this point public transportation was at an end, and I hired a horse to ride the rest of the way.

From Weeping Water to the basin I followed an Indian trail over the "divide," then an absolutely unsettled waste of rolling prairie — not a settler from Weeping Water until at Stephens creek William Shirley had a ranch, a log cabin of two rooms.

The older settlers know what an "Indian trail" is, but as I think some of the later ones do not, I will describe it to you. When the roving bands of Indians pass from place to place, they pile the coverings of their wigwams and their camp utensils upon their ponies' backs, and they fasten the tent poles to each side of the loaded pony, the ends dragging along behind on the ground. They often pile 150 to 200 pounds on the pony, and sometimes a squaw and papoose on top of all that. Another squaw leads the pony, and after forty or fifty have passed along in "Indian file," the sod is worn away so that it looks very much like a good wagon road. But ponies can pass where wagons cannot, as many a "tenderfoot" has found out to his sorrow.

I reached the present site of Lincoln toward evening of a warm day in September. No one lived there, or had ever lived there previous to that date. Herds of beautiful antelope gamboled over its surface during the day, and coyotes and wolves held possession during the night. Mr. Donovan, of whom Elder Davis has spoken, resided at the town (on paper) of Chester, about eight miles south. He (Donovan) did not remove to Lincoln until 1867.

About a mile west on Middle creek the smoke was rising from a camp of Otoe Indians, and down in the bend of Oak creek, where West Lincoln now stands, was a camp of about 100 Pawnee wigwams. I rode over, and that night slept upon my blanket by the side of one of them, and the next morning went over to the Salt Basin. The tread of civilization had not then marred its surface. It was smooth and level as any waxen floor. It was covered with an incrustation of salt about a quarter of an inch deep, white as the driven snow, while the water of the springs was as salt as brine could be. I had seen the basin for the first time, in its most favorable aspect, and was naturally quite enthusiastic over its prospects. A roofless and floorless log cabin stood upon the margin, built the year before by J. Sterling Morton, who had gone out from Nebraska City and "pre-empted" the basin; but it was deserted and desolate.

I immediately retraced my steps to Weeping Water, and there bought ox teams and wagons, and hired men, and went to work in earnest for the construction of salt works, which the following year I had in operation, and of the capacity of about two tons a day.

This salt found ready sale to the freighters from Denver and the mountain regions beyond, at two to three cents a pound. Until the railroads reached the Missouri river and brought Eastern salt into competition, it was quite profitable work. My first residence was a "dug-out;" that is, an excavation dug into the bank of a hill, or rather the creek bank, with a big cottonwood timber for a ridge pole, covered with poles, then topped with hay and soil. At the rear was a log fire-place. The front was of sod. Rather crude was all this, but yet quite comfortable.

The county of Lancaster was organized in the spring of 1863, and I had the honor of being chairman of the first Board of County Commissioners. An attempt had been made to organize the year before, but it had fallen through because there could not be found available men enough in the county to hold the necessary offices.

In the spring of 1864 the "Lancaster Colony" located at Lincoln, composed of the families of J. M. Young, Dawson, McKesson, Merrill, Giles, Harris, Lavender, Warnes, Humerick, Hudson, and one or two others whose names I do not just now recall. They staked out the town and called it "Lancaster," and soon afterward had the county seat established there.

The first postoffice in the county was established in 1863, and was named "Gregory's Basin." I was appointed postmaster, with a yearly salary of $3. I was also allowed $12 per year for carrying the mail weekly from Saltillo, then in Clay county.

The Lincoln postoffice pays a larger salary now, but I am not postmaster. In the fall of '63 and spring of '64 quite a colony of citizens of Northern Missouri came to the basin. The fortunes of war had made it unpleasant for the partisans of Jeff. Davis, particularly for those who had been suspected of indulging in an occasional shot from the bushes at neighbors of other political leaning; and they came up here to "Wait till the clouds rolled by;" but after the war closed, all went back to their Missouri homes.

About this time there came into our fold, from somewhere on the borders of Iowa, Mr. Alf. Eveland, and he became one of the "characters" of our early times. All you old settlers remember Eveland: a little, wiry, freckle-faced man, with hair as red as fire. He came to the basin and started a "saloon" at the cabin where he lived, with a keg of whisky, some beer, and a caddy of tobacco; but as he and his two sons-in-law, Jim and Kill Harmon, were its best customers, he didn't accumulate a fortune. But Eveland was ambitious. He wanted to be called "squire," so we elected him "justice of the peace," the first to hold that office in the county.

On the morning the Missourians pulled out for "home," one of them who had a lot of staves, of the value of about twenty dollars, came over to my works and sold them to me. I took the precaution to count and mark the staves, and took a receipt for the pay. A few days afterward, when I drove over to get them, I found Dr. Crimm (who had, you know, come up from Brownville, and had a bench of salt boilers in operation) loading these same staves. I asked him what he was doing with my staves, and he produced a receipt for pay of purchase price from this same Missourian, sold to him the same morning as to myself. We had been "sold" together with the staves, so we agreed to divide them equally. But just then the thought struck one of us that Eveland had been "squire" for several months and hadn't had a case, so we concluded to have a "law suit" and test the "squire's" capability. While I loaded up the property, Crimm rushed away, as angry as he could assume to be, and soon had a writ of replevin served. The day of trial came, and of course the whole settlement had to be present. As the doctor was plaintiff, he proved his case — that he had bought the goods of the owner, paid his money, marked the staves, and had a signed bill of sale on the morning the owner went away; upon which the squire announced that as he was entirely satisfied of the plaintiff's ownership, and should so decide in any event, it would be unnecessary for the defendant to take any further trouble in the matter; but we both insisted that the defense was entitled to their proof, and then it would be the duty of the justice to decide the ownership. So the trial proceeded, the evidence, of course, being identical with the plaintiff's. And then there was a puzzled squire, running his fingers through his "aburn" locks, and careful meditation brought no solution; and after vainly endeavoring to have "us boys" go and settle our dispute ourselves, offering to remit all costs if we would do so, he took three days to "consider." At the end of that time he was no nearer a determination, and asked our "terms" to take the case off his hands, which we finally agreed to do, in consideration that he should "treat" all our friends from his saloon. Well, we called in every one we could get word to in the county, and we bankrupted his business. That was the end of the first lawsuit and of the first saloon in Lancaster county. Eveland resigned his justiceship in disgust, and removed to a homestead down near where the Cropsey mill now stands; but he has now gone from there, gone away from us, but not from our memory.

During the winter of 1863, Mr. John S. Gregory, not having any other business to attend to, gave some attention to destroying some of the numerous wolves which then infested this region. He would insert a few grains of strychnine into little balls of fat, and then pass around a large circuit and drop the balls in the snow. The wolves would follow the trail, and snap up every ball. Every wolf that swallowed a ball was dead in a short time. He would then skin the animals, their pelts being valuable at that time. The carcasses he piled up in cords, north of Lincoln, to prevent the poisoning of domestic animals by eating the flesh. They were frozen stiff and stark, and corded up like wood. Toward spring Mr. Gregory had a couple of cords of carcasses piled up at one place. Then a lot of Pawnee Indians came along and stopped near the cords of wolf carcasses. Mr. Gregory, fearing they might eat the wolves, rode over to warn them of the danger. He found the squaws and papooses lugging the wolf carcasses into camp, and he at once expostulated with them, by signs, trying to make them understand it was dangerous to eat the wolves. The old chief thought he was demanding the return of the wolves because they were his property, and at the chief's command, the squaws and papooses lugged the carcasses back, and piled them up again. They were not well pleased at the prospect of losing a feast, and returned the wolf meat with long faces. Finally a member of the tribe, who could speak a little English, came along, and Mr. Gregory explained to him that he did not care for the wolf carcasses, but did not want the Indians to be poisoned. This explanation was made to the Indians, who set up a big guffaw, and the squaws at once began to gather up the wolf carcasses and take them to camp, laughing and indulging in expressions of great satisfaction. They cooked up the last one of the wolves, and had a great feast.

Mr. Gregory learned from the interpreter that the Indians were well acquainted with the use of strychnine in killing wolves, and were in the habit of eating animals killed in this way. They had no fear of the drug, and suffered no apparent damage from eating the wolves.

CHAPTER VI.

POLITICAL HISTORY OF THE COUNTY—A COMPLETE LIST OF THE STATE AND COUNTY OFFICERS FROM THE BEGINNING TO THE PRESENT.

The organization and political history of Lancaster county is, of course, of great interest, and valuable. Political contests in those early days were as warm as at present, and political canvasses were made with the same spirit of rivalry that now exists. For this part of the history of Lancaster county, the authors are indebted to Hon. Chas. H. Gere, editor of the *State Journal*, who prepared a chapter upon Lancaster county for W. W. Cox's "History of Seward County." The work is well and accurately done, as many of the dates and figures have been compared with the records and found to be correct, and the authors have no hesitancy in giving the subjoined extract as being a comprehensive and exact political history of the county. Mr. Gere's figures and reminiscences reach to and include the fall election of 1887, which have been supplemented by the authors from the records to bring the history down to date:

In the fall of 1859 the first movement toward county organization was made. A public meeting was held under the "Great Elm" that stood on the east bank of Salt creek, near the northwest corner of the B. & M. R. R. depot grounds, in Lincoln. Festus Reed was elected chairman, and after a strong speech predicting the future greatness of the little commonwealth they were preparing to organize on the frontier, the business in hand was proceeded with. A. J. Wallingford, Joseph J. Forest, and W. T. Donovan, were appointed a commission to select a location for a county seat, and they chose the present site of Lincoln, which was laid off in 1864, and named "Lancaster." An election was ordered by the Commissioners of Cass county, to which the unorganized county west was attached for election and judicial purposes, to be held at the house of William Shirley, on Stevens creek, and Judges and Clerks of Election duly commissioned. At this election, held on the 10th day of October, 1859, A. J. Wallingford, J. J. Forest, and W. T. Donovan, were elected a Board of County Commissioners; Richard Wallingford was elected County Treasurer; L. J. Loder, County Clerk; and John P. Loder, Recorder. No record of this election, or of the official proceedings of the county officers, are on file, except the certificates of the election and the qualification of L. J. Loder and J. P. Loder, in the archives of the county.

It is probable that little or no business was done under this organization. On the 9th of October, 1860, a general election took place, and was held at the house of W. T. Donovan for Lancaster county. Twenty-three votes were cast, and the following names are found on the official poll list:

Jeremiah Showalter, Richard Wallingford, J. D. Main, C. F. Retzlaff, Johnathan Ball, Hiram Allen, Benj. Eaves, Festus Reed, Daniel Harrington, James Coultard, Benj. Hemple, Wm. Shirley, James Moran, J. J. Forest, E. L. Reed, Michael Shea, L. J. Loder, John Dee, A. J. Wallingford, Aaron Wood, Lucius West, J. P. Loder, and W. T. Donovan.

For Delegate to Congress J. Sterling Morton received eleven votes, and Samuel G. Dailey twelve, showing a close contest. For Councilman, equivalent to a Senator in a State, T. M. Marquett received thirteen votes, and W. R. Davis two. For "joint," or float Councilman, Samuel H. Ebert received fifteen votes, and ———— Cozad one. For Representative, Wm. Gilmore had sixteen votes; Louden Mullen, fifteen; W. R. Davis, sixteen; Wm. Reed, sixteen; E. W. Barnum, twelve; and J. N. Wise, six.

For county officers the following were elected without opposition: Commissioners—one year, J. J. Forest; two years, A. J. Wallingford; three years, W. T. Donovan; Treasurer—R. Wallingford; Clerk—J. P. Loder. No candidate for Sheriff, Prosecuting Attorney, or Coroner, appears to have been running, and probably there was not business enough in the legal line to pay for the trouble of getting up a ticket. Festus Reed and R. Wallingford were elected Justices of the Peace, and C. F. Retzlaff and James Coultard Constables. Had all the offices to which the county was entitled been filled, they would have gone more than half way round the entire voting population. There are no records of any official acts of these officers elect.

On the eighth of October, 1861, the county election was held at the house of James Moran, and only fourteen votes were cast. The new names appearing on the poll list preserved in the office of the County Clerk, are: E. Galvin, E. L. Barrett, T. G. Maxwell, and Michael McDonald. Donovan, Wallingford, the Loders, Ball, Reed, Moran, Harrington, Dee, and Shea, again exercised the right of suffrage.

J. J. Forest was elected County Commissioner; Festus Reed, Probate Judge; L. J. Loder, Sheriff; J. P. Loder, Clerk; C. L. Barrett, Assessor; T. G. Maxwell and J. Moran, Justices of the Peace; and Jonathan Ball and C. F. Retzloff, Constables.

A record of an adjourned meeting of the County Commissioners, after this election, held May 1, 1862, is the first sign of official life in Lancaster county to be found in the County Clerk's office. This record occupies fifteen lines on a page of small commercial note paper, and informs us that the county was then and there divided into two election precincts, by a line running east and west through the center of "town 10;" and a petition for a road from the southeast corner of section 31, town 9, range 7, and another from the southeast corner of section 36, town 9, range 6, and one from the southeast corner of section 16, town 12, range 6, were received. In what direction and whither these roads were to run, the record saith not, and County Clerk J. P. Loder forgot to append his signature to the document. The Board adjourned till July first, but probably did not meet again till after the October election.

At the election of 1862, held on the fourteenth of October, the division of the county into two precincts was disregarded. Fourteen votes were cast, by Messrs

Cox, Mason, Foster, Calkin, Chatterton, Blunt, Wallingford, Ball, Chambers, Loder, Maxwell, Van Benthusen, Donovan, and Coultard. J. F. Kinney, Independent Democrat, received ten votes, and Sam. G. Dailey four, for Delegate to Congress. T. M. Marquett received twelve votes for Councilman for the district. Geo. L. Seybolt received ten, and J. E. Doom three votes, for joint or float Councilman. Five other Cass county statesmen received from one to seven votes for Representative, and T. G. Maxwell received thirteen, all, it is presumed, but his own suffrage, for the same office; but the other counties in the district not doing so well by him, he was not elected. Joel Mason was elected Commissioner.

The next record is of a meeting of the Board of County Commissioners, held November 3d, which ordered a special election to be held on January 17, 1863, to fill vacancies in the offices of Coroner, Surveyor, and Justices of the Peace and Constables, as those prviously elected had not qualified.

The next meeting was held February 5, 1863, and the officers elected at the special election sworn in. The Clerk was directed, at this meeting, to notify Judge Festus Reed to stop his depredations on the timber in the school section, in town nine, range six.

Another meeting was held September 12th, of the same year, and the county divided into four precincts — named Lancaster, Salt Basin, Stevens Creek, and Salt Creek, and the various places for holding elections were designated.

In 1863 the county election was held October 13th, and an entire new set of officers were elected, fifty-five votes having been cast in the county.

J. S. Gregory was elected County Commissioner for three years, William Shirley for two, and P. S. Schamp for one year. Clerk, Milton Langdon; Treasurer, R. Wallingford; Sheriff, Joseph Chambers; Surveyor, J. J. Forest; Coroner, Dr. John Crim; Probate Judge, J. D. Main.

J. S. Gregory was elected to the State Legislature, for the Representative district to which Lancaster belonged, and John Cadman, who lived in that part of the county then belonging to Clay, was elected for Clay, Johnson, and Gage counties, and took with him a petition from the residents of the northern and southern parts of Clay county for the wiping out of that county, and dividing it between Lancaster and Gage. This measure was consummated, and the addition to Lancaster made her a county of no mean proportions, extending thirty-six miles north and south, and twenty-four east and west.

The assessed valuation of Clay county at the time of its transfer was $36,129.82, of which $22,637.82 fell to the share of Lancaster. Her debt was $295.11, of which Lancaster assumed $185.70.

The Commissioners of Lancaster and Gage held a meeting at the house of H. W. Parker, Clerk of Clay county, near Olathe, July 19, 1864, and made a final settlement of the affairs of the county. The document setting forth the terms of this settlement was signed by Fordice Roper, F. H. Dobbs, and William Tyler, Commissioners of Clay county, and John W. Prey, of Lancaster, and attested by Oliver Townsend, clerk of Gage county, and duly filed. Copies of the official records of Clay county were made for Gage and Lancaster counties, but the latter were lost in Salt creek while en route, and have never been filed among the archives of the county.*

---

*John W. Prey was the Treasurer of Clay county when the division was made, and by some means had charge of the records referred to. When the division had been completed

At the time of the division of Clay county the principal settlements were in the extreme north and south of its territory, and a large majority of its tax-payers were undoubtedly favorable to its division. But after the lapse of a few years, when the central part was filled up with inhabitants, much discussion ensued as to the propriety of restoring the county, and several attempts have been made in that direction; but it is probable that the majority of the people in the territory involved are well satisfied with their present status. The clause on county division in the constitution adopted in 1875, will probably preclude any further agitation, and will establish our present boundaries for all time to come.

In 1864, at the Territorial election held October 11th, eighty votes were polled, of which P. W. Hitchcock received fifty-three, and George L. Miller twenty-seven, for Delegate to Congress.

John Cadman was elected to the House of Representatives for Lancaster county, and William Imlay for the Representative district composed of Lancaster, Seward, and Saline counties. Richard Wallingford was elected County Commissioner; P. S. Schamp, Surveyor; and Milton Langdon, Prosecuting Attorney.

At the general election, October 10, 1865, 125 votes were polled. August Kountze, for Territorial Treasurer, John Gillespie, for Auditor, received 100 votes each, and S. G. Goodman and John Seaton, their opponents, six votes each.

John Cadman was re-elected Representative for Lancaster county, and Joel Mason for the district of Lancaster, Seward, and Saunders counties.

The county officers elected were: Milton Langdon, Clerk; Luke Lavender, Probate Judge; S. S. Snyder, County Commissioner; William Guy, Treasurer; W. Ingram, Coroner; J. S. Gregory, Prosecuting Attorney; and P. S. Schamp, Surveyor.

June 2, 1866, an election was held under the State constitution, prepared by the Territorial Legislature of '65–'66, at which 165 votes were polled in the county, of which David Butler received 112, and J. Sterling Morton 53, for Governor; for the constitution, 95; against, 53. John Cadman was elected Senator to the first State Legislature, which met July 4th. James Queen, of Lancaster, was returned elected as Representative from Lancaster, Seward, and Saunders, and his seat was contested by his opponent, J. L. Davison, of Seward, and the contest was pending when the Legislature adjourned, after an eight-days' session. Ezra Tullis was elected Representative from the county.

At the October election of the same year, pending the admission of Nebraska as a State, 199 votes were cast, of which T. M. Marquett, (Republican,) received 129, and J. Sterling Morton, (Democrat,) 69 for Delegate to Congress.

J. E. Doom, of Cass, was elected Territorial Councilor and State Senator from Cass and Lancaster; E. K. Clark, of Seward, Representative from Lancaster, Seward, and Saunders; and E. H. Hardenberg, Representative from Lancaster county

---

he sent these records to Beatrice, to have the copies made. When the copy was ready for Lancaster county, Mr. Prey sent over to Beatrice a man named William Mills, a neighbor, with an order for the books. Mills's especial errand to Beatrice was to get a grist of flour. On getting this and the records Mills started home, late in the afternoon. When he reached Salt creek a tremendous rain had raised the waters very high, and not thinking of this, Mills plunged his team into the stream where he had comfortably forded it on his trip to Beatrice. The current was too strong, and the wagon box was floated off and upset, records, grist, and groceries, floating down the tide. Mills himself was nearly drowned, and was only rescued by the Prey family, whose residence was near the ford, rushing out and lending him assistance.

to both United States and State Legislatures. Hardenberg resigned at the close of the session of the Territorial Legislature, in March, 1867, and John Cadman was elected to fill the vacancy in the State Legislature, which was called immediately after.

John W. Prey was elected County Commissioner in the Third District.

At the county election of 1867, held October 8th, 235 votes were cast. The officers elected were: Silas Pratt, Commissioner; John Cadman, Probate Judge; S. B. Galey, County Clerk; J. H. Hawke, Sheriff; M. Langdon, Treasurer; Ezra Tullis, Surveyor; F. A. Bidwell, School Commissioner; and Emil Lange, Coroner.

At the State election of 1868, held October 11th, 460 votes were cast. David Butler, (Republican,) received 320, and J. R. Porter, (Democrat,) 123. C. H. Gere, of Lancaster, was elected Senator for the district composed of Lancaster, Saline, Gage, Pawnee, and Jefferson counties; Ezra Tullis, Representative from the county; W. K. Fields, County Commissioner.

Seth Robinson, of Lancaster, was appointed Attorney General by Governor Butler.

At the county election, October 10, 1869, 562 votes were cast. S. B. Pound, (Republican,) for Probate Judge, receiving 392; J. M. Bradford, (Democrat,) 170. Capt. R. A. Bain was elected Clerk; John Cadman, Treasurer; Sam. McClay, Sheriff; M. Langdon, Surveyor; Robert Faulkner and D. H. Sudduth, County Commissioners; Allen M. Ghost, Superintendent Public Instruction; Dr. D. W. Tingley, Coroner.

At the State election, October 11, 1870, 1,116 votes were polled. David Butler (Republican) receiving 798; John H. Croxton, (Democrat,) 318. Col. A. J. Cropsey, of Lancaster, was elected Senator for the district, and S. B. Galey Representative for the county.

An election was held May 2, 1871, for Delegates to the Constitutional Convention, which met in June, and Seth Robinson and J. N. Cassell were elected to represent the county; Col. J. E. Philpott, of Lancaster, from the Eleventh Senatorial District, of Lancaster and Seward; and W. H. Curtis, of Pawnee, for the Fourteenth Representative District, composed of Lancaster, Saunders, Johnson, Pawnee, and Gage.

At the election on the new constitution, held September 19th of the same year, 1,415 votes were cast —1,237 for the new constitution, and 178 against it. The constitution was not adopted.

At the county election of October 10th of the same year, 1,259 votes were cast. The officers elected were: J. D. Lottridge, County Commissioner; A. L. Palmer, Probate Judge; R. O. Phillips, Clerk; R. A. Bain, Treasurer; A. M. Ghost, Superintendent Public Instruction; J. T. Murphy, Surveyor; and Dr. J. G. Fuller, Coroner.

At the State election, October 8, 1872, 1,736 votes were polled. L. Crounse (Republican) receiving 1,189, and J. L. Warner (Democrat) 535, for Member of Congress. S. B. Pound, of Lancaster, was elected Senator for the Eleventh District; S. G. Owen and A. K. White, Representatives for the county; and M. H. Sessions, of Lancaster, Representative for the Fourteenth District. Henry Spellman was elected County Commissioner. J. J. Gosper, of Lancaster, was elected Secretary of State.

At the county election, October 14, 1873, 1,927 votes were polled. The officers elected were: J. Z. Briscoe, Commissioner; A. L. Palmer, Probate Judge; R. O. Phillips, Clerk; Charles C. White, Treasurer; Sam. McClay, Sheriff; Dr. J. O. Carter, Coroner; Tom I. Atwood, Surveyor; J. W. Cassell, Superintendent Public Instruction.

At the State election, October 13, 1874, 2,038 votes were polled, Silas Garber (Republican) receiving 1,382; Albert Tuxbury, (Democrat,) 287; J. H. Gardner, (Independent,) 170; and Jarvis S. Church, (Prohibition,) 139.

C. C. Burr, of Lancaster, was elected Senator for the Eleventh District; Alfred G. Hastings and Louis Helmer, Representatives for the county, and Thomas P. Chapman, of Saunders, for the Fourteenth Representative District.

Dr. H. D. Gilbert was elected County Commissioner, and A. G. Scott Superintendent of Public Instruction, to fill vacancy. On the question of a Constitutional Convention, there were 1,069 ayes to 558 noes.

At the election for members of the Constitutional Convention, held on the 6th of April, 1875, S. B. Pound and C. H. Gere, of Lincoln, C. W. Pierce, of Waverly, and J. B. Hawley, of Firth, were elected to represent the county.

At the State election under the proposed new constitution, and the county election, both occurring October 12, 1875, 2,360 votes were polled, S. B. Pound, (Republican,) of Lancaster, receiving 1,533, and G. B. Scofield, of Otoe, 727, for Judge of the Second Judicial District. Judge Pound was elected. The county officers elected were: W. E. Keys, County Commissioner; A. G. Scott, County Judge; William A. Sharrar, Clerk; Charles C. White, Treasurer; Sam. McClay, Sheriff; Dr. A. C. Gibson, Coroner; S. G. Lamb, Superintendent Public Instruction; J. P. Walton, Surveyor. For the new constitution, 2,119; against, 109. S. J. Tuttle, of Lancaster, was elected a Regent of the University.

At the State Election, November, 1876, 2,911 votes were polled, of which Silas Garber, (Republican,) candidate for Governor, received 1,947; Paren England, (Democrat,) of Lancaster, 712; and J. F. Gardner, (Greenback,) 252. The Senators elected from the county, which was now entitled to two, were Thomas P. Kennard, of Lincoln, and Cyrus N. Baird, of Oak creek. The Representatives elected were R. O. Phillips and W. C. Griffith, of Lincoln, John Cadman, of Yankee Hill, and Henry Spellman, of Saltillo. J. N. Wilcox was elected Commissioner.

At the county election of 1877, A. D. Burr was elected Clerk; Louis Helmer, Treasurer; J. S. Hoagland, Sheriff; J. B. Webster, County Judge; G. S. Lamb, Superintendent of Public Instruction; J. P. Walton, Surveyor; E. T. Piper, Coroner; H. D. Gilbert, Commissioner; and C. W. Pierce, State Senator, to fill vacancy.

At the State election of 1878, Albinus Nance, (Republican,) candidate for Governor, received 1,971 votes; W. H. Webster, (Democrat,) 433; and L. G. Todd, (Greenback,) 409. Whole number of votes cast, 2,818. Amasa Cobb, of Lancaster, was elected a Justice of the Supreme Court. M. B. Cheney and E. E. Brown were elected to the Senate, and S. G. Owen, W. W. Carder, M. H. Sessions, and T. R. Burling, to the House. John McClay was elected Commissioner.

At the county election, November, 1879, W. J. Weller was elected County Commissioner; J. E. Philpot, Judge; L. E. Cropsey, Clerk; Louis Helmer, Treasurer; Granville Ensign, Sheriff; A. D. Burr, Clerk District Court; E. T. Piper, Coroner; H. S. Bowers, Superintendent Public Instruction; and J. P. Walton, Surveyor. Amasa Cobb, of Lancaster, was re-elected Justice of the Supreme Court for the full term. S. B. Pound, of Lancaster, was elected Judge of the Second Judicial District for a second term.

At the State election of 1880, 4,778 votes were cast, of which Albinus Nance (Republican) received 3,397 and T. W. Tipton (Democrat) 1,381. The Senators elected were C. H. Gere and C. W. Pierce. Representatives, N. C. Abbott, C. O. Whedon, N. T. McClunn, and R. B. Graham. Commissioner, W. E. G. Caldwell.

At the county election of 1881 the following officers were chosen: Treasurer, R. B. Graham; Clerk, John M. McClay; Judge, C. M. Parker; Commissioner, H. C. Keller; Superintendent of Public Instruction, H. S. Bowers; Sheriff, Gran Ensign; Surveyor, J. P. Walton; Coroner, A. J. Shaw.

At the State election of 1882, 4,818 votes were cast, of which James W. Dawes (Republican) received 3,328; J. Sterling Morton, (Democrat,) 1,099, and E. P. Ingersoll, (Anti-Monopoly,) 391. Senators were E. E. Brown and P. H. Walker. Representatives, C. O. Whedon, A. W. Field, H. Wessenberg, J. W. Worl, M. H. Sessions, and M. H. Wescott. Commissioner, W. J. Miller. W. W. W. Jones, of Lancaster, was elected State Superintendent of Public Instruction, and C. H. Gere, a Regent of the university.

At the county election of 1883 the officers elected were: R. B. Graham, Treasurer; J. H. McClay, Clerk; E. R. Sizer, Clerk of District Court; S. M. Melick, Sheriff; C. M. Parker, Judge; W. E. G. Caldwell, Commissioner; J. P. Walton, Surveyor; H. S. Bowers, Superintendent of Public Instruction; N. J. Beachley, Coroner; Levi Snell, Senate, to fill vacancy. S. B. Pound was elected to a third term from this county, as a Judge of the Second Judicial District.

At the State and legislative election of 1884 the whole number of votes cast in the county was 6,101. Dawes, (Republican,) for Governor, received 4,012; Morton (Democrat) 2,180, and J. G. Miller, of Lancaster, (Prohibition,) 209. C. C. Burr and Alba Smith were elected Senators, and S. W. Burnham, Wm. B. Brandt, H. J. Liesveldt, A. W. Field, and J. B. Wright, to the House. Commissioner, H. C. Keller. Allen W. Field, of the Lancaster delegation, was, on taking his seat, elected Speaker of the House.

At the county election of 1885 the following officers were chosen: Treasurer, Jacob Roche; Clerk, O. C. Bell; Sheriff, S. M. Melick; Judge, C. M. Parker; Register of Deeds, J. H. McClay; Surveyor, J. P. Walton; Coroner, E. T. Roberts; Superintendent of Public Instruction, Frank D. McCluskey; Commissioner, Alba Brown. C. H. Gere was re-elected a Regent of the university, and Amasa Cobb was re-elected to the supreme bench.

At the State election of 1886 the whole number of votes cast was 6,834, of which John M. Thayer (Republican) received for Governor, 3,985; James E. North (Democrat) 1,424, and H. W. Hardy, of Lancaster, (Prohibition,) 925. R. E. Moore and S. W. Burnham were elected to the Senate, and J. L. Caldwell, J. Shamp, I. M. Raymond, J. Dickinson, H. J. Liesveldt, and G. W. Eggleston, to the House. Commissioner, H. J. Shaberg.

At the county election of 1887, the following officers were chosen: Treasurer, Jacob Roche; Clerk, O. C. Bell; Sheriff, S. M. Melick; Judge, W. E. Stewart; Register of Deeds, John D. Knight; Commissioner, Thos. Dickson; Superintendent Public Instruction, Frank D. McCluskey; Surveyor, J. P. Walton; Clerk of District Court, E. R. Sizer. Allen W. Field, of Lancaster, was elected a Judge of the second judicial district.

At the State election held on November 6, 1888, 9,962 votes were cast, of which Thayer, (Republican,) for Governor, received 5,440; McShane (Democrat) 3,610, and Bigelow (Prohibition) 811. At that election, Connell (Republican) was elected to Congress for the First Congressional District, receiving 5,355 votes, to 3,821 for Morton, (Democrat,) and 795 for Graham, (Prohibition.) For the State Senate, Raymond and Beardsley were elected, while for the House, Messrs. Hall, Caldwell, Dickinson, Severin, and McBride, were the successful candidates, all being Republicans.

R. D. Stearns was elected County Attorney, and Alba Brown, Commissioner.

CHAPTER VII.

THE SALT BASINS — GREAT EXPECTATIONS OF THE EARLY SETTLERS AND RESIDENTS OF LINCOLN — AN INTERESTING CALCULATION OF THE WEALTH-PRODUCING POWER OF THE WELLS — THE ATTEMPTS MADE TO REALIZE THESE EXPECTATIONS.

The first settlers in Lancaster county were attracted here by the fame of the Salt Basin, which in that early day had extended as far east as Plattsmouth and Nebraska City. The early settlers near the basins made many fanciful pictures of the wealth to be obtained from these same basins, and pictured to themselves a great city built near by, whose great source of wealth should be the working of the "salt wells." And it is safe to presume that one reason why the State capital was located at Lincoln (or Lancaster) was the fact that salt was one of the products of Lancaster county, and that the Commissioners believed that the manufacture of salt would, in the future, prove the foundation of a great business, which would attract capital to the little hamlet on the prairie. It is, however, certain that the early residents of Lincoln set great store by the basins, and that for years every intelligent man predicted wonderful results from the making of salt.

As proof of this it is here pertinent to quote from a little pamphlet of thirty pages, a history of Lincoln, the authorship of which is to be laid at the door of Hon. John H. Ames, and which was published by the "*State Journal* Power Press Print" in 1870, a few of the fancies and figures current in those days. Mr. Ames says:

"In the following remarks an effort will be made to furnish a knowledge of the facts and circumstances, established by experience, upon which it may be safe to base a final judgment. So far as known, no similar effort has previously been made; and while care will be taken that any information that may be contained herein shall be authentic, yet it must of necessity be less full and complete than may be desirable, or than it might be made if there had been any thorough and detailed official investigation and report thereon.

"In the absence of such assistance, recourse will be had to parties who are engaged in the business of making salt by solar evaporation, and in sinking the well for the purpose of testing the strength and value of the brine to be obtained beneath the surface at this place, any information derived from which sources may be relied upon as being entirely authentic and trustworthy."

After referring somewhat fully to a pamphlet published in 1869, by Augustus F. Harvey, entitled "Nebraska as it is," in which a description of the salt basins is given, and a prediction of the great undeveloped wealth which they represent is made, Mr. Ames continues:

"Previous to the time that the above passages were written, nothing like an extensive manufacture of salt at this place had been attempted. Some parties, however, had evaporated considerable quantities of the surface brine, both by means of solar and artificial heat, and the product obtained had been carefully analyzed by eminent chemists in New York City and other places, and the result, as declared by them, was as above stated. [Twenty-eight and eight tenths per cent of salt by weight; the product containing ninety-five to ninety-seven parts of pure salt, and three to five parts of chlorides and sulphates of magnesium, calcium, lime, etc.—ED.] But it is thought that the statement of Mr. Harvey in regard to the strength of the surface brine, although no doubt intentionally correct, is, nevertheless, inaccurate.

"During the summer months, and when a considerable interval of time has elapsed, characterized by an absence of rain and the prevalence of the warm, dry winds which he mentions, the constant evaporation from the surface of the wide, shallow basins or pools of salt water often suffices to reduce the brine contained therein to the strength of 28.8 per cent; and in fact, when such a state of the atmosphere has prevailed for a long time, the recession of water from the edges of the basin not unfrequently leaves thereon an incrustation, from a half an inch to an inch in thickness, of almost pure salt; but the brine, as it oozes from the soil, has not been found to exceed fifteen per cent in strength. It has been found that the rapidity of evaporation at Syracuse, and other Eastern springs, is in the proportion of two in the summer and one in the winter. Owing to the absence of heavy falls of snow, and the considerable prevalence of dry winds at the place during the winter months, it is believed that the proportional evaporation during this time will be greater.

"Early in the summer of 1869, Messrs. Cahn and Evans, having leased 640 acres of land from the State Government for that purpose, commenced work preparatory to sinking a well in the immediate vicinity of one of these salt springs, and at a distance of about one and one-half miles from the market square of the city; and having erected a derrick and procured an engine and the necessary machinery they proceeded early in the autumn to effect this purpose, keeping an accurate record of the rock and other formations through which they penetrated. By means of this record, with the aid of such knowledge as is obtainable of the ledges exposed in different localities, an approximate and reasonably definite conclusion may be formed as to the location of the center of the basin."

After giving the formations through which penetration was made, Mr. Ames continues:

"The ground near the wells is usually divided off into blocks, or squares, of several rods, between which are spaces or streets of convenient width, a map of the whole resembling the plat of a town. Across the squares, in one direction, are constructed vats or troughs, sixteen feet in width, and about eight inches in depth, in which the brine is exposed to atmospheric action. Covers, sixteen feet square, and adjusted with grooves or rollers, are provided, with which to prevent the brine from being diluted by falling rain. For the purpose of calculation, these covers may be taken to represent the number and size of the vats, and accordingly this is the size meant wherever the word vat is hereinafter used.

"As shown by the result of Mr. Harvey's experiment, six inches in depth of saturated or $33\frac{1}{3}$ per cent brine, that being the usual amount exposed in one of the vats, would, under ordinary circumstances, evaporate in thirty-six hours; or twice that quantity would be evaporated every three days, leaving as a product 144,456 cubic inches, or over 68.36 bushels of salt. This process repeated seven times every three weeks for twenty-one weeks, during the summer months, would result in the manufacture of 3,349.64 bushels, and repeated seven times every six weeks for thirty of the remaining thirty-one weeks in the year, would produce 2,392.60 bushels, which, added to the former, would make a total amount of 5,742.24 bushels, or 1,148.43 barrels of salt annually from one vat. Multiply this number by 1,000, the usual number of vats supplied from one well, and from the product subtract one-fifth of itself, as an allowance for the difference in the amounts of salt contained in saturated brine and brine of eighty degrees strength, and from the balance subtract one-twenty-fifth of itself, as an allowance for the smaller quantity of the weaker brine evaporated within the same time, (as a calculation sufficiently accurate for all practical purposes,) and the entire amount of salt which may be manufactured annually from one well will be seen to be 882,001.6 barrels.

"Supposing, what is not at all probable, that the brine should prove to be possessed of only sixty degrees strength, the rapidity of evaporation being the same, we will subtract from this amount one-fourth of itself, as an allowance for the difference in the product between equal quantities of the two brines, and from the balance subtract one-twenty-sixth of itself, as an allowance for the smaller quantity of the weaker brine evaporated within the same time, and it shows a result of 636,058.84 barrels annually. Change the supposition so that the strength of the brine will remain at eighty degrees, and the rapidity of evaporation will be reduced one-half, and we have only to divide the first product obtained by two, which leaves us an annual yield of 441,000.80 barrels. Uniting these contingencies, that is, supposing the strength of the brine not to exceed sixty degrees, and the rapidity of evaporation to be only one-half as great as it has been demonstrated to be by experiment, we will divide the second result by two, and there will be shown an annual product of 318,029.42 barrels. Making a deduction of one-fourth from each result obtained, as an allowance for loss of time consequent upon injuries to or breakage of machinery, and bad weather, and there will be left, in the order named, as follows:

	Barrels.
First	661,501.20
Second	417,044.13
Third	330,750.60
Fourth	238,522.60

"While the railways now being constructed and those projected will give us direct connection with the Eastern markets, and enable us to compete with Eastern salt manufactories upon their own ground, it is certain that we shall be called upon to supply all the vast territory lying between the Mississippi river and the Rocky mountains, so that $3 per barrel may be considered as an extremely low estimate for the minimum price at the wells. The cost of empty barrels furnished at the wells, due allowance being made for transportation, it is estimated cannot exceed forty-five cents each; to this we will add ten cents per bushel as the cost of manufacture, and deducting the whole from $3, it leaves $2.45 as the net value of a barrel of salt at the manufactory. This calculation exhibits the net value of the three annual yields, as above supposed, in their order, as follows:

```
First................................................................$1,356,077.46
Second...............................................................   977,940.46
Third................................................................   678,038.73
Fourth...............................................................   448,970.22
```

"The foregoing statement, in which every allowance is made for which any reason can be imagined, compares very favorably with any that can be made concerning the Eastern manufactories. The brine obtained from the wells in the Syracuse group varies in strength from sixty-four to seventy-four degrees, the average strength from them all being sixty-eight degrees. The brine obtained from the wells in the Saline group varies in strength from thirty-two to sixty-six degrees, the average strength from all being fifty-nine degrees. The average annual product of the wells at Saginaw is 72,000 barrels, while the rapidity of evaporation, as proved by experiment, is from two to three times as great here as at any of the places mentioned. * * * * It is certain, then, that unless the old maxim, 'figures won't lie,' can be successfully controverted, that the people of Lincoln have a valuable interest in the salt basin, vested and indefeasible, except by some unusual providential dispensation."

These quotations from Mr. Ames's work are given simply to show how highly the people of the early days valued the salt works, and what "great expectations" they had of the wealth to be secured from them. The complete history of the operations at the salt basins from the earliest times has been gleaned from Mr. J. P. Hebard, who had, at one time, considerable interest in the work. Mere mention of the salt basins has been made frequently in the past pages, but the subject has been deemed of sufficient importance to justify an entire chapter.

On the third day of May, 1854, the Kansas and Nebraska Act was passed, organizing and then creating the political bodies known as the Territories of Kansas and Nebraska. Soon afterward Congress, on the 22d of July, 1854, passed an act providing for the appointment of a Surveyor General for Nebraska, Kansas, and New Mexico, which provided in general terms that the President should have authority to survey the public lands of this then Territory, and should have the further authority, in course of time, to sell the same under the usual land restrictions affecting sales of public lands. The preceeding section of that act of July 22, 1854, said that "The President shall have no authority to sell the salt or saline lands within such Territory."

Salt springs, not exceeding twelve in number, were granted and passed to the State of Nebraska, by the act of February 9, 1867, when the State was admitted to the Union.

In October, 1857, these lands were surveyed and certified by the Surveyor General as being saline lands, and subsequently, in 1859, parties located land warrants on some of the saline lands, which, after the issuing of patents and finding them to be on saline lands, were afterward canceled.

As the county settled up, homesteaders came from miles around and camped out near the Salt Basin and evaporated brine to make their supply of salt for the year.

There have been several salt companies formed. On March 1, 1855, was incorporated the "Nebraska Salt Manufacturing Company," for the purpose of manufacturing salt from the salt springs near Salt creek, Nebraska.

On March, 16, 1855, was incorporated a company known as the "Saline Manufacturing Company," to establish salt works at or near the salt springs.

A third company was incorporated January 26, 1856, as the "Salt Spring Company," for carrying on the business at the salt springs discovered by Thomas Thompson and others, lying west of Cass county, Nebraska,

In 1861, W. W. Cox, now a resident of Seward county, and Darwin Peckham, of Lincoln, took possession of one of the log cabins, and commenced making salt. It was very scarce during war times, and was high in price, and of necessity many came to scrape salt.

They came from all the settled portions of Kansas, Missouri, and as far east as Central Iowa. If the weather was perfectly dry, they could get plenty of the salt, which could be scraped up where the brine had evaporated and left a crust of salt, but a few minutes of rain would turn it all into brine again. Some would arrive from a long distance just in time to see a shower clear off all the salt.

Small furnaces were built and sheet iron pans used for boiling salt, many of the farmers bringing their sorghum pans for this purpose. In dry time some would scrape up the dry salt, and accumulate a large supply, which found a ready sale to those unfortunate enough to reach there in wet weather.

Various other parties manufactured salt here in a primitive way, till the time of the formation of the State Government, in 1867. The creeks were then lined with scattering patches of timber, from which fire wood was secured for boiling purposes.

In March, 1868, the Governor leased to Anson C. Tichenor certain saline lands, including what is known as the Salt Basin.

On February 15, 1869, the lease was declared void by the Legislature, and the Governor was authorized to make a new lease to Anson C. Tichenor and Jesse T. Green, of the saline land which included the Salt Basin, for the period of twenty years.

A few iron kettles had been set in stone work, and salt made by boiling down the brine, being pumped from the basin by a windmill. In December, 1869, Horace Smith, of Springfield, Massachusetts, of the well-known firm of Smith & Wesson, being on a visit to relatives at Nebraska City, took a ride across the country to see the new town of Lincoln. Meeting Tichenor and Green at the hotel, the subject of manufacturing salt was naturally the principal theme in which he became interested, and before leaving town, made arrangements for the purchase of Tichenor's interest, and one-half of Green's, giving him a three-fourths interest in the lease.

On his return home, he stopped at Chicago, ordered an engine and pump, and several carloads of lumber for vats to evaporate brine, all to be shipped to East Nebraska City, that being the nearest railroad point, and from there all was hauled by wagon to Lincoln, in the spring of 1870. The engine was put on the shore near the basin, with a pump to bring the brine from the basin near by, and force the same into a large tank. From here it was distributed to the vats as needed.

The brine, as it ran from the basin when the tide was in — as it has a tide twice a day, regular in its hours, commencing at about 3 or 4 P. M., and reaching the largest quantity at about 6 P. M., and the same in the morning—would generally be about 35° to 40° by salometer, and on a warm day brine standing in the basin would register as high as 65° and 70°. Dykes were thrown up to confine the brine as it came up through the ground, and a canal conducted it to a small reservoir, where it was allowed to settle before being pumped into the tank. In the warm days of summer the evaporating was very fast. From a vat about 14 x 28 feet, in less than two weeks of evaporation about three thousand pounds of salt were taken. The vats were all supplied with covers, on wheels so that they could be run over the vats in case of storm. The brine from this basin is different from that of many manufactories, in that it requires nothing put in to purify it.

The salt from evaporation formed in cubes of different sizes, and when grasses were put in the brine a most beautiful cluster of crystals would be obtained in a few days' time. This salt, for general use, required to be ground in a salt mill. The kettles were also used, but scarcity of fuel worked against this mode; but salt thus made was fine as the dairy salt usually found for sale, and for dairy use was said to have no superior, as was the case with the coarser salt for curing meat.

The summer of 1870 was thus spent, when Mr. Smith sent his nephew, Mr. J. P. Hebard, to Lincoln to look after his interest and act with Mr. Green in developing the business. A large quantity of salt was made, finding a ready market for its utmost capacity of vats and boilers; and Mr. Smith visiting Lincoln that year, was so much encouraged by the results of the summer's work that on his return home he investigated the different modes of making salt, and spent a large sum in perfecting and trying a new process for manufacturing, in which all the heat was utilized, making a great difference in the expense of fuel, which was a large item where all the wood had to be shipped in.

Plans were made and partially completed for investing a large sum, in 1871, in improvements, vats, reservoirs, etc., for the making of salt on a large scale.

Mention was made of a party having located warrants on these saline lands, the patents for which the Government canceled, after finding them to be located contrary to law. One of the parties interested, J. Sterling Morton, attempted to gain possession of the buildings during the temporary absence of the lessees. Failing in this, suit was commenced in the district court against Horace Smith, J. T. Green, and the State of Nebraska, as defendants, to decide the question of title. Mr. Smith learning of this, and fearing a long litigation over the case, and uncertainty as to whether the State could maintain title to the land leased, and not wishing to invest capital under such uncertainties, decided to abandon the enterprise.

During the season of 1871, as all improvements were stopped, the works were run by Mr. Green at his own expense, netting a good return for the season's work.

In the October term of the District Court this case was tried, resulting in maintaining the State's title; but as Mr. Smith had given the matter up, and made other arrangements in matters of business, he transferred his interest to J. P. Hebard, who, on Mr. Green's refusing to take an interest in the summer's work, started the manufactory on his own account, and after accumulating quite a supply of salt in the bins, noticed that it suddenly commenced disappearing in large quantities. A friend of his in the dray business gave him some pointers, from which he soon found who was reaping the rewards of his labor, and where it was disposed of, and that the hauling was all done in the night time or early dawn.

Having learned, one Sunday evening, that another raid would be made in the morning, before daylight, he made it a point to be on hand. Before daylight, Monday morning, the teams were heard approaching from town, and on their arrival, one wagon backed up to the opening in the bin. Mr. Green accompanied them as the party interested in the results not of his own labor, and took his position in the wagon to shovel forward as thrown in at the end of the wagon bed. The owner of the salt appearing at this stage of the proceedings, the German teamster, who was shoveling out the salt, upon being informed of the kind of business he was engaged in, emphasized with a few flourishes of a good-sized ax-handle, and not understanding English perfectly, thought his life was threatened, and commenced hallooing: "I don't want to be kilt! I don't want to be kilt!" and stopped work. Mr. Green, finding no salt coming out, came into the building to find out what detained it, and meeting the owner, he was informed that his stealings were known, and had a few other facts called to his attention. He did not adopt the latest rules in such engagements, but started in on general principles to whip the owner, and being much larger than his opponent, he came down on the upper side. Having a long beard, the under man ran his fingers through the beard, and taking a twist on this, soon brought the belligerent to his terms, and Mr. Green returned to town with empty wagons. Suit was commenced for the full amount of the salt taken, judgment given, and the salt paid for.

Subsequently Bullock Brothers manufactured salt, but the works, after they closed up, remained idle for a long time.

A transfer of the former interest of Horace Smith was made to E. E. Brown and J. T. Green, and subsequently a company of Eastern capitalists was formed to develop the salt interest, and the State made an appropriation for sinking an artesian well, which was sunk to the depth of 2,465 feet. Aside from determining the different formations, this well did not result in any practical good.

The brine's having a regular tide twice a day would indicate that the supply from which it comes is not directly underneath. The brine oozes up through the muck on the basin, and if not confined by dykes, runs off into Salt creek. Where the basin is covered with brine when the tide is in, during the middle of the day it will be dry enough to walk over, and often a thin layer of salt will cover parts of the ground.

In the earlier history of Lincoln a well was sunk several hundred feet deep, on the east side of Oak, near, if not in, what is now known as West Lincoln. This was finally abandoned, as, like the artesian well in the postoffice square, no brine of sufficient strength was found that would answer for manufacturing purposes. On the banks of Salt creek may be found numerous small springs from which salt water flows, and it is probable that the material from which to make several hundred barrels of good salt per day, in good weather, all runs to waste. The water is fine for bathing purposes, and possesses medicinal qualities. As to the best means of utilizing this brine, there are different opinions, but no one has as yet solved the problem, and the question will remain for future determination.

CHAPTER VIII.

REMOVAL OF THE CAPITAL TO LINCOLN—LEGISLATIVE INCIDENTS PRECEDING THE ACCOMPLISHMENT OF THE WORK—CARRYING THE CAPITAL AWAY ON WHEELS.

The one great epoch in the history of Lincoln, the one event which, more than any other, gave the city its start, from which it has grown, by reason of its commercial advantages and the push and enterprise of its citizens, to its present size and importance among Western cities, the turning point in its career, so to speak, was the location of the State capital here, in 1867. And the incidents attending the location of the seat of government form one of the most interesting chapters in the history of the State of Nebraska.

In 1854, when the Territory of Nebraska was created, Francis Burt, of South Carolina, was appointed Territorial Governor by President Pierce. On the 7th of October of that year the new Governor arrived. Although ill at the time, he took the oath of office on the 16th, only to die on the 18th. Governor Burt, by the organic act, and the appointment of the President, was clothed with almost absolute power in the location of the Territorial capital; and although he was Governor but two days, he gave expression to sentiments and preferences that led the people to believe that had he lived Bellevue would have been the Territorial capital. After the death of Governor Burt, the Secretary of Nebraska, T. B. Cuming, became acting Governor, and soon after taking the oath of office, located the seat of Government at Omaha.

At that place the first Territorial Legislature met on Tuesday, January 16, 1855. Omaha continued to be the capital until the admission of Nebraska as a State, when the change was made to Lincoln, not, however, without much wrangling and a hard fight. Not that many attempts were not made to remove the capital to Bellevue, Nebraska City, Florence, and other places, for in many sessions of the Territorial Legislature "capital removal" was a cause of much bitterness—a bone of contention. The root of the whole trouble was a pretended

enumeration of the inhabitants of the Territory in 1854, on which the
representation in the first Legislature was based, that Legislature having the endorsing of Governor Cuming's location of the capital. The
North Platte fellows got away with those from the South Platte, and
hence carried their point. In 1857 an attempt was made to "remove,"
and again in 1858, when the exciting events which were just beginning in the East and South attracted the attention of the legislators
from their local bickerings. In a sketch, "The Capital Question in
Nebraska, and the Location of the Seat of Government at Lincoln,"
by Hon. Charles H. Gere, read before the State Historical Society,
January 12, 1886, he gives the incidents of these times very fully,
and from that sketch the account of the capital troubles during the
year 1867 is purloined:

"But the war came to an end, and when the last Territorial Legislature of 1867 met, the old question of unfair apportionment came
to the front again. The population of the South Platte section had
increased until it was about double that of the counties north of the
troublesome stream. But the superior tactics of the Douglas county
leaders held its representation down to such an extent that it had but
seven of the thirteen Councilmen, and twenty-one of the thirty-seven
Representatives. Two threads of policy had intertwisted to make
the resistance to a reapportionment based upon actual population, sufficiently strong to overcome the justice supposed to be latent in the
minds of statesmen.

"The first was the fear entertained by Douglas county of the reopening of the capital agitation. The North Platte was now about
a unit in favor of Omaha as against a southern competitor. The
second was a political consideration. A reapportionment meant a
cutting down of the representation from Otoe as well as Douglas
county, both Democratic strongholds. These counties, with the assistance of some lesser constituencies on the north of the Platte, which
sent Democratic delegations, were able to hold a very even balance in
the Legislature against the Republicans, though the latter had an
unquestionable majority in the Territory. Now that Statehood was
imminent, and there were two United States Senators to be elected by a
State Legislature, soon to be called, in case President Johnson should
not succeed in his plan of defeating our admission under the enabling
act of 1864, it was of immense importance to stave off a reapportion-

ment. Hence for capital reasons the Republicans from the North Platte and the Democrats from the South Platte worked in harmony with the Douglas county members in preserving a basis of representation in its original injustice. The usual bill for a new apportionment had been introduced, and passed the Senate, and came to the House, but the four votes from Otoe county being solid against it, it was sleeping the sleep of the just. In the Speaker's chair was William F. Chapin, of Cass, an expert parliamentarian, cool, determined, watchful, and untiring. The session was drawing to a close, and it was Saturday; the term expired at twelve o'clock, midnight, on the following Monday, and, as usual, the results of pretty much all the toil and perspiration of the forty days depended upon a ready and rapid dispatch of business during the remaining hours of the session.

"There was something sinister in the air. It was whispered about that morning that the reapportionment bill had at last a majority, in case Deweese, of Richardson, who was absent on leave, should put in an appearance. A vote or two had been brought over from some of the northern districts remote from Omaha, and anxious for Republican domination. 'Fun' was therefore expected. It came very soon after the roll was called on the opening of the session. The credentials of D. M. Rolfe, of Otoe, who had not been in attendance during the session, but who was an anti-reapportionist, were called up, and it was moved that they be reported to a special committee. The ayes and nays were demanded. Pending roll call, it was moved that a call of the house be ordered. The call was ordered, and the doors closed. All the members answered to their names but Deweese, of Richardson, and Dorsey, of Washington. Then the other side made a motion that further proceedings under the call be dispensed with. The ayes and nays were demanded, and there were seventeen ayes and sixteen nays. Speaker Chapin announced that he voted 'no,' and that being a tie, the motion was lost. An appeal was taken from the decision of the chair, and the vote resulted in another tie, and the appeal was declared lost. The rule is that an affirmative proposition cannot be carried by a tie vote, but that all questions are decided in the negative. The usual form of putting the question is: 'Shall the decision of the chair stand as the judgment of the house?' The negative would be that it should not so stand. But in that case a decision of the chair is reversed by less than a majority of the members voting, which is, of course, absurd. It was a deadlock. The result was a curious demonstration of the absurdity of manipulating a proposition by the use of misleading formulas, so that the negative side of a question may appear in the affirmative.

"The hours passed, but 'no thoroughfare' was written on the faces of the reapportionists. They said that until they had some assurance that a reapportionment bill would be passed before the adjournment, they would prevent the transaction of any more business. Secretly they expected Deweese, who was rumored to be well enough to attend, and they waited for his appearance, but he did not come. The Doorkeeper and Sergeant-at-Arms had orders to let no man out, and when noontide passed and the shadows lengthened, the members sent out for refreshments and lunched at their desks. The night came. Some of the refreshments had been of a very partisan character, and there was blood on the horizon. Many became hilarious, and the lobby was exceedingly noisy. From hilarity to pugnacity is but a short step. Arms and munitions of war were smuggled in during the evening by the outside friends of both sides, and it was pretty confidently whispered that the conclusion was to be tried by force of revolvers.

"A little after ten o'clock P. M., Augustus F. Harvey, of Otoe, rose, and moved that Speaker Chapin be deposed, and that Dr. Abbott, of Washington, be elected to fill the vacancy. He then put the question to a *viva voce* vote, and declared the motion adopted and Dr. Abbott elected Speaker of the House. The stalwart form of Mr. Parmalee, the fighting man of the faction, immediately lifted itself from a desk near by, and advanced, with Dr. Abbott, toward the chair, backed up by Harvey and a procession of his friends. As he placed his foot upon the first step of the dias, Speaker Chapin suddenly unlimbered a Colt's Navy, duly cocked, and warned him briefly to the effect that the Pythagorean proposition that two bodies could not occupy the same space at the same time was a rule of the House, and would be enforced by the combined armament at the command of the proper presiding officers. Daniel paused upon the brink of fate, and hesitated upon his next step. To hesitate was to be lost. The speaker announced that in accordance with the rules of the House in cases of great disorder, he declared the House adjourned until nine o'clock Monday morning, and sprang for the door. The Omaha lobby had promised faithfully, when the crisis came, to guard that door, and permit no rebel from the South Platte to escape. The first man to reach the door was said to be Kelley, of Platte, who had joined the forces of the reapportionists, and it is a tradition that he leaped over the legislative stove to get there in time. The door was burst open, and before the volunteer guard could recover its equilibrium, the seceders had escaped, and were out of the building, scattering to the four quarters of the globe. But they had a rendezvous agreed upon in a secret place, and in half an hour they were safely entrenched, and on guard against any Sergeant-at-Arms and posse that might be dispatched to return them to durance vile.

"The Abbott House immediately organized, admitted Rolfe, of Otoe, to full membership, and proceeded to clear the docket of accumulated bills. Members of the lobby trooped in and voted the names of the absent, and everything proceeded in an unanimous way that must have astonished the walls of the chamber, if they had ears and memory. About dawn, however, the situation began to lose its roseate hue, and an adjournment was had till Monday morning. Before that time arrived the hopelessness of the situation dawned on both factions. They perceived that nothing whatever would come of the deadlock. Neither party had a quorum. Deweese, of Richardson, could not be brought in to vote for reapportionment, and by common consent a peace was concluded, and Monday was spent in an amicable settlement of the arrearages of routine business."

These incidents, however, created a great sensation all over the State, and made sectional and partisan feeling run high. The adjournment took place on February 18th, and two days later, on the 20th, the State Legislature, (chosen at the same election at which the State constitution had been adopted under the enabling act, held June 2, 1866,) was called together by Governor Saunders, to accept or reject the "fundamental condition" insisted on by Congress as a condition precedent to the admission of the State. The condition was that the word "white" in the constitution theretofore passed by the Legislature and ratified by the people, should not be construed as debarring from franchise any citizen of Nebraska on account of race or color. On the 21st day of February, 1867, the second day of the session, the bill accepting these conditions passed, and was signed by Governor Butler, who had taken his seat that day. On the first of March President Johnson issued the proclamation declaring Nebraska a State, the State officers were sworn in, and Governor Butler began to prepare his call for a special session of the Legislature to put the machinery of the State in motion.

Quoting Hon. C. H. Gere again: "It was insisted upon by the leaders of the Republican party in the south and west, that a reapportionment of members of the Legislature should be one of the objects of legislation enumerated in the call. This was opposed by many Republicans in Douglas and other northern counties. It was also asked, this time by Democrats as well as Republicans, from Otoe as well as from Cass and Richardson and the southwestern counties, that a clause should be inserted making the location of the seat of government of the State one of the objects of the special session. The Governor was averse to commencing his administration with a capital wrangle, but thought it would be good policy to make use of the suggestion, for the purpose of securing a reapportionment without a repetition of the bitter struggle of the winter. He therefore opened negotiations with the Douglas county delegation to the coming Legislature, and promised them that he would leave out the capital question, provided they would pledge themselves to sustain a reapportionment. They flatly refused. They claimed that the Legislature could not constitutionally reapportion the representation until after the next census, and as for capital removal, they were not brought up in the woods to be scared by an owl. The Otoe delegation had, however, changed its base. The Senators had been elected and seated, and political considerations had lost their force with the democrats of that county. They wanted the capital removed south of the Platte, and they promised if the Governor would 'put that in' they would march right up and vote for apportionment.

"His Excellency had gone too far to retreat, and when his call was issued it embraced both capital removal and reapportionment, he having consulted a distinguished constitution constructor, Judge Jamison, of Chicago, on the latter point, and obtained an elaborate opinion that it was not only in the power of the Legislature, but its bounden duty, under the constitution, to reapportion the representation at its first session.

"The Legislature met on May 18th, and the lines were quickly drawn for the emergency. Reapportionment was a fixed fact, and after a few days spent in reconnoitering, a solid majority in both houses seemed likely to agree upon a scheme for capital location. Mr. Harvey, who had led the assault upon reapportionment at the late session of the Territorial Legislature, was an active leader of his late antagonists for relocation. Party affiliations were ruptured all along the line, and the new lines were formed on a sectional basis. The bill was prepared with deliberation, much caucusing being required before it would satisfy the various elements in the movement, and it was introduced in both houses on the 4th of June. It was entitled, 'An act to provide for the location of the seat of government of the State of Nebraska, and for the erection of public buildings thereat.' It named the Governor, David Butler; the Secretary of State, Thomas P. Kennard, and the Auditor, John Gillespie, Commissioners, who should select, on or before July 15th, (a date changed by a subsequent bill to September 1, 1867,) from lands belonging to the State, lying within the counties of Seward, the south half of the counties of Saunders and Butler, and that portion of Lancaster county lying north of the south line of township nine, a suitable site of not less than 640 acres lying in one body, for a town; to have the same surveyed and named 'Lincoln;' and declared the same the permanent seat of government of the State.

"The bill directed the Commissioners, after the site had been surveyed, to offer the lots in each alternate block for sale to the highest bidder, after thirty days' advertisement, and after having appraised the same; but that no lot should be sold for less than the appraised value. The first sale should be held for five successive days at Lincoln, on the site, after which sale should be opened for the same duration, first at Nebraska City, and next at Omaha. If a sufficient number of lots should not by this time be disposed of to defray the expenses of the selection and survey, and to erect a building as prescribed in the bill, further sales might be advertised and held in Plattsmouth and Brownville. All moneys derived from these sales, which should be for cash, should be deposited in the State Treasury, and there held by the Treasurer as a State building fund. From the proceeds of these sales the Commissioners should proceed to advertise for plans and contracts, and cause to be erected a building suitable for executive offices and the accommodation of the two Houses of the Legislature, that might be a part of a larger building to be completed in the future, the cost of which wing, or part of a building, should not exceed $50,000. The bill passed the Senate on the 10th day of June.

"Those voting for it were: Jesse T. Davis, of Washington; James E. Doom and Lawson Sheldon, of Cass; Oscar Holden, of Johnson; Thos. J. Majors, of Nemaha; William A. Presson, of Richardson; and Mills S. Reeves and W. W. Wardell, of Otoe.—Eight.

"The noes were: Harlan Baird, of Dakota; Isaac S. Hascall and J. N. H. Patrick, of Douglas; E. H. Rogers, of Dodge, and Frank K. Freeman, of Lincoln.—Five.

"The House passed the bill two days later, under suspension of the rules, forwarding it to its third reading. As in the Senate, so in the House, the opponents of the bill resorted to strategy for stampeding the friends of the measure, and offered numerous amendments to locate the capital, or the university, or the Agricultural College, at Nebraska City, or in the boundaries of Cass or Nemaha counties. But all amendments were steadily voted down by a solid phalanx. The gentlemen in the House, voting 'aye' on its final passage, were: David M. Anderson, John B. Bennett, William M. Hicklin, Aug. F. Harvey, and George W. Sproat, of Otoe; J. R. Butler, of Pawnee; John Cadman, of Lancaster; E. L. Clark, of Seward; W. F. Chapin, D. Cole, A. B. Fuller, and Isaac Wiles, of Cass; Geo. Crowe, William Dailey, Louis Waldter, and C. F. Hayward, of Nemaha; J. M. Deweese, Gustavus Duerfeldt, T. J. Collins, and J. T. Haile, of Richardson; Henry Morton, of Dixon; Dean C. Slade, and John A. Unthank, of Washington; Oliver Townsend, of Gage, and George P. Tucker, of Johnson.—Twenty-five.

"The noes were: O. W. Baltzley, of Dakota; Henry Beebe, of Dodge; George N. Crawford and A. W. Trumble, of Sarpy; Geo. W. Frost, Joel T. Griffin, Martin Dunham, J. M. Woolworth, and Dan S. Parmalee, of Douglas, and John A. Wallichs, of Platte.—Ten."

Early in the capital fight the Omaha newspapers made great sport of the removal scheme, and the departure of the Commissioners to hunt up a location was the cause of much merriment among them. It was not until the Commissioners had announced the location of the new capital that the newspapers woke up to the real situation, and then there was lively music in the air. Every little technicality that could be seized upon was used to defeat the scheme, but of course all efforts in that direction failed.

While the heated contest over the bill was in progress, every ruse, stratagem, and dodge, the North Platte party, and particularly the Douglas delegation, could devise, was employed to compass the defeat of the bill. It so happened that the Otoe delegation were Democrats, and Senator Mills S. Reeves, of Nebraska City, had been a bitter rebel, who had disliked the name of Lincoln more than he could that of Satan. The name of the proposed new town, as the removal bill was at first drawn, was "Capital City." Knowing the intense prejudice of Senator Reeves, Senator J. H. N. Patrick, of Omaha, rose in his place, and moved that the bill be amended by striking out the name "Capital City," and substituting that of "Lincoln."

Instantly Senator Reeves was upon his feet calling, "Mr. President!"

"The Senator from Otoe has the floor," said the President of the Senate.

"I second the motion of the Senator from Douglas," said Senator Reeves, in a quick, firm voice.

The South Platte men caught the spirit of the performance, and at once adopted the amendment. The bill was passed with the name of the illustrious Lincoln in it, and so the new capital became Lincoln. Thus Nebraska's capital bears the name it does as the result of an attempted sharp trick, designed to defeat the removal bill, and not owing to the admiration of the first State Legislature for the great war President.

During the fight the greatest bitterness was displayed on the part of the anti-removalists, and a great many amusing incidents are related of the men and times. During the great fight in the last Territorial Legislature, when pandemonium reigned supreme, and shotguns and revolvers played the most significant part in the Legislative proceedings, Jim Creighton (as he was called then) heard the noise of the contention at one of its fiercest parts, from below in the office of Auditor Gillespie. Rushing out with uncovered head, and flaming eye and cheek, he sought for some weapon of attack. An old mop stick belonging to Father Beals was found by the irate Creighton, and seizing this, he hurried to the door of the chamber, exclaiming, "I'll clean out the whole of those d———d South Platte people!" at the same time tearing the rag from the mop, in order to make of it a more murderous weapon. But before "Jim" got to the door, the South Platte people, led by the Speaker, with gun in hand, burst open the door of the chamber and escaped. Their numbers were too large for the valorous Creighton, and he dropped his mopstick and disappeared. Creighton undoubtedly had plenty of nerve, but nerve has a peculiar faculty of disappearing under the finger nails on certain occasions, and this was undoubtedly one of those occasions.

During the time the Commissioners were out on their tour of inspection, trying to decide where the capital should be located, they came to Ashland, and it is just as well to remark right here that Ashland lost the site of the capital because of the mosquitoes. There were a number of men with the party besides the Commissioners, and upon stopping at Ashland over night, the whole party was lodged in the upper story of a building, the windows guiltless of glass or blinds; that is, all of the party except Governor Butler. He was considered the big chief of the party, and was lodged in a lower room, in a bed surrounded carefully and completely with mosquito netting. The Governor slept soundly and refreshingly, but the other Commissioners and their friends spent a night of wild, uncontrollable emotion and vigorous action, trying as best they could to protect themselves against the little pests, whose musical wings and insatiable appetites kept the unfortunate ones awake. Morning dawned, and the weary ones, among whom was a preacher, together with the one whose sleep had been as peaceful and restful as that of a child whose innocence and youth bring it sweet dreams and quiet slumbers, departed to view the other landscapes. As the little village of Ashland faded into the mist across the prairie, the preacher broke the silence by exclaiming: " Well, there may be one man who will vote for Ashland, but if Governor Butler has any help in his vote, it will surprise me." The mosquitoes had fixed the business so far as Ashland was concerned. It may be that a few of those winged songsters yet linger around the old-time scenes of this classic (to Nebraska) town, but they can never do the harm their ancestors accomplished in the days of '67.

When the Commissioners had "swung around the circle," and had seen all the sites which aspired to become the seat of government of the new State, they returned by way of Yankee Hill, the site of John Cadman and the Nebraska City schemers. The Yankee Hill people had a banquet prepared, with all the delicacies of the season of 1867, on Salt creek. The feast was spread on a long table, which fairly groaned with the fine cooking of the Yankee Hill ladies. What astonished one Commissioner most was that the ladies had in some way supplied ice cream, doubtless the first ever seen in Lancaster county. How it was gotten out in the wild region of the Salt Basin, the officials never knew. Mrs. Cadman and her sister had managed the preparation of the feast, and when the Commissioners came over to Lancaster, the place which had beaten Yankee Hill for the county seat in 1864, and located the capital there, those ladies could hardly forgive them. They declined to recognize the Commissioners for six months or more, and they finally informed one of the officials that they did not see how he failed to be captured by such a feast as they had enjoyed at Yankee Hill. Mr. Cadman himself felt pretty sore over the success of Lancaster, but soon got over it, and became a business man in the new capital, and still so continues, in company with his son, on North Tenth street, between P and Q, though not a resident of the city himself. The business, that of hardware, is conducted by Mr. W. A. Cadman, the son.

The South Platte country never could have agreed on Yankee Hill, which was Nebraska City's site. Lancaster was taken as a compromise, to avoid a split in the section which had carried the removal bill, and was then trying to consummate the transaction. The compromise site was successful, being supported by Nebraska City, Plattsmouth, and Ashland, and now is three times as large as all of them combined.

But through all the discouragements, the worry, the difficulties, and the trials, the Commission persisted, and finally the capitol was located where it now stands.

The incidents attending the removal of the capitol are also interesting. The people of Omaha seemed to be determined to prevent the taking away of the Government effects, and hence it was deemed better to send the State library and other capitol belongings away by night, so as to avoid any opposition. Accordingly Auditor Gillespie secured a contract from Mr. J. T. Beach, of Lincoln, for moving the goods. Mr. Beach had arrived in the town in the spring of 1868, and the removal was made in the early winter, probably about the middle of December. Mr. Beach is now nearly fifty years of age, the fourth of October, 1889, completing the first half century of his existence, and he remembers the occurrences of those days very distinctly. Mr.

Beach was born in Brown county, Ohio, October 1, 1839, where he lived until he was ten years old. At that time his parents moved to Indiana, where he lived with them for a number of years. In 1861 he enlisted in the army, in the Tenth Indiana Infantry, and served three years. So that when Mr. Beach came to Nebraska, in 1868, he had had a recent training that well fitted him for the work which he undertook to do.

Securing the services of a Mr. Carr, yet a resident of Lincoln, to help him, Mr. Beach started with a two-horse team, and Mr. Carr with four horses, to move the capitol to Lincoln. They crossed the Platte at Ashland, the drifting ice making the crossing very difficult and dangerous. Along with these two men was Luke Cropsey, a son of A. J. Cropsey, who rendered valuable assistance during the trip. The trip occupied nearly a day and a half, for on the second morning, (Saturday,) at 11 o'clock, the party, with the two covered wagons, drove into Omaha, and put up at the old checkered barn, one of the early landmarks of the "city by the Big Muddy." In the afternoon Mr. Beach went to the State House, and had a conference with Mr. Gillespie, who strictly enjoined upon him secrecy as to his mission to Omaha, and made arrangements for loading the furniture. After night-fall of Sunday the library, furniture, desks, and everything else that was wanted at the new capitol, were loaded in the two covered wagons, ready for the return trip. At 4 o'clock Monday morning the start for Lincoln was made, and miles of ground had been covered before the people of Omaha awoke. Mr. Beach and his assistants came by the way of Plattsmouth. When that hamlet was reached the snow was coming down fiercely and heavily, and a stop was made until morning, as it was considered too dangerous to cross the river in the condition in which the ferry then was. About ten o'clock in the morning the ferry was repaired, and the party crossed the river with much inconvenience and considerable danger. The journey was continued until night-fall, through a blinding snow storm. As night approached Stove creek was several miles distant, and the only shelter visible was the dugout of a settler on the open prairie. Going to the door of this cabin Mr. Beach asked for shelter for the night for himself and two companions, and a place to shield their teams from the elements. The settler refused, on the ground of want of accommodations; but our travelers were not thus to be refused, and upon pressing their need were allowed to shelter their horses by a hay stack, and bunk themselves upon the floor of the cabin. The night passed, and when the morning came Mr. Beach informed his host that the party was without money, told him what their errand was, and offered to pawn two watches as security for the payment of the amount due for the night's lodging and breakfast. This the old settler refused, and the teamsters departed for Lincoln, which place they reached on Wednesday night, promising to send the pay for their lodging as soon as they reached Lincoln, which promise they kept. Five days the journey occupied, and when it was finished the whole of the State library and other needed capitol appliances were safely lodged within the walls of the building.

The cost of transfering this property was over $100. Mr. Beach took $60 in money with him and a check of $40 on a Lincoln bank. When the money was exhausted, in Omaha, Mr. Beach tried to cash the check, but the Omaha banks proposed to charge him a ruinous discount, and had it not been for the kindly assistance of Mr. Gillespie, who cashed the check free of charge, a row would have resulted. Mr. Carr avers that he has never been paid in full for the services of himself and his four-horse team while engaged in this enterprise, and as no one seems to dispute his claim, it is probable that some one, possibly the city of Lincoln, owes him more than a simple debt of gratitude. But the whole affair was conducted in a most satisfactory manner, and the capitol was in reality lost to Omaha.

At that time the people of Omaha were not very well pleased with the course events were taking, which the following incident will illustrate, and will also serve to show how carefully the work of removal was done. A few days after the library had disappeared across the prairie, John R. Meredith, of Omaha, dropped into Auditor Gillespie's office in the afternoon, and, noticing the empty shelves, inquired where the library had gone.

"It has gone to Lincoln," said Mr. Gillespie.

"Who sent it there, and by what authority was it sent?" was Mr. Meredith's next question.

"I sent it there," said Gillespie, "by the authority vested in me by the State Legislature."

Meredith left, and soon Gen. S. A. Strickland stormed into the Auditor's office, with about the same interrogatories, which were answered in about the same manner.

"Where is that library?" said the General.

"In Lincoln, the State capital," calmly answered Gillespie.

"By the eternals that library is coming back here, and it's coming right away," stormed Strickland.

All this bluster and blow did not disturb Gillespie, who quietly asked how the General's purpose was to be accomplished. Gen. Strickland then said that the library belonged to the Territory of Nebraska, and as Omaha was the capital of the Territory, the library belonged to Omaha, and that he would get an order from the Secretary of the Interior for its replacement in Omaha. Mr. Gillespie smiled, and merely asked that when Gen. Strickland received the letter he might be allowed a chance to read it, which the General readily acceded to. Matters quieted down, and remained so for some weeks, when one day Mr. Gillespie asked Gen. Strickland if he had heard from Washington yet. The General unwillingly admitted that he had, and that the reply was unfavorable to Omaha's claims. This ended the skirmishing and kicking. The capital was removed, and since then no attempt of alarming proportions has been made to have the capital location changed.

CHAPTER IX.

THE DIFFICULTIES EXPERIENCED IN BUILDING THE NEW CAPITOL.—HOW OMAHA OPPOSITION DELAYED THE WORK—THE FINAL SUCCESS AND MEETING OF THE FIRST LEGISLATURE IN LINCOLN.

The days of the capital removal, capital location, and capitol building, were full of stirring events, times of intense interest to the people then and now, when serious situations, which demanded prompt, energetic, and clear headed action, were often met with. During these times, Hon. John Gillespie, State Auditor, and one of the Commissioners to locate the capital, played an important part, and to him the authors of this history are indebted for the following, which was contributed entire by him:

The act authorizing the capitol location appointed the Governor, Secretary, and Auditor, Commissioners to seek a location, within the boundaries of Lancaster, Saunders, Butler, Seward, and the north half of Saline county, to be located upon State Lands, of not less than 640 acres in one tract, and to lay out and plat the same in lots, blocks, streets, and alleys, and make proper reservations for the several State institutions; when the same was completed to advertise the lots for sale at public auction to the highest bidder, and when the sales amounted to the aggregate of $50,000, then in that event to advertise for plans and specifications for a capitol building, and let the contract for building the same. The Legislature did not appropriate a dollar from the Treasury to carry out the provisions of the act, but all incidental expenses, as well as the completion of a capitol building, depended upon receipts from the sale of lots. The Commissioners well understood that the success of the enterprise depended upon a most favorable selection for the future capital of the State. Otherwise a most stupendous failure, that would result in ignominy to the movers, especially the Commissioners having it in charge, would follow. After the passage of the act, and before the Commissioners entered upon their work, difficulties multiplied, owing to the opposition of the North Platte people, and especially from the citizens of Omaha.

The citizens of that city were particularly opposed to the capital's removal from their midst, and commenced an opposition to prevent the carrying out of the enterprise. The Commissioners had to enter into a bond of $60,000 each for the faithful performance of duty. They did not hope or expect that Omaha citizens would sign their bonds, and had to look to other localities. Nebraska City was in full sympathy with the removal of the capital from Omaha to the South Platte country, and her best citizens volunteered as bondsmen for the Commissioners, an offer which was most duly accepted and appreciated.

But there arose another difficulty; the bonds had to be approved by one of the Judges of the Supreme Court, and to be deposited with the State Treasurer, Mr. August Kountze, of Omaha. Previous to filing the bonds, a Mr. James E. Doom, a member from Cass county, (who voted for the capital removal,) reported to the Omaha newspapers that the time prescribed by law for filing the bonds of the Commissioners had expired. So the Omaha *Republican* came out with a "double header," stating that the capital-removal enterprise had failed, by virtue of the Commissioners not having filed their bonds in time, as prescribed by law, and therefore could not give good title to the lands. The writer hereof had started that morning by steamboat to Nebraska City, to have the bonds approved by Hon. O. P. Mason, Chief Justice, preparatory to filing them. News had reached that city of the announcement made in the Omaha papers. In consultation with the Chief Justice, he said there was nothing in the statement, nor had the time prescribed elapsed. The bonds were returned to Omaha. Governor Butler and Secretary Kennard, accompanied by C. H. Gere and Col. C. S. Chase, repaired to the First National Bank of that city, and tendered the bonds to the State Treasurer for filing. Mr. Kountze said to them that he would not file the bonds, as they were not valid, the time for filing by law having passed; but he would place them in the vault. The proposition was satisfactory to the other two Commissioners, and they left.

The writer lived in Omaha at that time, and had to meet the abuse and denunciations of her citizens, who openly charged the capital removers as "land-grabbers" and enemies of Omaha. Several of her leading citizens tried by every means in their power to have me not file the bonds, and let the act become "null and void." One, now high up in authority in this State, spent several hours with me at my office, in the old capitol at Omaha, trying to persuade me not to file the bonds, and have the law become void, claiming that if carried out it would "disrupt the party." The interview was finally cut short by my informing him that "I was into it, and would see it through." The Commissioners, after looking the field over which was designated by the act, selected the site where the city now stands. This conclusion was arrived at by a careful examination of a State map and the general topography of the country. They concluded that in the future, when railroads were built south of the Platte, this point would be easily reached and accessible from any direction. And a further consideration, at that time deemed important, was the great salt deposits near by, considered valuable.

But in this selection no one, except the few homesteaders on the town site, was pleased. The citizens of Nebraska City wanted the capital located at Yankee Hill, on the line of the "steam-wagon road" west to the mountains. Plattsmouth wanted the capital at Ashland, her citizens offering to guarantee $50,000 worth of lots in case we located at Ashland. Brownville wanted the capital located at Camden, on the Blue river, as they had a railroad survey west by way of Camden and Fort Kearney. The Commissioners were beset by the friends of their favorite localities, all of which had their land "syndicates" formed; but the location made was upon neutral grounds, and one which proved the wisest selection, as the other interested localities compromised upon this one, which could not have been effected at any other point.

After having the town site surveyed and platted, the Commissioners appointed a day for the sale of lots at auction, to take place upon the grounds. Thereupon arose another serious difficulty, that seemed to threaten the defeat of the whole enterprise. The act required the Commissioners to deposit the money received from the sale of lots with the State Treasurer, to be designated, separate from any other fund, as the "State Building Fund," and all expenses for incidentals, buildings, etc., to be paid out by the Treasurer, upon the order of the Auditor, the same as other State funds. The writer was informed by a leading attorney of Omaha that some of the leading citizens of that city had requested him to commence suit by enjoining the Commissioners, and attaching the money in the hands of the State Treasurer as soon as deposited with him, and thereby tie up the same, and by years of litigation prevent the commencement of the capitol building. He informed me his fee was considered too large, and he was not employed, but that such action would be taken as soon as the money resulting from the sale of lots was duly deposited by the Commissioners with the State Treasurer. The Commissioners, after considering the possibility of such action by the enemies of the capital removal, thereby defeating the act of the Legislature authorizing the removal of the capital, called a meeting of the citizens signing their bonds, to be held at Nebraska City just previous to the day of the first sale of lots, and laid the situation before them. They advised us to proceed with the sale of lots, and prepared a written request, asking us not to deposit the proceeds of the lot sales with the State Treasurer, but to use the money in carrying out the provisions of the law, paying for the erection of a capital, and report to the coming Legislature our actions in full.

The sale of lots came off, and was reasonably successful; so much so that the Commissioners felt authorized to proceed to advertise for plans and specifications, and to let the contract for the building. The funds were kept in hiding, where no injunction or attachment could find them. I was often asked by certain parties of Omaha why the money for the sale of Lincoln lots was not placed with the State Treasurer, as the law directed. When pressed, one of the citizens said they wanted to enjoin the funds in the hands of the Treasurer from being paid out, and thus keep us from building the capitol at Lincoln. I informed the party that the funds would be turned over to the State Treasurer the next day to pay *his bill* for advertising. The bills of the *Republican* and *Herald* for advertising lot sales, for plans and specifications, and for letting the contract, had been handed in. I deposited with the Treasurer a sum sufficient to pay their bills, and if they wished to enjoin payment, all right. The orders of payment were given, the money paid out, the Treasurer receipting for the same, and acknowledged the authority of the Board by paying the money out on the order of the Auditor of State.

The first sale of lots took place in the fall of 1867. The following Legislature convened the first of January, 1869; hence the necessity of getting the capitol building under contract at as early a day as possible, having the summer of 1868 to complete the same. As there were no railroads, lumber had to be hauled from a point six miles east of Nebraska City, on the Council Bluffs & St. Joseph railroad. Stone quarries had to be found somewhere for building material. The Commissioners advertised for plans in the Omaha, Plattsmouth, and Nebraska City papers. The time drawing near, we found that the Omaha architects would pay no attention to our advertisement, and the result would be no plans offered, so we sent a copy of our "ad" to the Chicago *Tribune*, which caught the eye of a fifth-rate architect, Mr. James Morris, who could obtain no work in that city, and he hastily prepared a plan and presented the same on the day set. It being the only plan presented, the Commissioners were more than pleased to adopt it. The plan contemplated a central building, with wings to be attached afterward, which, if added, would have made a symmetrical building, but without the wings not very imposing. Consequently, in after years the Commissioners had to bear the brunt of many jeers on their architectural choice for a capital building.

We advertised for letting the contract, and as in the former case, but one bid was offered, that one by Mr. Joseph Ward, of Chicago, which was also accepted. He commenced at once, and had the excavation made and part of the foundation laid in the fall of 1867, intending in the spring of 1868 to push the work as fast as possible, and have the building completed in time for the Governor to announce by proclamation the completion of the capitol, and that the next Legislature would convene thereat on the first Thursday of January, 1869.

A stone quarry of blue limestone was found twelve miles south on Salt creek, and the contractor instructed to use the same; but after using it on the east side of the building, on the first story, it became shelly, and this quarry had to be abandoned. A man was sent out on horseback, who prospected a number of days all the streams in the vicinity for out-cropping stone without success, but finally visited Beatrice and reported a magnesia limestone in abundance, and easily dressed, which would harden by exposure. This stone was adopted, and all the teams that could be hired put on the road for Beatrice, (fifty miles,) to keep the work moving. This worked well for a short time, until we were notified by the contractor that the bridge over Salt creek had become dangerous, and that the owners of teams would not risk crossing, and that the County Commissioners refused to repair the bridge. This required our presence to get the Commissioners to repair the bridge; all of which, with bad roads and the interminable sloughs and mud-holes, made the getting of stone from Beatrice, and the lumber from Iowa, slow, difficult, and expensive, and the summer rapidly passing away. The Commissioners were fully impressed that in case of failure to complete the capitol in time for the convening of the Legislature the coming January, the session would have to be held at Omaha, and the strong probabilities were that Lincoln would never see a session held there, which no doubt would have been true. The contractor was constantly being urged to employ all the mechanics that could be worked to advantage, and consequently he had stone-cutters and carpenters sent out from Chicago.

About the 1st of June, 1868, I received a letter at Omaha from the contractor, that he had thrown up the job, and all work had stopped, on account of a difficulty with the architect; that a number of his stone-cutters had left for Chicago; and to come down and make settlement with him. This was a terrible crisis, and visions of a most glorious failure of the whole enterprise loomed up most too prominent for a calm view of the situation; but something had to be done, and done quickly. Unfortunately neither of the other two Commissioners were at Omaha at the time, the Governor being at his home at Pawnee, and the Secretary at his home at DeSoto. I sent a messenger from Omaha, by steam-boat, to Nebraska City, with an order to the "Elephant Stable" for a pony to carry a message to the Governor explaining the situation, and asking him to meet me at Lincoln the next day without fail. I took stage next morning for Council Bluffs, to take train for East Nebraska City, intending to take stage from that point to Lincoln, but owing to the stage sticking in the mud half-way between the two cities, I saw the train pull out, leaving several other passengers with myself behind. I returned to Omaha by the next stage, hired a livery team, and started for Lincoln *via* the rope ferry across the Platte river near Ashland, being delayed two hours in finding the ferryman. When I arrived at Lincoln, about 11 A. M. the next day, I found the citizens much disheartened, and fearful that the work on the building would not be renewed. I soon set their minds at rest on that point. Dunbar & Bailey, who owned the only livery stable in the city, and had the contract to deliver the stone, had drawn off all their teams, a number of the mechanics had left, and the prospect was blue enough. I waited all next day and the following day till noon for the arrival of the Governor. He did not put in an appearance. I called in James

Sweet, State Treasurer, who had just arrived from Nebraska City, to be present when I should summon the architect and contractor, and hear their differences, previously having refused to hear either one until the arrival of the Governor. I requested Mr. Morris, (architect,) to bring with him the plans and specifications, and meet me at my room in the Cadman House at 1 P. M. He repaired to the shop on the capitol grounds, and was in the act of taking the plans from the contractor's desk, when the contractor came in and kicked him out of the shop. Both being English, the backs of both were "high" when they reached my room. I first heard the architect, then the contractor. The *lie* passed frequently between them; but in getting at the facts I found the difference arose about the material to go into the interior walls of the building. The contractor claimed that it should be sandstone, as that material was at hand, and its use would enable him to proceed with the work. The architect claimed that the walls should be brick. I asked Mr. Sweet to turn to the specification, which said the walls should be brick, "if brick could *be had*, otherwise stone." I said I would settle that point, and as there were no brick here, nor none being made, instructed the contractor to put up the walls with stone. The architect objected, and said I was only *one* of the Commissioners. I told him *that was law*, and the other two would confirm the decision. I explained to both that if they did not propose to each do his duty, and push the work to completion, we would remove both. I was satisfied that the architect wished the contractor to leave, so he could become contractor as well. Both shook hands, and each promised to do his best to complete the building in time for the coming session. I instructed Dunbar & Bailey to hire all the teams they could get in the country, and rush the stone from Beatrice, and on my return to Omaha employed twelve stonecutters and sent them by wagon *post haste* for Lincoln, and work was resumed with considerable energy.

About two weeks afterward Mr. Ward, contractor, came into my office at Omaha with a Mr. Sweet, on his way to Chicago to buy doors, sash, glass, hardware, etc. He had an estimate for $2,600, of which $1,000 was to go to Mr. Sweet for money advanced to pay his men before leaving. It was then about four o'clock P. M. We had *no money* on hand, but I dare not tell him so, or else there would have been a "cyclone" at hand. I asked him where he was stopping.

He said at the "Planters," and that they would leave the next morning on the 4 A. M. train. I told him I would see him that evening at the hotel. Where the twenty-six hundred dollars was to come from, I did not know. After "bluing" over the situation for a short time, I went to the office of W. J. Hahn, County Treasurer, and asked if he had on hand any "State sinking funds" to be turned over. His reply was that he had. I told him I wanted $2,600, and as our next sale of lots took place the next week, I would turn that amount into the State Treasury at Lincoln and bring back the Treasurer's receipt. He gave me his check for $2,600 on the First National Bank of Omaha, and I started off to get it cashed before closing, but found I was too late. I explained the situation to Mr. Aug. Kountze. He said it was contrary to custom, but he opened the vault and paid me the money, which was carried to Mr. Ward, and delivered in a manner that conveyed the impression that the enterprise should not fail for want of funds. Thus this difficulty was bridged over, and the receipt of the Treasurer was forwarded Mr. Hahn the following week for the money deposited.

The next crisis to be met was more serious, and not so easily passed over. Our last sale of lots was to be in September, 1868. Hoping thereby to realize enough to complete and pay for the building, we had requested Sweet & Brock, bankers at Lincoln, to advance to the contractor money as he needed it, before the sale of lots took place, and also requested the contractor to put off paying for material until after the sale, hoping that we would not be pressed for funds. But in this we were disappointed. I received a letter from Nelson C. Brock that their bank had advanced $2,000 to the contractor, and calling for the return of the same at once; also by the same mail a letter from the contractor saying that he would discharge all the stone-cutters and laborers the coming Saturday, and would require $2,000 to pay them off. Unfortunately the other two Commissioners were not at the capital, and this emergency had to be met. I started for Nebraska City, and called upon James Thorn, County Treasurer, and found he had on hand sinking funds sufficient to meet the emergencies, and willingly offered to turn it over and take the Treasurer's receipt for the same. Thus this last difficulty was bridged over.

In 1871 a constitutional convention met in Lincoln and commenced to investigate County Treasurers, supposing they were loaning State funds. Mr. Thorn, with others, was called upon for a report of the collections and deposits. This circumstance was brought to light and he was asked to explain. He referred the explanation to myself. I went before the committee, of which General Victor Vifquain was chairman, and stated the circumstance that a crisis had arrived in the completion of the capitol; that no funds were on hand, and the "sinking fund" was used for six weeks to help out the "building fund." If such had not been done the capitol building would never have been finished, and Lincoln would not have been here to-day. The committee reported that no censure attached to any one.

After the election of 1868 and the Governor's proclamation had been issued announcing the completion of the capitol, and that the session of the Legislature of January following would convene at Lincoln, Hon. C. B. Taylor, Senator-elect from Douglas county, asked me if it was true, as set forth in the Governor's message, that the capitol was completed, and if there were any hotel accommodations at Lincoln. Being answered in the affirmative, he said they would "go down and adjourn the Legislature to Omaha, where they could have accommodations." On the first day of January, 1869, I opened the Auditor's office in the new capitol. On the day before convening, the Omaha and other delegations arrived in Lincoln, in a blinding snow storm, by private conveyances. I met Taylor at the Atwood House at dinner. He said he had been looking out to see the new capitol, but had failed to see it. I told him it was on account of the snow storm, but we had a capitol ready. He remarked that I had informed him correctly about the hotel accommodations, and if on presentation the capitol building looked as well, he would have no fault to find. After dinner I piloted him, Tom Majors, and other members, across the prairie to the capitol building. When we entered, the plasterers were finishing up in the lower halls. Taylor reminded me of the Governor's message issued some time previous, saying "the capitol was finished." Majors and others at once expressed their pleasure and surprise at seeing such a building. Taylor, after looking into the Senate Chamber, asked to see the Representative Hall. When he had seen these halls, with their new carpets, new chairs, and bright furniture, he was much impressed with the success which the Commissioners had achieved, and then and there promised that the Douglas delegation would make no fight on the capitol.

On organization of the Senate, C. B. Taylor was elected President. Next day he came into my office and drafted a bill appropriating $16,000 to grade and fence the capitol grounds and finish the dome of the capitol. A few days after he drafted a bill to continue the Commissioners for two years longer, to sell the unsold lots and blocks and build the State University, Agricultural College, and Insane Asylum. Both bills became laws.

After the meeting of the first Legislature confidence was established, and lots in Lincoln brought better prices at auction. There were no difficulties in the way to build the other institutions. When the next two years had passed the Commissioners reported the university and asylum completed, paid for, and over 300 lots unsold.

CHAPTER X.

AN INTERESTING DOCUMENT DEALING WITH CAPITAL REMOVAL—REPORT OF THE COMMISSIONERS APPOINTED TO SELECT A SITE FOR THE NEW SEAT OF GOVERNMENT.

One of the most interesting documents of the early days is the report to the Legislature of 1869 of the Commissioners appointed to locate the State capital. As far as known, there is only one of these reports in existence to-day, it being a document of fifty pages, bearing the imprint of "St. A. D. Balcombe, State Printer, Omaha, Neb.," and also bearing the legend, "Published by Authority." Through the kindness of Hon. John Gillespie the authors of this book are enabled to reproduce those parts of the report that are of especial interest, together with a synopsis of the other contents of the pamphlet. The document is as follows:

"REPORT OF COMMISSIONERS TO LOCATE THE SEAT OF GOVERNMENT OF THE STATE OF NEBRASKA.

"*To the Honorable the Senate and House of Representatives of the State of Nebraska:*

"In pursuance of the requirements of the act of the Legislature entitled, 'An Act to provide for the location of the Seat of Government of the State of Nebraska, and for the erection of public buildings thereat,' approved June 14, 1867, the Commissioners thereby appointed assembled at Nebraska City upon Thursday, June 18, 1867, and prepared for a personal examination of the district, viz.: 'The county of Seward, the south half of the counties of Saunders and Butler, and that portion of the county of Lancaster lying north of the south line of township nine,' within which a selection was to be made for the contemplated seat of the State Government.

"Having provided an outfit, and employing Mr. Aug. F. Harvey as surveyor, to ascertain the lines of the proposed sites, we left Nebraska City on the afternoon of the 18th day of July, and arrived at Lancaster, in Lancaster county, on the evening of the 19th. The

20th and 22d were occupied in a full examination of the town sites of Saline City, or 'Yankee Hill,' as it is more familiarly known, and Lancaster, the adjacent lands on both sides of Salt creek, and the stone quarries from two to eight miles south of the village.

On the twenty-third of July the Commissioners went down the valley of Salt creek, examining on the way a very beautiful and level plateau about six miles from Lancaster, and near Stevens creek, on the east side of Salt. Another site on the west side of Salt, on an elevated table near Rock creek, was shown us by parties living in the neighborhood, and who guided us on an examining trip around its lines.

"The 23d was spent in reviewing the townsite proposed on the high land west of and adjacent to the village of Ashland, in the southeast corner of Saunders county. The surface of this site declined gently to the north and east, sufficiently for thorough drainage, and is of such evenness that but little expense will ever be involved for grading. From any part of it a widely extended panorama is spread, embracing, as it rises, many square miles in the valley of the Platte and Salt creek. Timber is abundant, and inexhaustible quarries of fine rock outcrop along the bluffs near the mouth of Salt creek and along the Platte, within one to four and five miles from the town. Salt creek affords excellent water power for manufacturing purposes in Ashland. The distance of the site is about thirty-five miles from Plattsmouth, near the efflux of Salt creek to the Platte.

"On the 25th we went northwesterly along the old California trail through Saunders county, covering the Wahoo river near its head, and arriving at nightfall at the residence of J. D. Brown, in Butler county. Upon this route we observed no situation of commanding advantages.

"Leaving Mr. Brown's on the 26th, we looked over the flat prairie between the heads of Oak creek and the eastern tributaries of the Blue, in towns thirteen and fourteen north, range three and four east, in Butler county. Here is a wide tract of unbroken plain, upon which we drove for six hours without seeing a depression in the surface at either hand. We struck the Blue in town fourteen north, range two east, passing down that stream. After a drive that day, (including some diversions from the direct route to examine points which looked well at a distance,) of over seventy-five miles, we arrived at Seward Center, in the fork of Plum creek and the Blue, and opposite the mouth of Lincoln creek. All of the proposed site here could be seen at a glance. It lies on a high table between the streams named, is level, is surrounded by fertile valleys, adjacent to timber, stone, and first-class water power, and is remarkable for healthiness of situation.

"The advantages, indeed, are possessed in an equal degree by Milford, six to eight miles below Seward, and by Camden, in the fork of the Blue and West Blue, except that the last-named site was in a lower elevation. We remained in Milford over night, and on the 27th turned eastward, and arrived at Saline City in the evening.

"On the 29th we made a more thorough examination of 'Yankee Hill' and Lancaster, and their surroundings. At the last-named point the favorable impressions received at first sight, on the 19th, were confirmed. We found it gently undulating, its principal elevation being near the center of the proposed new site, the village already established being in the midst of a thrifty and considerable agricultural population, rich timber and water-power available within short distances, the center of the great saline region within two miles; and, in addition to all other claims, the especial advantage was that the location was at the center of a circle of about 110 miles in diameter, along or near the circumference of which are the Kansas State line, directly south, and the important towns of Pawnee City, Nebraska City, Plattsmouth, Omaha, Fremont, and Columbus.

"The State lands which we observed in our tour were mainly away from considerable bodies of timber or important water courses, and did not possess, to all appearances, any particular advantages, nor was the title of them so far vested in the State at that time (the report of the selection of lands by the Governor, under the acts of Congress admitting the State to the Union, not having then been certified or approved at Washington) as to warrant us in making a selection where there was a possibility that the title might fail, or in waiting until, by confirmation at Washington, the title had been secured.

"Under these circumstances we entertained the proposition of the people residing in the vicinity of Lancaster, offering to convey to the State in fee simple the west half of the west half of section 25, the east half and the southwest quarter of section 26, which, with the northwest quarter of section 26, (the last-named quarter being saline land,) all in town 10, range 6 east, the whole embracing 800 acres, and upon which it was proposed to erect the new town. In addition, the Trustees of the Lancaster Seminary Association proposed to convey to the State, for an addition to the site named in the foregoing proposition, the town site of Lancaster, reserving certain lots therein, which had been disposed of in whole or in part, to the purchasers thereof, and the owners of said lots reserved agreeing to a resurvey of the town site as an addition to Lincoln, and the acceptance of lots according to the new survey in lieu of those acquired from the Seminary Company and surrendered by them.

"James Sweet, Esq., was appointed conveyancer to the Commissioners, and after his report upon the sufficiency of the titles proposed to be made to the State, (which report will be found in the appendix hereto, marked 'A,') and a careful consideration of all the circumstances of the condition of the State lands, the advantages of the situation, its central position, and the value of its surroundings over a district of over twelve thousand square miles of rich agricultural country, it was determined to accept the proposition made by the owners of the land, if upon a ballot the Commissioners should decide upon a location at this point.

"In the afternoon of the 29th of July we assembled in the house of W. T. Donovan, of Lancaster, and after a comparison of notes and the discussion of advantages of the many points examined, proceeded to ballot for a choice.

"On the first ballot Lancaster received two votes and Ashland one. On the second vote Lancaster received the unanimous vote of the Commissioners.

"The Governor then announced the result to the people, many of whom were outside awaiting the decision.

"Having performed the business of the location of the seat of government, the Commissioners returned to Omaha, leaving Mr. Harvey at Lancaster to do the surveying necessary to locate the depressions and elevations on the town site, preliminary to his furnishing a design for laying off the blocks, streets, and reservations, and making a plat thereof. He completed that labor on the 12th of August, when he notified the Commissioners, and they again assembled at Lancaster, on the 13th day of August. On the 14th the Commissioners formally announced the founding of the town of Lincoln as the seat of government of Nebraska, in the following proclamation:

"To Whom it May Concern: Know ye, that on this the 14th day of August, A. D. 1867, by virtue of authority in us vested, and in accordance with an act to provide for the location of the seat of government of the State of Nebraska, and for the erection of public buildings thereat, approved June 14, 1867, we, the undersigned Commissioners, on this the 14th day of August, A. D. 1867, have by actual view selected the following described lands belonging to the State, viz.:

"S. E. ¼ of section 23; the W. ½ of the N.W. ¼, N.W. ¼ and the W. ½ of the S.W. ¼, of section 25, the W. ½ of section 25, of township No. 10 north, of range No. 6 east of the 6th principal meridian, and have located the seat of government of the State of Nebraska upon said described lands as a town to be known as Lincoln.

"Further, that we have, upon the day above mentioned, designated within said location the reservation for the Capitol Building, State University, and Agricultural College, parks, and other reservations contemplated in the aforesaid act, which will be properly designated upon a plat and filed in the office of the Secretary of State.

"Done at Lincoln, Lancaster county, Nebraska, this 14th day of August, A. D. 1867.

> DAVID BUTLER,
> THOMAS P. KENNARD,
> JOHN GILLESPIE,
> *Commissioners.*

"On the following day Messrs. A. F. Harvey and A. B. Smith, engineers, with a corps of assistants, who were sworn to perform faithful service, commenced the survey of the town. The design is calculated for the making of a beautiful town. The streets are one hundred and one hundred and twenty-five feet wide, and calculated to be improved on all except O and Ninth streets, and the other business streets around the Market Square and Court House Square, with a street park outside of the curb line; as for instance, on the one hundred foot streets, pavements of twelve feet wide and park or double row of trees, with grass plot between, twelve feet wide outside the pavements; and on the one hundred and twenty-five foot streets the pavement and park to be each fifteen feet wide. This will leave a roadway of fifty-two feet on the streets one hundred feet wide, and sixty feet wide on the wide streets, while on the business streets a ninety foot roadway will be ample room for all demands of trade.

"Reservations of nearly twelve acres each were made for the State House, State University, and city Park, these being at about equal distance from each other.

"Reservations of one block each for a Court House for Lancaster county, for a City Hall and market space, for a State Historical Library Association, and several other squares, in proper location, for Public Schools."

The Commissioners have also marked upon the book of record of lots, reservations of three lots each for the following religious denominations, viz:

Lots 7, 8, 9, block 65, for the Roman Catholic church.

Lots 10, 11, 12, in block 67, for the Methodist Episcopal church.

Lots 10, 11, 12, in block 87, for the Baptist church.

Lots 10, 11, 12, in block 89, for the Congregational society.

Lots 1, 2, 3, in block 91, for the German Methodist Episcopal church.

Lots 7, 8, 9, in block 97, for the Lutheran congregation.

Lots 10, 11, 12, in block 99, for the Protestant Methodist church.

Lots 16, 17, 18, in block 101, for the Christian church.

Lots 10, 11, 12, in block 119, for the Presbyterian church.

Lots 7, 8, 9, in block 121, for the Protestant Episcopal church.

These reservations were made with the understanding with the parties making the selection on behalf of the several denominations, that the Legislature would require of them a condition that the property should only be used for religious purposes, and that sometime would be fixed within which suitable houses of worship, costing some reasonable minimum amount, should be erected.

"The Commissioners have also reserved lot 13, in block 101, for the use of the Independent Order of Good Templars; lot 14, in block 101, for the Independent Order of Odd Fellows; and lot 15, in block 101, for the Ancient Free and Accepted Masons. We respectfully ask the Legislature to confirm our action in respect to all the reservations.

"The surveying of the town was done in the most careful manner, and with the utmost patience, and we believe that the lines are so well established that future litigation about 'lapping' of lots will be practically impossible. In every third street running north and south and every fourth or fifth street running east and west, there were set, at the center of intersection with every other street, a stone monument, even with the surface, in the top of which a mark was fixed at the exact point of crossing the lines. The work occupied Messrs. Harvey and Smith, and a double party of assistants, constantly, until the 10th day of September, when having staked off every lot in town, except in a few blocks in the northwest part of the northwest quarter upon the 'Saline land,' the work was completed.

"In anticipation of the completion of the survey, and to insure parties purchasing lots in time to build upon them for winter, and an early provision of the means of commencing work upon the State House, the Commissioners, upon the 17th day of August, issued their advertisement for the first sale of lots, to be held on the 17th day of September.

"This advertisement was authorized to be printed in such newspaper as could give it the widest circulation. Upon the day of sale the weather, which had been excessively disagreeable for nearly a week, culminated in a cold, drizzly rain, in consequence of which not more than one hundred persons were present, and but few of those the bidders we had expected. The aspect of affairs was disheartening. Persons who had loudly boasted of their great expectations in buying lots and building houses; others who had been lavish in prophecies of the unparalleled success of the enterprise; others who had been free with advice to us in regard to appraisements and sales — these, and still others, who were certainly expected to be on the ground and foremost in purchasing, had given us the cold shoulder, and were not present or within hearing. Indeed, your Commissioners almost felt that failure was after all to be the result.

"However, the first lot was put up, and after some delay in getting a bidder, it was sold to J. G. Miller, Esq., for an advance of twenty-five cents on the appraisement of $40.

"This small beginning was an index to the proceedings for the day, and when the evening closed, the sales footing up to about one-tenth of our expectations, our spirits or our hopes were in nowise improved.

"The second and third days gave a better result, and on the fourth and fifth, sunshine having come again, bringing more persons to the sales, and getting every one to feeling well, the bidding became encouraging, and the summing up of the five days' offering was nearly if not quite satisfactory.

"The sales here at this time amounted to about $34,000.

"The offering of lots was continued at Nebraska City from the 23d to the 27th of September, inclusive, and in Omaha on the 30th of September to the 4th of October.

"The sales at Nebraska City and Omaha amounted to about nineteen thousand dollars, and aggregated, with the amount at Lincoln, about $53,000, a sum sufficiently large to dispel all despondency and warrant renewed exertions.

"We again met an obstacle which for a little while promised a good deal of trouble.

"Under the 'Capitol Bill,' your Commissioners were required to pay over the amount received from the sales of lots to the State Treasurer, and pay all expenditures by warrants upon the State Treasurer building fund held by that officer. We have, in this regard, to plead guilty to a technical violation of law. Except the sum of $148, none of the money received by us has ever been paid over.

"As soon as the town was surveyed, there began rumors that the enemies of the enterprise were determined to defeat it if possible, and that nothing which could accomplish that end would be left undone.

"We were assured in the most reliable quarters that one of these defeating means would be the enjoining of the Treasurer against the payment of money upon warrants upon the building fund, an effort which, even if the injunction had not in the end been sustained, in the ordinary course of the courts would have prevented active operations until it should be too late to secure the erection of the State House.

"In consequence of this rumor, well founded as it seemed to be, hundreds of persons who would otherwise have invested largely in Lincoln lots, declined so doing; others who had purchased or bid off lots, hesitated about paying the money and taking their certificates; while others became so fearful of a bad result, that they even applied to the Commissioners for a restoration of the amounts paid and a cancellation of their certificates.

"At this juncture some friends of the enterprise, who were sureties upon our official bond, called upon the others, and prepared and furnished us with the following protest:

"[COPY.]

"NEBRASKA CITY, November 23, 1867.

"*To the Honorable David Butler, Thomas P. Kennard, and John Gillespie, Commissioners:*

"GENTLEMEN—The undersigned having become sureties on your official bonds for the faithful performance of your duties as Commissioners, respectfully beg leave to formally protest against the deposit of any of the funds received by you from the sale of State property with the State Treasurer, for the following reasons:

"1st. Because it has been repeatedly intimated by the enemies of the present capital location, that all moneys so deposited will be attached and held, so as to defeat the wishes of a majority of the people of the State by preventing the erection of the capitol buildings till after the sitting of the next Legislature.

"2d. Because we, having in good faith become sureties, not as a personal favor to the Commissioners, but to secure the success of the proposed location and early completion of the capitol buildings, are unwilling that the enterprise should either be defeated or delayed by useless litigation. We therefore, respectfully but earnestly request the Commissioners to withhold the funds which may now be in their hands, as well as those which may yet be received, and deposit them with those bankers who have made themselves sureties, and who may furnish the Commissioners satisfactory security for the prompt payment of the money deposited with them.   Very respectfully, your obedient servants,

"D. J. McCann.   Thomas B. Stevenson.
"Frederick Renner.   D. Whitenger.
"George Mohrenstecher.   S. McConiga.
"Samuel B. Sibley.   Robert Hawk.
"H. Kennedy.   James Sweet."
"John Hamlin.

"Under the circumstances which surrounded us, and being unwilling to jeopardize the money held by us as the representatives of the State in trust for the persons who had advanced it upon the risk of the success of the town of Lincoln, we felt that we could not do otherwise than accede to the demand and protest of our sureties, and having made satisfactory arrangements for the deposit and withdrawal of the funds with private bankers, we did so, and have assumed all the responsibility of the financial affairs of the enterprise.

"On June 17, 1868, we held a sale of lots at Lincoln, and realized about $9,000.

"On the 17th of September we again sold at Lincoln, and received about $13,580.

"At the sale in September, 1867, and June, 1868, we had offered lots only in the alternate or even numbered blocks, with those in four odd numbered blocks to make up for half of the reserved blocks, all of which, except the court house square, fell upon odd numbers. At the last sale, in September, 1868, we offered the lots in the odd numbered blocks on the old town site of Lancaster. The presumption of the authority to make this sale was upon the consideration of our occupancy of the ground. We accepted it from the proprietors as so much over the town of Lincoln proper, and excess beyond the section and a quarter which we had located as the capital, as an addition to the town, for the purpose of having no rival in the business of selling town lots upon ground adjacent to the capitol, and where having a village already established, the proprietors could easily have derived large profits, which otherwise would have been invested with the State. Besides, the building of the town had so far been accomplished in the direction of and upon that quarter that the appreciated value of property in second hands made it so probable that we could realize more money from a few lots there than from many upon the south side of the townsite proper; and standing in need of much more money than we had reason to believe these last-named lots would bring, we deemed it advisable to offer all that were then unsold.

"The lots were appraised prior to the first sale, according to the law, due consideration being had to their relative situation regarding the public reservation, and the probable business center, and their particular condition.

"This appraisement amounted to a total of..................................$68,000 00
"The appraisement on the lots sold was.. 63,475 00
"The advance on appraisement at all the sales was........................... 13,445 75
"Making the total sales at Lincoln, September, 1867...... ......$34,342 25
"At Nebraska City, September, 1867................................. 18,715 50
"At Omaha, September, 1867... 1,005 00
"At Lincoln, June, 1868... 8,970 00
"At Lincoln, September, 1868.. 13,553 00
                                                                                    ———
    "Total..$76,715 75

"Accompanying this report, appendix marked 'B' will contain a detailed statement of the purchasers of lots, of the lots purchased, and their prices.

"Appendix 'E' gives the list of lots unsold, of those appraised and offered at the public sales.

"On the 10th of September the Commissioners issued their notice to architects, inviting for a period of thirty days plans and specifications for a State House.

"In response Messrs. Taggart & W. R. Craig, of Nebraska City, and John Morris, of Chicago, submitted the drawings and specifications of designs.

"Upon the 10th of October, after a careful consideration of their merits severally we decided to accept that presented by Mr. Morris.

as being best adapted to the circumstances of construction and the wants of the State.

"On the same day Mr. Morris, having been appointed superintendent of construction, issued a notice to builders, inviting proposals for a term of three months, for the erection of the work.

"At the same time Mr. Morris was directed to commence such preliminary work, as excavation for foundations, delivery of material for foundation walls, and other arrangements as would facilitate the progress of the work after the contract was let.

"On the 10th of November the superintendent caused the ground to be broken, in the presence of a number of the citizens of Lancaster.

"The removal of the first earth was awarded, in the absence of any state officer, to Master Frele Morton Donovan, the first child born in and the youngest child of the oldest settler of Lancaster county."

"On the 11th of January the bid of Mr. Joseph Ward, proposing to furnish the material and labor and erect the building, for the sum of $49,000, was accepted, and from that time forward the work steadily progressed, with a few uncontrollable delays, to the completion of the work contemplated in the contract.

"For a report of the difficulties attending the work, and an estimate of the allowance proper to be made to the contractor for changes in material, increased amount of work, additional accommodation, and fittings, by Mr. Morris, the architect, is appended hereto, marked 'C.'

"The entire expenditures have been made by the Commissioners as in the following classification, for a detailed statement of which see Appendix 'D.'"

The red sandstone, referred to in the foregoing report, and out of which the Commissioners expected to build the capitol, proved to be rotten and worthless, and the blue limestone of Beatrice was substituted, at a necessary additional cost of several thousand dollars.

As a suggestion of the prices received for lots at the sales in 1867–8 and 1869, a few are given to represent the value of property at that time:

Lot 3, in block 55, the block bounded by N and O and Tenth and Eleventh, sold for $64. Lots 13, 14, 15, 16, 17, and 18, in the same block, sold to James Sweet for $353, or an average of $58.88 each.

Lot 7, in the block containing the Burr Block, sold for $80 to J. E. LaMaster. N. C. Brock bought lot 12, same block, for $61. The Capital National Bank corner sold to Jacob Blum for $86. These were average prices. Few lots sold at less than $40, and few over $150.

The leading buyers were Samuel E. Allen, Jacob Blum, S. R. Brown, Hawks & Bush, W. A. Brown, N. C. Brock, J. H. Bryant, David Butler, S. W. Burnham, Isaac Cahn, M. M. Culver, A. J. Cropsey, D. R. Dungan, Jacob Dawson, Wm. Findley, L. A. Groff, C. H. Harvey, U. S. Harding, Bob Hawke & Co., W. S. Horn, Thos. H. Hyde, C. J. Hull, H. S. Jennings, H. W. Kuhns, Levi B. Kennard, T. P. Kennard, J. E. LaMaster, Wm. Morton, J. J. Murphy, J. W. Millard, Jason G. Miller, J. D. McCann, Pat. O'Hawes, R. D. Presson, A. L. Palmer, Philetus Peck, George Ross, Amos Reid, J. M. Riddill, John Roberts, S. A. Strickland, James Sweet, John M. Taggart, Geo. P. Tucker, and Henry Witte. We notice such names among the buyers as John M. Thayer, who bought lot 1, in block 13, for $115; T. W. Tipton, John Taffe, and W. R. Vaughan. Five ladies bought lots, namely, Mrs. D. Babcock, Miss S. H. Chapman, Mrs. J. A. Harvey, Miss A. Peck, and Miss M. Wilson. The latter bought lot 5, in block 226, for $15. The ladies all looked out for bargains, or the men refused to bid against them. James Sweet was by all odds the heaviest buyer, his individual purchases amounting to $4,074, and as trustee, to $15,000.

CHAPTER XI.

THE CITY OF LINCOLN — THE EARLY BEGINNING — FROM PRE-HISTORIC
TIMES TO 1867 — THE TOWNS OF LANCASTER AND YANKEE HILL — THE
COUNTY SEAT CONTEST — THE BUILDING OF THE LANCASTER SEMINARY
— EARLY BUILDINGS AND REMINISCENCES.

In 1860, Government Square, Lincoln, was a rounded elevation. About the center of the square was a knoll about twelve feet higher than the present surface at the artesian well. Standing in summer on this graceful tumulus, as lovely a scene was spread out before the observer's eyes as ever was beheld in prairie landscape. To the west his hill of observation sloped evenly away to the valley of Salt creek. In the valley to the west of the creek, and north of O street, there was a beautiful grove of honey locust trees. South of O street there waved a little forest of stately elms and cottonwood, interspersed with a few honey-locust and hackberry trees. Besides, the stream in that direction was fringed with plum and other small trees and brush. Back from the trees the low ground between the hills was one sea of tall grass and yellow sunflowers. To the northwest could be traced the valley of Oak creek, also fringed with trees, and to the southwest the valley of Haines's creek, radiant with flowers. On the low ground directly westward the saline crust of the Salt Basin glistened in the sun like the surface of a lake, and far to the west the valley of Middle creek receded in a vista of green leaves, waving grass, and flowers. The valley of Salt creek could be traced for miles to the northeast, and the banks of the Antelope also had their fringe of grass, flowers, and trees, to the eastward. When the observer looked to the southward he saw his hill decline into a drain, almost deserving the name of a small ravine, in the vicinity of N street. This ravine originated in a basin of low ground in the locality a little distance to the northeast from the present site of the Burr block, and its course was southwesterly to Twelfth and O streets. Here it bent southward for a short distance and at the place where the alley south of Funke's opera house now is, it again turned westward. Its course then was southwesterly to a line now occupied by the Latta block, on Eleventh street. Here it was deepest and the descent into it pretty abrupt from either side. It crossed Tenth street at N, and was soon lost in the flat surface of the bottom land to the westward. In the vicinity of the Capital National Bank, at O and Eleventh, there was a depression, where water stood to a considerable depth when the street came to be graded across N street. More than one old settler can now tell how he or some other man had a vehicle swamped in the mud on Eleventh street in attempting to cross this drain in early days, the reputation of the slough in the vicinity of Eleventh street being particularly notorious.

Owing to this ravine, the elevation on which the capitol now stands looked higher, and the incline of its long, sweeping, northern slope more sharp, than at present. In all directions from the observer the distance faded away in a rim of hills, with gracefully undulating sides. In fact, it seemed that he stood on a conical elevation in a grand natural amphitheater, where surrounding heights were located at magnificent distances. The high ground on which the observer is supposed to stand, was covered with buffalo grass, as were all the high prairies twenty-nine years ago. Across the elevated surface sparse lines of blue joint marked the course of travel by ox teams from 1847 to 1860. The cattle of the west-bound trains had eaten the seed to the eastward and spread it along the trails in their journey toward the west. Indian ponies and buffaloes probably contributed to sow the seed also.

A few buffaloes could at times be seen, about this date, on the present city plat. The common deer and black-tailed deer were frequently seen on the site of the coming capital. Also the white-tailed and mule deer were occasionally observed. Herds of pronghorn antelope were often seen on the ground where Lincoln stands, in 1860, and during several years later. Elk had formerly been abundant. Prairie wolves, or coyotes, were numerous within the present city limits in 1860 and for years afterward. Pelicans, wild geese, ducks, prairie chickens, and quail, were seen in large numbers. Many small animals and birds made this region their home. Perhaps one thousand species and varieties of plant life could have been seen within the present platted limits of the city, twenty-nine years ago. This seems extravagant, but when it is known that the flora of Nebraska

10

comprises nearly 2,500 species and varieties of plants, it will not seem improbable.

With the landscape more beautiful than an ideal picture, the soil manifestly of unbounded fertility, and the land swarming with animal life, it can not be wondered that the early pilgrim who stood on the mound on post-office square and absorbed the prospect, thought that he had seen no spot so promising as this on which to found a city.

The land on which Lincoln now stands was surveyed in 1856 by the Government. The salt springs in the Salt Basin were then discovered and reported by the Government surveyor. Fabulous anticipations at once filled the minds of adventurers and enterprising men who then had begun to congregate along the Missouri river. In 1856 the Crescent Company was organized at Plattsmouth, and Captain W. T. Donovan, who commanded the steamer "Emma," from Pittsburg to Plattsmouth, was selected to represent the company at the Salt Basin. The captain and his family came on and settled on section twenty-three, on the west bank of Salt creek, and south of the mouth of Oak creek. The Crescent Company proposed to find out the value of the salt water flowage as a commercial investment. During the same summer William Norman and Alexander Robinson, representing a company similar to that of Donovan, came on and located for a time near the big Salt Basin, on section twenty-one. They soon became satisfied with their profits, and left the basin permanently. Owing to the threatening aspect of the Pawnee Indians during the latter part of 1858, Captain Donovan also abandoned the schemes of the Crescent Company, and removed to the Stevens creek settlement, where he remained until 1861, when he returned to the vicinity of the Salt Basin once more and located at Yankee Hill, a point nearly identical with the site of the present Insane Hospital.

In the autumn of 1859 a scheme for county organization was set on foot. At that time a large elm tree, with spreading branches, stood not far from what is now the Burlington Road round house. Under this tree the settlers met to take preliminary steps for the erection of county machinery. This caucus selected A. J. Wallingford, Joseph J. Forest, and Captain W. T. Donovan, as a committee to select a site for a county seat and lay out a town. That committee, with most commendable judgment, selected the present site of Lincoln, and called it "Lancaster," being named by Captain Donovan, probably, after Lancaster county, Pennsylvania. He named his first settlement at the Salt Basin, in 1857, "Lancaster." But the new town went without inhabitants for several years, and settlers came into the county very slowly until about 1864.

On July 2, 1861, Captain Donovan brought W. W. Cox, now of Seward county, to the Salt Basin, and on August 20th Cox and Darwin Peckham began to boil salt at the Big Basin, in section 21. They immediatly set up an extensive business by trading salt for all manner of useful commodities in the line of provisions, such as meat, flour, butter, potatoes, eggs, fruit, wood, clothing, etc. Salt was very scarce in the West, and during the war very high, so that people came even from near Des Moines, Iowa, for salt, and traded flour for the same, pound for pound. Settlers came from far and near to boil salt for themselves, and the Salt Basin was a lively place during the later months of 1861. No salt could be made in the winter time, and Mr. Cox wintered with Captain Donovan, at Yankee Hill. During the fall of 1861 such prominent men of the future as J. Sterling Morton, O. P. Mason, and Phineas W. Hitchcock, visited and inspected the Salt Basin. Mr. Morton then probably contracted some ideas that were unfortunate for him in after years. The Territorial Governor, Alvin Saunders, who had been elected in May, 1861, also visited the basin during the fall.

During the winter of 1861-2 the coyotes practically had the elevations where the city now stands all to themselves.

The season of 1862 passed much as that of 1861. Cox and others made salt at the basin.

John S. Gregory arrived during this year, and boiled salt by the Basin on section 21. Many others came and went, and the salt business was very prosperous. During the final week of May, Milton Langdon and family arrived, and settled on the north side of Oak creek, not far west of its junction with Salt creek. A county convention was held at the basin on the first of May, and it was attended by about every old settler in the county. An election was held in the fall, but there was nothing connected with it of particular interest in the history of Lincoln.

But there was one thing which did affect the destiny of Nebraska and this city which occurred in that year, and that was the final passage by both Houses of Congress of the Homestead Act. This had passed the Senate in February, and was passed by the House in May. This act brought settlers to Lancaster county with some activity during 1863.

During the winter of 1862–3, an old man named Van Benthusen was camped at the Salt Basin boiling some salt in a large open pan. An Indian hit him a rap over the knuckles with a ramrod, for a joke. The old man did not see the joke the same way, and flew into a rage and knocked the Indian over into the boiling salt, burning him fatally. The settlers went to the Indian camp in alarm, fearing this act had incensed the aborigines, but they were found making sport of the scalded Indian, who roared with pain in his dying agony. They called him a squaw, and pointed their fingers at him in scorn.

On August 20, 1862, a heavy frost killed the corn on low ground in Nebraska generally.

During the winter of 1862–3 a son was born to the family of Joseph Chambers, then camped at the Salt Basin. The child lived but a short time, but was, probably, the first child born within the limits of the present city. On March 3, 1863, Elmer E. Cox, now of Seward, was born at the basin.

The summer of 1863 found W. W. Cox and family still at the basin. During the spring of 1863 John S. Gregory built a frame house where West Lincoln now is, and made other improvements, and the same season he was made the first postmaster of this locality. The office was named "Gregory's Basin," but did not continue very long. Mr. Gregory received a salary of $3 per annum. During the summer of 1863 Mr. Gregory erected salt-making apparatus at the basin having a capacity of about two tons per day, for which he found a ready sale to pioneers and travelers in all directions, except, perhaps, to the westward. Few white men had then settled west of Salt creek. William Imlay also conducted a salt-manufacturing business in 1862–3, at the small basin near where the stock-yards are now located. Milton Langdon and others were engaged in making salt during 1862 to 1864.

John S. Gregory was elected to the Territorial Legislature for Lancaster county on October 13, 1863, and became a prominent figure in the county and city thenceforward for many years. Fifty-five votes were cast at this election. Mr. Gregory was probably the first permanent settler within the present city limits.

On the morning of July 4, 1863, Mrs. W. W. Cox proposed that the family celebrate Independence Day. Wild gooseberries were very plentiful along Salt creek, and Mr. Cox went out to pick a quantity to be used in the festivities. When he had filled his pail he heard some hallooing, and stepping out of the bushes to see what the disturbance was about, he saw a small group of men near by, and on closer inspection he found that it was the party of Elder J. M. Young, Rev. Peter Schamp, Dr. J. McKesson, E. W. Warnes, Luke Lavender, and Jacob Dawson. They were hunting for a good place in which to plant a colony. They at once joined in the celebration project. The neighbors were called in, dinner was served, the elder made a speech, and a small flag they had with them was raised; and this first patriotic event of its kind on the soil of the present capital, they do say, was a very soul-stirring occasion. Perhaps the flag then floated for the first time on the present site of Lincoln. The elder was looking for a place to locate a colony and establish a Methodist mission, and like most of the pioneer Methodist preachers, he was a very good judge of business possibilities as well as of yellow-legged chickens. After a careful inspection of all the surrounding region, he came back to the Salt Basin about July 10, 1863, and decided that the present site of Lincoln was the most desirable for his purpose of any spot he had seen. He dedicated a portion of section twenty three to colonial purposes, and christened it "Lancaster." But no attempt was made to settle the town until 1864, when the village life of Lancaster really began.

The winter of 1863–4 was one of intense cold, and the pioneers of the valley of Salt creek were threatened with starvation as well as with the rigors of the winter. But when spring came, settlers began to come in with renewed energy, and homesteading began in earnest, for it then became probable that the Union would be saved. People began to think they would risk this region, whose soil had so long been viewed with suspicion, owing to its radical contrast in appearance with that of States further east, and the libels long taught by ill-informed geographers. Jacob Dawson and John Giles took homesteads next to Young's new site of Lancaster in 1863. Captain W. T. Donovan had already taken a homestead — the first in the county — on January 2d, east of the Asylum. In 1864 Elder J. M. Young and his sons, Dr. J. McKesson, Luke Lavender, E. W. Warnes, and J. M. Riddle, made a permanent settlement on the town site of Lancaster. The southeast quarter and the east half of the southwest quarter, of section twenty-three, were platted by Jacob Dawson, and the plat is dated August 6, 1864. The streets were named North, Nebraska, Saline, Washington, Main, Lincoln, College, High, and Locust, from the north to the south side of the plat. From west to east they were numbered from one to twelve. The plat contained sixty-four blocks, of eight lots each. The streets were to be sixty-six feet wide; the alleys were to run east and west, and were twenty feet wide. The plat had a "Court-house" and a "Seminary" square. Three years later, when the capital commissioners replatted the town on a much broader scale, the original plat was practically discarded. Much of the prosperity of the early part of 1864 was lost by the scare caused by the Indian outbreak of that year, and most of the settlers left in September. Captain Donovan, John S. Gregory, and E. W. Warnes, stuck to the vicinity of the Lancaster plat. The Indians committed several butcheries west of the Big Blue, but did not molest the Salt creek settlement. Still, those who remained were in great fear at times lest they might be attacked.

The season of 1865 opened with but a few more settlers than that of 1864, on account of the Indian scare of 1864. Most of those who fled the fall before, returned in the spring of 1865, and others came and took homesteads.

Lancaster county had but one county-seat fight, which, owing to the few persons engaged, did not develop the exciting or sanguinary aspects that often grow out of such contests. When John Cadman and John S. Gregory were in the Territorial Legislature in the winter of 1864, Cadman was in a scheme to partition Clay county between Gage and Lancaster. Gregory at first opposed this hotly, but he finally came around and supported the scheme. The agreement to dismember Clay county was easy, comparatively. But when it came to the details of how it should be done, the problem was too much for Cadman and Gregory. It was an original case, this taking the life of a municipal government, and it required skill in law and the principles of civil and constitutional government not thought of when the scheme was hatched. At this point in the dilemma Cadman and Gregory called in T. M. Marquett, representing this county in the Council, and he was made a sort of referee, after much higgling, for the adjustment of the whole matter of division of territory, funds, and extinguishment of the life of Clay county. His work was so well done that it has never been questioned since.

This elimination of Clay county from the map was intended to fix the county seat of Gage county at Beatrice, and also that of Lancaster near where it now is. With Clay county in existence, the first would have had to go further south and the second further north. Cadman wanted the capital of Lancaster county at a point near the present Insane Asylum, which he at once staked off as a town site under the name of "Yankee Hill." Elder J. M. Young caused his site to be platted the same summer of 1864, and then thse two generals set out to capture the county seat of Lancaster county. Gregory had caused the Legislature to appropriate $500 for a bridge over Salt creek "to be located in Lancaster county," hoping to get the bridge opposite Lancaster. But Cadman was not asleep, and when the commissioners came to view the ground he plead so well for a bridge at Yankee Hill that the money was equally divided between the Yankee Hill and Lancaster bridge sites. With the addition of subscriptions, both sites secured a bridge over Salt creek, and were so far even in the fight. Lancaster had the Salt Basin and Yankee Hill had the freight road from the Missouri, making them about a tie. Yankee Hill secured a blacksmith shop and a small store, and was a little ahead on the count. But Elder Young was a shrewd and energetic leader, and Cadman was unfortunate in at least one particular. The settlers south on Salt creek had generally located near what they supposed would be the county seat of Clay county, and the prospective capital they had named Olathe. When Cadman joined hands with H. W. Parker, of Beatrice, and slaughtered Clay county in cold blood, he also annihilated the prospects of Olathe. The visions of the Olatheans suddenly went glimmering. Their anger against Cadman rose to a high pitch, and they "laid for him." And it is not recorded that Elder Young tried to smooth down the ruffled temper of the people of Olathe. So, when the people came to vote on the location of the county seat in the summer of 1864, Lancaster was victorious by odds. Olathe got even with Cadman. But Cadman did not long sulk in his tent. He joined with the people of Lancaster to make it a successful town, and was soon afterward a hotel keeper in Lancaster, and the justice of the peace of the place. He was elected to the next Territorial Legislature, and was a member of the first State Senate. He was also probate judge, sheriff, and treasurer of Lancaster county. At present he is residing in California, but he paid Lincoln a visit during July of the present year. He has a son residing in the city now, and another in Omaha.

Elder J. M. Young was a man of great enterprise, very large mind, and possessed of a warm heart. He was an antagonist whom most men could well afford to respect. He not only planted his colony on the sight of Lincoln, but was the inspiration which had much to do with inducing the commissioners to locate the State capital on his site rather than at Seward, or one of the other competitive points. He came to Lancaster county to found a female seminary when this region was almost literally a howling wilderness. Coyotes did the howling. So did the Pawnee and Otoe Indians. But he set about building his seminary, (in 1864, probably,) and had it in operation in 1866. It was built of the soft red sandstone of this region, and was about 30x50 ft. in dimensions, and two stories high. It stood on the rear part of the lot now occupied by the *State Journal* building, owing to the fact that the plat of Lancaster was totally disregarded by the surveyors who surveyed Lincoln, in 1867. It then became the school house, meeting house and public rallying point generally, until burned down in the spring of 1867. The first school on the site of Lancaster was taught in the "seminary" by Mr. H. W. Merrill, in 1866, in the latter part of that season, with an attendance of about thirty. School was continued in the "stone house" in 1866, when it was in charge of Mrs. Merrill, whose husband had a homestead on the Antelope. After it was burned, in 1867, John Cadman opened a hotel on its site, late in 1867, using the walls, in part, for his hostelry. This was the second hotel in Lincoln. Cadman afterward sold out to N. S. Atwood, who greatly enlarged the Cadman House, as a brick structure, and after running it for some time, it burned also. Before the Cadman House was built, the Pioneer House was erected on the southeast corner of Ninth and Q streets. It was the first hotel in Lincoln, and was well managed by L. A. Scoggin, who afterward mysteriously left, and has not since been heard from. The Pioneer was built in 1867, and was burned a few years later.

When T. M. Marquett ran for Congress in 1866, with J. Sterling Morton as opponent, Morton challenged Marquett to a campaign joint debate. The campaign was opened by the first debate, in the "seminary" just referred to, in August. The pioneers came from far and near, but this mass meeting numbered only about fifty persons. The meeting was a lively one, and the campaign resulted in the election of Marquett. So much for the history of the Stone Seminary.

The first term of the Territorial court in Lancaster county was held in November, 1864, at the house of Jacob Dawson. Dawson's house was a double log cabin, situated on the ground on west O street now occupied by the St. Charles hotel, between Seventh and Eighth, on the south side of the street. The officiating judge was Elmer S. Dundy, now United States District Judge for this district. Mr. Dawson acted as clerk, and Judge Pottenger, of Plattsmouth, was appointed Prosecuting Attorney for the Territory, at a salary of $75. T. M. Marquett, of Plattsmouth, was present as an attorney. Milton Langdon and John S. Gregory were the local attorneys, who were nearly always arrayed against each other in the local courts. The leading case of the term was that of Bird, or The Territory, against Pemberton. The latter had shot his revolver into Bird's house, and thumped Bird with it afterward, owing to some difficulty Pemberton had had with one of Bird's daughters. The Birds had talked, and Pemberton "did up" the father in consequence. After a good deal of trouble, a grand jury was impaneled, the venires for both grand and petit juries being exhausted in getting the panel. Then it took about three days to find a petit jury, owing to the lack of men. The eligible male inhabitants were nearly all on the grand jury. There were no professional jurymen in court on this occasion. The trial of cases was delayed about three days in the endeavor to find petit jurors.

The grand jury found several indictments. Pemberton was indicted and came to trial on a charge of "Malicious assault with intent to kill." T. M. Marquett defended him for a fee of ten dollars. He urged upon his honor, Judge Dundy, that his client should not be required to lie in jail, (there was no jail until 1868,) and should not be required to give bond, even if he could, if the Territory was unable to try him. It was not his client's fault that a jury could not be found. Citizens should not be made responsible for the failures of the Territory. He therefore moved to quash the indictment. Judge Dundy granted the motion, and Pemberton was discharged. Pemberton left, to avoid further trouble, Marquett assuring him that if he assaulted Bird again, that he would come to Lancaster and prosecute him. Another indictment was quashed in the same way.

This term adjourned on the day Abraham Lincoln was elected for a second term, November 8, 1864. There was a foot of snow on the ground, and the day was stormy. In returning to Plattsmouth, the court and attorneys were obliged to shovel through drifts. When within eight miles of Plattsmouth, the party learned of the election of Mr. Lincoln, and all five of them then and there gave three cheers. The drive to Plattsmouth was made in a single day. This long drive was frequently made in a day. Simeon Benadom made the drive in a day in 1868, when he brought his wife to the city. She was one of the first women who became a resident of Lincoln.

There was one term of court in Lancaster in 1865, and probably one court in 1866. The famous litigation of those early years was between John S. Gregory and his Uncle Eaton, of Plattsmouth. The war continued for several years, and was red hot. On one occasion Mr. Gregory expressed a decided opinion that Eaton would be a resident of Sheol in the future. Eaton promptly replied that he should, in such a case, be compelled to regret his misfortune, owing to the necessity he should be under of keeping such company as Mr. Gregory.

The next term of court in this county was held under the Government of the State of Nebraska.

On June 21st, 1866, an election was held to ratify the State constitution framed by the Territorial Leigslature early in the year. The people ratified the instrument all right, and the Legislature elected under that constitution met July 4, 1866. But the bill for the admission of Nebraska as a State, which passed Congress on July 28th, was vetoed by Andrew Johnson. This compelled the people to wait until 1867 for statehood. Congress passed another admission bill in January, 1867, which was also promptly vetoed by President Johnson, on the grounds that the Territory did not contain sufficient population to warrant it in claiming statehood; that the admission bill was at variance to some degree with the enabling act, and that the constitution had not been formed in the prescribed manner. It took Congress just two days to pass this bill over Johnson's veto: February 8 and 9, 1867. The Legislature met at Omaha, February 20th and ratified the provisions on which Nebraska was to be admitted; that she should enter into an obligation to deny no citizen the elective franchise on account of race, color, or previous condition of servitude. President Johnson proclaimed Nebraska a State on March 1, 1867. The Legislature immediately took steps to remove the capital from Omaha. How this was done is told in another chapter.

CHAPTER XII.

The Growth of the Village—The Change of Name—The Effect of the Location of the Capital—Early Business Houses and Residences—The Days of '67 and '68.

In 1864 Hon. John Gillespie returned from the army, in company with a son of Elder J. M. Young, on a furlough. When the steamer reached Nebraska City Elder Young was on the wharf watching for his son, whom he greeted cordially. He then gave Mr. Gillespie a neighborly reception, and the latter inquired whether the Elder was still living in Nebraska City. Mr. Young replied that he had located at Lancaster, in Lancaster county. Mr. Gillespie had a high opinion of Elder Young's ability and character, and expressed surprise that he should be incarcerated in the wilderness on Salt creek, and asked what he expected to do there.

"Oh, I am founding a colony out there," said the Elder, "and am building a female seminary. We will soon have the county seat, and will have the capital there some day."

The idea of founding a female seminary on the raw prairie, where there was scarcely a young woman to attend it, and of getting the Territorial capital out in the same nondescript region, struck Mr. Gillespie as visionary, if not actually absurd. But no fiction is so romantic and surprising as real human experience, especially in a new State, where almost anything within reason is possible.

Within about a year from the time that boat touched the Nebraska City wharf, John Gillespie was elected Auditor of the Territory of Nebraska. As Auditor he acted as one of three Commissioners, three years after the boat landed, to locate the capital of the State of Nebraska on Elder Young's colonial grounds, and in almost precisely three years from the time the Elder made the prophecy, the capital of Nebraska actually was in existence on the ground he had picked out for the site of "Lancaster" in 1863. His "seminary" was not very successful, but that was not very material, for in about five years from the date of his declaration to Mr. Gillespie that he proposed to found a seminary, the contract for the erection of the building for the University of Nebraska was let, and Elder Young lived to see all his dreams more than realized. His death occurred in 1884. Lincoln then was a city of about 20,000 people.

On the afternoon of July 29, 1867, the Commissioners finally met, at the house of Captain W. T. Donovan, to ballot on the location of the capital of Nebraska. The meeting was in the attic of the house. Lancaster had two votes on the first ballot and Ashland one. The one vote was by Mr. Gillespie, who said he feared that Lancaster was short on a water supply for a city of large population. But he was also influenced, doubtless, to vote for Ashland because that place was the favorite for a capital site of the Plattsmouth people, while Yankee Hill was the chosen site of the Nebraska City schemers. Plattsmouth was opposed to almost anything that Nebraska City favored. Mr. Gillespie was really in favor of Lancaster, and on the second ballot voted for it and made the choice unanimous. The citizens of the hamlet were gathered about the house awaiting the result in hopeful but anxious suspense. Presently Governor David Butler and Commissioners T. P. Kennard and John Gillespie came out of the house, and the Governor, standing on the east side to avoid the heat of the sun, formally proclaimed the decision of the Commission in favor of Lancaster. Of course the few settlers present rejoiced exceedingly.

On that historic July day the hamlet of Lancaster did not contain more than six or seven buildings, "shacks," log-houses, stone buildings, and all. The Commissioners then stood in front of Captain Donovan's house, which stood about sixty feet southwest of Opelt's Hotel, or near the southwest corner of Ninth and Q streets. This was a small stone and cottonwood frame house. Jacob Dawson's double log cabin of 1864 still stood on the south side of O street, between Seventh and Eighth, where the St. Charles Hotel now is. In the front end of this house S. B. Pound had set up a small grocery store in 1866, and it was still in existence when the Capital Commissioners came. Dawson also had the postoffice at that time, and took it "up town" with him when he removed two blocks east, in 1867. Milton Langdon resided in a little log-house near the southwest corner of Eighth and Q streets. Dr. and Rev. John McKesson, for he represented both the Methodist ministry and the medical profession, lived on his claim on the north side; his house was being erected at what is now W and Twelfth streets. The cottonwood grove now there was planted by McKesson, the trees at first being switches. The doctor added McKesson's Addition to Lincoln, and was offered $40,-000 for it in the early seventies, but declined to take it. He wanted more. He then went into the manufacture of a harvester he invented, and lost all his money, and now lives a poor man at La Cygne, Kansas. S. B. Galey, who came here in April, 1866, had a small stone building on P street near Tenth, on the site now occupied by John Sheedy's elegant block. Linderman & Hardenbergh, who next to S. B. Pound were the earliest merchants of Lincoln, had opened a small stock of goods at a point that would now be in Ninth street, near P, possibly partly in both streets. They had sold their shop to Martin and Jacob Pflug, early in 1867, who conducted it in the firm name of Pflug Bros. They kept a small stock of groceries, including a barrel of whisky, some hardware, and a few dry goods. Robert Monteith and his son John had a little shoe shop at what is now 922 P street. They soon after built the little frame building now on that lot and now used by M. Adler for a pawn shop. This is one of the few structures remaining of that date in the city, and when first built passed for quite a building.

Elder J. M. Young lived in what is now O and Eighteenth street. The sandstone house now on that corner was afterward erected by the Elder. Luke Lavender's log homestead residence was at O and Fourteenth, his eighty acres lying to the south and east. This house has been considered the first residence erected on the plat of Lincoln. If this is true, it must have been placed there before the fall of 1864, for it is positively known that Jacob Dawson's double log-cabin, on the south side of O street, between Seventh and Eighth streets, was completed before the close of October, 1864, for Judge Dundy held a term of court in that house during the first few days of November, 1864, and T. M. Marquett was in attendance as an attorney. Dawson's and Lavender's houses were, doubtless, built in the summer of 1864. Both men came to the county in company with Elder Young's exploring party, in July, 1863. William Guy, Philip Humerick, E. T. Hudson, E. Warnes, and John Giles, had homesteads near the plat of Lancaster, and the farms they then were opening are now all part of the city of Lincoln. The walls of Elder Young's old stone seminary stood on the rear part of the lots on the northeast corner of Ninth and P streets, where the *State Journal* block now stands. There may have been thirty inhabitants, all told, on the present site of Lincoln in July, 1867. Judging by the vote cast in the following fall election, there may have been five hundred people in the entire county. From thirty souls to fifty thousand inhabitants, in twenty-two years, is a record of rapid growth equaled by few cities of the world; but such has been the progress of Lincoln since 1867.

The Commissioners called the capital "Lincoln," according to the terms of the bill, which provided for the relocation of the seat of government of the State of Nebraska. How the name "Lincoln" came to be selected is told in the chapter on the removal of the capital.

When it became known that the Commissioners had selected Lincoln for the State capital, a number of men squatted on the site, expecting to bid in the ground they were on at the fall lot sales. But there was a good deal of doubt about the outcome of this capital venture. The North Platte people were generally unfriendly to the choice of the Commissioners, and Omaha was disposed to prevent the consummation of the removal, if such a thing were possible. The lot sales were not opened until September 17th, and the lack of confidence was so great that the sale, on the first day, was a failure. No lots could be disposed of. And the year of 1867 was practically closed before the sales were known to be sufficiently successful to assure the funds necessary to erect a capitol building. Had it not been for the courage of the Commissioners and the enterprise of the Nebraska City men, who were friendly to this as a site for a new capital, it is very doubtful if this removal scheme would have succeeded. Nebraska City considered it good strategy to get the capital out of Omaha, when it was thought that the latter town might be outstripped, and Nebraska City become the metropolis of the Missouri. It seems never to have occurred to the schemers, who were trying to protect themselves from Omaha, that the new capital would spring into such importance in twenty-two years as not only to overshadow Nebraska City, but even to rival Omaha herself. As Lincoln has passed all other towns on the river, she may yet pass Omaha. This is much more reasonable than a prediction of her present importance would have seemed in 1867.

The real business existence, in fact the real existence of Lincoln, dates from 1868. The lot sales had fairly succeeded. Confidence then had a substantial foundation; so that business houses and inhabitants came quite freely during 1868, and Lincoln became a town of about 500 people toward the close of the year.

Even now the records and traditions of 1868 are becoming dim — especially the traditions. It has taken days of patient inquiry to reproduce the landmarks of that year even with approximate correctness. Old settlers differ radically about various points. Certain buildings are located by some at one place and others feel sure they were somewhere else. But the village was substantially all confined to a space bounded on the west and east by Eighth and Twelfth streets, and on the north and south by R and N streets.

Jacob Dawson had left his historic double log-cabin on the present

SWEET'S BLOCK — NORTHWEST CORNER OF O AND TENTH.

site of the St. Charles Hotel, near O and Eighth, and had erected a large square stone and log house back some distance from the southwest corner of O and Tenth. The Sweet Block, on the northeast corner of O and Tenth, was finished early in 1868, by Darwin Peckham, who still is a leading mechanic of the city, and one of very few who did business on this plat in 1868. This building was just half its present size. Where the O street stairway now is there was an outside stairway for entrance to the upper story. The building was really three buildings erected together, by James Sweet, A. C. Rudolph, and Pflug Bros. Sweet and N. C. Brock opened the first bank in the city, in the southwest corner room, on the first floor, in June, 1868. This bank continued until 1871, when it was reorganized as the State Bank of Nebraska, by Samuel G. Owen, James

Sweet, and Nelson C. Brock. About the same time that the bank opened, A. C. Rudolph opened a grocery store in the next room north, and Pflug Bros. a stock of dry goods in the third room from the corner. The upper part was used for offices, and later on, part of the county offices were there, and the State Treasury was practically at the bank in 1869, Mr. Sweet then being State Treasurer. Bain Bros. opened the first clothing house in the city in 1868, on the southeast corner of Tenth and O streets. They had previously had a real estate office fronting Tenth street, to the south of their clothing house. D. B. Cropsey had a real estate office on the southwest corner of O and Tenth, where the State National Bank now is, his father, A. J. Cropsey, being with him. During that year Bohanan Bros. opened

SOUTHEAST CORNER O AND TENTH.

their meat market where it has been ever since, next to Cropsey's office, to the west, and where they have since done an enormous business. Squire Blazier also opened a meat market about where the postoffice now stands, postoffice block then being known as "Market Square." The square was used in those days for a camping ground for immigrants and land seekers, and was generally thronged with machinery, covered wagons, horses, cattle, and men. Here the early land agents found many of their customers. On south Tenth street, about where the Lancaster County Bank now stands, David May opened a small stock of clothing during the year. A little south of the alley R. R. Tingley opened a little drug shop; and a short distance south of this C. F. Damrow set up the first tailoring establishment in the capital. On the north side of this block, about the center, facing "Market Square," was Moll's grocery. S. B. Pound had removed his stock of groceries to what is now 915 O street, where he united with Max Rich, of Rich & Oppenheimer, of Nebraska City, in the grocery business during a few months of 1867 and 1868. The next year he sold his interest to Rich & Oppenheimer, who carried a general stock there for a number of years.

Judge Pound, as a merchant, was noted for his close application to his law studies. He really made his grocery business a sort of subsidiary arrangement to fill up the time while he prepared for the bar.

SOUTHWEST CORNER O AND NINTH.

He is a good example of success won by tireless application and industry.

On the northwest corner of this block a colored man named Moore had a barber shop, and near the southwest corner was the residence of L. A. Scoggin.

In the block bounded by O and N and Eighth and Ninth, there was one building, Dunbar's livery stable, located on the northeast corner of the block. It was a long low shed.

In the block bounded by O and P and Eighth and Ninth, there were two or three buildings. On the southeast corner, where the Humphrey Bros.' stately block now is, Dr. H. D. Gilbert, of Nebraska

City, had established a mercantile house, carrying the peculiar combination of books, drugs, and hardware. His little house stood beside the store to the north. Humphrey Brothers succeeded Dr. Gilbert soon afterward. Milton Langdon, the first County Treasurer of Lancaster county under the new order of things, lived a little back from the southwest corner of Eighth and Q. His milk house, which was a little to the southward, became the first city and county jail. When a citizen became too "wild and woolly," they "put him in the milk house." It is a question in dispute whether J. D. Minshall had a small store of dry goods and groceries on P, between Eighth

NORTHWEST CORNER O AND NINTH.

and Ninth, or not, in 1868. Simon Benadom says he is certain that he did. Charles F. Damrow thinks that he did, also. Others think he never was anywhere but on O street, between Tenth and Eleventh, south side. But he was doubtless there.

In the block bounded by P and Q and Eighth and Ninth, there were two or three houses. H. S. Jennings had put up a stone residence near the northeast corner. It is thought by several pioneers that there were two or three small houses on the south side, facing P, one of which was the Widow Gardner's dance house, which was a famous, or infamous, attraction during the legislative session of 1869. But these are not all fully authenticated. Near the northwest corner of Ninth and Q a story-and-a-half cottonwood frame stood. It was thirty-three feet square, and was partly used for public and partly for private purposes.

In the block bounded by P and Q and Ninth and Tenth, there were six or more structures of various sorts and sizes. At the northwest corner was the Pioneer House, the original hotel in Lincoln, kept by L. A. Scoggin. John Cadman had overcome his disappointment at not getting the capital, and having bought the lots at the southwest corner of the block, on which the walls of the old stone seminary stood, he built up that structure late in 1867, and opened it as the "Cadman House." He only owned it a few months, until he sold it, in 1868, to Nathan Atwood, who built a brick front to it of much larger proportions, and opened the "Atwood House," which was the principal hotel of the town for several years, but was burned down in 1879. On the northeast corner was the Methodist church, a low white building, erected late in 1867 or early in 1868. It was the largest audience room in town for several years, and was used for church services, political and business meetings, lectures, and similar public purposes. Its dimensions were about 25 x 40 feet.

Seth B. Galey having been appointed County Clerk in April, 1867, and been elected to that office in the fall of 1867, erected a small stone office on P street, where John Sheedy's block now is, in which he transacted the county's business belonging to his department. Next to him on the west was a little building in which S. B. Pound and Seth Robinson opened a law office. At 922 P street was the Monteith shoe shop, heretofore mentioned.

On the block bounded by Q and R and Eleventh and Twelfth, a short distance north of the southwest corner, was the "stone school-house." This was the first school-house in Lincoln. The stone school-house was the educational center during several subsequent years.

In the block included between O and P and Tenth and Eleventh streets the first saloon was started, by Ans. and George Williams. This was the first building completed on the east side of the Government Square. It stood north of the center of the block, and the upper floor was used for offices. The front room was Thomas H. Hyde's land office, where he transacted the leading land business of the town during 1868 and later. Mr. Hyde was an auctioneer at the State lot sales in 1868. His office was head-quarters for State officers and politicians, Governor Butler often resorting there to transact business. In after years the lower room became a notorious saloon, where more prominent men of the town drank whisky to their detriment than at any other place in the city. It is said that from fifteen to twenty leading men of Lincoln have snuffed out their prospects at that bar. This old cottonwood frame still stands, at 1320 O street, and is used as a second-hand store.

A good story is told on Colonel J. E. Philpott, who arrived in the capital about this time. When he looked around for a law office, he found empty the upper front room of the building in which the Williams boys had their bar. He took possession, and awaited the process of events. After a few days a tall, dignified-looking man came into his office, and said he was looking for a room in which to transact a land business. Colonel Philpott thereupon proceeded to lease the stranger a part of his office, and everything went on swimmingly, until it was developed, later on, that the stranger was the owner of the building, or Mr. Thomas H. Hyde, and Colonel Philpott had leased Mr. Hyde quarters in his own building. Mr. Hyde had been away on a land-exploring tour, and finding Colonel Philpott in his house on returning, played "tenderfoot" to have a little fun.

Dr. D. A. Sherwood had a real estate office near the southeast corner of this block, and a small stock of groceries in the same building.

Behind these shops, to the north and west, was located the first lumber yard in Lincoln. The proprietors of the yard were Monell & Larkley. Soon afterward Valentine Brothers opened a lumber yard on the ground fronting on Eleventh, from M to N streets, where Temple Block and the Billingsley Block now are. This firm supplied most of the lumber used in building the old State capitol. During 1868 and 1869 both yards employed teams to bring the lumber from the Missouri river, at a point about six miles above Nebraska City. Farmers and freighters going to the river with loads would return loaded with lumber, and the lumber trains were often long caravans.

A. J. Cropsey built a residence where the south end of the Capital hotel now is. Early in the fall of 1867 W. W. Carder had established the first newspaper of the town, near the middle of the east side of the block bounded by N and O and Tenth and Eleventh streets. This was the *Commonwealth*, which in the summer of 1868 became the

State Journal. A little west of Carder's office was the beer saloon of Joe Hodges, who is said to have dished out the first lager sold in Lincoln. Whisky had been sold for two years or more before this. Over on the southwest corner of this block William Shirley had erected a boarding house, and next to this building, on the north, was Cox's grocery and boarding house. About where Harley's drug store now is, at the southeast corner of Eleventh and O, stood William Rowe's harness shop, who was the pioneer horse furnisher of the town. About three lots east on O street was J. P. Lantz's land office. Mr. Lantz also conducted a real-estate monthly for about seven years, called the Nebraska *Intelligencer.* Of that he used to print an edition of 10,000 copies at times, and it was the means of inducing many to come to Nebraska. Mr. Lantz is still in the real estate business, on nearly the same spot he occupied in 1868. A couple of lots to the eastward was William Guy's residence. On the southeast corner of Twelfth and O streets was Charles May's bakery, where D. B. Alexander's block is now located. May baked 150 loaves per day in 1868. He also had a homestead. William Allen had a residence nearly opposite, north, near where the Burr Block stands. Leighton & Brown had a small drug store on the southeast corner of O and Eleventh, on the present site of the Richards Block. Seth H. Robinson lived on the northwest corner of Twelfth and P streets, where Mr. R. E. Moore now resides. It is said that Thomas Roberts had the first harness shop in town, near the southwest corner of Eleventh and O; but this is in dispute.

Such was Lincoln in 1868. There may have been a few small shops and residences in addition to those named, but those described substantially constituted the capital of Nebraska twenty-one years ago.

The ordinary trades were fully represented at this time. The professions were also. S. B. Galey, Seth Robinson, S. B. Pound, Ezra Tullis, Major Strunk, and J. E. Philpott, were the lawyers of this period. The first man admitted to the bar in this county was John S. Gregory, who became a disciple of Blackstone under the authority of Judge Dundy in 1866. He and Milton Langdon had practiced in the little legal affairs of Lancaster settlement back in 1864 and 1865, but they did this because they were somewhat more "posted" than the other pioneers of the neighborhood. Robinson was a man of brilliant mind, but not perfectly balanced. He became Attorney General of Nebraska in 1869. He died in California of quinsy a few years ago. S. B. Pound has since held the office of Probate Judge, [1871,] District Judge in 1875, and State Senator. He was a member of the Constitutional Convention of 1875, which framed our present State constitution. He formed a law partnership with L. C. Burr in 1887, having resigned the judgship at that time, owing to the low salary attached to it. Major Strunk was a resonant political orator of the early days, and slipped from the community in an unceremonious halo of social indiscretion. Col. Philpott is in the addition to the Sweet Block, having officed in the original block when some of the county and State officers were doing business there. It was here, in 1869, that the colonel became the unwilling victim of one of his own practical jokes. He was in partnership with Sam Tuttle, with an office at the east end of the block, on the upper floor. H. G. Brown, a good fellow, with a disposition to take things too seriously, was on the same floor, and was Deputy Clerk of both the District and Supreme courts. Philpott and Tuttle persuaded Brown to go down to the back yard at night to appropriate a little fire-wood for them from a pile belonging to the county. Brown obligingly went down for the wood, and Philpott slipped out and hid behind some sunflowers that grew further east in the yard. When Brown had filled his arms with wood, Philpott rose up suddenly and began to fire off his revolver, as if he had caught Brown stealing wood, expecting that the latter would drop the wood he had and run precipitately to cover. Then they would enjoy the joke on Brown at their leisure. This was the theory of the joke. But plans of jokers, like those of mice, do not always go the satisfactory way. No sooner had Philpott's gun flashed than Brown dropped his wood and wheeled toward Philpott's hiding place with the savage remark:

"Ah ha! you'll find that's a game that two can play at!"

And to Col. Philpott's dismay he began to reach for his hip pocket to get out his revolver. Col. Philpott saw that something must be done to ease the situation, and that in a hurry. So he sprang out into Brown's view and threw up his hands, gesticulating wildly while he protested with an intense earnestness he had not experienced for years:

"Don't shoot, Brown, don't shoot! It's me, Philpott—just a joke —that's all!"

Brown was not cooled down at once, and growled that "he'd a notion to shoot Philpott anyway, just on account of his blamed foolishness." Then Brown went off indignantly, and refused to be friendly for some time. All this time Tuttle was looking out of the window having all the fun there was in the performance.

In 1868 a drove of 1,000 Texas cattle passed through Lincoln northward bound. In going over the Salt creek bridge, at the foot of O street, the cattle broke the structure down, precipitating a lot of the long-horned bovines of Texas into the stream. The owner of the herd camped just across the creek, and the town trustees, Messrs. H. S. Jennings, S. B. Linderman, Dr. H. D. Gilbert, J. J. Van Dyke, and D. W. Tingley, donned their official dignity and proceeded toward the camp to require the proprietor of the herd to pay for the bridge. Major Bohanan and others of the population who were posted on the science of the Texas steer, followed at a prudent distance to see the fun. The trustees marched up to the steers in solemn state and artless innocence. The animals raised up their heads in audacious amazement, and began to move toward the officials of the city, who found it convenient to commence retracing their steps. This official retreat was at first conducted in good order, but the accelerated movement of the steers, and finally a charge from the animals, turned the retirement of the town officers into a precipitate rout, and they came pell mell back to cover with the steers in full pursuit. Having escaped, they then summoned the *posse comitatus*, and the owner of the steers was required to pay for the bridge; and their terms were not improved by the bad manners of his wild western cattle.

The doctors were here with the earliest comers. Dr. J. M. McKesson has already been mentioned as one of Elder Young's party, of 1863. Besides him there were in 1868 and 1869 Doctors H. D. Gilbert, George W. French, and J. W. Strickland. When the Lancaster County Medical Society was organized, on the 24th of May, 1869, the following-named resident physicians of the capital were present: D. W. Tingley, F. G. Fuller, J. M. Evans, H. D. Gilbert, L. H. Robbins, and George W. French. In the fall of the same year the following additional names were added to the roster: J. W. Strickland, John W. Northup, George A. Goodrich, and C. C. Radmore.

Politics in a new country never exhibits a character of tameness. Some one, probably Seth P. Galey, had organized the Republican party about 1866. Galey was a natural leader. He stood six feet in his stockings, and was as successful as he was large physically. He was county judge in 1867 and 1868. In 1870 he went to the Legislature, and in 1879 was chosen Mayor of Lincoln. He carried a hod to finish the stone seminary in 1866, and was attorney for the Atchison & Nebraska railroad in 1871 or 1872. He is now living in Portland, Oregon. There were many Union soldiers here in 1868, only three or four years out of the war, and they were intensely enthusiastic for their old leader, General Grant, in the Grant and Colfax campaign of 1868. So it was easy to stir up a hot discussion, especially with such candidates as Grant and Seymour, the latter's war record being decidedly unsatisfactory to the soldiers.

Some time during September, 1868, Simon P. Benadom, who had been appointed a postmaster in Jones county, Iowa, in 1856, by Buchanan, and was a warm Democrat, called a county convention of the Democratic party of the county. This was rather regarded as a joke by the Republicans. When the day came there were just three Democrats, besides Benadom, present in the old stone school house, two of whom were Irish stone cutters from the State Capitol building. Benadom was chairman and secretary of the convention, and an organization was effected. Benadom was selected for chairman of the county committee, and also of the senatorial committee, places he held for years afterward. It was decided to erect a Seymour and Blair "liberty pole" on Market Square, preparatory to holding a rousing Democratic rally there in October. A committee was selected to procure the pole, but on the appointed day not a man appeared but Benadom. He remembered the old story of the lark and the farmer, and immediately drove his lumber wagon to his woods, near Saltillo. There he found Matt Brackin, now commissary to the city jail, whom he invited to aid in getting the pole. Brackin was then and is yet a Democrat, and readily consented. They loaded three stalwart hickory saplings, and drove to Lincoln. Benadom welded iron rings, and the three poles were spliced together, and made a flag staff probably fifty-five feet high. It took all the Democrats in the town to raise it to a perpendicular position. But they planted it, a little to the southeast of the place where the Government Square artesian well now is. Benadom remembers this zealous work yet as a hot and difficult performance that almost sweat politics out of him for the time.

About three weeks afterward the Democratic rally took place around that pole. A platform had been erected at its base, and upon it Judge Savage, of Omaha, stood while he made a short and fiery speech to the assembled Democrats. Then A. J. Poppleton addressed the crowd for two hours, and it seemed to the followers of Seymour present that they had never heard a more eloquent speech. It established Poppleton's reputation as an orator of power, from that day to this, among Lancaster Democrats, and also among many Republicans. General Victor Vifquain, now Consul of the United States at Aspinwall, Panama, was present also.

This demonstration of the Democracy around the hickory pole, supposed to be symbolic of "Old Hickory," fired up the Republicans. They had to have a pole also, and to excel the Democrats. They sent to the river yards, (it was at that time told to the Democrats even to Chicago,) for several very fine pine timbers. The base timber was perhaps a foot square, and was left square. The next section was smaller, and was made with eight sides. The next was of less dimensions, and with more faces. The pole finally tapered off in a graceful round staff not larger than a man's wrist. When completed by Mr. Sam McClay, the leading Democrats admitted it to be the most graceful and lofty flag staff they had ever seen. It was so heavy and tall that the Democrats had to assist in planting it. It was so top heavy and flexible in the wind, that it had to be stayed by ropes. It penetrated the atmosphere to a height of one hundred feet. It cost the Republicans, it was reported at the time to the Democrats, three hundred dollars. This was perhaps a little higher than the facts. It was set up some distance north of the Democratic pole. The Republicans were very proud of the surpassing excellence of their pole, and probably took some pains to exult at the expense of the Democratic staff.

At any rate, toward the close of the campaign it was found one morning to have been broken in three pieces, and two fragments, with the flag, were on the ground. This fired the blood of the Republicans, particularly of the old soldiers. They thought their staff had been broken through political envy, or even malice. They suspected a stage driver named Pool with having committed this flagrant act, and a warrant was immediately procured of County Judge John Cadman for Pool's arrest. Sheriff J. H. Hawke brought Pool back to the city at the close of the day, and he was immediately arraigned before Judge Cadman in a little frame building, used for a saloon by Joe Hodges, on O street, between Tenth and Eleventh, where McConnell's brick block now stands. The room was packed with men, and the ground in front was occupied by an angry crowd of old soldiers and others, who freely declared they would hang Pool if found guilty; and very few who saw the menacing demonstrations doubted that they would carry out their threat.

S. B. Pound and C. H. Gere conducted the prosecution, and J. E. Philpott, H. S. Jennings, and Col. Van Armin, the defense. The trial had hardly opened before the floor broke down, and dropped the court, attorneys, prisoners, and reporters, to the ground, about a foot below. But a small affair like this cut no figure when a man was on trial for his life on a vague suspicion of having cut down a Grant and Colfax flag staff, and the trial went on. It soon developed that there was no evidence against Pool, and he was discharged, and was hustled off into the dark, by the back way. While the Grand Army men did not wish to hang a man who really had not committed the offense, yet Pool found it convenient to keep out of sight for a good while after this. The pieces of the broken staff had been arranged for a gallows in front of the court room, the rope was adjusted, and the whole aspect of affairs looked so like some one was going to be executed, that no one could blame him for feeling as though it was not conducive to long life to remain in the capital of Nebraska.

At the election following this fiery proceeding there were 460 votes cast in the county, of which the Republicans polled 320, and the Democrats 123.

This was not the only time that a man escaped by a hair's breadth from being taken from a Lincoln court and hung. In 1869 a man named Bill McClain was suspected of horse stealing. He was arraigned before Judge Cadman, and an angry crowd, led by Martin Pflug, the merchant, were actually uncoiling their rope; but the emphatic protestations of Simon Benadom and the size of Judge Cadman induced the mob to cool down and disperse. Judge Cadman was a very powerful man, and he told Benadom that he would have pitched out the leaders of the mob faster than they could come into the room where he was, had they attempted the assault.

After much labor and inquiry, a diagram of the town, as it appeared

EXPLANATION OF PLAT.

in 1868, has been prepared for this book. It shows where each house then in existence stood, as remembered by the pioneers now living. There is some difference of opinion about several buildings, and some may be omitted, but this chart is approximately correct. It is accompanied with a key, so that it can be readily understood.

The contract for building the old State capitol having been let, on January 11, 1868, to Joseph Ward, the work had progressed steadily all the season of that year, so that on December 3, 1868, Governor Butler announced by proclamation the removal of the seat of government from Omaha to Lincoln.

The United States land office was removed from Nebraska City to Lincoln in 1868, and Mr. Stewart McConiga, the popular Register, was kept as busy as a bee assisting immigrants to take homesteads. In fact, men stood in rows, awaiting their turn to take a claim.

So 1868 was a successful year for the new capital, and the future was full of hope. On petition of a majority of the citizens of the village, the County Commissioners, on April 7, 1868, ordered "that the town of Lincoln be declared a body incorporate, and that the powers and privileges be granted them as by the Statute in such cases are made and provided." Messrs. L. A. Scoggin, B. F. Cozad, Dr. Potter, W. W. Carder, and A. L. Palmer, were appointed Trustees of the corporation. An election was held on May 18, 1868, at which H. S. Jennings, S. B. Linderman, H. D. Gilbert, J. J. Van Dyke, and D. W. Tingley, were elected Trustees. But sixty votes were cast at this election, and the town government failed to continue the organization during that year.

The corporate existence of Lincoln, therefore, dates from 1869, and the events of that period of almost precisely twenty years, 1869 to 1889, will be the subject of the next chapter.

CHAPTER XIII.

LINCOLN FOR TWENTY YEARS, FROM 1869 TO 1889—ITS REMARKABLE GROWTH—THE INCREASE IN POPULATION BY YEARS—WATER WORKS, PAVING, SEWERAGE—EVIDENCES OF THE CITY'S WONDERFUL IMPROVEMENT—THE FLOODS OF 1868, 1869, 1874, AND 1889.

On petition of 189 citizens, the town of Lincoln was ordered incorporated by the County Commissioners, April 7, 1869, about twenty years and three months ago at this writing. The corporate limits were made to include section twenty-six, the west half of section twenty-five, the southwest quarter of section twenty-four, and the south half of section twenty-three, in town ten north, range six east. The town officers were as subjoined:

Trustees—H. S. Jennings, S. B. Linderman, H. D. Gilbert, J. L. McConnell, and D. W. Tingley.

Judges of Election—Seth Robinson, A. J. Cropsey, and J. N. Townley.

The town election was held on May 3, 1869, and a Board of Trustees were chosen, as follows: H. D. Gilbert, C. H. Gere, William Rowe, Philetus Peck, and J. L. McConnell. The officers of the Board were: H. D. Gilbert, *Chairman;* J. R. DeLand, *Clerk;* and Nelson C. Brock, *Treasurer.*

The year 1869 was a prosperous one for Lincoln. The lot sales had been wonderfully successful, assuring all needed State improvements to be derived therefrom. Land sales continued to be active, and population multiplied in town and adjacent country. Above all, the famously progressive Legislature of 1869 met early in the year at the new capitol, and not only approved all the splendid work of Governor David Butler and Commissioners John Gillespie and T. P. Kennard, but also made provision for further progress on a most wise and magnificent scale.

Hon. C. H. Gere, in his address to the Old Settlers' Association, at Cushman park, on June 19, 1889, tells of the deeds of this great Legislature in the following terms, which are none too complimentary:

The members of the first Legislature brought their cots, blankets, and pillows with them in their overland journeys in wagons (hired) or the jerkies of the stage line, and lodged, some in newly-erected store buildings, some in the upper rooms of the State House, while the wealthier law-makers boldly registered at the Atwood hostelry, and paid their bills for extras, including "noise and confusion" during the Senatorial mill between Tipton, Butler, and Marquett; and how they all agreed, after some preliminary hair-pulling, that the new capitol was a success, and ordered a dome erected thereon reaching the upper atmosphere, and confirmed the deeds, regular and irregular, of the Commission, and gave us a cemetery in which to bury our dead; how they passed a bill for the organization of the State University, and ordered a further sale of lots and lands to build the dome and construct a university building, a wing of an insane hospital, and a workshop for the penitentiary, and how they were all built in part or in whole of the old red sandstone of the vicinity, and came to grief soon after, may not be an interesting story to-day; but it was full of eloquence, fire, and significance for those who were on the ground at the time.

From the adjournment of that Legislature, the body that took in hand the building up of the new commonwealth and the laying of the foundation of its great institutions, so ably aided by the executive officers of our first State administration, to this memorial gathering, every six working days of every week of the twenty years has seen completed an average of ten buildings on the site of the city consecrated to the memory of the great emancipator and war President.

No body of men in forty days accomplished more. Every law passed by that memorable Legislature of '69 weighed a ton. Its work was original and creative, and it did it well. Its moving spirit was the Governor, David Butler. Some of its members came down to Lincoln from hostile localities, and had it in their hearts to destroy him and his works; but before the session was a fortnight old, his genial though homely ways, his kindness of heart, his sturdy common sense, the originality of his genius, and the boldness of his conceptions, captured them, and when the forty days were done, no man in the two houses avowed himself the enemy of David Butler.

The contract for excavating for and the construction of the basement of the State University was let to D. J. Silvers & Son, of Logansport, Indiana, on June 10, 1869, for $23,520, and work was immediately commenced. The corner-stone of the university was laid on September 23d, with Masonic ceremonies. The building was to be completed on or before December 1, 1870.

Messrs. Silvers burned the brick for the university building near where the Burlington & Missouri river dépot now is. They bought hundreds of cords of wood from the settlers, thus aiding them to obtain money for current expenses. The entire bottom in the region of the brick works was covered with cords of wood, sand, lime, clay, and brick. At times, during 1869, one hundred cords or more of wood would be in sight at one time. This was not the first brick burned in the county or city. Milton Langdon burned a kiln of brick, on the site of West Lincoln, as early as 1867, assisted by John S. Gregory, who supplied the wood. Simon Benadom burned a kiln of brick, on the ground where the Burlington dépot now stands, early in 1868, out of which a number of the chimneys were constructed. Seth Robinson used these brick to construct his residence, the same now occupied by R. E. Moore, on the northeast corner of Twelfth and P streets. Some of the same brick were used in building the Atwood House.

The contract for building the asylum for the insane was let to Joseph Ward, about August 15, 1869, for $128,000, and work proceeded soon thereafter.

Besides all this, the people of Lincoln still had a very high notion of the value of the Salt Basin as a commercial aid to the city. Mr. John H. Ames, who was the pioneer historian of Lincoln, having published a series of articles he had previously prepared for the *Statesman*, a Democratic newspaper of Lincoln; these were reprinted in pamphlet form in 1870 by the *Journal* "power press." In that work, the correctness of which is formally attested by the Governor, Auditor, and Secretary of State, Mr. Ames estimates that 882,001.60 barrels of salt can be made from a single well. Allowing for cost of barrels and every possible shrinkage, he calculates that a single well would produce salt to the value of at least $488,970.22. He casts his eye over the field and says that: "While the railway now being constructed, and those projected, will give us direct connection with the Eastern markets, and enable us to compete with the Eastern salt manufactories upon their own ground, it is certain that we shall be called upon to supply all the vast territory lying between the Mississippi river and the Rocky mountains, so that three dollars per barrel may be considered an extremely low estimate for the minimum price at the wells."

The foregoing estimate of the value of the wells seems a little fabulous at this time, but when Mr. Ames wrote, the faith in the salt wells was substantially represented by his views. Early in 1869 Messrs. Cahn and Evans leased a section of land from the Government, about one and one-half miles from the postoffice, expecting to open thereon extensive salt works. They were still drilling the well when Mr. Ames wrote his account.

REMARKABLE GROWTH AND IMPROVEMENTS. 167

With all these reasons for encouragement, Lincoln enjoyed a favorable growth during 1869. In reviewing the progress of the town early in 1870, Mr. Ames sums up the results as follows, in the work just quoted: "Only about two and one-half years have elapsed since the Commissioners, by official proclamation, called the town of Lincoln into existence. The village of Lancaster, which was included within its site, contained in all less than a half dozen buildings of every description. At the present time that number has been increased to over three hundred and fifty, and the number of inhabitants in town will not fall short of twenty-five hundred souls. The appreciation of real property, which was so slow at the time of the first public sales that the Commissioners nearly despaired of being able to make sufficient sales of lots to defray the expenses of building the State House, has risen to such an extent that means have been obtained from that source sufficient not only for the building of the State House, but also for building the State University, the Agricultural College, and the State Lunatic Asylum, and about six hundred lots belonging to the State yet remain to be sold."

In a following paragraph Mr. Ames continues: "The cash valuation of the real property of the town belonging to private individuals, as ascertained from the assessment roll, is $456,956. Nine of the church societies, for which reservations of town lots were made, as has been stated, have erected neat and commodious houses of worship, and edifices will be erected by the remaining societies early in the present autumn. Six societies, namely, the Methodist Episcopal, Protestant Methodist, Christian, Presbyterian, Congregational, and Catholic, have been duly organized for some time past, maintain pastors, and observe the regular stated services. Advantage is being taken of the facilities offered in the width of the streets for setting out trees for park rows. Two large hotels, in addition to the one large and many smaller ones now in use, have been constructed, while the business of building substantial residences and business houses is being engaged in to an extent difficult of belief to one who has not seen it. And one thing at least is evident; that is, that every one in Lincoln is confident that he has cast his lines in pleasant places, and where there is to be, within a few years, a large, prosperous, and beautiful city."

At this time, early in 1870, Mr. Ames explains that: "In Lancaster county there are no longer any Government lands subject to homestead and preëmption."

In a paragraph further on he remarks that "the cars are now running on four railroads, which are surveyed and in all likelihood will be built to Lincoln. The Burlington and Missouri River railroad is now completed to Lincoln, and will take a westerly direction to Ft. Kearney, with the Union Pacific, thus placing it at nearly the center of a great transcontinental thoroughfare."

During the summer of 1868 the *Commonwealth* had become the Nebraska *State Journal*, which now was a daily. The *Statesman* was a weekly Democratic paper, and the *Intelligencer* was a monthly real estate periodical.

In brief, the town had a continual run of progress — great progress, considering that it started in a wilderness in 1867. Then the wild and vicious Legislature of 1871 disorganized the condition of prosperity of the town greatly. It impeached Governor Butler, whose acts as Commissioner and Governor have seldom been equaled in history for sagacity, courage, and judgment in the founding of a city, and threatened to undo all that had been done. The public was led to believe that the location of the capital had been illegal, and property fell in value greatly, not to fully recover until after the grasshopper raids, which extended from 1873 to 1876. During the visit of these pests was the dismal period of Lincoln's history. Property fell to ruinously low prices, farmers had little to buy with, and hundreds not only left their farms, but the town of Lincoln also. But the more courageous of the people remained through the days of the scourge, and were well rewarded for their resolution. It was during the year 1873-74 that Mr. George B. Skinner was elected Street Commissioner for the purpose of giving a large number of men work to keep them from want. Mr. Skinner was fully equal to the situation, and proceeded to reconstruct the surface of the streets around Government Square, and where needed, and to make cuts and fills generally. Some criticised him severely and others applauded, but the needy grasshopper sufferers did what the people in later years conceded willingly; they admitted that he was a benefactor, without whose aid the wolf could not have been kept from the door of many a home.

But the locusts passed away in 1877, probably forever, and the city revived with phenomenal rapidity; so much so that the census of 1880 showed a population of 14,000. And from that day to this the growth has been both constant and rapid. The population of the city is now fully fifty thousand, as indicated by the city directory, the voting population, and the school census.

The growth of the city was so rapid that the wild animals of this region did not seem to appreciate the situation for several years, and failed to move westward away from civilization. Deer, wolves, and other wild animals, were captured within the present city limits as late as 1872, and Lincoln was a game and fur market for a number of years later. Mr. Simon Benadom was the wholesale fur and game merchant of Lincoln and all surrounding country for many miles, from 1869 for a subsequent period of ten years. In the winter of 1871 and 1872 he went east with his stock, and in a couple of months returned to find that Rich & Oppenheimer had purchased $2,000 worth of furs at their store, in course of business in his absence. He purchased these at once and bought $1,800 worth besides of Simon Kelly, who had taken a few barrels of whisky out on the Blue river and traded it for these furs with trappers he found there. Mr. Benadom used to buy furs to the value of about $20,000 a season along about 1870 to 1872. The best of the pelts he sold in New York, in person. Others were disposed of in Chicago and elsewhere. The fur trade was rather depressed in the winter of 1873–4, and to be busy Mr. Benadom bought prairie chickens and quail. In two months he shipped sixteen thousand of each to New York, packing them in boxes and barrels and sending them East in a frozen condition. It can be seen that this city was in a great game country fifteen years ago, whose natural wildness was not by any means subdued. In this connection we can illustrate by saying that Benadom alone killed fully fifty deer on the present plat of Lincoln during a few years after he came here, in 1868. He generally found them in the brush and tall grass of the Salt creek bottom, and his deer hounds having started one, he would catch the animal on the fly, being a precise rifleman. He also shot twenty-one wolves on the present plat of Lincoln.

The Government postoffice was begun in 1874 and completed in 1879, at a cost of $200,000. It is built of gray limestone from the Gwyer quarries on the Platte river. Its architecture is modern Gothic.

The Lincoln Gas Light Company was organized in 1872, with a capital stock of $60,000, and has grown and prospered ever since.

In 1880 the Lincoln Telephone Exchange was organized, with a capital stock of $10,000. At this time 615 instruments are in use in

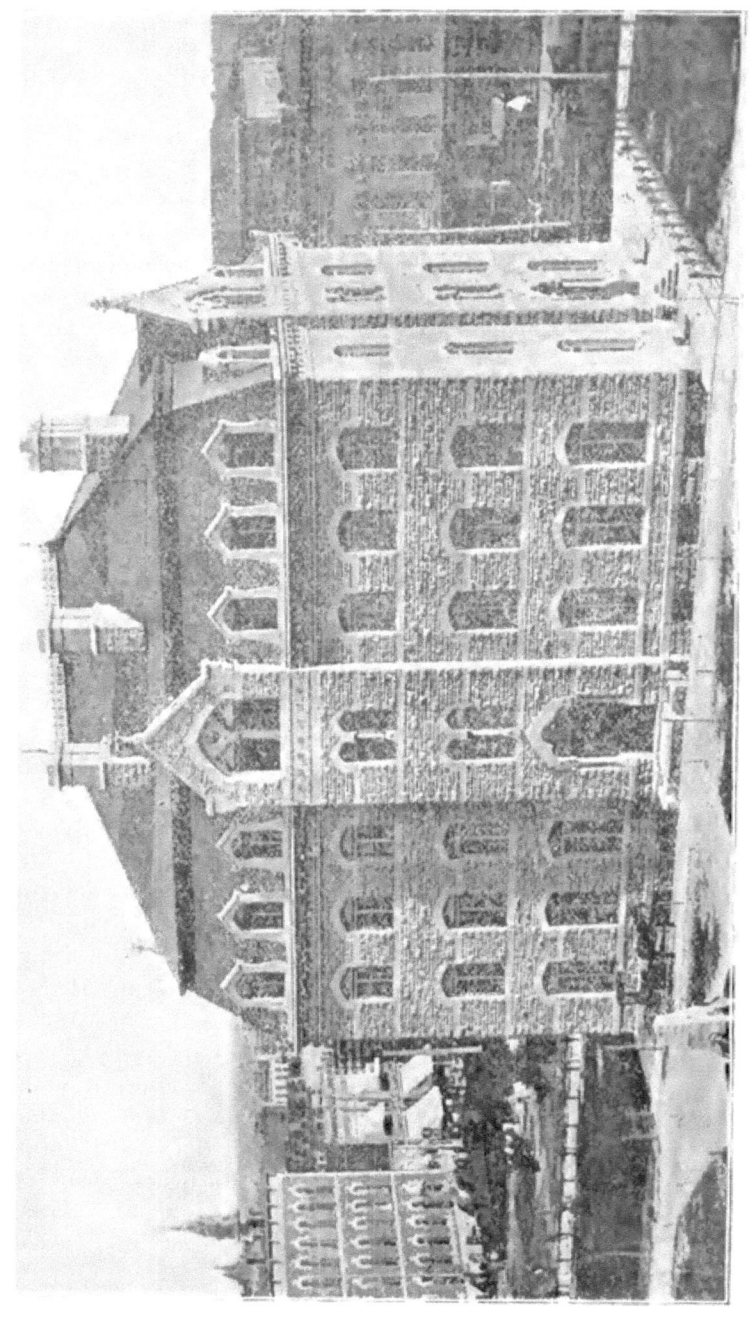

THE POSTOFFICE.

REMARKABLE GROWTH AND IMPROVEMENTS. 171

the city, with connections with fifty-seven towns in Nebraska and sixty-six towns in Iowa.

The city voted the Lincoln Street Railway Company right of way on the streets in April, 1881. Now that company has lines connecting all parts of the city, of which C. J. Ernst is the efficient manager. Besides, there are four other lines. The Rapid Transit line was built in 1887, and extended in 1888. At first its cars were operated with dummy engines, but these are now used only on the part of the line from U street to West Lincoln. The Rapid Transit connects West Lincoln with the asylum, by way of Twelfth street in the city. The Capital Heights line has its present terminus at O and Twelfth. It thence runs to N, thence to Eighteenth, thence to G, and eastward about two miles. This line was built in 1888. The Standard Street Railway was built in the fall of 1888, to connect the Lincoln company's line on North Twenty-seventh street with the Wesleyan University. The Bethany Heights line is being built this year, to connect the Lincoln company's line at V and Thirty-third with the Christian University. One of these companies has a capital of $1,000,000, and all now operate over thirty-one miles of track.

The City Water Works were begun in 1882, and consisted for seven years of a single well in the park bounded by D and F and Eighth and Sixth. The supply then was only about 1,000,000 gallons per day. This well proving inadequate to the demands of the growing city, an attempt was made in 1887 to increase the supply by sinking a pipe in the center of the well. This caused the water to become salty in taste. The same year Mr. Joseph Burns was employed by the city to attempt to construct a system of driven wells in Sixth street, and connect them with the pumping station. These wells were driven a little too deeply, perhaps, and most of them produced salt water after a few days' use. After great annoyance and much delay, it was finally decided to attempt to establish a well near N and the channel of the Antelope. This well was completed in July of the present year, and is now producing about 1,000,000 gallons of pure water daily, to the great satisfaction of the city. Operations for an additional supply in that vicinity are now going forward. During the last six weeks operations have been progressing at the park wells, and it is now believed that the trouble will be done away with, and that pure water will hereafter be supplied from that well also.

The pork-packing business was begun at West Lincoln in 1881, with a capacity of 10,000 hogs. Now there are two large packing houses there, capable of handling all the hogs that can be bought for many miles around. The dressed beef business is also carried on there, having been begun last year. The packing business of the city is growing constantly, and will soon be one of the most important commercial interests of Nebraska. There are extensive stockyard facilities connected with the packing houses.

The Board of Trade was organized January 16th, 1880, with a large membership, designed to benefit the city in every possible way. It is now in a very prosperous condition, and has several hundred members. It raised $10,000 by subscription this summer to advertise the city, and is a most enterprising organization, from which the city will reap great benefit for years to come. The officers of the board are given elsewhere in this chapter.

In 1887 a contract was awarded to H. T. Clarke and Hugh Murphy to pave the central portions of the business part of the city, from N to S on Seventh, Eighth, and Ninth, and from N to Q on Tenth and Eleventh, and from N to P from Eleventh to Fourteenth, the outside streets named being included, and all comprising the first and second paving districts. The city had had no experience in paving whatever, and when the contractors were ready to lay blocks, it was found that gas pipe, water mains, sewer pipe, and street car tracks, must all be put down before paving could go on. This required a vast amount of work and expenditure, and delay upon delay accumulated until the patience of the public was wholly exhausted. The newspapers were filled with criticisms of the council, board of public works, and contractors. The streets presented the appearance of a fortified city, with ditches, trenches, heaps and ridges of earth, and business men were blockaded for entire blocks, for weeks at a time, with no outlet but the sidewalk, and in many cases with no crossings for pedestrians. The streets were frequently flooded with water to settle them. The worst siege was around Government Square. The Capital Hotel was confronted with a small swamp for several months.

But the work was finally done, in 1888, and everybody agreed that the results were worth the worry. The city was beautified, verily transformed from a raw-looking western town, with sidewalks full of ups and downs, and a general evidence of disorganization and lack of system. The paving was followed by a general leveling down and extending of the walks to conform to the line and grade of the curbstone, and now the city is as beautiful as any place of its age in the United States. During 1888 and the present year, Stout & Buckstaff, who have contracted for paving districts three, four, five, six, seven, and eight, have added several miles of paving, so that over eight miles of the streets of the city are now paved, and about fifteen miles are under contract. Much of the paving has been done with cedar blocks, but that now being constructed is being laid with vitrified brick, manufactured for the purpose in this city by Stout & Buckstaff. It is believed that this kind of paving will prove durable and successful.

The sanitary sewerage of the city is an extensive system, now in perfect operation. The storm-water sewers perform the service intended, in the heaviest storms. The water service of the city is very complete in all but the supply, and that defect will be fully remedied within a short period.

In brief, Lincoln is in a condition to continue its prosperity, and afford such enjoyment to its inhabitants as only a completely-built city can do, possessed of such ample improvements and acquirements in the way of educational, commercial, social, and religious facilities. With equal progress, relatively, for ten years, such as Lincoln has made in ten years past, it will be one of the most beautiful home cities in the Nation. The real value of the property of Lincoln is now not far from fifty million dollars. Owing to the pernicious system of assessment in vogue, it appears much less; but it is believed that a careful calculation will show that the genuine worth of the property within the city limits is fully equal to the sum stated.

The county is now erecting a court house in the city, to cost about $200,000. It will probably be completed the present year. The Board of Trade announces the material progress of the city during 1888, taken from official sources, as follows:

Public buildings erected	$395,000 00
Public improvements made	627,368 00
Semi-public improvements	88,500 00
Railway improvements	64,950 00
Business blocks erected	159,000 00
Residences erected	1,014,100 00
Churches erected	18,500 00
Colleges and School buildings erected	156,500 00
Factories built	297,500 00
Total improvements for 1888	$2,821,418 00

The State Fair is located at Lincoln, and has been very successful ever since it opened at this point. Funke's Opera House, at the southwest corner of O and Twelfth, is a first-class theatre, and supplies all the leading attractions. It is now under the direct and very skillful management of Mr. Robert McReynolds, who, with Mr. L. M. Crawford, of Topeka, Kansas, organized a large theatrical circuit in 1888, covering Nebraska, Kansas, Colorado, and several other States. Companies can be engaged at the Lincoln office for all the theatres in the circuit, which includes all the principal towns, and may be billed through without further trouble to their managers.

In 1888 Mr. E. H. Andrus supplied a great need to the city by improving a well watered and amply shaded tract of land, about three and one-half miles west of the city, with conveniences for outdoor recreation. He has since conducted it as a park where picnics, conventions, camp-meetings, games, and all manner of excursions, can resort and find pleasant accommodations at all times. Outings of an entire week are often held there, and excursions of twelve and fifteen hundred people frequently visit the park, especially on Sunday, when excellent musical and appropriate programmes are carried out by the leading musicians and speakers of the city.

The city possesses a public library, founded in December, 1875, which is supported by taxation. It contains over 5,000 volumes, designed for common use, and most of the leading periodicals of the day are in its files. It is open every day in the week.

The State Library, at the capitol building, comprises over 30,000 volumes, mainly on legal subjects. As a law library it is considered very complete.

The State University library includes over 10,000 volumes of miscellaneous books. Its list of works on science and special subjects is very elaborate.

The Young Men's Christian Association has also begun to found a library, so that Lincoln is well supplied with scholastic appurtenances for a place but twenty-two years old.

Lincoln is at the point of confluence of five or six small streams of different sizes, which together drain a surface of over 700 square miles. During Monday, August 12, 1889, and part of the following night, the rain poured down over all this territory. The combined waters began to gather at the Lincoln basin during Monday,

and rose rapidly all night, covering much of the low land near the
city and along the creek to various depths, depending on the elevation.
From one to two thousand families live on this low ground,
mostly in little cottages, and before Tuesday morning many of these
houses were surrounded by water, and in many cases partly submerged,
though generally the water only covered the first floor but a
few inches. In many cases, however, the water rose to the depth of
two or three feet in the buildings, and in a few instances even to
greater depths. Hundreds of people were not aware of the rapid rise
of the water until it began to penetrate their houses, and then there
was a general hurry to escape; but wading to high ground over submerged
and mirey streets in the dark, was no easy task, and many did
not dare attempt it. The waters continued to pile up until Tuesday
morning, and then the police, city officers, and many citizens, came
to the rescue, and the frightened residents of the valley were gathered
on shore, along the hill. Many came to dry land on small rafts, others
in boats, and still others waded. The unfortunate people whose
homes were flooded were generally poor, and they presented a forlorn
spectacle as they huddled along the margins of the advancing floods,
and watched the progress of the threatening waters. During the day
Mayor Graham and other city officials threw open the Park schoolhouse
and other buildings to the refugees, and they were cared for the
best that circumstances would permit. All were rescued by Tuesday
noon. The water reached its height toward evening on Tuesday, the
13th, and before morning began to recede, and continued to fall slowly
until within usual limits, which required most of the week. Fortunately
the weather was warm and pleasant after Tuesday morning.
After the flood the houses were wet, the yards sloppy, and the streets
mirey, in the flooded district, and it required several days for the
people to get back into their homes. Not much damage was done the
houses, though gardens were ruined, furniture partly spoiled, and
the atmosphere rendered unhealthful and disagreeable. No lives were
lost.

Many factories, lumber-yards, and similar business institutions,
were flooded and damaged. The water was over most of the tracks
south of O street, and trains were delayed on all lines. The Union
Pacific to Beatrice did not use its own track for three or four days, and
the Burlington road to Tecumseh was impassable for a longer time,

Within the city the damage to railroad property was not very severe. A rise of a foot or two more would have proved very disastrous.

The water did not quite cover the crown of the pavement at the crossing at Seventh and N streets. The blocks on that corner were nearly all displaced, and the pavement had to be repaired a little distance north on Seventh and east on N. Boats landed against the bank on the west side of the northwest corner of the park, at F and Sixth streets.

This was not the highest that Salt creek has been since Lincoln was founded, though it was vastly the most damaging flood the city has known, owing to the development of property on the low lands. In fact, big freshets have been frequent, and the waters have piled up in front of Lincoln in a formidable way on several occasions, especially since the stream was blocked by dams below the city. There was a good deal of a flood in 1868, and a deluge in 1869, when a prominent editor of the city went boating, fell in, and was tortured with cramps for hours afterward. The torrent of 1874 was especially memorable, the water being made very high by a gorge of brush and drift below the town. Boats landed at the foot of the hill, Eighth and O streets, and a son of William Hyatt was drowned on the block bounded by Seventh and Eighth and O and P streets. A man named T. W. Taylor was also drowned near the city during this freshet. But Mr. M. G. Bohanan, who had particular reason to observe the relative rise of the creek on account of the location of his slaughterhouse, is sure that the flood in April, 1887, following the winter of almost unprecedented snow fall, surpassed all other freshets before or since by a foot or two. Owing to the accumulations of ice, and succeeding cold weather, it was the hardest deluge to contend with, though it affected the city but little, as there was but little settlement and few factories on the low land at that time.

Salt creek has shown a disposition to flood the flat land once or twice since, but there has really been no freshet of the formidable character of that of the present summer for several years past.

CHAPTER XIV.

LINCOLN POLITICALLY FROM THE BEGINNING TO THE PRESENT—HER PUBLIC IMPROVEMENTS—PAVING, SEWERAGE, AND WATER-WORKS—SEMI-PUBLIC WORKS—HER FIRE DEPARTMENT—THE POLICE FORCE—THE PRESENT CITY OFFICERS AND OFFICERS OF THE BOARD OF TRADE.

As has been stated in an earlier chapter, the town of Lincoln was organized in 1869.

In 1870 the Town Trustees elected were C. N. Baird, D. S. Smith, D. A. Sherwood, C. H. Gere, and H. J. Walsh. C. H. Gere was elected Chairman, R. O. Phillips was chosen Clerk, and N. C. Brock was continued as Treasurer of the board.

On March 18, 1871, the town was organized as a city of the second class, under a charter. The election occurred on the third of the following April, and the officers then chosen were: W. F. Chapin, Mayor; C. H. Street and R. E. Moore, Police Judges; A. E. Hastings, Marshal; T. F. L. Catlin, Clerk; G. W. Ballentine, Treasurer; Councilmen—First ward, L. A. Scoggin and C. C. Burr; Second ward, D. A. Sherwood and J. M. Creamer; Third ward, J. J. Gosper and J. L. McConnell; T. T. Murphy, City Engineer. Thereafter, until 1889, the city officers elected were as follows:

1872.—The city officers of 1872 were: Mayor, E. E. Brown; Councilmen—First ward, J. R. Fairbank (two years) and L. A. Scoggin, (one year;) Second ward, William McLaughlin (two years) and D. A. Sherwood, (one year;) Third ward, G. G. Owen (two years) and J. J. Gosper, (one year;) Clerk, Thomas L. Catlin; Treasurer, William A. Coleman; Marshal, John McManigal; City Physician, J. O. Carter; Police Judge, R. E. Moore; Engineer, Tom L. Atwood.

1873.—Mayor, Robert D. Silvers; Councilmen—First ward, L. A. Scoggin and J. R. Fairbank; Second ward, T. P. Quick and William McLaughlin; Third ward, N. S. Scott and S. G. Owen; City Clerk, R. N. Vedder, (resigned September 2d, and E. P. Roggen appointed to fill vacancy;) Treasurer, William Coleman; Marshal, Brad Ringer; Engineer, Thomas L. Atwood; City Physician, S. W. Robinson; Police Judge, Lewis A. Groff, and C. Green, Police Judge to fill vacancy; Street Commissioner and Fire Warden, George B. Skinner; and T. P. Quick, Chief of the Fire Department.

1874.—Mayor, Samuel W. Little; Councilmen—First ward, L. A. Scoggin and John Eaton; Second ward, William McLaughlin and T. P. Quick; Third ward, R. O. Phillips and N. S. Scott; Clerk, E. P. Roggen; Treasurer, William A. Sharrar; Marshal, P. H. Cooper; City Engineer, A. Roberts; Police Judge, J. H. Foxworthy; Street Commissioner and Fire Warden, George B. Skinner; Chief of the Fire Department, T. P. Quick, and Gran. Ensign Assistant.

1875.—Mayor, Amasa Cobb; City Clerk, R. W. Charter; Treasurer, B. F. Fisher; Police Judge, R. W. Taylor; Marshal, P. H. Cooper; City Engineer, A. Roberts; Cemetery Trustee, Philetus Peck; Councilmen—First ward, James Ledwith, and J. R. Fairbank to fill vacancy; Second ward, Fred. W. Krone; Third ward, O. Kingman; T. P. Quick, Chief of Fire Department.

1876.—Mayor, R. D. Silver; City Clerk, George V. Kent; City Treasurer, James McConnell; Marshal, P. H. Cooper; Police Judge, John McLean; City Engineer, J. P. Walton; Cemetery Trustee, Israel Putnam; Councilmen—First ward, John Monteith; Second ward, L. W. Billingsley; Third ward, C. M. Leighton and E. W. Morgan; T. P. Quick, Chief of the Fire Department.

1877.—Mayor, H. W. Hardy; Clerk, R. C. Manley; Treasurer, James McConnell; Police Judge, J. S. Dales; Marshal, Thomas Carr; Engineer, J. P. Walton; Cemetery Trustee, J. J. Turner; Councilmen—First ward, James Ledwith; Second ward, Rufus Yard and J. B. Wright, (elected in September to fill vacancy;) Third ward, J. K. Honeywell; T. P. Quick, Chief of the Fire Department.

1878.—Mayor, H. W. Hardy; Clerk, R. W. Jacobs; Treasurer, James McConnell; Marshal, Thomas Carr; Police Judge, J. S. Dales; Engineer, J. P. Walton; Cemetery Trustee, A. M. Davis; Councilmen—First ward, James H. Dailey; Second ward, R. P. R. Millar, Third ward, Austin Humphrey; Isaac M. Raymond, Chief of the Fire Department.

1879.—Mayor, Seth P. Galey; Clerk, M. Nelson; Treasurer, D. B. Cropsey; Police Judge, J. S. Dales; Marshal, I. L. Lyman; City Engineer, J. P. Walton; T. P. Quick, Chief of the Fire Department. Councilmen—First ward, W. C. Griffith and James Ledwith; Second ward, R. P. R. Millar and John B. Wright; Third ward, Austin Humphrey and H. J. Walsh.

1880.—Mayor, John B. Wright; Clerk, R. C. Manley; Treasurer, D. B. Cropsey; Police Judge, J. S. Dales; Chief of Police, I. L. Lyman. Councilmen—First ward, R. Grimes and J. Ledwith; Second ward, J. L. Caldwell and J. Frederick Krone; Third ward, H. J. Walsh and John Doolittle; City Engineer, J. P. Walton; Chief of the Fire Department, T. P. Quick.

1881.—John B. Wright, Mayor; R. C. Manley, City Clerk; A. C. Cross, Treasurer; J. S. Dales, Police Judge; N. S. Scott, City Engineer; Cemetery Trustee, L. J. Byer, and to fill vacancy, A. M. Davis. For Councilmen—First ward, C. C. Munson; Second ward, S. B. Linderman; Third ward, J. H. Harley.

The total vote cast at this election was 1,400.

The question of voting the Lincoln City Street Railway Company right-of-way over north and south streets from Seventh to Seventeenth, and on east and west streets from A to R, was carried in favor of the license by a vote of 841 to 405.

1882.—At the city election of April 4, 1882, 1,899 votes were cast, with the following result: Mayor, John Doolittle; City Clerk, R. C. Manley; City Treasurer, A. C. Cass; Police Judge, B. F. Cobb; City Engineer, J. P. Walton; Cemetery Trustee, A. M. Davis. Councilmen—First ward, H. Shaberg; Second ward, Fred Krone; Third ward, C. L. Baum.

1883.—At the city election held on April 3, 1883, 1,705 votes were polled. The election resulted in the choice of the following officers: Mayor, R. E. Moore; City Clerk, R. C. Manley; City Treasurer, John T. Jones; Cemetery Trustee, Lewis Gregory; Councilmen—First ward, W. C. Lane, Second ward, S. B. Linderman; Third ward, Charles West; Fourth ward, W. J. Cooper long term, and J. H. Harley short term.

1884.—The city election of 1884 was held April 1st, and 1,550 votes were cast. Mayor, R. E. Moore; Clerk, R. C. Manley, and Treasurer, John T. Jones, held over. The elected officers were: Police Judge, M. Montgomery; Cemetery Trustee, H. J. Walsh. Councilmen—First ward, N. C. Brock; Second ward, H. P. Lau; Third ward, J. W. Winger; Fourth ward, J. R. Webster.

1885.—At the city election held on April 7, 1885, 2,347 votes were cast. The officers elected were—Mayor, C. C. Burr; City Clerk, R. C. Manley; City Treasurer, John T. Jones; Cemetery Trustee, A. M. Davis. Councilmen—First ward, James Dailey; Second ward, L. W. Billingsley; Third ward, A. E. Hargreaves; Fourth ward, W. J. Cooper.

At this election Burr received 1,115 votes, Fitzgerald 1,085 votes, and H. W. Hardy 247 votes. The votes were counted on the 9th of April, and on the evening of the 10th the Council met to consider a notice of contest by John Fitzgerald. The attorneys for Fitzgerald, Whedon, Sawyer & Snell, objected to the jurisdiction of the Council to hear and determine the contest. On motion of Billingsley and Webster, the objection was sustained, and the Mayor and Clerk were ordered to issue certificates to candidates having a majority on the face of the returns. Attorney Whedon gave notice that he would apply to the Supreme Court for a perpetual injunction to restrain those officers from issuing the certificate; but the matter was dropped without further proceedings.

1886.—The city election of 1886 was held on April 6th. Police Judge, Cemetery Trustee, and Councilmen, were elected, as follows: Police Judge, A. F. Parsons; [removed from office and place filled by appointment of H. J. Whitmore;] Cemetery Trustee, Lewis Gregory. Councilmen—First ward, N. C. Brock; Second ward, John Fraas; Third ward, H. H. Dean; Fourth ward, R. B. Graham. The total vote cast was 2,668.

1887.—The city election of 1887 took place on April 5th, and 3,919 votes were cast. E. P. Roggen was the regular Republican nominee; A. J. Sawyer, the independent reform movement nominee, and A. J. Cropsey, the straight-out Prohibition nominee. This election was carried on without regard to party affiliation. Roggen received 1,478 votes; Sawyer, 2,013 votes, and Cropsey, 428 votes. The election resulted as follows: Mayor, A. J. Sawyer; Clerk, R. C. Manley; Treasurer, J. T. Jones; Cemetery Trustee, L. J. Byer. Councilmen—First ward, J. H. Dailey; Second ward, L. W. Billingsley; Third ward, J. M. Burks; Fourth ward, W. J. Cooper; Fifth ward, long term, Gran. Ensign; short term, J. Z. Briscoe; Sixth ward, long term, (two years,) L. C. Pace; short term, (one year,) Fred. A. Hovey. The question of voting right-of-way on the streets to the Rapid Transit Street Railway Company was settled at this election in favor of the license by a vote of 2,571 to 43. C. A. Atkinson was appointed City Attorney, and P. H. Cooper Chief of Police, or Marshal.

1888.—The city election of 1888 was held on April 3d, and the total vote was 4,063. The following officers were elected: Police Judge, W. J. Houston; Cemetery Trustee, A. M. Davis. Councilmen—First ward, A. Halter; Second ward, John Fraas; Third ward, H. H. Dean; Fourth ward, R. B. Graham; Fifth ward, Louie Meyer; Sixth ward, H. M. Rice. G. M. Lambertson was appointed City Attorney.

1889.—At the city election of April, 1889, R. B. Graham was elected Mayor; D. C. Van Duyn, Clerk; Elmer B. Stephenson, Treasurer; O. N. Gardner, City Engineer; I. L. Lyman, Water Commissioner.

The Legislature of 1889 gave the city a new charter, which provided for an Excise Board, designed to have exclusive control of the liquor licenses of the city, instead of the Council, as theretofore. The first board, elected in April at the city election, were John Doolittle and C. J. Danbach. The Mayor is an *ex-officio* member of the board, so that Mayor Graham is the third member of the first board. The Councilmen chosen at this election were: First ward, P. Hayden; Second ward, J. C. Saulsbury; Third ward, William McLaughlin; Fourth ward, F. A. Bochmer and W. S. Hamilton; Fifth ward, H. M. Bushnell; Sixth ward, L. C. Pace.

Having become a candidate for Mayor, Mr. R. B. Graham resigned his chair in the Council before the election. Mr. W. J. Cooper was nominated for the place, and elected. But it afterward seemed that there was some technical invalidity in his election, and it was thought best to go through the formality of an election again. So the Mayor called a special election; and, there seeming to be no opposition to Mr. Cooper, less than half the vote in the ward was polled. But during the day some schemers quietly put W. S. Hamilton in the field against Cooper, and to the surprise of the city he was elected. His friends had completely surprised and taken the camp of the Cooper people. This and other causes led up to the appointment of a committee of Councilmen, by the Council, to investigate allegations of corruption on the part of the Council of 1887 and 1888. The committee consisted of W. S. Hamilton, H. M. Bushnell, H. H. Dean, L. C. Pace, and William McLaughlin. After intermittent sittings for several weeks in May and June, during which numerous witnesses were examined, it appeared by the report of the committee that nothing of much consequence could be charged against any one. The city bonds had been fairly well handled, the storm-water sewers had been well constructed, and the charges against Councilmen of having been subsidized were not sustained. It appeared that W. J. Cooper had sold material to the city at high prices, while Councilman, under the name of one of his men; and this was about all that seemed worthy of criticism. The atmosphere now cleared up, and no more was heard about the matter.

The entire list of city officers, including the officers of the Board of Trade, for 1889, are as follows:

CITY ORGANIZATION.

Hon. R. B. Graham, Mayor.

Councilmen.—First ward, A. Halter, P. Hayden; Second ward, John Fraas, J. C. Saulsbury; Third ward, H. H. Dean *President*, William McLaughlin; Fourth ward, F. A. Boehmer, W. S. Hamilton; Fifth ward; L. Meyer, H. M. Bushnell; Sixth ward, H. M. Rice, L. C. Pace.

Other City Officers.—D. C. Van Duyn, City Clerk; R. H. Townley, Deputy; E. B. Stephenson, Treasurer; R. C. Hazlett, Deputy; G. M. Lambertson, City Attorney; W. J. Houston, Police Judge; O. N. Gardner, City Civil Engineer; I. L. Lyman, Water Commissioner; L. J. Byers, Street Commissioner; W. W. Carder, Chief Police; W. H. Newbury, Chief Fire Department; V. H. Dyer, Sewer Inspector; Joseph McGraw, Gas Inspector; Wm. Rhode, Inspector Live Stock; A. H. Bartram, Health Officer.

Board Public Works.—A. Humphrey, Chairman; R. C. Manley, W. J. Marshall.

Excise Board.—R. B. Graham, President; D. C. Van Duyn, Clerk; John Doolittle, C. J. Daubach.

BOARD OF TRADE.

President, R. H. Oakley; Secretary, C. A. Atkinson.

Directors.—R. H. Oakley, *President;* T. P. Kennard, T. W. Lowrey, J. J. Imhoff, Eli Plummer, Joseph Boehmer, C. J. Ernst, A. E.

Hargreaves, Mason Gregg, M. L. Trester, A. H. Weir, C. W. Mosher, C. T. Brown.

Committees.—A. H. Weir, Chairman Railroads; Jacob Rocke, Chairman Live Stock; J. J. Imhoff, Chairman Miscellaneous; C. W. Mosher, Chairman Rules; M. L. Trester, Chairman Membership; Joseph Boehmer, Chairman Finance; C. J. Ernst, Chairman Executive; T. W. Lowrey, Chairman Transportation; T. P. Kennard, Chairman Manufactories; Eli Plummer, Chairman Reception; Mason Gregg, Chairman Market Reports; H. D. Hathaway, Chairman Papers and Periodicals; C. T. Brown, Chairman Real Estate; A. E. Hargreaves, Chairman Arbitration; C. A. Atkinson, Chairman Advertising.

FIRE DEPARTMENT.

The Fire Department has kept pace with the growth of the city, and to-day is recognized by the Board of Underwriters to be one of the best organized, disciplined, and equipped, departments in the West; in fact, second to none. The first volunteer fire company was organized in 1875, and was named the Phœnix Hook and Ladder Company. In 1872 the growth of the city demanded better protection, and a Silsby steam fire engine was purchased, and named The W. F. Chapin, the Hon. W. F. Chapin being the Mayor of the city in that year. Two hose carts, and 1,000 feet of rubber hose, were purchased at the same time, and a company called the Chapin Hose Company was organized, with a roster of fifty men. In 1880 it was found necessary to increase the strength of the department, and a second size Silsby steamer was purchased and added to the equipment. No changes were made in the department until 1882, when the Chapin Hose Company was disbanded, (the Hook and Ladder Company having disbanded in 1879.) Two new hose companies were organized, known as the Merchants' Hose Company No. 1, and the Fitzgerald Hose Company No. 2. The "Fitzgeralds" have a national reputation, having won the Nebraska State championship belt and cart in the years 1884 and 1885, and the world's championship at the city of New Orleans in 1886. On January 4, 1886, the department was reorganized, Hon. C. C. Burr, Mayor, by Fire Warden Newbury, and five full-paid men appointed and a two-horse, four-wheel hose carriage purchased and put in service. In January, 1887, the Merchants' and Fitzgerald Hose Companies were disbanded, thus ending the life and useful career of the volunteer fire department of Lincoln, which had performed faithful and efficient service for twelve years. But the rapid growth and increasing area of the city demanded a change, and a metropolitan system, with trained and experienced men, constantly on duty, was placed in service. In the month of January, 1887, Hon. A. J. Sawyer Mayor, the department was reorganized by Chief W. H. Newbury and placed on a solid and substantial basis. The fire department at present consists of thirty-five full-paid men, the organization being as follows: one Chief of Fire Department, one Assistant Chief, three Captains, two engineers of steamers, and twenty-eight men. Salaries: Chief, $110.00 per month; Captains, $75.00 per month; engineers of steamers, $75.00 per month; drivers, pipemen, linemen, $70.00 per month. Apparatus in service: Two four-wheel two-horse hose carts, one hose wagon, two four-wheel two-horse chemical engines, hook and ladder truck, one aërial hook and ladder truck, one chief's buggy, one supply wagon, nineteen horses. Annual expense of maintaining department, present equipment, $35,000.00.

The engine houses are large double houses, fitted up with all the modern and best improved electrical appliances, and will contain four pieces of apparatus each. Fire department headquarters—Engine house No. 1 is situated at the corner of Tenth and Q streets. Engine house No. 2, corner of O and Twenty-third streets, and engine house No. 4, at F street, between Twelfth and Thirteenth streets.

The first chief of the volunteer department was the Hon. Seth Linderman. His successor was T. P. Quick esq., who held the position for about ten years. The Hon. N. C. Abbott, Hon. I. M. Raymond, Hon. Gran Ensign, and Hon. I. L. Lyman, gentlemen who have represented the State, county, and city, in different positions of trust and honor, were at different times chief of the volunteer organization. The present chief, Wm. H. Newbury, was appointed Fire Warden of the city in July, 1885; appointed Chief of the Fire Department in April, 1887. Through his untiring efforts the city of Lincoln has to-day a fire department of which it is justly proud. No city in the country of the same size has had so small a percentage of loss from fire as Lincoln has had since the organization of the paid department.

The roster of the the Fire Department, as at present constituted, is as follows:

Chief—W. H. Newbury. Captains—J. Morrow of company No.

1, G. H. Priest of company No. 2. Drivers—F. Maden, P. Kuykendall, and R. Malone. Engineer—J. Heberling. Stoker—Frank Strattan. Firemen—H. Stratton, C. W. Clyter, B. H. Floyd, J. C. McCune, A. B. Hosman, G. R. Slat, F. G. Fawcett, F. McMillan, J. Fitzgerald, and S. S. Smith.

One of the most successful institutions of the city is the Red Ribbon Club, which was organized by John B. Finch in November, 1877, at a place on the east side of Tenth street, about four doors north of Tenth and N streets. For years it held its meetings in "Red Ribbon Hall," at the northwest corner of Twelfth and M streets. Every Sunday afternoon in the year Mr. George B. Skinner, who has been president, manager, and inspiration to the organization from its beginning, would be found on the platform directing the meeting. The programmes consisted of singing from "Gospel Hymns," or similar musical books, and voluntary addresses by persons in the audience, though Mr. Skinner would often call upon men or women whom he thought could make short, useful addresses. Hundreds of drinking men have been induced to sign the pledge by this club, and by it assisted to keep the good resolution. The club now meets at a large assembly room on T street, between Eleventh and Twelfth street. The roll of the organization now numbers fully 17,000 persons, including many of the leading men and women of the city and State. For twelve years it has lived and expanded, and is now, perhaps, the largest, oldest, and most successful, association of its kind in the United States. For all this growth and power it is substantially indebted to George B. Skinner.

Lincoln has hotel accommodations for fully 2,000 persons. A sketch of the earliest hotel history has already been given in another chapter, where reference is made to the "Pioneer," the "Cadman," and the "Atwood."

In 1869 — — Wilson constructed a store foundation on the southwest corner of P and Eleventh streets. This lot and one other to the southward, were sold to James Griffith, who still resides in this county, who disposed of them to Cropsey & England. That firm passed the property over to Dr. Scott, who completed the building on the foundation already there, and opened a drug store in it about 1869. In 1870 he converted the building into a hotel, which was managed by John Douglas, and it was called the "Douglas House." Mr. Douglas conducted it until November, 1873, when Mr. J. J. Imhoff bought it, called it the "Commercial Hotel," and at once greatly enlarged it. Its patronage increased constantly under his control, and he was obliged to enlarge it to its present dimensions of 150 x 108½ feet, and to three stories in height, so as to possess a capacity to accommodate easily 300 guests. It soon became the political headquarters of the State and the principal rendezvous of politicians, associations, and public affairs generally. Mr. Imhoff owned the hotel until the opening of 1886, when Mr. C. W. Kitchen bought it, changed its name to "The Capital Hotel," and managed it until May 1st, 1887. Then Hon. Edward P. Roggen became its landlord, Mr. W. H. B. Stout having bought it, and so continued until March, 1889, when Mr. G. F. Macdonald, formerly of the Millard Hotel in Omaha, bought an interest with Mr. Roggen, and since that date the house has been managed by Roggen & Macdonald. It still continues to be the political hub of the State, being Republican State headquarters annually. It possesses all modern conveniences and improvements and is the best known hotel in Nebraska. Mr. Richard W. Johnson, who was chief clerk with Mr. Imhoff, occupied the same position with Mr. Kitchen, and has been the chief clerk with Mr. Roggen and Messrs. Roggen & Macdonald. He is one of the worthiest and best hotel men in Nebraska, and one of the best known.

Next in order of origin is Opelt's Hotel, at Ninth and Q streets, which was built by Mr. J. S. Atwood, who completed it in 1880. It was then named the "Arlington" house. It was the largest hotel in Nebraska at that date, and yet ranks among the most spacious and excellent hostelries in the State. Mr. Joseph Opelt, its present landlord, became its first landlord and conducted it until 1881, when it was purchased by J. S. McIntire, who managed it for a short time, and it passed into the hands of Capt. Wm. Ensey, who controlled it about three years. It then was without a landlord for about three months, when Mr. Joseph Opelt, on March 15, 1886, again became its lessee and landlord, and so continues to the present time. He has always had a large and profitable business. The house is fitted up with modern improvements and has an easy capacity of about 250 guests. Mr. Stanley C. Wicks is the efficient chief clerk of this excellent hotel. It is now owned by W. H. Atwood, of Kinderhook, N. Y., the son of the builder.

THE CAPITAL HOTEL.

The next large hotel built in Lincoln was the Windsor, at first called the "Gorham House," located at the southeast corner of Eleventh and Q streets. This hotel was erected by Mr. T. F. Barnes, in 1884, and was opened January 5, 1885, by Gorham & Brown, who managed it about a year, when it passed into the hands of Glass & Montrose, who also conducted it about a year. Then it came into the control of its presentable managers, Messrs. E. K. Criley & Co., Mr. E. K. Criley being in immediate charge. In his hands it has been much improved, and its business and capacity extended. The same firm controls the "Paddock House" at Beatrice, and other noted hotels in the West. The Windsor is equipped with the most improved hotel facilities and has a capacity of over 200 guests. It is still owned by Mr. T. F. Barnes. Mr. S. J. Whitmore is the chief clerk of the Windsor, and is an excellent and capable man in the position.

The "Lindell Hotel" is an excellent hostelry, located at the northwest corner of Thirteenth and M streets. This is a pleasant, quiet, home-like place, new and tidy, and managed by Dr. A. L. Hoover and his son, Mr. S. C. Hoover, under the firm title of Hoover & Son. It is a favorite resort for people who wish excellent accommodations away from the noise and disturbance of the business part of the city. The site of the Lindell has been a hotel location for twenty years. In 1869 J. N. Townley opened a boarding-house there, which was managed by John Douglas for a short time before he took charge of the "Douglas House," at Eleventh and P streets. The property passed through various vicissitudes, and finally came into the hands of Dr. Hoover, in 1885, who removed the old frame to one side for a kitchen and erected a brick structure in 1886, which the growing business of the house required to be enlarged in 1888. It has a capacity of over 100 guests, and is furnished with the leading hotel conveniences. It discards a bar.

The "Tremont Hotel," at the southwest corner of P and Eighth streets, is an excellent public house, possessed of steam heating, electric light, and other facilities of that kind, and its rates are very low for the accommodations it offers. It is conducted by Mr. R. W. Copeland, and can accommodate about 100 guests.

The "St. Charles Hotel," on the south side of O street, between Seventh and Eighth, is a well-known hostelry of the city, long conducted by Mrs. Kate Martin, who still owns it. Mr. Jacob Rocke

THE WINDSOR HOTEL.

is now the landlord and lessee. It enjoys a good trade, and can accommodate 150 guests. It is managed by Mr. Chris. Rocke, brother of Jacob Rocke, the County Treasurer.

The "Transit," on Twelfth between O and P, Wright & Marey, proprietors, has accommodations for fifty guests.

The "Washington House," on the southeast corner of M and Ninth, and the "Peoria House," on the northwest corner of Q and Ninth, are frame hotels, of smaller capacity, with rates at $1.00 per day. The "Ideal Hotel," on the west side of Fourteenth street, between N and O, is conducted by W. C. Trott as a hotel and select boarding-house, and has a capacity of about 100 guests. There are a number of smaller public houses in the city, so that Lincoln can comfortably entertain a large number of persons of all tastes as to accommodations and price.

The regular police force of Lincoln consists of but seventeen men, or one to about each 3,000 inhabitants. Yet few cities in the United States are better policed, owing to the high grade of the citizenship in the city as well as to the excellent class of men on the force and the effective discipline maintained. The criminal record of Lincoln ranks with the minimum records of the very best governed cities of equal population in the world. The excellence of the police discipline was largely effected under the administration of Mayor A. J. Sawyer, by Marshal P. H. Cooper, and Captain W. T. B. Ireland, both being officials of long experience, the latter being especially efficient in the administrative details of the department. Officers A. L. Pound, C. M. Green, and J. K. Post, were also men of experience and fine record on the old force, and Officers Splain and Kinney also deserve praise as guardians of the city.

In June, 1889, the force was reorganized by Marshal W. W. Carder, who came into office at that time. Marshal Carder has already added a number of features of excellence to the department, and the force is in a most effective condition for the duties belonging to it. It now consists of nine night men and eight day men, including the Marshal. The roster of the force is as follows: Marshal—W. W. Carder. Night Captain—C. M. Green. Sergeant—F. A. Miller. Officers—George F. Sipe, James Malone, A. L. Pound, J. K. Post, W. T. B. Ireland, M. F. McWilliams, William Splain, Joseph N. Snyder, W. H. Palmer, Thomas Carnahan, Louis C. Otto, J. E. Kinney,

John Keane. Special—W. S. Crick. General Police Officers—Health Commissioner, A. M. Bartram; Meat and Live Stock Inspector, W. C. Rhode; Driver of the Patrol Wagon, John H. Simpson.

Hon. Robert B. Graham, chief executive of the city of Lincoln, is one of the best known and most highly respected citizens of Lancaster county, a man who has done much to advance the material interests of both city and county. That he is of Scotch parentage can readily

HON. ROBT. B. GRAHAM, MAYOR.

be told at a glance, his sturdy, well knit frame and kindly face proclaiming the nationality of his birth. Mr. Graham was born in New York City on the 17th of May, 1842. His early youth only was passed in that city, his parents removing to St. Louis when he was only five years of age. Here his youth and early manhood were passed and here he married. The early education of Mr. Graham was obtained at the public schools of St. Louis, where he was in almost constant attendance until he was fifteen years of age. In 1859, when in his seventeenth year, the young man entered the Baptist College at Burlington, Ia., and pursued his studies there uninterrupted for two years. But at that time the same circumstances that spoiled the college life of so many young men of the land, that changed the whole course of life for so many hundreds of the loyal men of the North, intervened to cut short his college years; for although under age, he enlisted in the sixty-seventh Illinois infantry at the beginning of the war and was soon sent to the front. His army experience only lasted for eighteen months, he being discharged at the end of that time on account of disability. After his discharge he returned to St. Louis, where he lay sick for some time. When he recovered sufficiently to be able to work, he entered the steam cracker factory of Thomas Miller, as bookkeeper, and after a year was admitted to partnership, the firm then being Thomas Miller & Co. The firm then took a government contract for furnishing hard tack, but in 1863 the factory burned out, and was never rebuilt. From that time until 1867 Mr. Graham was engaged with the firm of Tossig, Livingston & Co., traveling through the South and Southwest buying wool, etc.

On the 12th of March, 1868, Mr. Graham was married to Miss Mary E. Hilton, of St. Louis, soon after which he moved to Glenwood, Ia., where he engaged in the milling business, buying an interest in a steam flouring mill at that place. At the end of a year he sold his interest in this mill and turned his face again westward, locating in the spring of 1869 in Lancaster county, in the northwestern part, in what is now Mill precinct. Mr. Graham's coming to Lancaster county was upon the suggestion of George Harris, the original B. & M. land commissioner, well known to many of the pioneers of the early days. From the spring of 1869 Mr. Graham has been a continuous resident of the county, and has, during that time, been connected closely with its growth and development. In 1870 Mr. Graham and his brother built a flouring mill in Mill precinct, the third mill built in the county, which he operated for a number of years.

In 1880 the people of the county concluded that Mr. Graham's sphere of usefulness could be profitably enlarged, and hence he was elected a member of the House of Representatives of the State Legislature, that being the sixteenth session. The result was very satisfactory to his constituents, as he displayed much ability in dealing with questions of legislation. As a legislator he was careful, watchful, and prudent, taking broad and conservative views of all questions requiring his attention and decision. In 1881 Mr. Graham was elected County Treasurer, being reëlected in 1883. As county treasurer his duties required his presence in Lincoln, and hence his residence here dates from his first election to that office. Mr. Graham showed great financial ability in dealing with the money matters of the county, and is entitled to great credit for his work during his two terms. By bringing to his duties as treasurer the same care, prudence and thorough business methods that had made his private business a success, he succeeded in so improving the finances of the county that all warrants or other evidences of indebtedness, except bridge warrants, were paid in cash, something before unknown. This result he accomplished by a close and careful collection of taxes, and a carefully arranged system of accounts. The system inaugurated by Mr. Graham has been followed by Mr. Roche, the present Treasurer, so well that all warrants, including bridge, are now paid on presentation.

In 1886 Mr. Graham was elected a member of the City Council from the Fourth Ward, and was reëlected in 1888. The duties of this office he discharged most satisfactorily to the people until he resigned, in the spring of 1889, to take the office of Mayor, to which he had been elected on April 13, 1889. No man, as member of the City Council, has done more hard work for the good of the city—work that was always well and honestly done. And his three years' experince in that body has enabled him so far to avoid many of the mistakes of his predecessors. As chief executive of the city, he is energetic, yet conservative, mindful of all interests and classes. He is particularly safe and able in guarding the reciprocal relations and welfare of the business and working people, to the end that everything shall work together for the general present prosperity and the continued development of the city. Mr. Graham and family belong to the most respected social circles of the city.

Hon. Elmer B. Stephenson, Treasurer for the City of Lincoln, holds one of the most responsible offices in the city government. As a representative young man, citizen, and official, a short biographical sketch of his life has a very appropriate place in this volume.

His father, John M. Stephenson sr., was born in Kentucky, on a plantation, his father being the owner of slaves. While yet a young man the father emigrated to Southern Illinois, and became a pioneer farmer near Mount Vernon. When the war came on he enlisted in the Seventh Illinois Cavalry, though a positive Democrat in politics. His son, John Stephenson jr., joined the same company, though a mere stripling, and both served during the great conflict with honor to themselves. John Stephenson jr. was daring to the point of audacity, and on one occasion while on a foraging expedition, he captured three rebel soldiers single handed, although his gun was so out of repair as to be useless. Later on he was himself seized while out foraging, and

HON. E. B. STEPHENSON.

lay in Libby prison until reduced to a mere skeleton from disease and starvation. He finally escaped through a tunnel, and reached the Union lines, almost dead with sickness and exhaustion. The father of the Treasurer was a friend and admirer of John A. Logan, and was acquainted with Abraham Lincoln, who practiced law before the war in Mr. Stephenson's county.

Before marriage the mother of the Treasurer was a Miss Esther Melcher. She was born in Maine, and her mother was a cousin of S. F. B. Morse, the great electrician. When young she removed with her parents to Mt. Vernon, Illinois, and there grew up from childhood with John M. Stephenson sr. In her young womanhood she was a successful school teacher, and her characteristics are those of persistent industry, courage, and love of learning and progress. In political sentiment she was always a Republican. Her brother, Josiah Melcher, is a prominent minister in Bloomington, Illinois, who has written several works on theology.

Elmer B. Stephenson, the Treasurer, was the third son and child, and was born at Troy Grove, La Salle county, Illinois, on December 7, 1858. When a child his father's family removed to a farm near Troy Grove, where he spent his boyhood life. His occupation was that of attending the district school in winter, as soon as old enough, and working on the farm in the summer season. And while a farmer he performed many a month of hard work, doing the labor of a full hand in harvest field, corn gathering, or elsewhere, from the age of fifteen to eighteen.

When eighteen years of age he entered the office of Dr. W. G. Houtz, with the intention of studying medicine, and while there gave the subject some investigation, and also devoted some time to the improvement of his education. When twenty-one years of age he made a year's tour of the Southern States, exploring as far south as Texas. Upon returning he found that his old friend Dr. Houtz had removed to Lincoln, Nebraska, and upon the doctor's urgent invitation, Mr. Stephenson followed him to Lincoln, in 1880.

Not having the means with which to pursue a professional career, and finding it difficult to secure remunerative employment, his first three years were spent in incongenial labor at low wages. To add to his discouragement, if his natural unflagging resolution had allowed him to get discouraged, the end of the first and second year each found him prostrated with severe illness. Having succeeded in saving a little money during the third year, he was enabled to unite with Mr. D. W. Moseley in the real estate business in 1883, under the firm style of Moseley & Stephenson.

But wealth did not rush in to overwhelm the firm immediately, and the first year was a hard contest to make expenses. But 1885 was a year of high-tide prosperity to Lincoln, and Moseley & Stephenson, having laid a careful foundation, were rewarded with a successful business. This continued during 1886, and they were able to close up the year's work with the balance sheet decidedly in their favor. While together Messrs. Moseley & Stephenson placed upon the market, for a syndicate, the lots of both Belmont and Riverside additions to the city of Lincoln.

The following year, in 1887, Mr. Stephenson severed his business connection with Mr. Moseley and entered into a partnership with Mr. Whitney J. Marshall for the transaction of the real estate business. This association was continued with profit to both members until Mr. Stephenson was elected to the office of City Treasurer in April last, having been nominated to that over several strong competitors. He was elected by a majority of about 1,500. Mr. Marshall, his partner, was fortunate also, having been appointed a member of the Board of Public Works by Mayor Graham, who was elected on the same ticket with Mr. Stephenson.

The success of Mr. Stephenson has not been due to favoritism nor the influence of powerful friends, nor to accident. It has been accomplished in the face of many discouragements, and a man of less persistent determination would have failed. Hard work, courage, and good management, have won for Mr. Stephenson a comfortable fortune and an honorable position, which he now occupies with prudence and efficiency.

Hon. G. M. Lambertson, City Attorney for the city of Lincoln, is a leading attorney of this city, and a gentleman of State-wide reputation.

His father was Samuel Lambertson, who was born in Pennsylvania in the year 1815. Though not an educated man, he is a lover of books, learning, and progress, and has never neglected any opportunity to secure additional knowledge or advance the education of his family. Early in life he was apprenticed to the tailor's trade, and having learned the art thoroughly, he opened a merchant-tailoring house at Franklin, Indiana. He followed this occupation most of the time for fifty years, and accumulated a little fortune at it. He never held any political office, but was at one time a Knight Templar in the Masonic fraternity, and has for many years been a member and officer in the Baptist church. He was naturally a patriot. In politics he was first a Whig, when the Whigs were the best party. Then he became an Abolitionist; then went into the ranks of the Republican party. When the war began he was early in the field as a staunch defender of the Union. He promptly organized Company F of the Seventh Indiana Infantry, with the opening of hostilities, and became its captain. During the first two years of service, he participated in eighteen important battles, including those of Antietam and the second Bull Run. At the close of his second year he returned to his home county to encourage enlistments, and succeeded in raising a regiment of thirteen companies, which were called the "Home Guards." These

HON. G. M. LAMBERTSON.

he equipped, and then was elected Colonel of the regiment. The "Home Guards" were immediately called into service by Governor Morton to repel the invasion of Indiana by John Morgan, which the guards aided to thoroughly accomplish.

He now resides with his daughter, Mrs. G. H. Elgin, at Southport, Indiana, and is enjoying the well-earned profits of a busy early life.

The mother of Mr. G. M. Lambertson was born in Kentucky, in 1818, and was the daughter of a Baptist minister, who preached in Kentucky and Indiana, named Lewis Morgan. She was a woman of energy, courage, and positive thought, and had power to influence those with whom she came in contact. She was devoted to works of charity, religion, and the elevation of her fellow man. Her death occurred in 1877, at the age of sixty years. Her children were G. M. Lambertson, Mrs. G. H. Elgin, now of Logansport, Indiana, now aged thirty-seven; Mrs. U. M. Chaille, living at Indianapolis, aged thirty-five; Mrs. L. B. Lavelle, of Louisville, Ky., aged thirty-three; and Dr. O. F. Lambertson, of Lincoln.

Genio Madison Lambertson was born at Frankfort, Indiana, May 19, 1850. He began his education in the public schools of his State, and later became a student in the Baptist college at Franklin, Indiana. He then attended Wabash University, at Crawfordsville, Ind., for six months, and then entered Chicago University, from whence he graduated, in 1872.

He then studied law with Messrs. Overstreet & Hunter, leading attorneys of Franklin, Indiana, and having carefully fitted himself for a legal career, he selected Lincoln for his future home, and located here June 1, 1874.

He began his life work as a clerk in the law office of Lamb & Billingsley, and later became a member of that firm. In December, 1878, Mr. Lambertson was appointed United States District Attorney for the District of Nebraska, by President Rutherford B. Hayes, and continued in that position for eight years, with high credit to himself. In this position he made a State-wide reputation. At the close of his second term he was tendered a temporary reappointment by President Cleveland, but this he declined.

From the expiration of his second term, in February, 1889, he has been steadily engaged in the practice of his profession in this city. He now ranks among the most able and successful attorneys of Lincoln. Among his most recent important achievements was the procurement of a writ of *habeas corpus* from the Supreme Court of the United States for the liberation of the Councilmen from the jail at Omaha, wherein they were incarcerated by order of Judge Brewer, of the United States Circuit Court, for alleged contempt. Mr. Lambertson also represented the city before the Inter-State Commerce Commission, in its suit to require the Union Pacific railroad to deliver shipments from San Francisco at Lincoln as cheaply as at Omaha, when the merchandise passed through Lincoln in reaching Omaha, and pro rata when shipped otherwise. The Commission sustained the proposition advanced by Mr. Lambertson and the city secured the relief demanded. He was appointed City Attorney in 1888, and Mayor Graham reappointed him to the same office in the spring of 1889. In this position the business men of the city consider him a prudent and safe adviser.

Mr. Lambertson was married on June 10, 1880, to Miss Jane Gundry, daughter of Mr. Joseph Gundry, a prominent capitalist of Mineral Point, Wis. She was born at Mineral Point, Wis., August 29, 1855, and was educated at Kemper Hall, Kenosha, Wis. Mr. and Mrs. Lambertson rank justly among the most respected people in the best social circles of the city. Their children are Margery Elizabeth, born August 23, 1881, and Nancy Perry, born August 26, 1883.

Mr. Lambertson is a prominent and respected member of the Baptist Church in this city, and he is ever ready to contribute to the progress of the city and welfare of mankind by both voice and deed.

CHAPTER XV.

LINCOLN'S RAILROADS—WHEN BUILT AND THE BONDS VOTED THEM—THE TERRITORY INTO WHICH THEY PENETRATE—THE COMMERCIAL ADVANTAGE GIVEN LINCOLN BY HER RAILROAD LINES—HER TELEGRAPH AND EXPRESS SYSTEMS.

As a railroad center all must concede that Lincoln stands at the head among Western cities. Her great lines of road reach out in every direction, controlling for her the trade of a territory vast in extent, unlimited in resources, and wonderful in its possibilities. The showing which can be made demonstrates conclusively that Lincoln is the heart of the most complete system of railroads over which commerce passes to and from any trans-Mississippi city, and the best distributing point in the western half of the United States. That such is the fact makes it of interest to consider in detail the lines of road over which our commerce passes, when they were built, how they came to be built, the inducements offered them to come, and the other facts in connection therewith which suggest themselves to the inquiring mind.

First, let attention be called to Lincoln's Eastern connections. Three great trunk lines from the East operate their own tracks into the city: the Chicago, Burlington and Quincy, the Fremont, Elkhorn and Missouri Valley, (Northwestern,) and the Missouri Pacific. Lincoln is the terminus of the Missouri Pacific's northwestern line, which gives the city an outlet direct to the Gulf and the Atlantic. In addition to these the Omaha & Republican Valley branch of the Union Pacific is virtually an extension of the Rock Island and Milwaukee roads, and it may be considered a certainty that the Rock Island will come into Lincoln soon over its own track. Thus it will be seen that this is virtually the terminal distributing point for seven great railroads. There is no distributing point west of Lincoln in all the vast region that lies between the Missouri and the Rocky mountains, and Lincoln and the cities on the Missouri reach too easily into the territory of Denver on the west to leave a field for the growth of any new city of importance in the intervening territory.

Prior to 1869 the sound of the locomotive engine was unheard on the prairies of Lancaster, nor had its shrill notes echoed through the streets of Lincoln. But at that time a change was accomplished. The Legislature of 1869 started the building of four roads by appropriating 2,000 acres of land to each mile of road constructed in the State within two years. These four roads started from points on the Missouri river and headed for Lincoln. The first was the Burlington & Missouri River Railroad in Nebraska, which started from Plattsmouth; the second, the Atchison & Nebraska, from Atchison; the third, the Midland Pacific, from Nebraska City, and the fourth, the Omaha & Southwestern, from Omaha. To-day these all belong to the same system; but they started as competitors, and the race was to get for each as much as possible of the 250 miles that would exhaust the 500,000 acre appropriation.

The B. & M. had a further inducement to come in the shape of bonds voted by the county to the amount of $50,000.

Then the Atchison & Nebraska was voted county bonds to the extent of $120,000, and the Midland Pacific was tempted by a bonus of $150,000.

The Midland Pacific gave promise, in consideration of so large a bonus, to locate large car shops in Lincoln, but the promise was never carried out. The road was, however, extended to York, and the $150,000 has proved to be a good investment.

When these lines had been completed into the city from the east and southeast, and the B. & M. had been extended west to Kearney, the people began to realize that the city was already a prominent railroad center, and could be made the hub of the State by a continuation of the efforts to attract new roads. Great enterprise was shown in this direction, and the reward came in due season. For several years hard times and poor crops interfered with railroad building seriously, and no change was made in the map until 1879. In that year the city gave $25,000 in bonds to aid the Lincoln & Northwestern in starting its line to Columbus, and when that road was under way the Union Pacific retaliated by sending a branch of its own down from Valparaiso, and extending it to Beatrice a few years later. An extra inducement in the shape of a bonus was given by the city for the Valparaiso line.

When the revival of business and restoration of confidence came, between 1876 and 1878, the B. & M. began a movement that made it the greatest system in the State. The Nebraska railway was leased, and important extensions were projected. Among the first was a line from Hastings to the Republican Valley, which in time developed into a great through road to Denver.

The Lincoln & Northwestern, a northern branch of the A. & N., was built from Lincoln to Columbus, in 1879, and in the following year the B. & M. secured possession of the entire property. This was not regarded as favorable to the city at that time, but later events have shown that it considerably increased the importance of Lincoln, considered from a railway standpoint. The city became the hub of the B. & M. system, six lines belonging to that company running out in all directions. The operating head-quarters were located here, and in time the offices of the general superintendent, the superintendent of telegraph, the general baggage agent, the chief engineer, the stationer, the car accountant, and other officers, whose duties extend over the entire B. & M. system, were removed from Omaha and Plattsmouth and permanently located in the fine building erected in 1880 for a passenger depot and head-quarters building.

After the Union Pacific had been secured and had been extended south to Beatrice, and into Kansas, there were still a number of roads that the city greatly desired. The roads were willing to be courted, and the wooing went on for several years. The Missouri Pacific was the first to capitulate, building a line from Weeping Water to the city in 1886, after receiving a donation from the city of $70,000. But a few months later the Fremont, Elkhorn & Missouri Valley was also completed to the city, coming from Fremont, and receiving a bonus from the city of $50,000. The effect of the building of these roads was tremendous. The following spring saw the greatest activity in real estate the city has ever known.

THE BURLINGTON ROAD.

Lincoln is particularly interested only in that portion of the B. & M. system west of the Missouri river. The total length of the various B. & M. lines is 2,753 miles, and it is practically traversed by traveling men representing Lincoln jobbing houses. On only a few miles of road southwest of Omaha, a few miles west of Atchison, and a short stretch of road east of Denver, are the jobbers of Lincoln unable to do a profitable business.

B. & M. DEPOT.

The impregnable position held by Lincoln as the distributing center of all the vast territory covered by this system, can be better understood by studying a Burlington map than by reading pages of argument. It will show that the main C. B. & Q. line from Chicago enters Nebraska at Plattsmouth, twenty miles south of Omaha, comes directly to Lincoln and west to Denver. Lincoln is situated almost midway between these great cities, being 555 miles from Chicago and 484 miles from Denver. From this city four additional trunk lines extend in as many directions. These, as well as the main line, cover a large territory with their branches. Taken in the order of their importance to the city, the Wyoming branch ought to be considered first. This is an extension of the old Midland Pacific from York through Aurora and Grand Island, up into Custer county, and on to the new city of Alliance, in Box Butte county, 360 miles from Lincoln. From Alliance, a branch is now being constructed to the Black Hills, in Wyoming, 168 miles to the northwest. Another line will, without doubt, be pushed west from Alliance, perhaps to the Yellowstone region, and on to a connection with the Northern Pacific. This road traverses a very promising region. Between Lincoln and Broken Bow the country is famous for its fertility. Between Broken Bow and Alliance the live stock industry will always thrive. The Box Butte region is excellent for agricultural products again, and Wyoming is rich in minerals and has inexhaustible beds of coal. Lincoln is the terminus of this road. All trains are made up here, and the entire line is managed from this city. Two passenger trains each way as far as Ravenna and one the remainder of the distance to Alliance, enable the people along the line to communicate easily with Lincoln. Freight trains are obliged to make an early start in the morning for the northwest, and in the shipment of goods on this line the Lincoln jobber is from twenty-four to forty-eight hours ahead of all competition. The entire road looks naturally to Lincoln for supplies.

Another long line on which the city finds a ready market, reaches to Cheyenne, Wyoming, a distance of 488 miles. The natural course of traffic on this line is west to Crete, twenty miles on the main line, south to De Witt, thirty miles, thence west through Strang, Edgar, Blue Hill, and Holdredge, all junction points for north and south branches of the same system, and into Colorado and Wyoming, where

Cheyenne is the present terminus. The country traversed is exceptionally fertile, and the towns are thriving. Lincoln jobbers sell goods on the entire road.

The main line west ought to be mentioned as the road upon which the best cities of the western part of the State are situated. It runs to Denver, 484 miles, and the Lincoln jobber is able to cover 400 miles of it with profit to himself and his customer.

It will thus be seen that the B. & M. has three great lines running west out of Lincoln, which extend the entire distance across the State, which are connected by branches at frequent intervals.

The Burlington is moving toward northern Nebraska. Branches have been extended from Central City in three parallel lines, and it is probable that the road now in operation from Lincoln to Columbus will also be pushed into the North Platte region.

The southern and southeastern portions of the State are gridironed with B. & M. lines, and as all roads once led to Rome, so they now lead to Lincoln. Nebraska City, fifty-five miles east, on the Missouri river, has the original Midland Pacific branch, which is now connected with the "Q" system in Iowa by means of a magnificent steel bridge opened in the past year. This gives Lincoln another connection with Chicago.

The Atchison & Nebraska became a part of a system connecting St Joe, Kansas City, and Atchison, with Lincoln, and also with Denver, by means of a line through the southern tier of counties of Nebraska, meeting at Oxford with the main line from this city. From this southern trunk three important feeders extend into Kansas.

Some idea of the strategic position of the city with respect to these lines may also be gained from a visit to the offices and yards and shops. Nearly 100 trains enter the city daily on the various lines, but not a single locomotive passes through. The train crews have their head-quarters here, and the number of employés stationed here to look after the business of the company is nearly 800. The yards are the most extensive in the entire system, forty-two miles of track being inside of the yard limits.

The Lincoln passenger depot is the best owned by the system, and is the center of more business than any depot occupied by a single railroad in the country. Twenty-five passenger trains arrive and depart every day. One-half of the people entering the State come through the gateway called Lincoln.

As a means of showing the business done here by the B. & M. system and the increase of business during the past three years, the following table will be of service:

YEARS.	NO. CARS.	TONNAGE.
1886	12,651	136,565
1887	20,889	217,518
1888	23,477	257,690
Totals	57,017	611,773

During 1888 the average number of men employed on the B. & M. in Lincoln was 793, to whom an average monthly wage of $43,443.50 was paid. Within the city limits are forty-two miles of track, a very large showing for a city of this size.

THE UNION PACIFIC.

This road has usually been considered an Omaha road, and many are now firm in the belief that the U. P. would do nothing for Lincoln beyond that which is absolutely necessary to its own welfare; but the facts are that the Union Pacific is becoming a more important road to Lincoln every year, and the management is looking toward Lincoln with favor as time passes. The road appreciates that Lincoln is an important and growing commercial center, and is willing to give all the facilities that are afforded by its immense system of road in Nebraska and Kansas. As evidence of this, the treatment given Lincoln upon the opening of the K. C. & O. railway may be cited. This road was built to occupy vacant territory in the southwest. Extensions were made from Fairfield west to Minden, and thence southwest to Alma. At the same time the road was built east and north to a connection with the O. & R. V. at Stromsburg. During the building of this line Lincoln looked upon it with suspicion. It was to be a part of the U. P. system, and that, in the minds of many people, meant that its business must go either to Omaha or Kansas City. It was something of a surprise, then, when the road upon completion was operated as a line running directly out of Lincoln. Through trains were put on running from Alma to Lincoln by way of Stromsburg and Valparaiso. A car goes to Omaha, but the solid train, with this exception is run through to Lincoln. That it increases the railroad business of the city not a little is shown by the fact that this train carries, according to the statements of the conductors, 150 passengers per day on an average. Equal facilities are given for reaching that line with freight, and thus it turns out that one of the most important extensions made by the Union Pacific for several years is practically a new line out of Lincoln.

This city is situated on the branch connecting the Nebraska and Kansas divisions of the road, and is about midway between them. Direct connection is made with the roads traversing the northern tier of counties of the State of Kansas, and distributing rates are given that enable the Lincoln jobber to reach that territory on advantageous terms. The Union Pacific system in Nebraska includes the main line from Omaha west and a number of important branches. On all of those lines the Lincoln merchant has nearly the same facilities and rates as are enjoyed by Omaha. In connection with the Rock Island the road forms a through line to Chicago, and a good portion of the "in" business comes over this road. For "out" business this system is very important. The main line and branches traverse nearly forty Nebraska counties, nearly all of them favorably located and capable of sustaining a large population. Lincoln goods go out over the system to Wyoming, Colorado, Utah, and Idaho, according to the statements made by the jobbers and also by the agents of the company. The buiness of the Lincoln offices has increased steadily since the road was built into the city. When the Missouri Pacific and the Elkhorn were completed to this point, they shared with the older roads the Eastern traffic. The Union Pacific was able to give them a liberal portion of it and still receive for its own share a much larger tonnage in 1886 than in 1885, and a still greater increase in the two following years. Although the exact figures of the business cannot be given, the local agent, Mr. Miller, gives the information that the increase has been most wonderful in the past three years. This city has through trains or excellent connections on all the roads of the Union Pacific system, which includes over 1,000 miles of road in this State and fully as much in Kansas, Wyoming, Colorado, Utah, and Idaho, all regularly traveled by salesmen from Lincoln jobbing houses.

THE MISSOURI PACIFIC.

When Gould built his first Nebraska extension, in 1880, he thought that Lincoln was too insignificant a city to reach with his main line, and he therefore passed it thirty miles to the east. This was a mistake, as the managers of the road soon discovered. In a few years a Lincoln branch was projected, and in 1886 it was completed to this city. This line caused not a little of the unparalleled prosperity of the last three years. By giving a direct road to St. Louis shorter than the Omaha line, it placed the jobbers at an advantage which they understood and knew how to use. Freights on all southern business are now the same as to Omaha, and as the out rate is lower than from Omaha, the Lincoln jobber is very well cared for on all goods from the southern market. The road was also important in opening up the coal fields of the south, and in bringing the yellow pine and oak and other hard woods of the Missouri and Arkansas to Lincoln. The importance of the traffic from that region is great, and it is swelling in volume from year to year. The system includes about 7,000 miles of road. Kansas City and St. Louis are reached by two daily trains. Through cars run from Lincoln to Kansas City, where close connections are made for trains to all points on the system, east, west, and south. This has become a favorite route for the traveler who does not care to pass through Chicago, but would prefer to visit the cities further south. The road has also done a large California business in Lincoln, taking the traveler over the southern route.

The Missouri Pacific was wanted by the city because it was thought that it would be particularly valuable in bringing in coal and lumber. The books of the freight office show that it has filled every promise in this regard. Yellow pine, hard wood, coal, and southern products, form the bulk of the business. A considerable amount of miscellaneous freight is also brought from the east *via* St. Louis. By comparing the record of the year month by month with that of 1888, it is found that the business of the Lincoln freight office has increased fully fifty per cent for the entire year.

THE NORTHWESTERN.

Previous to 1886 the wholesale trade of the city of Lincoln was confined to the south half of the State of Nebraska. The territory occupied was known to be by far the most fertile portion, but still it was felt that much advantage would result from a connection with the entire State. A line reaching the Fremont, Elkhorn & Missouri Valley was particularly desired, as that would not only give access to the entire Elkhorn system in Nebraska, but the Northwestern system reaching to Chicago and to the great lumber districts of the north. At one time a company was organized to build the Lincoln & Fremont road, in order to secure such a connection, but the enterprise failed. It is, perhaps, well that it did, for in a short time the city was able to attract a branch of the road.

Lincoln became a city on the Northwestern lines in 1886, the Elkhorn railway building a branch from Fremont. Direct connection was thus obtained with a system of road covering 7,005 miles, 1,252 miles of this belonging to the Elkhorn, over 1,000 being in Nebraska. The main line extends from Blair, on the Missouri river a short distance north of Omaha, to Fremont, on the Union Pacific in Dodge county. From that point it follows the valley of the Elkhorn river toward the northwest, and traverses the entire northern portion of the State. At Chadron, in the extreme northwest, a branch diverges to tap the Black Hills, while the main line continues until the Wyoming coal fields are reached. There are numerous feeders; one connects Lincoln with Fremont, another gives Omaha connection with the main line. It will be seen that the branch to this city is in general direction a continuation of the main line. It places Lincoln practically the same distance away from the main line as Omaha. The two competing cities have the same out rates and the same train service. They are on an equality in battling for the business of Northern Nebraska.

In the year 1885 the State Legislature of Nebraska passed a law adopting the commissioner system of railroad control, a system which so far has proved to be the best devised for regulating and controlling the operations of railroads. The State Constitution expressly forbids the creating of any new State offices, and hence to get around this constitutional impediment, the law provides that the Board of Commissioners shall consist of the Secretary of State, Auditor of Public Accounts, Attorney General, Treasurer, and Commissioner of Public Lands and Buildings, who shall appoint three secretaries, to whom the duties of the board are in a large degree delegated. Accordingly the present "State Board of Transportation" is composed of Hon. G. L. Laws, T. H. Benton, William Leese, J. E. Hill, and John Steen. The secretaries are J. R. Gilkeson, L. W. Gilchrist, and W. S. Garber. The law of 1885 provided that the Auditor, Secretary of State, and Attorney General should constitute the board, but the law of 1887 added to these officers the Treasurer and Commissioner of Public Lands and Buildings.

Taken all together Lincoln's railroad facilities are unsurpassed in the West, and the extent to which the business done by her roads has grown is the surest and best indication of the wonderful growth of the business of the city.

As Lincoln is well equipped with railroad lines, so is she with telegraph lines and express facilities. The Western Union is, of course, here, and has been ever since the coming of the first railroad. The Pacific Mutual, or the Postal Telegraph Cable Company, has been in operation in the city for nearly four years, and does a thriving business.

At the time of the settlement of Lincoln, the express business of all the country west of the Missouri river was by common consent of all the other express companies, conceded to be the exclusive territory of the Wells-Fargo Express Company, with headquarters at San Francisco. That company established an office in Lincoln early in 1868, with Austin Humphrey as agent. He conducted the business in one corner of the Humphrey Brothers' hardware store, in the old frame building that stood on the northwest corner of ninth and O streets, on the ground now occupied by the five story brick block of the same firm.

In a few years the increased business requiring the exclusive time of an agent, W. H. Wallace, an experienced expressman, was sent here to take charge of the business, opening a regular office on ninth street, between O and P, with a new wagon, and Morris Turner as clerk.

In the summer of 1875 the Union Pacific Railroad Company decided to do the express business of its line, and as this was the only railroad upon which the Wells Fargo operated, and as the territory was isolated from the headquarters at San Francisco, and as the business of the company was greatly reduced by the grasshoppers of 1873, 1874, 1875, the company on July 1, 1875, withdrew from its business, and abandoned all its territory east of Ogden. Its place was immediately filled by the Union Pacific Express Company, on the Union

Pacific railroad; the American Express Company, then operating on the C. B. & Q. system, taking the B. & M.; the United States Express Company, operating on the Chicago, Rock Island & Pacific and Kansas City & Council Bluffs, taking the Midland Pacific from Brownville to Seward, and the A. & N. from Atchison to Lincoln.

The American Company took the office and fixtures, with the agent of the Wells-Fargo Company and the United States Company occupied a frame building on Tenth street, back of the First National Bank, with Mr. DeKay as agent. The frame building referred to had done duty for years on the corner now occupied by the First Na-

THE HUMPHREY BLOCK.

tional Bank, as a first class family grocery, kept by Thomas Sewell. In November, 1875, J. S. Atwood having extended the Union block on O street to the alley between Tenth and Eleventh, the American Express removed its office to the room next the alley, the agent living in rooms above, stairs leading down into the office.

On July 1, 1876, Mr. Wallace was succeeded by S. W. Chapman, who held the agency until December 1, 1880, when he was succeeded by S. J. Roberts. During this time the growth of business of the companies was more than 300 per cent. In February, 1877, Mr. DeKay, agent of the United States Company, was succeeded by J. E.

R. Millar, who still holds the place; and the office was moved to the Union Block, on O street. In May, 1884, Mr. Roberts, agent of the American Company, gave place to J. L. Hopkins, who held the place until June, 1887, when he was succeeded by C. S. Potter, who was in turn succeeded in January, 1888, by C. R. Teas, who now occupies the position.

When the Southern Pacific completed its connection with the Santa Fé at Deming, N. M., the Wells-Fargo Company began a systematic warfare to recapture the West Missouri territory abandoned by it five or six years previous. After fighting more than a year with the Adams Express Company on the Sante Fé road, the Wells-Fargo Company finally succeeded in driving its competitor out of the territory west of Kansas City, and then demanded the surrender of Nebraska. The American Company retired from the B. & M., but the United States Company for several months held on to the A. & N., it and the Wells-Fargo running opposition, with two messengers on each train, and two agents at each station. At length the United States Company grew tired, and the Union Pacific railroad being completed to Lincoln in 1880, the United States Company turned its business, with agent, office, etc., over to the Pacific Express Company, and retired from all the field west of Omaha. Early in 1886 the Missouri Pacific came into Lincoln with the Pacific Express Company, which had worked on to that line, giving the city direct communication with St. Louis and all the lines belonging to that great system. In the fall of the same year the Elkhorn line came in with the Wells-Fargo Company in connection with the American Express, opening Lincoln to the Black Hills, Minneapolis, Chicago, and all the 5,000 miles of the Chicago & Northwestern system.

Lincoln now has in name but two express companies — the Wells-Fargo and the Pacific — although really with the advantage of the four; the Wells-Fargo and the American being under the control of one company, and the Pacific and United States being consolidated.

CHAPTER XVI.

STATE INSTITUTIONS.—THE PENITENTIARY—HOSPITAL FOR THE INSANE—HOME FOR THE FRIENDLESS—THE PENITENTIARY REVOLT—WARDEN NOBES'S STORY OF THAT OCCURRENCE—SOME OF THE PRINCIPAL ACTORS—NEW INCIDENTS OF THE REVOLT—THE EXPLOSION AT THE ASYLUM.

At the time the Commissioners had in consideration the selection of a site for the location of the capital, Messrs. W. T. Donovan, of Lancaster, Nebraska, and Hon. G. H. Hilton, of Cincinnati, O., as an inducement to the Commissioners to select the present site, offered to donate to the State forty acres of land, situated about two and one-half miles south of the town of Lancaster, upon the express condition that said land should be reserved by the Commissioners, and used by the State as the site of the proposed penitentiary. Upon the final decision locating the seat of government, this grant was accepted and the reservation and location made accordingly, it being understood that in case the State Penitentiary should not be erected upon this site, the same should revert to Mr. Hilton, in whom the legal title was then vested. This explains why the penitentiary is located in a hollow instead of being on the hill either this side or beyond.

Among the subjects for legislation named by the Governor to be submitted to a special session of the Legislature, called to meet in Lincoln, in February, 1870, was that of erecting a State Penitentiary, and providing for the care and custody of State prisoners. Accordingly an act to provide for both these objects was passed at that session, and received the approval of the Governor on the 4th day of March, 1870. The act provided for the election of three State Prison Inspectors, who were to take charge of the sale of lands for the raising of the necessary funds, and also of the erection of the buildings. A temporary building was immediately erected on the ground to accommodate the present necessities, which did duty until the new building was completed, and which now stands within the prison walls.

The three Inspectors, Messrs. W. W. Wilson, W. W. Abbey, and F. Templin, set to work immediately upon their selection. W. H. B.

Stout, then of Washington county, Nebraska, and J. M. Jamison, of Des Moines, Ia., were granted the contract for $312,000. The work, as far as the contract extended, was completed in the fall of 1876, but since then numerous additions have been made to the capacity of the institution. At the opening of the penitentiary the number of prisoners was 18, but at present nearly 100 boarders are accommodated.

Henry C. Campbell was the first warden, appointed and he was succeeded by William Woodhurst, in 1873, during whose wardenship occurred the famous "revolt" among the prisoners, on January 11, 1875.

About four o'clock in the afternoon of that day, Deputy Warden C. J. Nobes stood with his hand upon the latch of the door that gave admission to the old stable which was then used as a shop for the convict stone-cutters. The window panes near by were covered with frost. Had they been clear, so that he might have seen into the shop, or had he seen the eyes that peered out at him through the little holes that had been scraped through the frost, he would not have entered. But no suspicion of anything wrong had entered his mind, and he opened the door quickly and stepped in. If his pulse did not beat a trifle quicker as he did so, his must have been an extraordinarily imperturbable nature. As he closed the door there stepped quickly from behind it twelve men whom he recognized by a hasty and comprehensive glance as the most desperate convicts in the prison. Wm. McWaters, who was afterward killed by a guard while attempting to incite a revolt, stood immediately in front of Mr. Nobes, with the muzzle of a revolver which he had taken from the guard almost touching the warden's face. Quin Bohanan, afterward a murderer, stood near by with a pick raised over the warden's head. Grouped around them, armed with stone-hammers, which their vengeful and determined faces showed they would not hesitate to use, were Warrel, McKenna, Thompson, Gerry, Elder, and five others, equally desperate but not as well known as these leaders.

A glance was sufficient to reveal everything to the warden. A conspiracy to take the prison had been formed, the guards in the shop had been overpowered and disarmed, and the conspirators had lain in wait for the warden. Their plan had worked admirably, and when Mr. Nobes was invited to surrender, he replied, "All right boys; what do you want?"

"Take his six-shooter," said one of the conspirators.

"He hasn't any," said McWaters.

Nobes had always conveyed the impression that he did not carry a "gun," and his heart gave a throb of hope at McWaters's remark. "I began to work my hand around to my hip pocket, kind of careless like," he says when he tells of the experience, "but Bohanan soon discovered what I was doing, and catching my hand, with the remark, 'I'll take care of that,' took my revolver from my pocket."

"Take off your clothes," said McWaters.

"No, I won't do it," replied Nobes. "You can undress me if you want to, but I won't do it myself."

The conspirators let him have his own way about it, and soon had him stripped to his underclothes. It was suggested that they put a striped suit on him, but he told them they could not do that, and they contented themselves with dressing him in a teamster's clothes. It was then suggested that they shave him, but he declared that he would not submit to it. It was finally put to a vote, and Elder and Jennings voted to shave him, while the other ten voted against it. The barber, who had been brought in, was accordingly not called upon to exercise his art upon the warden.

The convicts sat their prisoner in a chair, tying his hands behind it, and tying the chair to a post. The guard was disposed of in the same way at the other end of the shop.

McWaters then arrayed himself in the warden's clothes, and blacked the sides of his face with the stove poker, so as to represent the warden's whiskers. Taking Nobes's heavy cane, McWaters formed seven of the men in line and marched them across the yard to the cell house and warden's quarters. The guards on the walls saw the moving group, but as they marched in the usual manner, each with his right hand on the shoulder of the man in front, and as McWaters was dressed in the deputy's suit and carried his cane, nothing was suspected.

The convicts found the doors open, and had no difficulty in making Warden Woodhurst and the guards prisoners. They then went to the armory, sending one of their number to Nobes for the key to the door. He pointed out the key to the dispensary, and declared that it was the key to the armory, knowing that if they had to force the armory door open they would be likely to alarm the guards on the walls, whom, of course, they had had no opportunity of capturing. They did have to batter down the door, but the guards had in the meantime been alarmed in quite another manner.

Four men had been left to watch the deputy warden, the guard Cochran, and Mr. C. B. Fox, who were in the stone shop. Besides the mutineers, there were about twenty other convicts in the shop, who took no part in the revolt, but kept on working. When McWaters and his seven fellow-conspirators had gone, Nobes called a convict named Johnson to him and asked him to untie him. The four conspirators left to guard him told Johnson they would kill him if he did. "You are not afraid of these fellows," said Nobes; "you untie me and I'll protect you." Johnson was a fellow of a good deal of nerve, but he looked at the four desperate men before him, calculated on his chances with McWaters and his seven comrades, and said that he believed he would not take sides in the trouble either way.

It has always been supposed that Mr. Nobes succeeded in loosening his bonds himself, and that statement has been made in every account of the revolt. The truth is that he was released by one of the mutineers who was left to guard him. This man's name was Warrell. Observing that the deputy was struggling to free himself, Warrell came back to him with his hammer in hand and said: "You had better keep quiet, or I'll have to tap you with this hammer."

"You wouldn't hit anybody," replied Nobes. "A man with only four years to serve here is a fool to go into a scheme like this. You untie me and I'll get you out of here."

"I don't dare to. They'll kill me if I let you go," said Warrell.

"They needn't know it at all," said Nobes, "and if you let me loose, McWaters and his gang will not get back here. You come down here and swing your hammer over my head and swear you'll kill me, and then get down behind the chair and untie the straps, while pretending to tighten them. I tell you I will get you out of here if you'll do it."

The noise made by the hammers of the men who were working enabled the convict and the imprisoned deputy to carry on this conversation without being overheard. Warrell followed the deputy's directions, and after threatening to brain him with the hammer, got down behind him, and while apparently tightening his bonds, loosened them. The other convicts were in front of the deputy, and could not see what Warrell was doing. But the deputy's feet were also tied, and there was no way of loosening them without immediate detection. Fortunately, as Warrell rose and moved away, two shots were fired at the cell-house. Two of the mutineers went to the window, and, scratching away the frost, pressed their faces close to the window. Another one, Edwards, who stood in the door, was also watching the cell-house. All of them had forgotten their prisoner for the moment. It was a valuable moment, and Nobes made the most of it. His hands were free, and he soon succeeded in untying his feet. Lying near him was a hoe. As he sprang up and seized this, Edwards, who stood in the door, saw him and gave the alarm; but it was too late. The deputy swung the hoe into the air and knocking Edwards, crowbar and all, over a pile of stone, escaped from the shop and ran across the yard to the stable. Getting out of range of the convicts' guns, he called to a guard to throw him a six-shooter, and taking this in hand, he went back to the stone shop. Arrived here, he made Thompson, one of the mutineers, untie the guard, and the two got outside the walls.

There was a board wall at the southwest corner of the yard, and the plan of the mutineers was to dress themselves in citizens' clothes, procured from the warden and guards, secure arms from the armory, kill the guard at the southwest turret, and escape at nightfall. The two shots which attracted the attention of the conspirators left to guard the deputy, and which gave him the opportunity to escape, were fired at the guard in this turret. His name was Julius Grosjean. The first shot cut his vest and the second wounded him slightly in the leg.

It took the deputy warden but a short time, when he had regained his liberty, to get the guards together and dispose of them to the best advantage. They were stationed at knot-holes and other improvised port-holes where they could command the yard, and were instructed to shoot the first man who came into the yard with a gun. Innings, one of the mutineers, appeared at the kitchen window with a gun, and the deputy himself drew a bead on him and fired. The man disappeared. After the surrender Nobes learned that he had gone up stairs and surrendered to the warden. A bullet-hole in the casement and a scratch on Innings's neck gave evidence of the accuracy of the deputy's aim.

It was but a short time after the revolt was discovered by the guards on the walls until the report had reached the city, and citizens with

15

arms began to arrive. The Governor was also promptly notified, and secured an almost immediate order for the movement of the 23d U. S. infantry from Omaha to the scene of the revolt. "The citizens had nerve enough," says Mr. Nobes, "but they were not used to discipline and you could not count on them. You might station a man at a certain point and in five minutes find that he had gone somewhere else. I tell you I felt a good deal better when I heard the measured tramp of the regulars, and the orders of the officers which I knew would be obeyed to the letter."

The company of regulars under Major Randall arrived about one o'clock in the morning, and at once proceeded to throw a line of guards about the walls. The warden and his wife, and two guards, in the meantime, were the prisoners of the mutineers. The latter made one or two experiments in the way of going into the yard, but a fusilade from the guards convinced them that such experiments were far from safe. They discussed many plans during the night, which were overheard by the imprisoned guards and the warden and his wife. One plan was to go out to the gates with the imprisoned guards in front of them, and another was to secure still more certain immunity from being shot by forcing Mrs. Woodhurst out ahead of them. These plans were abandoned, however, as impracticable, and they gradually lost their courage and hope as the slow hours of the night wore away.

About six o'clock in the morning Mrs. Woodhurst appeared at the southwest window of the chapel, much to the relief of her husband and sons, (who were separated from her during the eventful night,) as well as her many friends among the citizens before the walls. She stated that she thought the mutineers could be persuaded to surrender to her. The troops were making preparations to enter the yard and storm the building occupied by the mutineers, but before they started the convicts agreed to surrender to Mrs. Woodhurst, stipulating only that they should receive no excessive punishment.

The conduct of Mrs. Woodhurst through all that trying experience is spoken of with the highest praise. When she was allowed by the convicts to go to her own room and stay there, she made her way to another room whence she was able to alarm the guards on the walls, and thus prevent them from coming to the house, where they would have been captured. Her behavior was marked by the utmost intrepidity and presence of mind throughout the entire night. At one time she secured the arms of the mutineers, hid them in her wardrobe, and concealed their ammunition in a bucket of water. She gave them back their arms, however, when they began to batter down the door of the wardrobe where she had concealed them.

Deputy warden Nobes kept the promise which he made to Warrell, the convict who untied him when he was a prisoner in the stone shop. On April 5, 1875, Governor Garber granted Warrell a full pardon, and the deputy had the pleasure of reciprocating the favor done him at a time when he needed it desperately, by opening the prison gates and letting the convict who had saved him step out into the world a free man.

McWaters was a restless, irrepressible character, and, not discouraged by the failure of this revolt, set immediately to work planning another. The plan for this one was discovered through the dropping of a note, which one of the conspirators had written to another. The attempt was to be made on the 26th day of May. Kolkow, the keeper of the wash-house, was to be killed. The deputy warden was then to be disposed of, and a rush for liberty made. When the 26th of May came the convicts were kept in the main building all afternoon. The next day they were marched out, but the guards were under special instructions to keep a close lookout, and to shoot any convict who made any suspicious demonstration. A short time after the convicts had gone to work, John Geary was granted leave to go to the privy. Just as he was returning McWaters held up his hand, and was given permission to go. He met Geary just under the guard's cage, and touching him, said something. The guard did not hear what it was, but the fact that anything was said was warning that something was wrong, and he was at once upon the alert. When McWaters stooped and picked up a stone and made a motion to throw it at the guard, the latter fired. McWaters stood upright a moment, without making any outcry, and then walked forward about twenty feet, where he was caught by Cochran, the overseer. The blood was gushing from the carotid artery, and within a few seconds from the time he staggered into the overseer's arms, he died. The ball from Hugh Blaney's gun had passed through McWaters's left jaw, entered the neck, severed the carotid artery, passed down through his body, and came out just above the left kidney.

After firing upon McWaters, the guard immediately re-cocked his gun, and ordered Geary back to work. He then gave the alarm by ringing the bell in the yard, and those in the warden's and deputy's rooms. The alarm brought out the warden and deputy, and after the convicts had been allowed to work long enough for the excitement to subside somewhat, they were marched into the main building and an extra guard set over them.

McWaters was not the only one of the mutineers who was a figure in a subsequent tragedy. Quin Bohanan's term expired October 13, 1877. On the 19th of February, 1882, in a quarrel with James Cook, at Waverly, over the spelling of the word "pedlar," he killed Cook. He was tried and sentenced to the penitentiary for life, but after serving a short part of his time, he succeeded in getting a new trial. The result was far from being what he expected, for the jury brought in a verdict of murder in the first degree, and he was sentenced to be hanged.

He was confined in the Otoe county jail, awaiting some further judicial proceedings, his case having been appealed to the United States Supreme Court; but on the 22d day of June, 1887, he escaped, and has since succeeded in eluding the officers, spurred on as they are by a heavy reward.

Bohanan was of that peculiar temperament that either could not appreciate disgrace and the apparent hopelessness of his situation, or, appreciating them, could not be depressed by them. He seemed never to allow the idea of escape to leave his mind. An incident occurred during his second trial which Mr. Nobes never made public, because Bohanan's attorneys feared it might prejudice his case. When Nobes took Bohanan into the buggy to bring him to the city for trial, he fastened his handcuffs to an iron in the buggy seat. When about half way to town he suddenly discovered that Bohanan had taken off the nut which held the iron, and was almost free. As the team was a very spirited one, the situation was somewhat critical. Looking Bohanan sternly in the eye, he ordered him to put the nut back, which he did.

"Now," said Nobes, "if you make the slightest move toward getting away, I'll kill you."

"For God's sake, Mr. Nobes, don't shoot me!" exclaimed Bohanan, who saw that Nobes was a good deal agitated, and evidently feared that he might conclude to act as executioner without further delay.

"Oh, I won't shoot you," replied the deputy; "I will just cut your heart out."

Bohanan probably believed it, for he made no further attempt at escaping.

Elder, who was also one of the mutineers, went to Kansas City after his term expired. "I was sitting in a hotel at Kansas City one day," says Mr. Nobes, "when somebody tapped me on the shoulder and spoke to me. I looked up, and before me stood Elder, arrayed in the height of fashion and sporting a pair of eye-glasses and a shiny silk hat. He asked me if I had been to breakfast. I told him that I had, and he said he would see me after he had breakfasted. When he came out he asked me to take a walk with him. He took me down town to a good office building, and following him up stairs, I found myself in an elegantly-furnished room, the windows of which proclaimed that it belonged to 'Dr. Elder.' He was working a patent-medicine fake, and was making plenty of money and flying high. He asked me not to give him away, and as I had no particular reason for doing so, I left him to practice his improved style of villainy undisturbed."

In March, 1875, L. F. Wyman was made warden, and he served until October, 1877, when he was succeeded by Henry C. Dawson, who acted in that capacity until September 7, 1880.

C. J. Nobes was the next warden, and under his management, which continued for six and one-half years, affairs moved very smoothly; the discipline of the prison was greatly improved and its sanitary condition carefully looked after.

Mr. Nobes was succeeded in 1887 by R. W. Hyers, who held the office until January 1, 1889, when he resigned, his place being filled by the appointment of Dan Hopkins, who is the present warden. Mr. Hopkins seems to be especially fitted for the place he holds, as is evidenced by the continued good order prevalent at the penitentiary and by the respect with which he is treated and the esteem in which he is held by the prisoners. Mr. Hopkins is a man of just a little over forty-three years of age, having been born August 30, 1846, in Rushford, Alleghaney county, N. Y. His parents both came from Vermont. Mr. Hopkins's early life was passed quietly, without special incident worthy of note. He lived in Alleghaney county until he was twelve years old, when his parents moved to Catarangus county,

N. Y., where he finally resided until 1871, or until Dan, as he is familiarly called, was twenty-five. On September 23, 1863, Mr. Hopkins being then under the age required, enlisted in the service of his country, to help fight her battles and throttle the treason that seemed for a time to have a death grip on the nation's throat. He enlisted in the Ninth New York Cavalry, Col. Nicholls commanding. This regiment was assigned to duty in the Shenandoah valley, in the Second Brigade of the Cavalry Corps of the First Division, under command of Gen. Merritt. Gen. Deven was in command of the division, the officer of Company I, Hopkins's company, being Capt. Putnam. Mr. Hopkins prides himself upon the fact that he is one of the very few remaining high privates who now survive the years and ravages of disease. When he went into the service he weighed only ninety pounds, and, of course, being only seventeen, had to stretch the truth one year to be allowed to enlist; but like a good many other boys whose patriotism rose with danger, this little prevarication was counted as nothing. What he wanted was to get a shot at a traitor, and the end justified the means.

Mr. Hopkins's battle experiences are those of every soldier who fought and skirmished with the enemy up and down the beautiful Shenandoah valley from 1863 to 1865. If these experiences were rightly written they would make a volume of rare interest—war, tragedy, love, adventure, defeat, and victory, all mixed together in one grand plot. He was, of course, in Sheridan's command, but was not permitted to be present at Lee's surrender, as his horse had been condemned and he, together with hundreds of others, had been ordered back to Remount camp, below Harper's Ferry, as a guard for prisoners taken during the campaign, and to get a fresh mount. After the remount he went back to the valley, where his division did patrol duty to the end of the war. He was mustered out of the service at Winchester, on June 1, 1865, having staid in the service without a wound or accident until the close of the war.

Returning home at the close of the war, he engaged in farming and stock buying until March 16, 1871, when he married, and with his bride started for the West. Mrs. Hopkins's maiden name was Morrill—Miss Jennie Morrill—closely connected with the family of Senator Morrill, of Vermont, on her father's side, and on her mother's side with that of Secretary Seward. Mr. Hopkins proceeded directly to Lone Tree, now Central City, where he took a homestead six miles southwest of the village, perfecting his homestead right in the usual manner. In August, 1873, during the trying grasshopper times, he temporarily abandoned farming, (as did many Nebraska farmers, of necessity,) and went to Wyoming in the employ of the Union Pacific railway. He remained in the employ of this company, holding a responsible position, until December, 1875, when, with his family, he went back to New York, where he remained only a year; but that was long enough to give him a disastrous experience in the oil country. In December, 1876, he came back to Nebraska, a wiser if not a sadder man. He went on his farm, but only stayed there a short time, moving soon into Central City, where he was appointed Deputy Sheriff of Merrick county in 1877, which place he held for two years. In 1879 he was elected Sheriff, and again, in 1881, was chosen by the people for the same position. In 1883, on retiring from office, he engaged in the implement business in Central City, and continued that two years. But at the end of that time he accepted a flattering offer from the Great Northwestern Stage Company, and in February, 1886, went to Denver, the company's headquarters, as Superintendent of that company's lines in Wyoming and Colorado, spending a considerable portion of his time traveling over the routes and inspecting the lines.

Until March 15, 1887, Mr. Hopkins remained with this company, when he resigned on information received of his appointment by Governor Thayer as deputy warden. With his family he arrived in Lincoln April 1, 1887, and immediately entered upon the discharge of his duties. This place he filled in a most satisfactory manner until the resignation of Warden Hyers, on January 1, 1889, when Mr. Hopkins assumed the duties of warden, on appointment of Gov. Thayer. Mr. Hopkins has dispensed with the office of deputy warden, V. U. Heiner acting as principal keeper. Elder P. M. Howe is the chaplain.

The position of warden in the Nebraska penitentiary is a difficult one to fill. In fact, the duties of warden of any prison require great care, judgment, a knowledge of human nature, firmness, and yet kindness. It is a trying place, but Mr. Hopkins has shown himself possessed of these qualifications in a large degree, and the result is seen in the smoothness with which affairs within the walls move.

Mr. Hopkins's family consists of a wife and one daughter, Miss Inez, now in her sixteenth year.

By the act providing for the sale of the unsold lots and blocks in

Lincoln, and the erection of the State University, the Commissioners were directed to locate, on or near the site of said town, a site for a State Lunatic Asylum, and from the proceeds of such sales the sum of $50,000 was appropriated and directed to be expended, under the supervision of the Commissioners, in the erection, upon such plan as they should adopt, of the necessary building. Accordingly, a site containing about 160 acres, and situated about two miles southwest of the site of the old town of Lancaster, was set apart for that purpose; and after having issued the notices required by law, and having adopted the plan of Prof. D. Winchell, an architect from Chicago, the contract for the construction of the building was let, on the 15th day of August, 1869, to Joseph Ward, also formerly of Chicago, who stipulated for its completion on or before the first day of December, 1870, the contract price for the work being $128,000. On December 22, 1870, the asylum was opened for the reception of patients. A little while before this it was set on fire, near the roof, but the flames were extinguished before much damage was done. Dr. Larsh, of Nebraska City, was appointed the first Superintendent, and had twenty-six patients when he took charge. On the night of April 18, 1871, the building was burned to the ground. Whether set on fire, or ignited by a defective flue, has not been determined. Two or three of the insane persons at the time in the building were burned to death. The city of Lincoln made temporary arrangements to accommodate the patients thus rendered homeless, advancing $1,500 for that purpose. This sum was afterward repaid by the State.

The burned asylum building had been insured for $96,000. The insurance companies took their option and rebuilt the building, the contract price being $71,999.98. William H. Foster, of Des Moines, Iowa, was the architect of the second building, and R. D. Silvers the contractor for the erection of the main building and one wing. The contract called for a facing of limestone ashlar, rough finish, but this was changed later on to Carroll county (Missouri) sandstone, with rubble-work finish and rustic joints. It was finished on October 2, 1872.

The building was crowded as soon as completed, and the Legislature of 1875 appropriated $25,000 for an additional wing, which was at once erected, under the supervision of the trustees. Three more wings have been added since that time, which, with kitchen, boiler-house, and other improvements, have cost in the aggregate $196,618, and the plant had cost, on January 1, 1889, as estimated by the Secretary of State, the sum of $272,413. The asylum is credited with additional property valued at $70,668.05.

On February 5, 1889, one of the boilers in the boiler-house of the asylum exploded, killing one engineer and two patients, and wrecking the boiler-house. The Legislature was then in session, and an investigation indicated incompetency in the engineers. An appropriation was made at once for rebuilding the boiler-house, and the work has been completed.

The present number of patients is nearly 400, and the average weekly expense of their maintenance was $4.66 per capita during 1887 and the first eleven months of 1888.

The institution is now under the management of Superintendent W. M. Knapp, M.D., with Dr. J. T. Hay as first and Dr. Miss Helen B. Odelson as second assistant physician. Mr. J. Dan. Lauer is the steward, to whose management is due much of the financial success of the institution, and Mrs. Mary Magoon, the matron.

The State Legislature, by an act of February 28, 1881, established a Home for the Friendless, to be controlled by the Board of Lands and Buildings, at or near the town making the largest donation for the Home. Lincoln contributed $2,050, and secured the institution, and the State expended the $5,000 appropriation in buildings and grounds. The Legislature of 1883 appropriated $2,000, that of 1885 $10,000, and the session of 1887 $11,895.30, making the cost of the plant, to date, $28,895.30. The Home has other property valued at $5,988.80.

The Home is supported in part by benevolent contributions from generous people, and is managed by the Society for the Home for the Friendless, a band of women organized about fifteen years ago, and since incorporated under the laws of the State and subject to a general control of the State Board of Lands and Buildings. This is one of the most commendable charities in the State, and the ladies at its head deserve the highest praise for their practical work in the cause of humanity.

The Home now maintains about 100 children, some of them infants but a few days old. Good homes with families are found for these children as fast as possible. The Home is now under the immediate management of Mrs. A. B. Slaughter, Superintendent; Miss Alice Huff, Physician; and Mrs. Elizabeth Moore, Matron.

CHAPTER XVII.

LINCOLN'S EDUCATIONAL INSTITUTIONS—HER PUBLIC SCHOOLS—EARLY TIMES—THE WONDERFUL GROWTH NOTICED—THE NUMBER OF SCHOOL BUILDINGS AND TEACHERS, AND THE ANNUAL COST OF CONDUCTING THE WORK—THE HIGHER INSTITUTIONS OF LEARNING—OTHER SCHOOLS.

The schools of Nebraska have closely followed the earliest settlement of the State. This was true of Lancaster, which became Lincoln. In fact, Elder Young's Lancaster Seminary Association came to this region for the very purpose of founding a school, and a female seminary at that.

The "Lancaster Colony" laid out "District No. 1" in the latter part of 1864, the same year that Lancaster was platted. This district was six miles square. The first board of directors were Jacob Dawson, John M. Young, and Milton Langdon. The following year, 1865, District No. 2 was organized at Yankee Hill, with John Cadman, W. R. Field, and W. T. Donovan, as directors. In this district, in the dugout home of John Cadman, not far from where the Insane Asylum now is, one of the first schools in this vicinity, and probably in the county, was taught, in the winter of 1865-6, by Robert F. Thurston, with about fifteen scholars in attendance. Judge A. W. Field and his sister, Mrs. J. E. Philpott, four of Cadman's children, three of Donovan's, and others, were pupils in this school. It is probable that a school was in progress at the same time at Saltillo. Probably late in 1866 the Stone Seminary was so far completed in Lancaster that it was decided to open a school in one room in this building, which occupied the ground on the northeast corner of Ninth and P streets, where the *State Journal* block now stands. The interior of the building was not finished by any means. In fact, but one room was in condition to use, and carpets and other cloths had to be hung up to keep the wind out and make the place tenable. There was no floor except the ground, and the partitions were merely lathed up. Here, however, Mr. H. W. Merrill conducted the first school in

Lancaster, in the latter part of 1866. The term concluded with an "exhibition." About thirty pupils attended this school of twenty-three years ago. Early in 1867 Mrs. H. W. Merrill taught a term of school in the stone seminary. She was a lady of a good deal of culture, being possessed of a good academic education and could sing well besides. The directors were anxious to find a teacher, and urged Mrs. Merrill to take the school. She said it would be impossible, as she had a baby only about a year old. The directors told her to take it to school with her, and to this arrangement she finally consented. So Mrs. Merrill labored with the youth of Lancaster with a baby in her arms part of the time. She lived in one end of the building, and John Montieth had a shoe shop in another part. Rooms were scarce in those days. During her term, just after an old-fashioned spelling school, the stone seminary caught fire from a misconstructed flue, and the woodwork of the building burned to the ground. That was the last of the stone seminary as an educational institution. The walls stood there until the fall of 1867, when John Cadman rebuilt the woodwork and opened the "Cadman House."

In the fall of 1867, soon after the first sale of lots, the directors of the district caused a small stone school house to be erected near the northeast corner of Q and Eleventh streets. In this, during the fall of 1867, Mr. George W. Peck taught the first school in the town after it became Lincoln. Mr. Peck still resides in the city. His average attendance was about thirty-five pupils. In the winter of 1868-9 school was continued in the stone school house, with Prof. ———— James as teacher. The attendance had grown to about sixty-five, and the directors then bought the Methodist church, at the southwest corner of Q and Tenth streets, and divided the school, and instruction was begun on May 5, 1869, in both places, with T. L. Catlin teacher in the church. Both schools were well attended. The stone school house became a town jail about 1873, and the old Methodist church continued a school house until the present summer of 1889, being known first as the South School House, and for years past as the "J Street School." It stood near the northeast corner of Eighth and J streets, and was removed during the present summer.

During the spring of 1869, Miss Griswold, afterward Mrs. S. B. Galey, taught a select school. In 1870 the schools had grown to three, and the following spring the question of bonding the district for $50,000 of ten per cent bonds, to build a "high-school building," began to be discussed. Finally, on the 17th day of June, 1871, an election was held at the "White School House" to vote on the bond question. At this election Messrs. C. M. Parker, W. A. Colman, and B. W. Ballard, were judges, and 211 voters were out, of which 151 were for bonding the district and sixty against. We find on the polling list of this election such familiar names as R. E. Moore, C. M. Parker, R. P. Beecher, Geo. B. Skinner, T. H. Hyde, W. J. Hyatt, J. E. Philpott, L. E. Cropsey, H. J. Walsh, John McConnell, P. Way, T. P. Quick, Amasa Cobb, D. B. Cropsey, D. L. Peckham, A. Humphrey, P. H. Cooper, C. M. Leighton, A. M. Davis, G. Ensign, John McManigal, J. H. Ames, and J. P. Hebard.

On August 19th an election was held to determine the location of the proposed $50,000 high-school building. There were three sites before the election from which to choose. One was block sixty-three, where the high school now is, between streets Fifteenth and Sixteenth, and M and N; another was block 155, bounded by F and G and Fifteenth and Sixteenth; and the third was block 120, bounded by J and K and Eleventh and Twelfth. There were 235 votes cast, of which 185 votes were cast for block sixty-three, thirty-two votes were cast for block 155, and eighteen votes for block 120. So block sixty-three won the location. The board this year was composed of Philetus Peck, Moderator; S. J. Tuttle, A. L. Palmer, John Lamb, A. L. Pound, and W. T. Donovan. Palmer or Tuttle acted as secretary of the meetings for several years after this.

On September 9th the board held a meeting, and "Elder Lamb was authorized to answer the Citizens' Bank at Sidney, Ohio, that they could have twenty thousand dollars in bonds at 90 cents on the dollar." The same meeting records that Mr. Lamb was appointed "to procure a strip of breaking for shade trees and to save the building from fire." Some of those shade trees can now be seen around the high-school block, and it would be difficult for a prairie fire to get at the building at the present time. Mr. Palmer also records that the board ordered a "Webster's Unabridged Dictionary and Lippincott's Gazette," probably meaning Gazetteer.

On December 23, 1871, the board adopted the plans and specifications for the new school house offered by Roberts & Boulanger, at a cost of $1,300, the architects to superintend the work. On February

15, 1872, the board decided to advertise for bids on the construction of the high-school building, to be completed by September 1, 1872. On March 11th the bid of Moore & Krone for doing all the brick, stone, iron, and masonry work on the house, was accepted. Also Mr. Parcell's bid to do the carpenter work for $12,300 was approved. Parcell was of the firm of Parcell & Dehart. The stone, brick work, etc., were to cost $30,760, or the building, finished, $43,060. The contractors were to give bond on or before March 18th. On the 1st of April, 1872, S. J. Tuttle was reëlected to the board and J. M. Jamison in place of A. L. Pound, after a hot fight to prevent Jamison & Stout from getting the school-house contract.

On June 11, 1872, J. W. Cassell was employed as Superintendent of the city schools for the ensuing year, at a salary of $1,400 per year. Probably a corps of seven teachers served with him, at "the Stone School House," the stone church, at the northwest corner of Twelfth and J streets, the "South School House," and the new high-school building, during 1872–3.

On September 26 the board authorized the erection of "a suitable number of lightning rods" on the new building. But the carpenters working on the structure dragged along, and it was not completed until the first of January, 1873. Then, on January 9th, arrangements were made by the board to occupy the new school house, and abandon the old stone school house near Eleventh and Q.

From this time the real prosperity of the city schools dates. New maps and charts were ordered. The German language was ordered taught in the new building, on January 9, 1873. The school had a bell, a janitor, and Prof. Leland was employed to teach music at a salary of $10 per month.

On February 6, 1873, we find the board allowing the following bills to teachers for one month past:

Miss E. P. Rockwood	$65 00	Miss Priscilla Nicholson	$50 00
Miss Jennie Roberts	60 00	Miss Mary Sessions	50 00
Miss S. G. Lamb	60 00	Alice Roberts	37 50
Mrs. A. S. Newcomer	60 00	M. A. Whyman	26 25
Mrs. E. Mollie Powers	55 00	Supt. J. W. Cassell	140 00
Miss Hortense D. Street	55 00	Geo. B. Holmes	11 25
Miss Emma Williams	41 25	J. Holdegroff	33 75
Miss May Bostater	55 00		

In September, 1874, Prof. W. W. W. Jones took charge of the

schools as superintendent, and occupied that position until about the close of the year of 1880, when Prof. S. R. Thompson became superintendent, with a corps of over twenty teachers. He was followed by Prof. J. M. Scott, who held the place until June, 1883. District No. 1, Lancaster county, had, some time before this, become the School District of Lincoln.

Of late years the schools have made rapid strides in every respect, as the subjoined exhibit of facts and figures showing the status of the schools of to-day will demonstrate. In brief, the schools of Lincoln exhibit superior development for a city so young. A most wonderful growth has taken place in the last ten years, and the methods of work have kept even pace with the growth in numbers. To Supt. E. T. Hartley, who has had charge of the schools for the past seven years, is due very much of the splendid condition in which they are to-day. Prof. Hartley is a man of wonderful energy, great tact, thorough business methods, and liberal education, and these qualifications, to which must be added his great love for the work, make him a man peculiarly qualified for the place he holds.

The number of school buildings has grown to sixteen, with rooms for ninety schools, and possessing a seating capacity for 5,000 pupils. The total enrollment for the past year was 4,748, of whom 2,375 were boys, and 2,373 were girls. It required over eighty teachers to instruct these five regiments of pupils. The total amount of money paid out for the support of the city public schools for the year ending July 8, 1889, was $98,451, of which sum $43,175 was disbursed for teachers' salaries.

The elementary schools cover eight years of work, and have been arranged in sixteen grades. All the common-school branches are completed in the eight years, including United States history, an eight years' course in music and drawing, temperance hygiene, and four years oral instruction in English language preparatory to the systematic study of grammar.

The high school curriculum comprises four parallel courses of three years each, the English, the Latin, the German, and the Classical. These courses include instruction in algebra, book-keeping, geometry, botany, human physiology, physical geography, chemistry, physics, geology, English composition, word analysis, technical grammar, orthoepy, elocution, history and development of English literature, rhetoric, political economy, civil government, elements of commercial law, general history, three years each in Latin, Greek, and German. It will be seen that the public schools furnish a good practical education, well rounded out, even if the pupils do not go to college, and if they expect to enter a higher institution, they are prepared to do so.

The work of the High School is arranged in departments, and employs nine instructors. Special reference libraries are supplied for the departments of history and English literature, and a working laboratory in chemistry and physics is provided, enabling pupils to perform their own experiments. The department of physiology is well equipped with fine skeletons and a series of plaster and papier-maché models. In addition to the general reference library, each department has a special library. A feature of the Lincoln schools is a circulating library, from which the pupils made 35,510 loans last year, a remarkable record considering the other public and private libraries of the city.

The corps of teachers of the city schools for 1888–89 is as follows:

E. T. Hartley, M. A. .... *Superintendent.*
H. S. Bowers .... *Assistant Superintendent.*
J. C. Miller .... *Special Instructor in Music.*

CENTRAL BUILDING—HIGH SCHOOL.

S. P. Barrett, M. A., Principal,
   Mathematics.
Lawrence Fossler, B. S.,
   German and Biology.
Geo. B. Frankforter, M. A.,
   Chemistry and Physics.
Marian Kingsley, B. A.,
   Rhetoric and English Literature.
Mary M. Pitcher, M. A.,
   Latin and Greek.
Mina F. Metcalf, M. A.,
   General History.
Mate Treeman, B. S.
   History and Civil Government.

ELEMENTARY SCHOOLS.

Louise Adams.
Mrs. Marie Fielding.
Ella Kaufman.
Beth Brenizer.
Ella Conard.
Flora A. Beecher.
Ina Fay Risely.
Lulu Sumner.
Mrs. S. N. Franklin.

T STREET SCHOOL.

G. W. McKinnon, Principal.
Dora M. Neihardt.
Mrs. Mary McKinnon.
Frances Duncombe.
Helen W. Chapin.
Clara Pettigrew.
Eva Lamb.
Lillian Upham.
Mrs. Lulu Wilson.
Susie Hoagland.

Q STREET SCHOOL.

Anna Shuckman, Principal.
Alla Lantz.
Lena Smith.
Mrs. Hattie Musselman.
Lizzie C. Jones.

Etta Erb.
Mrs. Lizzie Gleason.
Dora Brooks.
Jennie Cole.
Ottie Rathbun.
Jennie Marine.

CAPITOL SCHOOL.

Mrs. A. P. Tiffany, Principal.
Mrs. Jeannie Hard.
Mrs. Emma R. Cropsey.
Bertha McCorkle.
Kate Folsom, (Mrs. Ralston.)
Seba Dewell.
Mrs. L. H. Davis.
Mara L. Byam.
Alice Todd.
Sarah Riley.
Mrs. Emmeline Tucker.
Louise Tucker.

C STREET SCHOOL.

Mrs. Elizabeth Bowen, Principal.
Mary Stevens.
Manie Sawyer.
Mrs. Abbie Chamberlain.
Edna Scott.
Emma Smith.
Jessie Love.
Mrs. T. E. Hardenburg. (Died July 24, 1889.)
S. Alice Lease.
Gertrude Aitken.

PARK SCHOOL.

Cora Hardy, Principal.
Edith Long.
Ada Buck.
Mrs. Anna R. King.
Lydia Welch.
Minnie Welch.
Emma Bing.
Sallie Cox.
Lottie Eckhardt.

ELLIOTT SCHOOL.

Mrs. Emma W. Edwards, Principal.
Alice Russell.
Lutie Thomas.
Nettie Taylor.
Laura Roberts.
Medora Smith.
Alice Cronley.
Sarah Shea.
Alice Orr.

OUTLYING SCHOOLS.

J. Oliver.
Kate Stoddard.
Margaret Pryse.
J. C. Pentzer.
May Taggart.
Genia Stillman.
Orra Reeder.
Mary Dolan.
Lizzie Bond.
Olive Roberts.

The board of education is composed as follows:

J. A. Wallingford,
   President.
W. W. W. Jones,
   Vice President
A. G. Greenlee,
   Secretary.

Miss Phœbe Elliott.
Lewis Gregory.
W. J. Marshall.
Sam D. Cox.
W. A. Lindley.
O. E. Goodell.

The instruction for 1889–90 will be under the direction of the following officials:

E. T. Hartley..*Superintendent.*
Burr Lewis...*Principal of High School.*

PRINCIPALS OF WARD SCHOOLS.

Mrs. A. P. Tiffany, Capitol.
Miss Anna Shuckman, Q Street.
Mrs. Elizabeth Bowen, C Street.
Mrs. Emma W. Edwards, Elliott.
Miss Cora Hardy, Park.
Miss Alice Russell, T Street.
Mrs. Jeanie Hard, Cherry Street.
Miss Jennie Marine,
Special Instructor in Vocal Music.
Miss Lydia Welsh,
Special Instructor in Penmanship and Drawing.

A notable feature of the high school is a series of lectures on subjects directly or indirectly connected with the course of study, given by persons prominent in educational circles, and occurring once or twice per week throughout the year. Among the lecturers have been the Governor of Nebraska, and other State officers, the Chancellor and other members of the faculty of the State University, lawyers, ministers and physicians of Lincoln, and the instructors of the high school.

THE STATE UNIVERSITY.

The high standard of general intelligence which has made Nebraska able to boast of having a less percentage of illiteracy among her citizens than any other State in the Union, is as old as the settlement of the Territory. The founding of the present State University came through a process of evolution. To found a university seems to have been the highest ambition of many of Nebraska's earliest politicians, and to become the home of a great educational institution, the goal for which nearly all of her earliest towns strove earnestly and well.

In the first session of the Legislature charters were granted to Nebraska University, located at Fontanelle; Simpson University, located at Omaha city, and the Nebraska City Collegiate and Preparatory Institute, located at Nebraska City. In the next session Simpson University asked for a renewal of its charter, and charters were granted to the Nemaha University, at Archer; Washington College, at Cuming City; the Plattsmouth Preparatory and Collegiate Institute, and the Western University, at Cassville. In the third session the Legislature added to the list the Brownville College and Lyceum, the Salem Collegiate Institute, the Rock Bluff Academy, the Dakota Collegiate Institute, the Nebraska University at Wyoming, the Omaha Collegiate Institute, St. Mary's Female Academy, the University of St. John, the Omaha Medical University, and amended the charter of the Western University. In the fall session of the same year charters were granted to the University of Nebraska, Wyoming College,

DeWitt Collegiate Institute, Falls City College, the Literary Association of the Elkhorn, the Dodge County Lyceum and Literary Association, and the State Historical Society. In 1858 Dempster Biblical Institute and the Lewis and Clark College were chartered.

There was a general impression that the chartering of universities was a good thing, and the Legislatures of those early days had a blank form of charter which became a bill for the creation of a university, ready for introduction as soon as the name of the prospective institution was inserted.

THE STATE UNIVERSITY.

In a very complete paper on the university, read by Professor H. W. Caldwell before the State Historical Society at its 1889 meeting, and from which the foregoing facts have been taken, it is recorded that the bill organizing the University of Nebraska was introduced into the Senate February 11, 1869, by Mr. Cunningham, of Richardson county. It was referred to the Committee on Education, of which Hon. C. H. Gere was chairman, and was reported back the next day, with amendments, and passed. It was passed by the House and signed on the 15th, having become a law within four days from its introduction. A bill was passed about the same time in the session, providing for the sale of unsold lots and blocks in the town site of Lincoln, and for the erection and location of a State Lunatic Asylum and a State University and Agricultural College; and as an illustration of the jealous care with which the State's educational interests have always been guarded, it may be mentioned that on February 12th the bill was amended, on motion of Mr. Tullis, of Lancaster, by striking out the words, "lunatic asylum" before the words, "university" etc., and inserting them after those words. The original charter of the university provided for a board of twelve regents. Nine of these were to be chosen by the Legislature in joint session, three from each judicial district, and the Chancellor, Superintendent of Public Instruction, and Governor, were made *ex-officio* members of the board. In 1875 an amendment was passed providing that the Chancellor should not thereafter be a member of the Board of Regents, and at the same time provision was made against an increase of the number of regents by an increase in the number of judicial districts. The constitution of 1875 creates a board of six regents, to be elected by a direct vote of the people.

The charter of the university provides for five colleges, viz: A college of literature, the sciences and arts; a college of law; a college of medicine; a college of agriculture and the practical sciences; and a college of fine arts. The contract for the erection of the building was let August 18, 1869, the corner-stone was laid September 23d, the building was accepted January 6, 1871, and the university was opened with an enrollment of about ninety students January 6, 1871. The corner-stone was laid with Masonic ceremonies. "Major D. H. Wheeler," says Mr. Caldwell's paper, was master of ceremonies. A brass band from Omaha headed the procession. In the evening a grand banquet was given, Governor Butler made a few remarks, Mr. Wheeler a short speech, then Attorney General Seth Robinson gave an address on "Popular Education." There was a banquet attended by a thousand people, and dancing was indulged in from ten till four o'clock.

The record of the doubts and fears of the Board of Regents and citizens of Lincoln as to the safety of the university building, forms an interesting chapter in the history of the institution. Before the doors were even opened to students the rumor gained currency that

RESIDENCE OF HON. A. J. SAWYER.

the building was unsafe, and in June, 1871, three professional architects were secured to examine it. They reported that it was safe for the time being, and that a few inexpensive repairs would render it safe beyond a doubt for years to come. The repairs were made and the university opened. In March, 1883, at a special meeting of the regents, a report was received from another set of architects, and a new foundation was ordered put under the chapel, and this was done. June 26, 1877, the Chancellor in his report called the attention of the board to the condition of the building. This time four architects were employed — one from Omaha, one from Nebraska City, and two from Lincoln, and on the strength of their report the regents resolved, July 6, 1877, to tear down the building and erect a new one at a cost of $60,000, $40,000 to be raised by the citizens of Lincoln, and work was to commence immediately on securing the above amount. The citizens of Lincoln were not satisfied, and sent to Chicago and Dubuque for architects, who examined the building and pronounced it easily repaired. August 15th a committee of Lincoln citizens met the regents, and upon the new light presented by them, the resolution to tear down was reconsidered, and a new foundation and other repairs were ordered, to be paid for by the citizens of Lincoln. The repairs were made at a cost of $6,012. Various attempts have been made to secure an appropriation to reimburse the citizens of Lincoln for this expense, but all have failed.

Mr. Caldwell's paper states that on June 3, 1869, a committee consisting of Regents C. S. Chase, Supt. Beals, and Rev. D. R. Dungan, was appointed to secure names of suitable persons for Chancellor. January 6, 1870, the salary of the Chancellor was fixed at $5,000, and A. R. Benton was selected on the second ballot. H. S. Tappin, J. D. Butler, E. B. Fairfield, and A. Barns, each received one vote on the first ballot. The next year the Chancellor's salary was reduced to $4,000 and the salaries of professors fixed at $2,000. The first faculty was elected April 4, 1871, as follows: Ancient Languages, A. H. Manley; Mathematics, H. E. Hitchcock; English Literature, O. C. Dake; Sciences, H. W. Kuhn, who declined and recommended Rev. Samuel Aughey, who was unanimously elected at the June meeting. June 13, 1871, a tutor was authorized, and G. E. Church was chosen as the first tutor at a salary of $1,000. Finally the first faculty was completed, by the election, September 6, 1871, of S. K. Thompson to the chair of agriculture, with the condition that he was not to enter upon the discharge of his duties for at least one year. From this modest beginning of four professors and one tutor the faculty has developed into a body of twelve professors, two associates, two adjunct professors, two instructors, two tutors, two lecturers, and the principal of the Latin school, besides assistants in the laboratories and the teachers in art and music.

The character of the development of the university course of instruction can not be better summarized than by quoting the words of Prof. Caldwell: "Two sharply-marked principles have governed in the formation of the courses of study. The first period was characterized by an almost inflexible course of study; there were practically no electives. The classics and mathematics formed the backbone of the work. A term or two of history and of English literature, a couple of years of some modern language, and a text-book study of two or three sciences, were switched in, with no expectation of securing more than a mere outline knowledge of these subjects. They were not supposed to be able to give mental culture; the scientific course even was not made to secure a mental development; its object was to give practical knowledge. In short, whether for better or worse, the ordinary college course of the *renaissance* type, only slightly impregnated with the modern scientific and historic spirit, was the only one recognized.

"The second period begins in 1880 and marks an entire revolution in ideas. An elective course was introduced and the principle recognized that all studies may be made about equally valuable for purposes of mental culture, and therefore the courses were planned with reference to continuity of work in each line. The pamphlet announcing the change says: 'The elective system is the one that insures the greatest interest and profit in every study, and it is the only system that allows a student to become a special scholar in any one department, while still leaving to him the option of a general education.'"

The progress of the university, under the system introduced in 1880, has been steady and rapid, and the institution has become widely known for its original work in several departments of investigation. The department of history is especially strong, and with the possible exception of the Michigan and California universities, no institution west of the Alleghanies has developed its equal. The work which has just been published by Prof. George E. Howard, the head of this department on "Local Constitutional Government in the United States" has been most favorably received by the great historians of the world, and gives him high rank among specialists in historical investigation.

The income of the university is derived from the interest on the proceeds of the sale of the Agricultural College and University lands, donated to the State by Congress, from the rental of unsold lands and from a university tax, levied by the State. The total grant of lands amounted to 135,576.31 acres. The income from this source in 1888 was about $38,923.64. It is estimated that under the present policy of disposing of these lands, the total permanent investment will be about $1,000,000.

The unity of the educational system of the State is recognized both by the university authorities and those who have the direction of the common schools. The high schools of the State are gradually and systematically being brought into close relations with the university by being accredited as preparatory schools whose graduates are admitted to the university without examination.

The university has passed the dangers of the formative period. It has a well-defined policy and course of study established upon the broadest and most modern basis. It has passed safely through the period of sectarian intermeddling, and the dangerous reaction which followed, and the spirit which controls its management now is one which, while recognizing the Christian element which pervades all our institutions, is broad and tolerant. There is no reason why, with the development of the State, the institution shall not become the equal of any in the United States.

THE CHRISTIAN UNIVERSITY.

This institution, which, from its prosperous beginning, promises to be one of the leading schools of higher education in the West, had its origin in the following manner:

In July, 1887, a proposition was made to the Nebraska Christian Missionary Board to donate certain lands, in or near the city of Lincoln, on condition that a university of the Christian church be established thereon. After investigation and consultation, a committee especially appointed, decided to locate the proposed university on what was known as the Hawley farm, adjoining the city on the northeast. The donations of land received consisted of three hundred and twenty-one acres of land and city lots valued at four thousand dollars. At a meeting of the committee, held February 14th, articles of incorporation were adopted and a subcommittee appointed, of which J. Z. Briscoe was chairman, to consider plans and specifications of a main building to be begun on or before May 1, 1888.

THE CHRISTIAN UNIVERSITY.

The corner-stone of the first building was laid with appropriate ceremonies, April 30, 1888. The building consists of Milwaukee brick, trimmed with Michigan red sandstone. It is four stories high, exclusive of basement; one hundred and eight feet front by seventy-eight in depth.

The action of the committee in inaugurating the enterprise was confirmed by the State Convention held at Lincoln, August 28th to 30th 1888. A board of trustees was elected, to be known as the Nebraska Christian Educational Board. It consisted of J. Z. Briscoe, *President;* Ex-Governor Alvin Saunders, *Vice President;* C. R. Van Duyn, *Treasurer;* Porter Hedge, *Secretary;* and W. P. Aylsworth, W. T. Newcomb, Ira Titus, C. J. Hale, Thos. Wiles, J. T. Smith, C. C. Munson, E. T. Gadd. Subsequently the contracts were let for the first building, aggregating a cost of $65,000, to be completed about the first of January, 1890. The work thus far has progressed very satisfactorily, and is nearing completion. All expenses have been promptly met by the sale of lots.

At a meeting of the Board in April, 1889, it was decided to open the school October 1, 1889. The following-named persons will constitute the first faculty:

W. P. Aylsworth, A. M., *Acting President, Dean of the Biblical Department, and Professor of Hebrew and Biblical Literature.*
A. M. Chamberlain, A. M., *Professor of Ancient Language and Literature.*
J. A. Beattie, A. M., *Professor of Pure and Applied Mathematics.*
E. D. Harris, A. B., *Instructor in Preparatory School.*
A. T. Noe., M. D., *Instructor in Physiology, Anatomy, and Hygiene.*
Mrs. W. P. Stearns, *Instructor in Vocal and Instrumental Music.*

The present prospects of the enterprise are very bright. Already several buildings have been erected and others are under way. A boarding hall for the accommodation of the students has been ordered built to be ready for the spring of the school year October 1st. A street-car line has been projected and material ordered, connecting the city directly with the university campus, known as "the Bethany Heights street-car line." The prospective endowment is thought to be not less than one hundred and sixty-five thousand dollars. Twenty-five thousand of this amount is a donation by J. J. Briscoe, which is designed to be used as a basis of support for the Chair of Biblical Literature.

THE NEBRASKA WESLEYAN UNIVERSITY.

By an agreement entered into by the three Nebraska Annual Conferences of the Methodist Episcopal Church a commission, was appointed, consisting of members of each Conference and representatives of the Boards of Trustees of the then existing colleges, for the purpose of considering the matter of locating a central university, under the control and patronage of the Methodist Episcopal Church in Nebraska.

The commission met in Lincoln, in December, 1886, and selected Lincoln as the location of the future university. Trustees were chosen, and they entered upon the work of preparation at once.

The corner-stone of the first university structure was laid in September, 1887, and the institution was opened for students in September, 1888.

The property of the university consists of an endowment fund of one hundred thousand dollars, and five hundred lots in University Place, and a campus of forty-four acres.

THE WESLEYAN UNIVERSITY.

The cost of the building was about seventy-five thousand dollars. The building is fully completed, and is being thoroughly furnished for the best class of work.

There are three regular courses of study—classical, scientific, and philosophical—besides complete courses in music, art, and elocution. There are eight regular professors, besides tutors.

The total number of students enrolled since September, 1888, is about 150.

The village of "University Place" was incorporated in 1888, and is rapidly developing as a first class educational center. The elements that cluster about it are such as to insure its future character as a village of exceptional morality and intelligence.

The Nebraska Wesleyan University, by the terms of the "Plans of Agreement" adopted by the "commission," became the head of all the colleges, academies, and other schools, existing or to be hereafter organized under the control of the Methodist Episcopal Church in Nebraska.

THE LINCOLN BUSINESS COLLEGE.

The Lincoln Business College was founded in 1884 by Prof. F. F. Roose. The following year Prof. D. R. Lillibridge was admitted, and since that date the college has been conducted under the firm name of Lillibridge & Roose. It has been uniformly successful, its patronage growing constantly and the scope and efficiency of its instruction improving all the time. It is now recognized as one of the best schools of its class in the West, possessing a complete and thorough business course, including full short hand, normal, penmanship, type-writing, and telegraphic departments. That it is a superior school is shown by the fact that its attendance was six hundred students during the past year. The entire third floor of the Academy of Music block, at the southwest corner of Eleventh and O streets, is now required for the accommodation of the various departments. Students attend this excellent school of practical instruction from Nebraska, Colorado, Dakota, Kansas, Iowa, Illinois, and Minnesota, those States being its regular field of patronage. Occasional students come from all parts of the Union. Seven teachers are employed regularly in the college.

The graduates of its various departments readily find employment in the lines of work for which the school has given them special training. In securing situations the managers of the institution offer constant and cheerful assistance. The Lincoln Business College is one of the most excellent institutions of this city. Messrs. Lillibridge and Roose are among our most popular business men and citizens. Mr. Lillibridge is now Commander of Appomattox Post of the Grand Army of the Republic, and holds other prominent social positions. Mr. Roose is Deputy Head Consul of the Head Camp of Modern Woodmen of America, the highest official, save one, in that order. He is also a prominent member in other orders.

THE CATHOLIC SCHOOLS.

One of the successful schools of the city is the Catholic Seminary, located east of Fourteenth street, between U and V. The building was originally built by a stock company as a dormitory for the State University, but it did not pay, and was sold at sheriff's sale in 1882, and was bid in by Mr. John Fitzgerald. He sold it to the Sisters of

the Holy Child Jesus, who opened a general school there, and have conducted it ever since. For some time it did not fully pay expenses, and Mr. Fitzgerald generously supplied the shortage from his own pocket. It now is self-sustaining. Mrs. John Fitzgerald has labored constantly to encourage the school, and establish it; and owing largely to her kind offices, and the good work done by the sisters, the school has become one of the permanent and growing institutions of Lincoln. It will continue partly a general and partly a select school until September, 1890, when the parochial school building, now being erected near the pro-cathedral, at the northeast corner of M and Thirteenth streets, under the direction of Rt. Rev. Bishop Bonacum, will be completed.

This building will cost about $35,000, and a school with preparatory and academic courses will open there in the fall of 1890, for young men. It will be conducted by the Brothers of the Christian Schools, and will open with a corps of five teachers. The curriculum will include a full commercial course of study and other practical instruction. When this school is opened the grade of instruction in the young ladies' academy will be raised, the advancement having now been made in part, with a high standard of excellence in every particular. Young ladies from all parts of Nebraska, without regard to religious belief, will be received and taught on equal terms.

OTHER SCHOOLS.

An important educational institution is now being founded by Prof. O. B. Howell, of this city. This is the Nebraska Conservatory of Music. A three-story building of cut stone and brick, 50 x 132 feet, with massive towers, is being erected at the southeast corner of L and Thirteenth streets, in which is to be opened, this fall, a college of music and fine arts. The conservatory will be incorporated under the laws of the State, with a Board of Trustees, and graduates will receive diplomas. Students who are given special training as teachers will receive certificates.

A full corps of the best teachers will be engaged. Each department will be in charge of a principal, who will be assisted by competent instructors. Private instruction will also be given. A home will be furnished in the building for young ladies attending from a distance. This home will be under the supervision of the director, preceptress, and matron. At the beginning of each school year one free scholarship will be given some person in the State who has natural ability but not the means to acquire a musical education.

It is needless to state that this institution will be an important addition to the educational advantages of Lincoln, and, indeed, of the entire State. Professor Howell is a man of energy and ability, and will doubtless make the conservatory successful.

In this connection it is proper to state that in 1887 the first of a series of annual musical festivals was attempted, and it was so successful that it was repeated and improved in 1888, and again in the spring of 1889. The last festival was received with every mark of popular approval, and drew crowded houses for three successive nights. Such music as the "Hallelujah Chorus," and some of the famous oratorios, were rendered by able singers from abroad, assisted by the best home talent. The credit for the success of these musical events was largely due to Mrs. P. V. M. Raymond, a most estimable lady of Lincoln.

Elder Johnson established a denominational school for the Seventh-day Adventist Church, at the corner of Fifteenth and E streets, in 1887, which still continues, with a moderate attendance.

A number of private schools of more than ordinary excellence are also conducted.

It will be seen from the foregoing that Lincoln's claim of being the educational center of the West is well founded, and that the pride of her people in their institutions of learning is fully justified by the facts as they exist to-day. And the future holds much in store.

CHAPTER XVIII.

LINCOLN'S CHURCHES—THE BROOKLYN OF THE WEST—HISTORICAL SKETCHES OF ALL THE CHURCHES OF THE CITY—THE Y. M. C. A. ORGANIZATION.

Lincoln is preëminently a city of churches. As an educational center the city is not equaled in the West. And while this is true, it is equally true that no city in the West can equal this in the number of its church organizations and the beauty of its churches. The present chapter is devoted to historical sketches of the various churches, which number about forty. A former chapter has given an account of the very early church work in the town of Lancaster, and the present will deal with the churches now occupying the field.

In harmony with the spirit of Methodism, as soon as the emigrants' wagons had made a permanent halt on the prairies of Lancaster county, the Methodist Episcopal itinerant was on his track, and in 1867 Rev. Robt. Hawks was appointed to what was then called Lancaster Circuit. He formed a Methodist class at Lancaster, and at the close of the conference year, Lancaster class had sixteen members. During the year 1867, the town Lancaster was changed to Lincoln, and the capital of the State located at Lincoln. No sooner was this done than the prophetic eye of Methodism took in the situation, and was laying plans to meet the emergency. In the spring of 1868, Lancaster class was made a station, and the society named the First M. E. Church of Lincoln, and Rev. H. T. Davis was appointed its pastor. When Elder Davis arrived on the ground he found a society of sixteen members, a small shell of a church on Tenth street, just inclosed, with a $400 mortgage on it, and no parsonage. Among the sixteen original members can be mentioned Captain Baird and wife, John Cadman and wife, Wm. Cadman, A. K. White and wife, J. Kimball and wife, Mrs. J. Schoolcraft, with J. Kimball as class leader. At the end of the first year the little church on Tenth street was too small for the people. It was cleared of the $400 mortgage and sold for school purposes, and a larger building, costing

$3,000, built on the site the large St. Paul stone church now occupies. Elder Davis stayed three years, and closed his pastorate with a membership of 202. Rev. J. J. Roberts was the next pastor. He came in 1871, from the Genesee Conference, N. Y. He came to Nebraska with hopes of improving his health, which was poor; but instead of his health being improved, he continued to grow worse, and at the end of one year he was compelled to give up work. His pastorate, though short, was successful, the membership having grown to 300, and a parsonage having been built—the present parsonage, less an addition since made. In 1872, Rev. G. S. Alexander was appointed to this church, and his pastorate is remembered because of the prominent part he took in the Woman's Crusade. In 1874, Rev. W. B. Slaughter was sent to the Lincoln M. E. Church. He came from Brownville and remained three years, the full pastoral term. His pastorate was a very successful one, and the increase in membership, and the growing audiences, demanded more room, and another wing was added to the church. Mr. Slaughter was succeeded by the Rev. H. S. Henderson, of Iowa, who came in 1877, and served the church two years. The Young People's Meeting was organized during Mr. Henderson's pastorate, with Dr. Paine as leader. Rev. A. C. Williams was the next pastor. He came in 1879, and remained the full pastoral term, three years. The A street society was formed during Mr. Williams's term, and a church built, but this was done contrary to his judgment and wishes. There was quite an opposition to the movement, though a majority thought the time had come for this church to enlarge its borders and establish another church. Owing to the strong opposition to the movement, or from some other cause, this church made no growth or advancement till, at a later day, it was moved and changed to Trinity, as will hereafter be noticed. Rev. R. N. McKaig succeeded Rev. Williams in 1882. Rev. McKaig was an inveterate worker, and the church took a new impetus at once on his arrival. The congregation grew, and the question of a new church, which had been contemplated during Rev. Williams's pastorate, now revived, and the sentiment for a new church was strong. On April 23, 1883, an official meeting of the church was held, and it was decided to proceed at once to the erection of a new house of worship. Committees were then appointed to look after the various departments of the work. On June 11th the plans of a Mr. Wilcox, of Minneapolis, were accepted, the cost of the proposed building to be $25,000. Excavating for the new church was begun on July 1st. It was soon found that the church would cost much more than contemplated, but it was decided to go on with the work as arranged, and a committee was appointed to solicit subscriptions for the excess of cost. The corner-stone of the church was laid by Dr. Marine, since pastor of the church, in the spring of 1884, and the church was dedicated by Bishop Bowman on Sunday, August 23, 1885. The church cost $45,000 instead of $25,000, but this amount was soon paid in, leaving the church free from debt. This church was then called, as it had first been named, the First M. E. Church, which name was changed, in the fall of 1883, to the St. Paul M. E. Church.

Rev. C. F. Creighton, of Circleville, Ohio, succeeded Rev. Mr. Williams by appointment. He came in 1885, and remained two years, being elected Chancellor of the Nebraska Wesleyan University in the fall of 1887. The first year of Rev. Creighton's pastorate was doubtless the most successful in the history of the church. It was during this year that the great Bitler revival took place. This large revival swelled the church membership, including the probationers received from the meeting, to about 1,200. This large membership was too much for one pastor, and Rev. J. S. Bitler, the evangelist, was elected as assistant pastor till conference. It was during this year, on March 19th, that the church decided to build a new church, east of the Antelope. A site was selected, and a temporary tabernacle erected for services till a new church could be built. This new church was commenced on the corner of R and Twenty-seventh streets, and work on it was pushed with all possible speed. In less than four months from its commencement it was ready to be turned over to the trustees.

At the annual conference held the following September, J. T. Minehart was appointed pastor of the new church. The society was named Grace M. E. Church, and the new church building, costing $11,000, was dedicated September 19th, 1889, by Bishop Warren, free from debt. The second year of Rev. Creighton's pastorate, 1886, was an eventful one. Grace Church had become well established, and was moving on, but still there were calls from South Lincoln and West Lincoln for help on new churches, and during this year Trinity M. E. Church was established, which absorbed the old

A street church, heretofore mentioned. A new site was selected, and a new church built on the corner of A and Sixteenth streets. At the next conference, Rev. H. T. Davis, the present pastor, was appointed to Trinity Church, and since Elder Davis's connection with it, it has steadily grown, and is to-day one of the most prosperous church societies in the city, having a membership of upward of 260.

This same year, Asbury M. E. Church, at West Lincoln, was built by the assistance and under the guardianship of St. Paul M. E. Church. This was dedicated in November, 1887, and Rev. Clay Cox was appointed its pastor. This church cost, with furniture, about $2,000. The Nebraska Wesleyan University thrust itself on St. Paul Church this year, and its pastor was the leading spirit in the interests of Lincoln, and every one seemed to look to him for leadership.

When the university was located, Dr. Creighton was elected its president, and resigned the pastorate of St. Paul's. He was succeeded by Dr. Marine, who was transferred from the Indiana conference. His transfer was a very unfortunate one, on account of his health. The church, especially at the time of his coming, needed a man of great physical activity to shepherd the people and gather up the scattered ones. Dr. Marine took sick in the summer of the first year, which developed into brain trouble, and for weeks he laid at death's door. He finally recovered, contrary to the expectations of every one, and was able to attend the annual conference. He thought he was as well as ever, and on the statement of his physician that he was able to take the work, he was returned to St. Paul Church for the second year.

On September 10th, 1888, W. H. Prescott was elected by the official board as associate pastor and financial secretary, and was appointed by the Presiding Elder. On the return of Dr. Marine for the second year, he found himself able to occupy the pulpit only occasionally, and he soon was taken down with another serious attack of brain trouble, which entirely unfitted him for the duties of pastor. The official board granted him a vacation of three months, for him to go East, in hopes of his recovery. On February 4th, 1888, Rev. W. H. Prescott resigned as assistant pastor and financial secretary. The pulpit was supplied by transient ministers for several months. Dr. Marine's health was made worse by his trip East, and he soon returned, worse

ST. PAUL M. E. CHURCH.

than when he left. It now being evident to himself that he would not be able to assume his duties again, he tendered his resignation as pastor, which was accepted April 1st, 1888. The official board then requested the Presiding Elder, with the aid of the Bishop, to secure a new pastor for St. Paul Church as soon as possible, and at a meeting of the Bishops at Delaware, Ohio, in May, several united in recommending Rev. F. S. Stein, of Milwaukee, Wis., who was appointed. His transfer to the Nebraska Conference was arranged, and on June 1, 1889, Rev. Stein was on the ground as pastor. The membership of St. Paul's is now nearly 600.

The Rev. Father Emmanuel Hartig, O. S. B., the present German pastor of Nebraska City, is the founder of the Catholic Church of Lincoln. He was born at Inchenhofer, Bavaria, May 1, 1830. In September, 1857, he came to the United States, and went to St. Vincent's monastery, Westmoreland county, Penn. Here he remained until September, 1860, when Rt. Rev. Abbott Wimmer sent him to Atchison, Kansas. At this place he was ordained priest by Rt. Rev. John Miege, first Bishop of Leavenworth, July 10, 1861. His Superior, Rev. Augustine Wirth, sent him on the same day to take charge of Nebraska City mission. From Nebraska City he administered for several years to the spiritual needs of all the Catholics in the South Platte country, including Salt creek. When, in 1867, Lincoln became the capital of the State of Nebraska, he came hither in the interests of his charge. He found but few houses in Lincoln; at one of these, the house of Mr. Daily, he held service until the erection of the first church, in 1868, a frame building, 24x50, costing $1,000. On the completion of this church Lincoln had service once a month. Rev. Father Hartig being no longer able to operate successfully over so broad a field, Rt. Rev. Bishop Fink sent him an assistant in the person of Rev. Michael Kaumley. From August, 1868, to February, 1869, either Rev. Father Hartig or Rev. Father Kaumley held service in Lincoln once a month. At the latter date, Rev. Father Kaumley was recalled and his place taken by Rev. Father Michael Hofmeyer, of St. Vincent's Abbey, Westmorland county, Penn. For some time he attended Lincoln from Nebraska City, but finally located at the capital, and thus became the first resident Roman Catholic priest of our city. He added thirty feet to the church and began to keep the parish records of Lincoln. Until his arrival the records had been kept at Nebraska City. The first marriage mentioned in the Lincoln records is that of Silas Huff and Catherine Curtin, in the presence of Thos. G. Murphy and Honora Murphy, Rev. Father Hofmeyer being the minister. The first interment was that of Henry Armon, who died in October, 1869. The first recorded baptism took place September 26, 1869. The last record made by Rev. Father Hofmeyer is that of a marriage on December 26, 1870. During his charge at Lincoln he performed seven matrimonial and sixty-five baptismal services.

Rev. Father Hofmeyer was succeeded by Rev. William Kelly. Rev. Father Kelly's first recorded act is that of the marriage of John J. Butler and Mary J. Kennedy, which took place, May 16, 1871; his last official act was a baptism on April 29, 1874.

From this date the growth of the church has been steady, keeping pace with all the other interests of our city.

Within the past ten years the growth of the Catholic population of Lincoln and of the whole South Platte country became so pronounced that the Rt. Rev. James O'Connor, Bishop of Omaha, petitioned the Bishops of the Third Plenary Council, of Baltimore, to erect the South Platte country into an independent diocese, with the See at Lincoln. The wishes of the learned prelate were acceded to. Rt. Rev. Thomas Bonacum was appointed to the new See.

Rt. Rev. Thomas Bonacum was born near Thurles, Tipperary county, Ireland, January 29, 1847. During his infancy his parents emigrated to the United States and settled at St. Louis. His early education was conducted by the Christian Brothers until his fifteenth year, when he entered the ecclesiastical seminary of St. Francis de Sales, near Milwaukee, Wis. At this renowned institution, during a period of six years, he applied himself to the classics, English literature, and the sciences. He devoted himself to the studies of philosophy and theology under the Lazarist Fathers, at Cape Girardeau, Mo., until the time of his ordination. He was ordained June 18, 1870, at St. Louis. Some time after this he went to Würzburg, Bavaria, and spent a number of years in the profound theological course, the study of canon law, and German literature. At the end of this course he made the tour of Europe. When he returned to the United States, he successively had charge of various missions, all of

THE CATHOLIC PRO-CATHEDRAL.

which he administered in a manner commendable to himself, beneficial to the interests of religion, and satisfactory to his ecclesiastical superiors. In 1881, as an appreciation of his success in more contracted fields, he was appointed rector of the very important parish of the Holy Name of Jesus, in St. Louis. Here he continued to labor successfully until his election to the See of Lincoln.

In 1884, The Most Rt. Rev. Richard Kenrick chose Rev. Father Bonacum as one of the two theologians who always go with a Bishop to a council. This choice, coming from one of so distinguished sagacity, marked the Rev. Father Bonacum as one who would soon receive even still more remarkable favors. The subsequent facts soon verified this anticipation. The fathers of the Third Plenary Council, of Baltimore, decreed to divide the diocese of Alton, locating the See at Belleville, in Southern Illinois. By the unanimous consent of the assembled fathers, Rev. Father Bonacum was chosen to preside over the new diocese. Rome, at that time, did not ratify the erection of the proposed See, and the matter was held in abeyance. Nevertheless Leo XIII did not overlook the young candidate proposed by the council of Baltimore. When, therefore, the request of Rt. Rev. Bishop O'Connor was granted by Rome, Rev. Father Bonacum, the previous choice of the fathers of the council for Belleville, was appointed Bishop of the See of Lincoln.

The bulls were issued August 9, 1887, by Leo XIII, and the consecration took place November 30, 1887, at St. Louis, in St. John's pro-cathedral, in the presence of a vast concourse of prelates, clergy, and laity. The Venerable Peter Richard Kenrick, Archbishop of St. Louis, was the consecrator. The general approval of the choice of Rome was evidenced by the largest gathering of prelates and priests that ever took place on a similar occasion in that sacred edifice.

Rt. Rev. Bishop Bonacum's reception, which took place at Funke's opera house, December 20, 1887, will long be remembered by all who were present as one of the most notable events connected with the history of our city. With the coming to Lincoln of the Rt. Rev. Bishop Bonacum, a new and powerful energy was infused into all the Catholic enterprises of the South Platte country. Not less than thirty churches have been dedicated in the period of twenty months. But it is in the city of his See, as one would naturally expect, that the most remarkable proofs of his zeal are to be found. The enlargement of the pro-cathedral, the furnishing and decoration of the interior, the procuring of suitable sacred vestments, etc., were the first objects of his solicitude. All these ends were attained at a cost of about $18,000. While this work was in progress, the organization of a German congregation, and the building of St. Francis de Sales Church for this people, was part of his occupation. The erection of St. Francis de Sales Church has effected a complete reunion and revival of German Catholic interests. The Rt. Rev. Bishop soon saw the great need of a hospital in so large a city as ours, and set himself to the task of getting one worth his accustomed energy and firmness of purpose. With this object, he purchased the beautiful home and grounds of J. A. Buckstaff, for $20,000. He gave charge of the sick to the Sisters of St. Francis, trained nurses, who opened the hospital September 1, 1889. The purchase was made June 15, 1889.

On the acquisition of this handsome property, he entered into a contract with the city by which he assumed the care of the sick for a period of seven years. The terms of the contract on the Bishop's part are exceedingly moderate. The getting of the hospital was a gratification to all humane people.

Weighty and various as these cares were, they could not divert the mind of the Bishop from one of the subjects of his deepest anxiety: the establishment and promotion of the cause of Christian education among his people. Reverently obedient to the instructions of the Third Plenary Council, of Baltimore, that the Bishops of the United States should supply all parishes with schools, he commenced the splendid school building which is in course of erection between the pro-cathedral and the pastoral residence, on M street. Whatever skill and experience can devise will be done to make the edifice one of the most complete of its kind in the State. The cost will range between $20,000 and $25,000. The Rt. Rev. Bishop has a very efficient body of clergymen, on whom he was dependent for the accomplishment of the works we have enumerated.

Rt. Rev. Bishop Bonacum is an early riser and late worker; very methodical in all that he does. He is simple in all his tastes and habits. In manner he is dignified and courteous; in etiquette he is very considerate of the wishes of others. Hospitality is a pronounced trait of the Bishop's. As a prelate he is very broad and far-seeing, thoroughly equipped with all the spiritual and worldly knowledge necessary for his exalted position. He has a mind which, while comprehensive, has a singular facility for grasping details. He is pliant enough when principle is not involved, but where it is a matter of right or justice, he is inflexible and inexorable.

The First Presbyterian Church is one of the most prominent, prosperous, and influential, of the leading churches of Lincoln. It was organized with eight members April 4, 1869, by Rev. J. C. Elliott, of Nebraska City. It was not until January, 1870, that the church secured the regular services of a minister, the Rev. H. P. Peck commencing his labors January 15, 1870, with "only five effective members" on the ground. January 26, 1871, Rev. H. P. Peck was elected the first pastor of this church, and was duly installed on the last Tuesday of April, 1871. The first church edifice was erected near the corner of Eleventh and J streets, on lots donated by the State, and was dedicated to the worship of Almighty God October 9, 1870, the Rev. T. H. Cleland, D. D., (then of Council Bluffs, Iowa,) preaching the sermon. This first sanctuary was built at a cost of $5,000, and with various improvements from time to time, continued to be the house of worship for the First Presbyterian Church until December, 1884. Ground was broken for the erection of the present church edifice at the southwest corner of Thirteenth and M streets, in April, 1884; its vestry room was completed in September, 1885, and was occupied as a place of worship till the middle of January, 1886, when the main auditorium was finished and immediately set apart to its sacred uses. This new and beautiful sanctuary, costing $40,000, was formally dedicated to the worship of God July 18, 1886, the Rev. A. V. V. Raymond, D. D., (now of Albany, N. Y.,) preaching the sermon.

The following minsiters have served the church either as pastor or stated supply:

Rev. A. P. Peck.......................January, 1870,.......................June, 1874.
Rev. J. W. Ellis........................April, 1875.......................March, 1876.
Rev. S. W. Weller....................April, 1876.......................July, 1878.
Rev. James Kemlo...................January, 1879.......................December, 1879.
Rev. John O. Gordon................July, 1880.......................November, 1882.
Rev. Edward H. Curtis, D. D........January, 1883.......................

It now has a membership of nearly 500, and a large and successful Sunday School, at the First Church, of which Mr. Milton Scott is

THE FIRST PRESBYTERIAN CHURCH.

Superintendent, Mr. W. G. Maitland First and Miss L. W. Irwin Second Assistant Superintendent. Mr. Charles A. Hanna is Secretary and Treasurer. Its Ladies' Aid Society, Ladies' Missionary Band, Young Ladies' Mission Band, Young People's Society of Christian Endeavor, and Children's Bands, are all prosperous and doing good work. The officers of the First Church are as follows:

Edward H. Curtis, Pastor.

Elders—N. S. Scott, C. S. Clason, Wm. M. Clark, J. J. Turner, C. M. Leighton, C. A. Barker, John R. Clark, H. E. Hitchcock, J. K. Barr.

Trustees—T. H. McGahey, F. W. Bartruff, M. D. Welch, W. G. Maitland, C. A. Barker, W. H. McCreery, Wm. M. Clark, J. W. Winger, C. W. Lyman.

This denomination has also established a mission in North Lincoln, where a Sunday School is maintained, with Mr. —— —— Osborn as its Superintendent. A church will probably be organized there in the near future.

The First Presbyterian Church building is one of the six fine structures erected by the leading denominations of the city, costing on an average $45,000, exclusive of grounds, and taken together perhaps are not equaled in a city of twenty-two years of age on the continent. An additional half dozen costly and elegant church buildings exist in the city, although not so fine as the first six referred to. All the church buildings are of modern architecture, and exhibit great liberality on the part of the people of Lincoln.

In October, 1888, a number of persons interested in the work of the Presbyterian Church, met in a vacant store building near the corner of O and Twenty-seventh streets and organized a Sabbath School. At this meeting there were sixty-four persons enrolled as members of the school, and Mr. Thomas Marsland was chosen Superintendent, Mr. George G. Waite Secretary, and Mr. Almon Tower Treasurer, and a full corps of teachers selected, and classes organized. Preaching services were held in this store-room every Sabbath by different ministers until February 14, 1889, when the school moved into the basement of a church being erected on the corner of Twenty-sixth and P streets, on lots donated in part by William M. Clark. On the evening of March 13, 1889, those interested in the work convened and formally organized a church, to be known as the Second Presbyterian Church of Lincoln, Nebraska. This organization was entered into by forty-six charter members. The officers elected were as follows:

Elders.—Myron Tower, Thomas Marsland, W. C. Cunningham, and William M. Clark.

Trustees.—Walter Hoge, J. H. Mockett jr., George A. Seybolt, and H. C. Tullis.

On April 1, 1889, Rev. Charles E. Bradt, by invitation of the church, took charge of the work. The society has gone steadily on, until at present the church has an enrolled membership of eighty-seven, a Sabbath School numbering above 200, and a strong, growing, Young People's Society of Christian Endeavor. The Church is still worshiping in the basement of what is to be the lecture-room of the church building. This basement has been put in at a cost of about $1,200, with the hope that the superstructure may soon be erected to meet the growing demands of the church and congregation.

Prominent among the prosperous and influential religious societies of the city is the Congregational Church. The First Congregational Church, whose elegant building stands at the northwest corner of L and Thirteenth streets, is one of the pioneer religious organizations of the city. The Official Manual of the church for 1889 contains the following historical sketch:

"This church was organized August 19, 1866, with six members. At that time, according to the records of the Council assisting the organization, there were in the town seven buildings, viz., one seminary, four dwellings, one store, and one blacksmith shop.

" Rev. E. C. Taylor was pastor of the church from its organization until October, 1867. The members of the church at its organization were F. A. Bidwell, John S. Gregory, Mrs. Welthy P. Gregory, Mary E. Gregory, Philester Jessup, Mrs. Ann M. Langdon.

" Rev. Charles Little accepted a call to become pastor of the church on November 8, 1867, and continued until April, 1870. During his ministry the first meeting-house was erected. It was built in 1868 and furnished in 1869. An Ecclesiastical Society, to have charge of financial affairs, was organized April 11, 1868, which surrendered its authority to the church and disbanded January 16, 1873. The church was incorporated January 23, 1873. Rev. Lebbeus B. Fifield was called to the pastorate September 12, 1870, and resigned June 4, 1872.

THE FIRST CONGREGATIONAL CHURCH.

August 1, 1872. Rev. Samuel R. Dimock was asked to preach. He was installed by Council January 2, 1873, and dismissed on advice of Council January 15, 1875. During his pastorate (1873) the meeting-house was considerably enlarged. A call was extended to Rev. Lewis Gregory September 16, 1875. He was installed by Council November 23, 1876. The church building was repaired and refurnished in 1878. April 29, 1883, the church voted to build a new meeting-house. The plan for the present building was adopted September 20, 1883. Work began November 6, 1883. The basement and chapel were occupied for Sunday services January 17, 1886, and the auditorium on February 7, 1886. The building was formally dedicated January 9, 1887.

"Since its organization different officers have served the church in order of time as follows:

"*Clerks.*—J. S. Gregory, J. P. Hebard.

"*Deacons.*—F. A. Bidwell, E. J. Cartlidge, L. H. Fuller, G. S. Harris, J. S. Gregory, Geo. McLean, J. C. Leonard, W. C. Hawley, Geo. McMillan, Elisha Doolittle, M. B. Cheney, W. Q. Bell, S. H. Burnham.

"*Trustees.*—F. A. Bidwell, W. R. Field, A. L. Palmer, Lindus Cody, S. M. Walker, O. W. Merrill, J. P. Hebard, S. B. Galey, R. P. Beecher, Geo. S. Harris, S. L. Coffin, J. C. Leonard, H. C. Babcock, T. H. Leavitt, Geo. McMillan, L. E. Brown, W. W. Peet, Charles West, T. F. Hardenburg, A. S. Raymond, M. B. Cheney, A. E. Hargreaves, B. F. Bailey.

"*Treasurers.*—Albert Biles, J. R. Webster, L. A. Groff, Aldus Cody, R. P. Beecher, E. J. Cartlidge, Geo. McLean, T. F. Hardenburg, Elisha Doolittle, Charles West, J. C. Leonard, T. H. Leavitt, J. W. Bell, W. Q. Bell."

The First Congregational church now has between 300 and 400 members, maintains a large and prosperous Sunday School, and successful missionary societies and Society of Christian Endeavor.

During the first week in August, 1887, a low, rough board house was erected, at the instance of Rev. Lewis Gregory and under his direction, near the northwest corner of Seventeenth and A streets. The work of construction required but two days, and with the chairs to seat it, cost only about $200. On the following Sunday, services were held there, under the direction of Rev. E. S. Ralston, and religious exercises continued to be held there regularly until the first Sunday in November, 1887, when the society was organized as the Second Congregational Church of Lincoln, and it was so incorporated. But at the first business meeting in 1888, the name was changed to that of "Plymouth Congregational Church."

This primitive tabernacle first built was used as a meeting house until December, 1888, when the new church building, on the same corner, was so far completed that it could be used in part. On Easter Sunday, 1889, the main auditorium was first used. When fully completed this building will be a commodious, complete, and handsome structure, worth $10,000. The lots are valued at $5,000 more.

Rev. E. S. Ralston has had charge of this congregation from its organization, and was regularly installed as its pastor on May 8, 1888.

Plymouth Church now has a membership of over 100, and a Sunday School of about 200. The membership of both church and Sunday School is constantly growing. It has an active Society of Christian Endeavor, the second organized in Lincoln, the first having been founded in the First Congregational Church. Its Ladies' Aid and Missionary Society and Young Ladies' Missionary Society are doing good work.

The present officers of the church are: Rev. E. S. Ralston, Pastor; J. A. Wallingford, Clerk; W. A. Hackney, Treasurer. Trustees—J. A. Lippincott, W. A. Selleck, J. A. Wallingford, J. P. Walton, and W. A. Hackney. Deacons—J. A. Lippincott and Newton King.

A Congregational church mission is now doing active work on the north side of N street, between Twenty-first and Twenty-second. A Sunday-school is held there, of which Miss Jennie A. Cole is Superintendent. A small building was opened there for the mission on the last Sunday in July, its dimensions being about twenty-five by fifty feet. This mission promises to soon grow into the third organized Congregational society in Lincoln. It has been named the "Pilgrim Congregational Church."

The German Congregational Church was organized in the spring of 1889, by Rev. Adam Frandt, and services have been held at the corner of Eighth and J streets. Though one of the latest societies formed in the city, it appears to be prosperous and growing in membership.

The first service of the Episcopal church was held in Lincoln in May, 1868, by the Rev. R. W. Oliver, D. D. On the 17th day of November in the same year, the Rev. Geo. C. Betts, of Omaha, held the second service, and of those who were present only one was a member of the church. Subsequently the Rt. Rev. R. H. Clarkson, D. D., Bishop of the diocese, visited the city, holding services and preaching. About this time the Rev. William C. Bolmar was appointed missionary in charge. In January, 1869, steps were taken toward the organization of a parish. A meeting was held, at which were present: Michael Rudolph, A. F. Harvey, John Morris, J. J. Jones, H. S. Jennings, E. Godsall, A. C. Rudolph, John G. Morris, R. P. Cady, J. C. Hire, Wm. C. Heddleson, S. L. Culver, and J. S. Moots, who signed a petition which was sent to the Bishop, praying for permission to organize a parish, under the title of "The Church of the Holy Trinity." The Bishop's consent having been granted, on the 10th of May the same year another meeting was held, at which a parish organization was effected, by the election of a vestry consisting of Michael Rudolf and A. F. Harvey, warders; and J. J. Jones, A. C. Rudolf, H. J. Walsh, Dr. L. H. Robbins, and J. M. Bradford.

The parish was admitted into union with the council of the diocese in September of the same year. The congregation worshiped at various places in the city until 1870. The Rev. Mr. Bolmar left the parish in February, 1870, and in May of that year the Rev. Samuel Goodale took charge. Measures were at once adopted for the erection of a suitable place of worship, and a sufficient sum was subscribed to proceed immediately with the work.

A church edifice costing $4,000 was erected at the corner of J and Twelfth streets, on lots belonging to the parish. It was consecrated March 5, 1871. At the end of a year the Rev. R. C. Talbott, now at Brownville, succeeded the Rev. S. Goodale, and continued in the rectorship until October, 1875. In April, 1876, the Rev. C. C. Harris became the fourth rector, and served the parish for seven years. During that time many improvements were made. A rectory was built, trees were planted, the church was repainted, a pipe organ was purchased, the church edifice enlarged, and the number of communicants rose to one hundred and four.

The Rev. J. T. Wright came in November, 1883, and after one year gave way to the Rev. Alex. Allen. During the rectorship of

Mr. Allen steps were taken for the erection of a new and larger church. With this in view, Mr. Guy A. Brown, a most zealous and generous churchman, issued a small parish paper, the purpose of which was to awaken interest in the enterprise. On June 14, 1888, the cornerstone of the new church was laid by the Grand Lodge of Freemasons of Nebraska, Bishop Worthington also taking a prominent part in the ceremonies. The building is just about completed at this writing. It is built of Colorado red sandstone, Gothic, cruciform; will cost about $35,000, and will accommodate about 500 people. Holy Trinity Church is the mother of two other organizations in the city. In the spring of 1888 the old church was removed to a lot on Twelfth street, between U and V, and a congregation was organized under the ministry of the Rev. R. L. Stevens, and took the name of "The Church of the Holy Comforter. In 1889 the Holy Trinity Chapter of St. Andrew's Brotherhood came into possession of the house of worship which had been used by the Baptists, and moved it to a lot on the corner of Washington and Eighth streets. Regular services are held here by the rector of Holy Trinity and a lay reader.

The working agencies of the church of the Holy Trinity at this time are: 1. The Holy Trinity Chapter of St. Andrew's Brotherhood, thirty-six members. 2. The Woman's Aid Society, forty members. 3. The Woman's Auxiliary to the Board of Missions, 110 contributors. 4. The Altar Guild, twenty-eight members.

There are about 120 children in the Sunday School, of which Mr. W. L. Murphy is Superintendent; about 150 communicants, and about 600 individuals connected with the parish.

At this time, July, 1889, the vestry consists of the following named gentlemen:

H. J. Walsh, Sen. Warden; J. C. Kier, Jun. Warden; D. R. Lillibridge, Secretary; W. L. Murphy, Treasurer; R. H. Oakley, J. F. Barnard, E. P. Holmes, James Hearn, and C. H. Rudge. The Rev. John Hewith became rector March 1, 1889, before the completion of the new church.

Prominent among the religious denominations of the city is the First Baptist Church. The Baptist Society is one of the most prosperous and progressive in the city, and its new edifice at the northwest corner of K and Fourteenth streets is a beautiful structure costing about

THE FIRST BAPTIST CHURCH.

$40,000. The new and handsome parsonage is situated on a lot immediately west of the church. A brief historical sketch of this society in Lincoln is here given.

The First Baptist Church of Lincoln, Neb., was organized August 22, 1869, with fourteen members. The first pastor was Rev. O. T. Conger, who began his labors here in June, 1870, and remained four and one-half years, until January, 1875. During his pastorate the church edifice on the corner of Eleventh and L streets was erected, and 169 persons were received as members of the church.

In October, 1875, Rev. S. M. Cramblet became the pastor, and remained two years, during which time fifty-six members were received.

In May, 1875, Rev. W. Sanford Gee began a pastorate of three and one-third years, during which the parsonage on L street was built, and 110 members were received.

In January, 1882, Rev. Dr. Chaffee began his pastorate, which continued one and three-fourths years, during which 115 members were received.

May 4, 1884, Rev. C. C. Pierce began his labors with this church. During the latter part of his pastorate, a large subscription for the purpose of erecting a new church edifice was secured, and three lots at the corner of K and 14th streets were purchased. Rev. Mr. Pierce resigned September 5, 1886, having received 120 members into the church during his pastorate.

The church immediately extended a call to Rev. O. A. Williams, who accepted it, and began his labors in November, 1886. Under his ministry the church has been very prosperous. About 200 members have been added since he commenced his pastorate here; the large church building has been erected, and branches of the denomination have been organized in other parts of the city, of which he has general charge. A prosperous Sunday School is maintained, besides the usual subordinate organizations that are associated with all leading church societies. The membership is large and numbers many of our best and most influential people.

The officers of the First church are as follows:

Rev. O. A. Williams, Pastor; S. P. Bingham, Treasurer; P. S. Chapman, Clerk; L. C. Humphrey, Treasurer of Building Fund. Board of Trustees: C. W. Sholes, chairman; Geo. H. Clarke, L. G. M. Baldwin, L. C. Humphrey, E. E. Bennett.

Three Baptist Missions have been organized in the city, where Sunday Schools are maintained, and of which Rev. O. A. Williams is the mission pastor. One of these missions is at the corner of J and Twentieth streets, Mr. L. G. M. Baldwin being Superintendent of its Sunday School. The North Lincoln Mission is quite prosperous, and will soon build a church to cost $3,000. Mr. H. J. Humphrey is Superintendent of its Sunday School, which is held at the corner of Twelfth and Butler avenue.

The East Lincoln Mission is located at the corner of Twenty-seventh and W streets, and Mr. S. S. McKinney is Superintendent of its Sunday School.

The Central Church of Christ in the City of Lincoln was organized with twenty-eight charter members, on January 24th, 1869. Their first place of meeting was in the house of J. M. Yearnshaw, who was also their first regular minister. Miss Julia McCoy, now Mrs. Marshall, and still a member of this congregation, was the first person immersed by them in Lincoln. The private house becoming too small, their place of meeting was changed to the old capitol building, and here they spent the fall and winter of '69. Joseph Robinson was the first elder of the church, and Bros. Hawk and Akin its first deacons. On July 3d, 1869, out at Crabb's mill, on Salt creek, the initial steps were taken toward the erection of a house of worship. G. W. French, J. M. Yearnshaw, and J. H. Hawk, were appointed a building committee. Slowly, and yet with patient persistence, the work went on, until on July 3d, 1870, the church house now standing on the northwest corner of K and Tenth streets was dedicated. Here, with varying success and failure, with mingling lights and shadows, the church has worshiped until this writing.

On April 23, 1871, the first Sunday School of any moment was organized, with J. Z. Briscoe as Superintendent and C. C. Munson as assistant.

Since the time of J. M. Yearnshaw the church has enjoyed the pastoral labors of D. R. Dungan, J. Z. Briscoe, J. B. Johnson, J. Mad. Williams, J. M. Streator, B. F. Bush, Chas. Crowther, R. E. Swartz, R. H. Ingram, and Chas. B. Newman, the last named occupying its pulpit now.

The history of the Church of Christ in Lincoln would be sadly in-

THE CHRISTIAN CHURCH.

complete without special mention of Bro. Barrow's counsel and patient, helpful care ever since its organization.

The history of the years from '71 until '87 is about such as comes to the average church. The church now numbers some 460. It has a house and lot in West Lincoln, and also a good lot in East Lincoln. Regular preaching and Sunday school services are held at all of these places, and are well attended.

The church has an "Auxiliary to the Christian Woman's Board of Missions," and an efficient "Aid Society." It has a large "Young People's Society of Christian Endeavor," and a "Young Ladies' Mission Band." Its present official board comprises the following:

Elders.—J. Z. Briscoe, Geo. Leavitt, G. E. Barbar, E. D. Harris.

Deacons.—Porter Hedge, J. M. Webber, J. A. Reynolds, C. R. Van Duyn, W. S. Mills, S. S. Young, S. M. Dotson, L. G. Leavitt.

Deaconesses.—Mrs. Martha Hallett, Mrs. Martha Hedge.

Evangelists.—Chas. B. Newman, R. W. Abberly.

Of its Sunday School Chas. C. Munson is the efficient Superintendent.

In the fall of 1886, realizing that it would soon be necessary to provide larger and more commodious quarters, the church purchased two lots on the northeast corner of K and Fourteenth streets, and early in 1887 steps were taken looking toward the erection of a new house of worship. Finally, after much consultation and delay, on October 25, 1887, plans were chosen and a building committee, consisting of J. Z. Briscoe, G. E. Barber, O. C. Bell, Porter Hedge, and C. C. Munson, was chosen. The corner-stone was laid July 3, 1888, President A. R. Benton, of Indianapolis, making the address. The church was dedicated on Sunday, August 25, 1889, with impressive services. It is a most beautiful structure, one of which the church may well be proud.

The First Free Baptist Church of Lincoln was organized May 2, 1886, with eighteen members, electing Rev. A. F. Bryant pastor, A. D. Baker deacon, and G. W. Sisson secretary.

Land was purchased on the corner of F and Fourteenth streets, and a church house erected in the same year of the organization, and was occupied, though not wholly completed. Meanwhile Rev. Bryant removed, and Rev. B. F. McKenney succeeded to the pastorate, remaining one year. Rev. O. E. Baker, of Providence, R. I., was elected, and commenced his labors with the church April 1st, 1888.

By the liberality of friends, and the aid of the Home Mission Board, the church house was completed and dedicated in June, 1888, the pastor preaching the sermon, and Rev. E. H. Curtis, D. D., of the First Presbyterian Church, and Rev. O. W. Williams, D. D., of the First Baptist Church, assisting.

The First Universalist Society of Lincoln was organized at the residence of J. D. Monell, September 1, 1870, with W. W. Holmes, S. J. Tuttle, J. N. Parker, Mrs. Sarah Parker, Mrs. Julia Brown, Mrs. Laura B. Pound, and Mrs. Mary Monell, as charter members. About this time the property now in the possession of the society, on the corner of Twelfth and H streets, was secured by grant from the Legislature of the State. A subscription was also begun, looking toward the erection of a chapel. In the meantime the society held occasional services for worship in the Senate Chamber, in the old Capitol building. During the month of December of this same year Rev. Asa Saxe, D. D., General Secretary of the Universalist denomination, visited Lincoln for the purpose of ascertaining whether it would be advisable to make this a missionary point. His decision was favorable to such a movement. Consequently, with the financial aid of the denomination, the society was able to call Rev. James Gerton, then of Illinois, to be its first pastor. He accepted the invitation, and began work in September, 1871. The following October the corner-stone of the chapel was laid, and on Sunday, June 23, 1872, it was dedicated.

All this was brought about largely through the efforts of one devoted woman, Mrs. Mary Monell. It was she who first gathered the few scattered Universalists in the place together. Unaided she raised the subscription to build the chapel; she collected the funds, saw that the work was done, and paid the bills. The early records of the society reveal the zeal and fidelity with which she did her work, the many difficulties with which she had to contend, and her final triumph. Mrs. Monell must always be looked upon as the patron saint of the First Universalist Society of Lincoln.

In 1873 the denomination was so badly crippled by the panic of the year before that it was unable to continue its financial aid to the society; and as the society was not strong enough to support a pastor of its own accord. Rev. Mr. Gerton, after remaining two years, was forced to resign his charge. For nearly ten years after this the society had no settled pastor. Preaching services were held only occasionally and as Universalist clergymen were passing through the city, or stopping in it for a short time. During a portion of this time the chapel was rented to other religious organizations. The society continued in existence, however, and in the spring of 1883 the trustees of the Universalist General Convention made arrangements with Rev. E. H. Chapin, the present pastor, to come to Lincoln and take charge of the work. Rev. Mr. Chapin has now been with the society something over six years, and during that time has quite thoroughly identified himself with the intellectual, moral, and benevolent, interests of the city. Year by year the society has continued to gather to itself numbers and strength. The parsonage, now standing on one of the church lots, was completed in 1886. Connected with the church as auxiliary organizations are the Unity Club, the Ladies' Aid Society, and the Young People's Missionary Association.

Trinity German Evangelical Lutheran Church was organized November 24, 1881, with five members, Rev. F. Koenig, now of Seward, Neb., presiding. The present pastor, H. Frincke, took charge of the congregation in April, 1882. During the first year services were held in a small church building corner N and Thirteenth, the present site of the new Y. M. C. A. rooms. The following three years the congregation assembled in the Universalist church, on Twelfth, between H and J streets. In the spring of 1886 the new church was occupied, located on H, between Thirteenth and Fourteenth streets. In the rear of this church building a school-room accommodating ninety pupils was built. This department of the church work is under the direction of teacher F. Hellmann, whose school now numbers seventy pupils, who attend the school daily, except Saturday and Sunday. This gentleman, together with the pastor, is sustained solely by the congregation.

The unaltered Augsburg Confession, and its Apology, the Formula of Concord, the two catechisms of Luther, the Apostolic, Nicene, and Athanasian Creeds, form the confessions of this church. It belongs to that great Lutheran organization, the Missouri Synod. The present officers are: Messrs. H. Herpolsheimer, H. Witte, Peter Grafelmann, trustees and elders. The status of the congregation is as follows: Souls, 400; voting members — *i.e.*, male members of and above the age of twenty-one years — 60; communicants — *i.e.*, all such as are allowed to partake of the Lord's Supper — 285. The current expenses amount to about $1,500 annually. The valuable property is free from all incumbrances. Services every Sunday at 10 A. M. and 3 P. M. Evening services every other Sunday at 8 P. M.

The African Methodist Episcopal Church was organized in 1872, by Rev. G. W. Gaines, Presiding Elder of the Nebraska district. The pioneer organization was composed of but eleven members. Its place of worship was located upon the north side of E street, between Tenth and Eleventh, in 1873, on lots donated by the State, where the home of the society still remains, including the parsonage. A large and handsome building is now being erected there, which will cost, when completed, $6,000.

The society is now in a prosperous condition, and has a growing membership, numbering 110. The Rev. J. W. Braxton is the pastor in charge. He is a popular and successful man with his people.

A prosperous Sunday School is now maintained by this society, comprising 100 scholars, with a library in connection therewith numbering four hundred volumes.

There are two other colored church societies in the city, but they are in a weak and disorganized condition.

Besides the churches already mentioned, there are a number not so well established, but which deserve a place in a descriptive sketch of Lincoln. Among these is the Mount Zion Baptist Church, located at the corner of F and Twelfth streets. This church maintains regular services and a pastor, Rev. J. L. Cohron.

Besides the German Evangelical Lutheran, there are other societies belonging to the Lutheran denomination. One is Our Savior's Danish, located at 216 South Twenty-third street, of which Rev. P. L. C. Hanson is pastor, and H. J. Nellson clerk. Another is the Swedish church, located on K, between Thirteenth and Fourteenth, Rev. F. N. Swanberg pastor. A third is St. Paul's German, at F and Thirteenth, Rev. H. Heiner pastor.

All these churches enjoy regular service, and support Sunday Schools.

The Swedish Methodist Society is just becoming well organized.

A prosperous church has been started at Wesleyan University, which maintains the usual services, and of which Dr. C. F. Creighton is pastor.

The Reformed Hebrew Congregation is the society of the leading Hebrew people of the city. S. Seligsohn is President, M. Oppenheimer Vice President, W. Meyer Secretary, and I. Oppenheimer Treasurer.

During the present year the Salvation Army disbanded.

The Seventh-day Adventists hold services at the corner of Fifteenth and E streets. Rev. L. A. Hooper is pastor.

The Swedish Mission is located at 233 South Ninth street, with Rev. C. G. F. Johnson as pastor.

The United Brethren Society holds its meetings at Eleventh and B streets. Rev. J. Olive pastor.

The Young Men's Christian Association of Lincoln was organized in January, 1880, with thirteen members. The following officers were elected: President, A. O. Geisinger; Vice President, Richard George; Secretary, W. W. Peet; Treasurer, M. L. Easterday.

Robert Weidensall, the veteran Secretary of the International Committee, was present at the organization, and has ever since had a deep interest in the progress of the association. After four years' experience the association decided that the only way to keep abreast with like associations in other cities was to employ a competent General Secretary. After considerable correspondence, and through the help of the International Committee, the present General Secretary, Jas. A. Dummett, was recommended as a suitable young man to carry forward the work. Mr. Dummett is a graduate of Adrain College, Michigan, and had been an active worker in the Pittsburgh, Penn., Y. M. C. A. for five years. On the sixth day of August, 1884, Mr. Dummett arrived in Lincoln, and during his five years of faithful and efficient service, has succeeded in building up one of the strongest associations west of Chicago. The association during the past five years has kept pace with the rapid growth of the city. When the present Secretary arrived the association was occupying rooms for which they were paying the sum of $12.50 per month, with a membership of one hundred. To-day the association is pleasantly situated in a handsome suite of six rooms in the McConnell block, 144 South Tenth street, with a present membership of five hundred. The association has entirely outgrown its present surroundings, and on the 24th day of July the contract was let for a $60,000 association building, to be erected on the southwest corner of N and Thirteenth streets, to be completed by September 1, 1890.

Y. M. C. A. BUILDING.

The building will be a very handsome structure, and when completed it will not only be an ornament to the city, but a great blessing to the multitudes of young men who need just such privileges as the association can offer them in a building specially adapted to its work.

The following well-known business men constitute the present officers and directors: J. H. Mockett sr., President; John R. Clark, First Vice President; S. H. Burnham, Second Vice President; John L. Doty, Third Vice President; Capt. J. W. Winger, Recording Secretary; M. L. Easterday, Treasurer. Dr. Benj. F. Bailey, A. R. Talbott, E. E. Bennett, Chas. West, J. J. Imhoff, A. S. Raymond, J. Z. Briscoe, A. H. Weir, C. C. Munson, Directors.

The following members of the board constitute the Building Committee: John R. Clark, Chairman; C. C. Munson, Secretary; A. H. Weir, Treasurer; Chas. West and A. R. Talbott. Ferdinand C. Fiske is the architect, and Louis Jensen the contractor.

CHAPTER XIX.

SECRET ORDERS—THE FIRST LODGE ORGANIZED IN LINCOLN—HISTORICAL SKETCH OF ALL THE PRINCIPAL ORDERS NOW IN THE CITY—OTHER SOCIETIES DESERVING MENTION.

The characteristic of man to plant his hearth-stone and religious institutions as soon as possible upon settling in a new country, manifests itself almost equally in reference to his social and benevolent institutions. Hence we find that almost as soon as the early residents of Lincoln had established their homes, secret orders were founded, the first one to set up its altars in the city being the Independent Order of Odd Fellows. The history of Odd Fellowship in Lincoln commences almost at the time of the founding of the city, the first lodge being organized on the 21st of April, 1868.

Two of the State Commissioners appointed to locate the capital— Gov. David Butler and Secretary of State Thomas Kennard—were members of the order in good standing. Their duties, however, in giving the initial impetus to a new State, and laying the foundation of its capital, occupied their time to such an extent that the organization of the first subordinate lodge was left mainly to other men and members.

The lodge first organized was Capital Lodge No. 11, and its charter was committed to the hands of W. H. Stubblefield, Max Rich, Samuel McClay, L. A. Onyett, and Samuel Leland. At the organization Max Rich was installed as N. G.; Samuel McClay, V. G.; Samuel Leland, Secretary; and L. A. Onyett, Treasurer. W. H. Stubblefield was appointed District Deputy Grand Master.

The lodge was instituted by the Hon. George H. Burgert, of Nebraska City, who was at that time Grand Master.

Three members were received into membership at that time, viz., L. Lavender, by deposit of card, and S. B. Pound and Seth Robinson by initiation.

The lodge was instituted in the limited second story of a frame building standing on the ground now known as No. 123 South Tenth street, the first floor being occupied as a drug store kept by Mr. Tingley.

On the 18th day of October, 1870, the Grand Lodge, I. O. O. F., of Nebraska, held its thirteenth annual session in Lincoln, using the Senate Chamber of the old capitol building.

At that session, upon the petition of Bros. M. Rich, S. McClay, John Lamb, R. A. Bain, Charles Hasbrouck, M. G. Bohanan; and Sisters S. E. Lamb, R. Oppenheimer, P. E. Helman, A. Bain, and L. E. Bax, a dispensation was given to organize a lodge of the degree of the Daughters of Rebekah, to be known as Charity Lodge No. 2.

On the evening of the 19th the lodge was duly instituted by Grand Master John Hamlin, supported by the officers and members of the Grand Lodge. After adjournment a reception and banquet was given the Grand Lodge and the members of No. 2, by Governor David Butler and his wife, at which many ladies and gentlemen of Lincoln were present. In memory of this occasion, and as an appreciation of its lasting fitness, the lodge has ever, with eminent success, kept up the social feature inaugurated on that evening.

In 1871, among the members of Capital Lodge and those of other lodges sojourning at Lincoln, a number were found who desired an organization in which they could work in the higher or encampment degrees of Oddfellowship. Accordingly, on the 7th day of April of that year, a charter was granted by the Grand Lodge of the United States, giving authority to organize a subordinate Encampment in Lincoln, to be known and hailed as Saline Encampment No. 4. On the 12th day of May the encampment was instituted by District Deputy Grand Sire St. John Goodrich, of Omaha.

The officers were Samuel M. Clay, C. P.; W. P. Ensey, H. P.; J. C. Ford, S. W.; M. G. Bohanan, J. W.; Charles Purcell, Scribe, and Isaac Oppenheimer, Treasurer.

Success has crowned its labors since the time of its organization.

On the first day of July, 1872, the Grand Encampment of the Patriarchal Branch I. O. O. F. of Nebraska, was instituted, in the hall of Capital Lodge, the hall being then located in the third story of No. 1023 O street. The Grand Encampment was composed of the Past Chief Patriarchs of the then five Subordinate Encampments in the State. It was instituted by St. John Goodrich, the District Deputy Grand Sire.

The grand officers were D. A. Cline, of No. 1, Grand Patriarch; John Hamlin, No. 1, Grand High Priest; W. L. Wells, No. 3, Grand Senior Warden; John Evans, No. 2, Grand Scribe; D. H. Wheeler, No. 3, Grand Treasurer; H. A. Wakefield, of No. 5, Grand Junior Warden; and St. John Goodrich, of No. 2, Grand Representative to the Grand Lodge of the United States.

In 1873 the order had progressed so far that it was deemed expedient to organize another lodge. Accordingly about the 1st of May fifteen members, belonging to as many different lodges in different parts of the county, united in a petition to the Grand Lodge of Nebraska for a new subordinate. The petition was granted, and on the 5th day of June, 1873, the lodge was instituted by D. D. Grand Sire St. John Goodrich, to be known as Lancaster Lodge No. 39.

The first officers were J. H. Wheeler, N. G.; J. C. Ford, V. G.; O. M. Druse, Secretary; and M. K. Fleming, Treasurer.

J. H. Harley was the first initiate. The lodge has succeeded according to expectations.

The next lodge, Germania No. 67, was instituted for the benefit of those who could best work in their native German vernacular. The lodge was instituted with ten charter members, on the 11th of December, 1877, by Hon. H. W. Parker, of Beatrice, who was Grand Master of the order at that time. The first officers were: George Webber, N. G.; G. Rasgarshik, V. G.; Aug. Droste, Secretary; and G. R. Wolf, Treasurer. Seven parties were initiated. The advantages it brought, and its success in more closely fraternizing a large number of the German element in Lincoln, demonstrated that the judgment that gave existence to the new lodge was well founded. It has, perhaps, dispensed as large a benefice, both material and attentive, as any lodge in the city.

March 29, 1881, a charter was granted for what is known among Odd Fellows as a degree lodge. On the evening of the same day it was instituted by Grand Secretary D. A. Cline, acting under a special commission. It was known as Magic Degree Lodge No. 2. It existed but a short time.

On the 14th of February, 1885, Ford Uniformed Degree Camp No. 2 was instituted by Isaac Oppenheimer, Grand Patriarch. The members procured an expensive uniform and acquired great proficiency in the peculiar drills of the order, which are of a military character. James Tyler was elected captain. This organization continued and prospered until March, 1887, when it was merged into an organization of more enlarged purpose and of much grander proportions, known as the Patriarchs Militant, I. O. O. F. The style of the uniform was materially changed. From that time Ford Uniformed Degree Camp No. 2 was, and still is, known as Canton Ford No. 2 P. M. Chevalier James Tyler again took the office of captain.

As Lincoln grew in size and importance as a city, so did the Independent Order of Odd Fellows as one of its benevolent and fraternal institutions, until a new lodge was deemed to be necessary. Accordingly, on the 22d day of January, 1886, Grand Master Arthur Gibson, of Fremont, placed the charter for Lincoln Lodge No. 138 in the hands of the following members: J. E. Douglas, L. C. Dunn, Charles J. Heffley, C. D. Hyatt, O. P. Dinges, E. T. Roberts, D. F. Dinges, A. H. Hutton, John Hill, S. M. Hartzell, S. W. Long, T. F. Lasch, J. D. Hurd, and W. D. Fowler, and organized them into a lodge. It prospered as all the lodges have up to this date.

In an organization where the beneficial feature distinguishes it particularly, each lodge must make it a chief object not only to have money in its treasury, but a reserve in the shape of real estate or in some productive form, so as to make good all its promises and pledges to members in their day of need. With such an object in view, numerous schemes were proposed and debated from time to time by the lodges. It was granted that something was needed which would at the same time afford accommodations as a lodge room and as a source of revenue. Until the spring of 1881 but little was accomplished. On the 3d day of May, 1881, articles of incorporation were adopted, executed, and filed, which brought into existence "The Odd Fellows' Hall Association, of Lincoln, Neb.," with a capital stock of $20,000. The stock was soon taken. On the 1st day of June the first regular meeting of the stockholders was held for the purpose of forming a permanent organization. At this meeting D. A. Cline was elected President; Charles T. Boggs, Secretary; W. W. Holmes, Treasurer, and a board of directors composed of nine stockholders, to hold their office for three years.

Land was secured on the northeast corner of L and Eleventh streets, and by the summer of 1882 a fine-appearing and substantial brick edifice, four stories in height, with two business rooms, was completed, when the different Odd Fellow organizations then in the city found themselves housed with all the comforts and conveniences necessary.

The scheme proved a success, and placed the two lodges participating in the ownership, Nos. 11 and 39, on a solid financial basis.

In the year 1868 Pythianism first obtained a foothold on Nebraska soil, through the efforts of Captain George Crager, who, coming direct from the birthplace of the order, planted its good seed with vigor and earnestness. August 28, 1871, John Q. Goss, the Grand Chancellor, assisted by P. G. C. George Crager, G. K. of R. and S.; E. E. French, G. M. A.; T. J. Lane, and Knight Henry Lauer, visited Lincoln and instituted Lincoln Lodge No. 8, K. of P., the first lodge in this city and the only one instituted that year in the State.

The lodge flourished in numbers and finances, and the members were the most honored citizens of the then small but flourishing capital city. In 1873 the lodge succumbed to financial reverses and other causes, and surrendered its charter in November of that year.

In December a few of the old Knights strong in the spirit, with others, petitioned for a new charter. This was granted December 3, 1873, by Judge J. W. Carter, Grand Chancellor, and the first meeting for institution was held in the attic of the old opera house. The first officers were: C. C., A. Meyer; V. C., G. B. Harris; K. of R. and S., D. Kalor; M. of Ex., F. E. Smith; M. of F., M. J. Percival; P., P. H. Cooper. The lodge has met with various reverses and successes. It moved from place to place until finally it settled in the old Masonic Hall, corner of Tenth and O streets, which is now completely fitted up with lodge room, banquet room, kitchen, etc., for lodge purposes. It has been honored by the Grand Lodge in the selection of six of its members to the office of Grand Chancellor, and with eighteen subordinate offices. Its present membership is 186, and it possesses property valued at $3,800. Its present officers are: P. C., H. M. Shaeffer; C. C., T. M. Cooke; V. C., S. A. Warner; P., H. C. Fredericks; K. of R. and S., Banks Stewart; M. F., J. W. Percival; M. of Ex., M. Hooker; M. A., Wm. Chichester; I. G., J. J. Young; O. G., C. A. Risings.

In the year 1884 some of the young blood of No. 16 conceived the idea that another lodge of Knights of Pythias would be of benefit to the order in this city. A petition to the Grand Chancellor resulted in a dispensation, and Apollo Lodge No. 36 sprang into existence, on August 18, 1884. The lodge flourished from the start, and as a result of its work and influence, the growth of both Nos. 16 and 36 was large, nearly doubling in membership in one year. Its representatives have taken high rank in the councils of the Grand Lodge, and are placed upon the most important committees. It has been honored in the choice of Richard O'Neill as Grand Chancellor, now the sitting Past Grand. It has a membership at present of eighty-three, eleven Past Chancellors, and one P. G. C. Its finances are in good condition. The present officers are: P. C., Walter Keens; C. C., Ed P. Keefer; V. C., F. B. Harris; K. of R. and S., T. D. Scudder; M. of F., J. North; M. of Ex., H. W. Kelley; M. of A., J. J. McClellan; I. G., Winnie Scott; O. G. Wm. P. Gronen; Trustees, J. E. Douglas, T. W. Tait, Phelps Paine.

A. D. Marshall Lodge No. 41 was organized June 18, 1885, by G. C. J. C. McNaughton, with twenty-three members. The lodge was named after the lamented A. D. Marshall, one of the earliest and most enthusiastic Pythian workers of the city, and by good work and careful selection has to-day a membership of 105. The present officers are: P. C., W. H. Berger; C. C., L. T. Gaylord; V. C., Ed. R. Sizer; P., J. C. Davis; M. of Ex., Jno. F. Hayden; M. of F., H. E. Chapel; M. A., A. Katzenstein; K. of R. and S., F. Hornetius; I. G., Wm. Webb; O. G., Chas. Posky. This lodge has already accumulated considerable property.

Capital City Lodge No. 68 was instituted February 9, 1887, during the term of Grand Chancellor John Morrison, as a testimonial to him of the esteem in which he is held by the order in the Capital City of the State, with the large number of 135 petitioners, the largest list ever presented to a Grand Chancellor for approval, and embracing State, county, and city officials, and leading citizens. This lodge has continued its work with such success that to-day it strives with the mother Lodge, No. 16, for supremacy in numbers, in quality of membership, and in wealth; and ranks second only in members in the State, having at this time 183 Knights, five Past Chancellors, and a District Deputy Grand Chancellor, S. J. Dennis. The present officers are: P. C., Prof. F. F. Roose; C. C., C. W. Hoxie; V. C., G. S. Foxworthy; P., Charles Burton; M. of Ex., R. Wackerhagen; M of

F., Fred A. Miller; K of R and S., Q. L. Martin; M of A., A. G. Kellum; I. G., W. G. Stamm; O. G., L. D. Van Kleek. Trustees: W. L. Cundiff, R. B. Graham, F. A. Miller. Financially it ranks well with any lodge in the city.

The Uniform Rank, Knights of Pythias, has its headquarters for the State in Lincoln, the first division being organized here in 1879, from members of Lincoln Lodge No. 16. From this start this branch of the order has grown into a brigade of four regiments and thirty-six divisions, with the following officers, who are Lincoln residents: Brigadier General Commanding Nebraska Brigade Uniform Rank, Knights of Pythias, W. L. Dayton; Col. and Chief of Staff, W. C. Lane; Col. and A. A. G., H. S. Hotchkiss; Col. and Asst. Commissary Gen'l., John B. Wright, Lincoln.

First Regiment Nebraska Brigade, Uniform Rank Knights of Pythias, Col. H. F. Downs, Commanding; Lieut. Col., J. E. Douglas; Lieut. and Adjt., John Jenkins; Lieut. and Quartermaster, W. N. Rehlaender; Captain and Chaplain, Rev. E. C. Ralston; Quartermaster Sergeant, Walter Keens.

Lincoln Division No. 1, Uniform Rank Knights of Pythias, was instituted in 1879, with thirty-two members. The division has been in many contests for honors, and on many occasions has won trophies which now adorn its armory, and at the meeting of the Supreme Lodge of the World, at Toronto, Ontario, in 1886, won the honorable distinction of third prize in competition with divisions from all over the country. The present membership is seventy-seven. The present officers are: Sir Kt. Capt., A. A. Lasch; Sir Kt. Lieut., J. W. Percival; Sir Kt. Herald, F. A .Miller; Sir Kt. Guard, Nelson Westover; Sir Kt. Sent., F. A. Harris. It has upon detached service Brig. Genl. W. L. Dayton, Chief of Staff, Col. W. C. Lane; Col. and A. A. G., H. S. Hotchkiss; Col. John B. Wright, Commissary Genl. Wm. N. Rehlaender, Lieut. and Quartermaster of 1st Regt. Rev. E. C. Ralston, Capt. and Chaplain of the 1st Regt.

A. D. Marshall Division No. 10, was organized September 28, 1886, with twenty-nine members. This Division, by hard work, is steadily coming to the front, and has a record of three prizes, and the Capt., W. H. Berger, winning at Columbus during the Brigade encampment of 1889, an elegant sword as the best commander. The Division is the proud owner of a handsome flag, with emblems of the Uniform

Rank worked in silk, and valued at $200, presented to it by its lady friends and admirers. It has a membership of thirty-nine, composed entirely of Knights of Marshall Lodge No. 41. The present officers are: Sir Kt. Capt., Wm. H. Berger; Sir Kt. Lieut., H. E. Chapel; Sir Kt. Herald, G. E. Maxwell; Sir Kt. Guard, M. D. Clary; Sir Kt. Sent., H. Yanow; Sir Kt. Treas., J. F. Hayden; Sir Kt. Recorder, G. E. Van Every. Of its members there are on detached service, Ed. R. Sizer, Col. and A. D. C. to Maj. Genl. James R. Carnahan, Comdg. the Uniform Rank Knights Pythias of the world, and also of the same rank on the staff of Gov. John M. Thayer, of the State of Nebraska; H. F. Downs, Col. Commanding 1st Regt. U. R. K. P., Nebraska Brigade; and John Jenkins, Lieut. Adjt. of the 1st Regt.

Apollo Division No. 11 was instituted October 11, 1886, with thirty members. The Division has had a short but brilliant career, seventeen of its members participating in the contest at Toronto in July, 1886. The Division won first prize at Hastings, October 13, 1886, in a State contest, two days after institution, and first prize again the following year at Omaha, in a contest open to the world. Later on it was presented with a gold medal at Omaha for excellence in drill, and bears the proud honor of being the best drilled Division in the State. The present membership is forty-one. A beautiful flag presented to it by A. E. Hargreaves, is highly valued by its members. There are on detached service, J. E. Douglas, Lieut. Col. 1st Regt. U. R. Neb. Brigade, and Walter Keens, Quartermaster Sergeant. Its membership is entirely from Apollo Lodge No. 36, and Diana Lodge No. 106, Beatrice. The present officers are: Sir Kt. Capt., C. M. Keefer; Sir Kt. Lieut., W. E. Churchill; Sir Kt. Herald, Frank B. Harris; Sir Kt. Guard, T. W. Tait; Sir Kt. Sent., Walter Keens; Sir Kt. Treas., R. O'Neill; Sir Kt. Recorder, J. E. Douglas.

In the year 1888, through the exertions of Brother J. E. Douglas, P. C. of Apollo Lodge No. 36, a Board of Relief was organized for the aid and assistance of sojourning Knights who might be in need. This board is composed of representatives from each lodge, to whom all cases are referred, each lodge contributing, in proportion to its membership, to the fund of the board. The meetings are held on the second Friday of each month, or the board may be convened at any time, if necessary, by the President or upon call of two members. It has already proved a very desirable adjunct to the order in this city. The following are the officers:

President—J. E. Douglas. Address, 25 City Block, Eleventh St.
Vice President—W. C. Lane, 1034 O street.
Secretary—H. E. Chapel, 1115 P street.
Treasurer—Prof. F. F. Roose, Academy of Music.

Endowment Rank Knights of Pythias, Section 657, was established February, 1888, with twenty-five members, carrying over $50,000 of insurance, and is in successful operation.

The Ancient Accepted Scottish Rite of the United States, its Territories and Dependencies, Lincoln Consistory No. 54, Chapter of Rose Croix, Council of Princess of Jerusalem, and a Lodge of Perfection, were organized April 23, 1889, with fifty members, by Joseph McGrath, of New Jersey, Grand Inspector General of the Rite as organized A. D. 1807.

The officers of the consistory are: A. G. Hastings, Commander; James Tyler, 1st Lieutenant Commander; A. E. Kennard, 2d Lieutenant Commander; Austin Humphrey, M. of S. and G. O.; J. H. Peebles, G. C.; M. R. Davey, G. T.; L. D. Woodruff, G. S.

The Chapter of Rose Croix has the following officers: S. G. Owens, P. M.; L. D. Woodruff, S. W.; E. O. Miller, J. W.; J. G. Chapin, Orator; M. R. Davey, Treasurer; J. C. Seacrest, Secretary.

The Council of Princess of Jerusalem is officered as follows: W. R. Carter, G. M.; A. E. Kennard, D. M.; G. H. Peebles, S. W.; M. L. Hunter, J. W.; M. H. Day, Treasurer; A. L. Shrader, Secretary.

The Lodge of Perfection has the following officers: W. S. Bloom, M.; James Tyler, D. G. M.; J. C. Seacrest, S. W.; F. P. Lawrence, J. W.; G. H. Peebles, Orator; J. H. Agers, Secretary; M. R. Davey, Treasurer.

Lincoln Lodge No. 19, York Rite, Ancient Free and Accepted Masons, was organized 1868, and has about 160 members.

Lancaster Lodge No. 54 was organized in 1874.

Lincoln Chapter No. 6, Royal Arch Masons, was organized April 28, 1868, and has a membership of 170.

Mount Moriah Commandry No. 40, Knights Templar, was organized in 1871, and has now a membership of 125.

The Ancient Arabic Order of Nobles of the Mystic Shrine, Sesostris Temple, was organized in 1880, and now has a membership of 125.

It is now about twenty-three years since Dr. Stephenson formulated the plans for the organization of the Grand Army of the Republic, an organization which should bind together by ties fraternal those who had survived the dangers of the late war, and which should be charged with the care of those who might need the assistance of a brother's hand in time of distress. The founder of the order has long since gone to rest, and his body sleeps in the beautiful cemetery at Springfield, Ill.; but his work still goes marching on. Not until September 8, 1879, however, was a post of the G. A. R. established in Lincoln. At that time Farragut Post, of thirty-four charter members, was formed, the following being the list:

S. J. Alexander, L. W. Billingsley, R. C. Hazlett, Lyman Wood, A. D. Burr, W. S. Latta, Henry Masterman, W. A. Daggett, D. B. Howard, G. K. Amory, C. H. Gere, A. P. Tarbox, J. E. Philpott, R. O. Philips, Silas Sprague, W. R. Kelley, W. H. Beach, Sam McClay, P. A. Smith, W. J. Cooper, N. Carpenter, Jas. Bolshaw, S. P. Richey, T. B. Dawson, Levi Gable, D. C. Reynolds, E. G. Clements, C. C. Harris, A. Masterman, J. Curry, M. L. Hiltner, J. W. Owens, Thos. Sewall, R. N. Wright.

The first officers were: Commander, S. J. Alexander; S. V., L. W. Billingsley; J. V., C. H. Gould; Chap., H. Masterman; Adjt., Geo. K. Amory; Q. M., A. D. Burr; O. D., R. C. Hazlett; O. G., Al. Masterman. The successive Commanders have been: C. H. Gould, J. C. Bonnell, R. C. Hazlett, Guy A. Brown, S. V. Hoagland, Jos. Teeter, Harry S. Hotchkiss, and O. C. Bell.

The post grew rapidly in numbers, at one time reaching over 500 in good standing, and to-day has a membership of 250, with the following officers: Commander, H. C. McArthur; S. V., J. H. Foxworthy; Jr. V., Silas Sprague; Adjt., P. A. Gatchell; Q. M., Martin Howe; Surgeon, J. R. Haggard; Chap., Henry Masterman; O. D., Jos. Teeter; O. G., J. W. Bowen; Sergt. Maj., T. B. Beach; Q. M. Sergt., Wm. M. Gillespie.

This is the largest post in the State, full of energy, whose charity and kindness is being felt by many worthy comrades and by the widows and orphans of fallen comrades. The members of Farragut Post are known by Nebraska comrades for their whole-souled comradeship and efficiency in the work of the order. The meetings of this post are usually attended by between 100 and 150 members.

Appomattox Post No. 214 was organized January 28, 1886, at which time the following officers were duly elected and installed: Lieut. Edgar S. Dudley, P. C.; Hon. H. A. Babcock, S. V. C.; Hon. W. W. W. Jones, J. V. C.; Col. Brad P. Cook, Adjt.; D. R. Lillibridge, Q. M.; Prof. L. E. Hicks, Chap.; J. O. Carter M. D., Surg.; Hon. S. J. Alexander, O. D.; Prof. Geo. B. Lane, O. G.; Hon. C. H. Gere, Serg. Maj.; and Maj. N. G. Franklin, Q. M. Serg. The membership in the post is not large, some forty-five members comprising its entire roster, but it is, perhaps, fully equal, intellectually, to any organization in the State. The regular meetings of the post are held the first Saturday evening in each month.

Art. 4, Sec. 3, of its by-laws, reads as follows: " On the death of a comrade, not over three months in arrears, the sum of one hundred dollars (to be drawn from the relief fund) shall be paid to his widow or legal representative, for funeral expenses. Should there be no legal representative, the post shall take charge of the funeral, the expenses of which shall not exceed one hundred dollars, to be paid from the relief fund." Thus it will be seen that Appomattox Post is a benevolent insurance organization to a certain extent, and no worthy comrade who applies to any of its members for assistance goes away empty-handed.

Its present officers are: D. R. Lillibridge, Post Commander; C. W. Lyman, S. V. C.; John Gillespie, S. V. C.; Brad. P. Cook, Adjt.; O. E. Goodell, Q. M.; N. G. Franklin, O. D.; L. J. Alexander, O. G.; J. H. McClay, Q. M. Serg. The post is one of the best in the State, and is in a prosperous and flourishing condition.

The fraternal and benevolent order, the Ancient Order of United Workmen, was started in Lincoln by the organization of Lincoln Lodge No. 9, on the 17th of December, 1885. From this beginning there has been a steady growth, until to-day it has three English and one German lodge, with an aggregate membership of 315, whose protection amounts to the grand sum of $630,000. There have been but three deaths in this membership since its organization four years ago, showing the care in selection of membership.

The present officers of No. 9 are: P. M. W., J. W. McMillan; M. W., Dr. G. H. Simmons; Foreman, Art. Masterman; Overseer, W. J. Conley; Recorder, Wm. Helmer; Financier, F. W. Bartruff; Receiver, A. D. Guile; Guide, J. P. Masterman; Watchman, George Fowler; Representatives to Grand Lodge, J. W. McMillan, F. W. Bartruff.

Upchurch Lodge No. 15, A. O. U. W., was named after the founder of the Order, and instituted April 18, 1887. It now has forty-five members, and is increasing in membership. P. Zook is the present Master Workman. Representative to Grand Lodge, F. F. Roose.

Capital City Lodge No. 80, A. O. U. W., was organized May 15, 1886, by E. W. McDonald, Grand Lecturer, with a charter list of about thirty. The membership is energetic and pushing. It has been largely instrumental in building up the order in this city, and through its work the Improvement Association of the A. O. U. W. was formed, resulting in giving the order a hall of its own, nicely furnished, and at a moderate cost. It has to-day 127 members, who have the reputation throughout the State of doing the best degree work. It has a "team" organized for that purpose, the only one in the State. The present officers are: P. M. W., W. S. Houseworth; M. W., T. J. Berky; Foreman, Wm. Clark; Overseer, Frank Pynchon; Recorder, James Farrell; Financier, W. McClellan; Receiver, John Rivett; Guide, Wm. Brannon; I. G., Charles Deahne; Representatives to Grand Lodge, W. S. Houseworth, Henry Mayer, E. W. McDonald, E. L. Holyoke.

Concordia Lodge No. 151, A. O. U. W., was organized May 17, 1888, with twenty-four charter members. It works entirely in the German language, and is composed of our best German citizens. It has a membership at present of forty-seven, and has work ahead. The present officers are: P. M. W., Carl Schmitt; M. W., Louis Vieth; Foreman, P. Andressen; Overseer, A. Kroner; Recorder, Paul Prigel; Financier, R Heminghaus; Receiver, R. Hahnermann; Guide, Joseph Fraas; I. W., Emil Motz; Representative to Grand Lodge, Carl Schmitt.

Logan Legion No. 8, Select Knights A. O. U. W., was organized in May, 1887. The object of this branch of the A. O. U. W. is additional protection to the amount of $3,000 if desired, and for a representative display of the order.

Improvement Association, A. O. U. W., was formed for the purpose of procuring a hall and furnishing the same for the use of A. O. U. W. lodges. It is composed of members of the order who are stockholders to the amount of $1,500, shares of which are $5. The stock can be increased at any time if desired. The association has furnished an elegant hall over 1114 O street, which is used by the A. O. U. W. and kindred societies. The stock is paying eight per cent. and is bought by the lodges when offered for sale. The officers are: J. T. Rivett, President; J. W. McMillan, Vice President; W. S. Houseworth, Secretary.

The "Modern Woodmen of America" is a fraternal, beneficiary, secret organization. Its founder is Hon. J. C. Root, of Iowa, who organized the first camp in January, 1883, since which time the order has grown with wonderful rapidity. Not until April 27, 1886, was a lodge of Woodmen organized in Lincoln. At that time Capital City Camp No. 190 was instituted with a large charter membership, which has since grown to 225 members. The present officers of this camp are: V. C., W. J. Bryan; W. A., T. P. Converse; Clerk, C. C. Calkins; Banker, S. K. Hale; Escort, C. Van Raden; Assistant Escort, E. H. Whiteside; Sentry, C. J. Olson; Examiner, Dr. J. R. Haggard; Managers, W. A. Manchester, F. F. Roose, D. T. Cook; Delegate, W. J. Bryan.

Antelope Camp No. 916 was instituted April 4, 1889, with one hundred names on its petition. It erected, in East Lincoln, a hall for its own use, which was dedicated the following July. M. W. of A. was the first order to organize a local society in East Lincoln. Its officers are: V. C., I. H. Strawbridge; W. A., M. Ewing; Clerk, F. C. Smith; Banker, A. W. Field; Escort, S. D. Woodley; Watchman, F. Risser; Sentry, R. C. Jones; Managers, Dr. Pogue, H. Royer, F. W. Homan.

F. F. Roose Camp No. 969, M. W. of A., organized May 2, 1889, started out under the most favorable circumstances. Among those who enrolled as charter members are many of Lincoln's most prominent citizens. The petition for a charter was signed by 190 persons. While the camp is young, its officers and members have entered into the work with the same spirit characteristic of the whole order — push, enterprise, enthusiasm, business, and fraternity. The following are its present officers: V. C., A. R. Talbot; W. A., O. C. Bell; Clerk, Chas. G. Burton; Banker, F. S. Kelly; Escort, A. B. Bumstead; Watchman, N. King; Sentry, A. L. Church; Managers, Ed. Young, E. R. Sizer, O. F. Lambertson; Delegate, W. M. Woodward. The camp was named the "F. F. Roose Camp" in honor of F. F. Roose, Head

THE MONTGOMERY-BILLINGSLEY BLOCK.

Adviser, the second highest officer in the Supreme Camp, and an upright and respected citizen of Lincoln.

The entire Woodmen membership in Lincoln is over 500.

Prof. Franklin F. Roose, one of the proprietors of the Lincoln Business College, is one of the most enthusiastic "secret order" men, not only in Nebraska, but in the entire West. He is connected with a number of orders, but his position in the order of Modern Woodmen entitles him to more than a passing notice in this work. In the summer of 1886 Mr. Roose was elected by Capital City Camp No. 190, Modern Woodmen of America, as delegate to the Head Camp, at Sterling, Ill., which met the following October. At that camp he was elected Head Clerk, and before the session closed was elevated to the place of Head Adviser, the second highest rank in the Supreme Camp. At the Des Moines session of the Head Camp, held in November, 1888, he was elected for another two years' term, his reëlection being by acclamation. Prof. Roose was born at Moline, Ill., July 3, 1855. His early education was received in the common schools of Rock Island. During the war he used to visit the rebel prison on Rock Island and trade with the soldiers, also with the Indians confined at Davenport for their depredations and murders in Minnesota.

The father of Mr. Roose was a carpenter, and owned a lath and shingle mill in which was employed a number of men, and it was in this saw-mill that the young man began work, at the age of nine years. He continued at this work for seven years, when he moved with his father to a farm a few miles from Edgington, Ill. He there worked for five years, or until the spring of 1876. At that time Mr. Roose, being twenty-two years of age, bought a team, wagon, plows, harrows, etc., rented ground at $5 per acre, and began farming on his own account, in order to obtain money to complete his education. One year's work gave him, after selling off all his farming implements, $400, and with this amount he started, in the spring of 1877, for Bloomington, where he entered the Illinois Wesleyan University. Here he remained two years. While attending that school an incident occurred which shows the esteem in which he was held by his fellow students. The last and only money he owned was $25, and one night this, together with two concert tickets which he had procured for himself and the lady who was afterward to be his wife, was stolen.

Hearing of this loss, the senior class of the college made up the entire amount and presented it to Mr. Roose, also making good the loss of his tickets.

In the fall of 1879 Mr. Roose engaged as an instructor in Chaddock College, Quincy, Ill., at the same time carrying on his private studies. While connected with this institution he was secretary of the faculty, member of the board of trustees, and secretary of it and

PROF. F. F. ROOSE.

of the executive board. In the summer of 1880 Prof. Roose and Miss Elizabeth Morrison, who afterward became his wife, both graduated in the Gem City Business College, and soon after, on September 7, their marriage took place. A week later Prof. Roose took charge of the commercial department of the McKendree University, Lebanon, Ill., which he conducted for two years. At the end of that time Prof. and Mrs. Roose each received the degree of B. S., having completed all the studies of this course.

On June 20, 1882, the professor and his wife sailed for South America, where he had engaged to teach in the Collegio Americano, at Pernambuco, Brazil. He occupied that position six months, and then for six months was secretary to the Hon. Henry L. Atherton, United States Consul at that place. Afterward he was auditor for the Recife and Caxangá Railway Company, which position he retained until January, 1884, when he resigned and returned to North America, the intense heat of that tropical country proving disastrous to his health.

In the fall of 1884 Prof. Roose, his health having been restored by a summer's residence on a farm, came to Lincoln and founded the Lincoln Business College and Institute of Penmanship, Short Hand, Type Writing, and Telegraphy. In 1885 McKendree University gave Prof. Roose and his wife both the degree of M. S., and in 1886 the Iowa Wesleyan University conferred upon them the degree of A. M. *pro merito*. His work in Lincoln has been remarkably successful, and while a resident of the city he has built up a social and business standing of the very best.

Prof. Roose is a busy man; few minutes can go to waste with him, as will be seen by the immense amount of work which he does daily; and yet he always has time to say a few pleasant words to the friends he meets upon the streets or who call at the pleasant home of Prof. and Mrs. Roose on D street. In addition to the work of his business college, in which enterprise he has associated himself with Prof. D. R. Lillibridge, Prof. Roose has charge of the commercial department of the Nebraska Wesleyan University; is the editor and publisher of the *Western Workman*, the official organ of the A. O. U. W., and one of the editors of the *Lincoln Monthly*, an educational journal. In addition to these duties Prof. Roose attends to the duties which necessarily fall upon him as a prominent member of several secret orders, and the secretary of several associations. He is Head Adviser, Modern Woodmen; Past Chancellor Commander of Capital City Lodge No. 68, K. of P.; representative to the K. of P. Grand Lodge of Nebraska for 1889 and 1890; a member of the Masonic order; member of the Select Knights of America; one of the managers of Capital City Camp No. 190, M. W. A.; member of the Phi Delta Theta, the A. O. U. W., and the Nebraska Press Association; Vice President of the A. O. U. W. Building Association, and was Secretary and Treasurer of the Northern Relief Association, A. O. U. W., for one and one-half years. He is also Vice President of the M. W. A. board of directors for the State of Illinois, and of the executive council; Past Master Workman and Deputy Grand Master Workman of Upchurch Lodge No. 45, A. O. U. W., and was a member for 1887 and 1889 of the A. O. U. W. Grand Lodge. The foregoing list is sufficient to show that no man in the West is more thoroughly identified with the work of secret orders than is Prof. Roose, and the numerous positions of honor and responsibility to which his fraternal brothers have elevated him shows in what esteem and confidence he is held by them.

A new secret society in which Lincoln is especially interested is the "Order of Delphians," whose Supreme Lodge is located in this city, and the first work of which was done here. This order was instituted in February, 1889, in Lincoln, and is an association designed to promote the interests of mankind by improving the welfare of those engaged in teaching. To this end the teachers are banded together to advance their social relations, provide libraries for their benefit, to promote harmony in the work of the teacher by adapting the instructor to the places he can best fill. In brief, it is intended to keep, at the Supreme Lodge, a bureau of information for the benefit of all teachers as well as school boards. Through the subordinate lodges places needing teachers, and teachers seeking situations, together with information concerning the merits of the teachers and circumstances surrounding the places to be filled, are to be supplied to the Supreme Lodge. To this bureau all teachers can apply for employment and boards and directors can come for teachers. In this way it is believed teachers can be located in situations they can best fill, thus promoting the general welfare of all concerned.

Lincoln began with a subordinate lodge of twenty-eight members. The Supreme Secretary, Mr. W. S. Bloom, occupies a suite of rooms on the second floor of the Latta block, at 133–9 South Eleventh street.

The Lincoln Division of the Ancient Order of Hibernians was organized on January 21, 1885, by Brother Richard O'Keeffe, of Omaha, and John Rush.

Patrick Egan was elected County Delegate, but on October 1, 1885, he was called on to explain why he did not comply with the constitution, and approach the sacraments with the Division on September 10th, as had been decided on at the previous meeting. (September 3d.) Mr. Egan explained the reasons why he could not consistently abide by the laws compelling members to approach the sacraments in a body, as he felt that there was too much ostentation in parade. Mr. Egan said he was sorry to say that through circumstances he was constrained to tender his resignation.

Mr. Egan's resignation was accepted on November 8, 1885, and Mr. James Kelly was thereupon elected County Delegate, which office he still holds.

The Division has made good progress since its organization, and now numbers about ninety members. In the fall of 1888 the Division presented a magnificent pulpit to Right Rev. Bishop Bonacum, for the pro-cathedral. The officers at present are: Thomas McShane, President; Frank Sheppard, Vice President; Michael Corcoran, Recording Secretary; Edward M. Maher, Financial Secretary; Thomas McGivern, Treasurer.

Lincoln Lodge No. 35, Independent Order of Good Templars, was organized May 10, 1868. The lodge grew very rapidly, attaining a membership at one time of 250. Since its organization it has enrolled about 1,500 members.

Lincoln Lodge No. 35 can boast of having sent out into the field some of the best temperance workers of this country, Mr. and Mrs. John B. Finch, John Sobieski, Joe Critchfield, J. G. Wolfenbarger, and Mr. Sibley, being a few among the number.

The officers of Lincoln Lodge No. 35, for the summer term of 1889 are as follows: C. T., L. A. Willis; V. T., Nellie Hodge; S. J. T., Emma Hedges; Sec'y, G. H. Crandall; A. Sec'y, Mamie Gulick; F. Sec'y, C. E. Hedges; Treas., Carrie Brown; Chap., Mr. Flucard; M., Mr. Cooper; A. M., Addie Bundy; Guard, Mr. Dill; Sentinel, Sam B. Ijams.

The Ancient Order of Foresters meets on the first and third Fridays of each month, in the K. of P. Hall, at 1007 O street. The list of officers at the opening of the year were: W. Robertson, J. P. C. R.; E. A. Stephens, C. R.; G. R. Knowles, S. C. R.; F. Cather, F. Sec;

G. Leavitt, Rec. Sec.; H. A. Stephens, Treas.; M. Seivers, S. W.; J. Leister, J. W.; R. Scheape, S. B.; D. N. Stephens, J. B.

The Knights of Tabor meet at 1024 O street. The officers for 1889 were: J. Wright, C. M.; J. Williams, V. M.; E. Brown, Secretary; J. F. Malone, Treasurer; J. H. Washington, C. O.; A. Johnson, C. G.

The Knights of Labor first organized in this city in 1881, under Assembly Number 2659; but the order lapsed in a short time, and was reorganized in 1885 as Assembly 3774. The organization grew rapidly to about 700 members, but failed to continue. A second reorganization was effected in 1887, out of which grew two locals, one being the Lincoln Assembly No. 2659, which meets over 1023 O street, in the A. O. H. hall, and the other being Stephens Assembly 573, named after the National Master Workman of the order. This assembly meets in Central Labor Union Hall, at 1125 O street. Both assemblies are prosperous, and together now number about 800 members. Of Assembly No. 2659 George W. Black is Master Workman and M. Corcoran Secretary. Of 573 J. H. Craddock is Master Workman and S. J. Kent Secretary. It is expected that there will be six locals in the county before the close of the year.

Lincoln has two principal social clubs, the Union and the Elks. The Union Club was organized May 29, 1879, with the following officers: Edgar S. Dudley, President; Thomas Sewell, Vice President; J. H. Alford, Secretary; George C. Newman, Treasurer; J. H. Fawell, Master of Ceremonies. On the 19th of May, 1888, the club was incorporated under the laws of the State of Nebraska, with a capital stock of $5,000, divided into shares of $25 each. This allows the club a membership of 200, the present membership being 122. The present officers are: E. B. Appelget, President; J. F. Barnhart, Vice President; J. A. Marshall, Secretary; W. W. W. Jones, Treasurer. Board of Directors—R. A. Perry, C. O. Whedon, R. C. Outcalt, Thomas Sewell, O. W. Webster, and J. H. Harley. The club occupies elegant rooms at the northwest corner of N and Twelfth streets, fitted up in a most complete manner.

The "Elks" Club was organized March 10, 1888, with sixty-five charter members, which have been increased to 105 at the present time. The officers of this organization are: W. J. Houston, E. R.; H. R.

THE BURR BLOCK.

Wiley, E. L. K.; E. B. Slosson, E. L. K.; W. H. Axtater, E. L. K.; A. E. Hargreaves, Treasurer. This club is elegantly quartered in the Shaberg Block, southeast corner of P and Eleventh streets.

Prominent among the associations of the city is the Haydon Art Club, designed to promote a taste for the fine arts.

There are also tennis, lacrosse, and wheel clubs, and supposed to be a press club, but this is not active.

Among social clubs may be mentioned the Harmonie, Pleasant Hour, Pleasant Hour Jr., Swedish Social and Literary, and Yorke.

Lincoln is the center of the organization designed to carry the prohibitory amendment at the election of 1890, known as the "Nebraska Non-partisan Prohibitory Amendment League." Mr. C. A. Atkinson is the President of the State League, and Mr. Charles Robbins Secretary. Messrs. Atkinson, John M. Stewart, and C. F. Creighton, are members of the State Executive Committee.

Lincoln is also the residence of Mr. A. G. Wolfenbarger, representing Nebraska in the National organization of the Prohibition party.

Among the most worthy benevolent societies of the city is the Woman's Christian Association, designed to aid women in the work of self-support and protection. Also for the help of the needy. It now maintains a Woman's Home, on Eleventh street, between K and H.

The Willard and Lincoln Branches of the Woman's Christian Temperance Union are active contributors to the Christian charities of the city, the former having done noble work for a couple of years past in the management of the city hospital.

Company D of the First Regiment Nebraska National Guards is the best drilled militia company in the State. Captain, L. H. Cheney; 1st Lieutenant, W. M. Decker; 2d Lieutenant, C. H. Foxworthy. The company has forty-nine men.

CHAPTER XX.

The Irish National League—Lincoln as the Head-quarters of this Powerful Organization—Sketch of the Lives of the Lincoln Men who are Prominent in the League.

Lincoln having been for five years past the headquarters for the Irish National League of America, a brief sketch of that powerful organization will not be out of place.

Since the first attempt of the English to subjugate the Irish people, hardly a generation of Irishmen has passed without protest against the usurpation of Ireland's national rights by an alien government. Through many centuries the story of this national resistance drags its bloody trail, down to the last great rising of 1798, when Antrim, Presbyterian, and Wexford, Roman Catholic, made a daring attempt to establish an Irish republic on Irish soil. They failed; but the memory of their heroism lived on to inspire the patriots of later years.

The agitation of O'Connell had sunk into lethargy; the brave spirits of '98 had gone to other lands, with all their energy and all their genius; famine and pestilence had made Ireland a grave yard; and the world witnessed the greatest exodus of a people since the national migrations of antiquity. Gavan Duffy, sailing for Australia, said he left Ireland a corpse on the dissecting table; but the indomitable heart of the gallant little nation was still beating, though feebly. Then it was that James Stephens sewed the seeds that grew into the formidable Fenian Brotherhood. Alas! the curse of dissension made its appearance; the powerful conspiracy was forced into precipitate action, and failure was again written on Ireland's struggles for freedom. Among the gallant spirits sent to penal servitude for Fenianism was a dark-faced, thoughtful young man, who, though deprived of his right arm, was destined to work great things for Ireland. Michael Davitt, the one-armed young patriot, was sentenced to seven years incarceration in a British dungeon. Better for the enemies of Ireland if they had hanged him. During the lonely hours he thought out the Irish question, and he studied the causes of Ireland's constant failures. He became convinced that it was only madness to dream of encountering England's armies in the field. But he was familiar with the social miseries and inequalities of privilege that formed the common inheritage of the British and Irish masses, and he believed that an agitation in Ireland, going as far as but not beyond the limit of revolution, for the destruction of the Irish land system, combined with a demand for the establishment of a parliament in Ireland to legislate for local needs, would touch a sympathetic chord in the hearts of the British masses and prove much stronger than merely argumentative pleadings in parliament, and more likely to succeed than armed insurrection. He would agitate without, and proper representatives should voice the people's cry within the walls of the British parliament. When the prison doors were opened, Davitt went to work to put his ideas into practical shape, and the result was the establishment of the Irish Land League in 1879. Davitt and Thomas Brennan, now of Omaha, were its evangelists. Patrick Egan became Treasurer, and Charles Stuart Parnell, the parliamentary and *de facto* leader of the Irish people, at once espoused the new organization. Soon thereafter branches of the league were formed in America, and the Irish Land League of America became a strong organization. Though Irishmen were not numerous in Lincoln at that period, they made up in energy what they lacked in numbers, and a branch of the Land League was formed here with the following officers: President, Hon. John Fitzgerald; Vice President, Rev. M. A. Kennedy; 2d Vice President, General Victor Vifquain; Secretary, Thomas Carr; Treasurer, E. P. Cagney. It may be remarked, incidentally, that in 1867, the gallant General Vifquain went to Ireland to give the Irish cause the service of his well-tried military experience.

In 1882 the Land League was suppressed in Ireland, and Parnell organized the existing Irish National League. Early in 1883 a great convention of Irishmen and descendants of Irishmen was held in Philadelphia, and the American Land League was merged into a new organization known as the Irish National League of America, the objects of which are simply to sustain in every necessary way, the constitutional policy of Parnell in his efforts to secure Home Rule for Ireland. Alexander Sullivan, Rev. Dr. O'Reilly, of Detroit, and Roger Walsh, as President, Treasurer and Secretary respectively, constituted the first executive officers of the league. At a convention held in Boston in 1884, Patrick Egan, then a resident of Lincoln—where he settled after escaping the clutches of Dublin Castle officials, who on any pretext would have hanged him as a recompense for his patriotic devotion—was elected President, and with Mr. Egan the headquarters of the league came to Lincoln, where it has since remained. In January, '86, Secretary Walsh having resigned, Jno. P. Sutton succeeded him and became a citizen of Lincoln. The third convention of the Irish National League of America took place in Chicago in August, 1886, and our fellow townsman, Hon. John Fitzgerald, was elected to the Presidency by an overwhelming vote, Treasurer O'Reilly and Secretary Sutton being reëlected to their respective offices without opposition. The Irishmen of Lincoln have done good service to the Irish cause. In December, 1885, Lincoln contributed $2,100, and in 1888 $1,171, besides nearly $600 for the sufferers in the blizzard of January, 1888. The meetings of the League are features of Lincoln life, and are largely attended. The present local officers are P. O. Cassidy, President; E. P. Cagney, Treasurer, and John P. Sutton, Secretary. The local ex-Presidents are John Fitzgerald, Patrick Egan, and J. J. Butler.

As the names of Fitzgerald, Egan, and Sutton, have been so prominently connected with the League for years, and all being residents of Lincoln, it is eminently proper that this work should give some extended personal notice of these men.

Hon. John Fitzgerald was born over fifty years ago, in Limerick, county, Ireland. His father was a tenant farmer holding at the same time a small piece of free-hold property, the remnant of a more ample estate that had once been in the possession of his ancestors, but which had been reduced to a few acres by the operation of laws that had proved only too successful in bringing the old landed proprietors to beggary and ruin. Edward Fitzgerald, the father of the subject of our sketch, was evicted from his farm, and seeing the poverty and decay that surrounded him on all sides, leased his little free-hold, and with his sons sailed for the United States, back in the "forties."

At that time there was considerable prejudice against Irish immigration to America, and if the immigrant from the Green Isle found a fair field, he could also say that he found no favor. Americans of that day are not to be lightly blamed. American literature was in its

HON. JOHN FITZGERALD.

infancy. The mental food of the people was mainly derived from English sources, and the character of the Irish people was delineated by men imbued with racial hatreds. Reared in this atmosphere of distorted teachings, and fed upon unrefuted calumnies, it is no wonder that the mass of Americans felt prejudiced toward the Irish race, whose most numerous representatives were the unlettered and poverty-stricken victims of a tyranny described by Edmund Burke as the most perfect system ever devised by the perverted ingenuity of man to drive a nation mad. The immigrants, too, had their serious faults, which, though doubtless the engendered results of a century of oppression, helped to increase the aversion prejudice had already excited against them. Intemperance was painfully prevalent, and faction-fighting was a vice that long baffled the efforts of the priest and patriot to destroy it. Americans are a just people, and are quick to fling away their prejudices when convinced that they are in error, and few are more ready to recognize and reward true merit.

The Fitzgerald family, after arriving in New York, pushed westward, to find employment in the great public works which eventually made New York and Pennsylvania the leading States of the Union. They quickly developed qualities of mind and heart which won the confidence and respect of the leading contractors of that day. John Fitzgerald was then a youth of seventeen summers, with a strong, muscular frame, and a vigorous constitution. He was then, and always has been, a strict disciple of Father Mathew, from whom he had received the pledge while yet almost an infant. A salient feature of his character is his incontrollable desire to be doing something.

In those early days, after the close of the open season, it was usual for the great armies of canal builders to withdraw for the winter to the neighboring towns, waiting for the spring to resume work. Only too many frittered away in these idle days, all the money they had accumulated by hard labor in the burning heat of summer. The Fitzgeralds were men of a different stamp, and did not believe in making their summers pay for their winters. They sought such work as could be found, even if the remuneration hardly paid their living expenses. It was on one of these occasions that John Fitzgerald accepted work from a farmer for his board and seven dollars per month. At another time he was working for a farmer, digging ditches, when his quick perception showed him how he could do the work by conract, make money for himself, secure better wages for his companions, and give greater satisfaction to the farmer. He made his proposition to the latter, and it was accepted.

In twenty-four hours John Fitzgerald was a contractor, his fellow-workmen became his employés, and he stood on equal ground with his former employer. The job was finished much quicker than the farmer had calculated, and the work was done to his complete satisfaction. The laborers received higher wages than their agreement with the farmer had called for, and John Fitzgerald had a good round sum of money to the credit of his profit and loss account. That was Mr. Fitzgerald's first contract, and to-day he speaks of it with greater pride than of all the enterprises of magnitude he has since completed.

The reputation achieved by Edward Fitzgerald and his sons did much in the districts wherein they labored, to raise the character of the Irish in American opinion, and contractors were glad not only to employ them, but to sublet to them large portions of their work.

After the death of their father, in New York State, the brothers, Edward and John, turned their attention to the construction of railroads. After satisfactorily completing important contracts in New England during the war, they gradually worked westward until they reached Wisconsin, where they built several hundred miles of railroad. Following the star of empire, the brothers penetrated through Iowa with their iron highways. After the death of his brother Edward, John assumed control of what had become a vast business, and after building the greater part of the C. B. & Q. in Iowa, crossed the Missouri and took up work for the B. & M. and Union Pacific roads, until his name became inseparably bound up with the history of railroading from the Atlantic to the Rocky mountains.

Mr. Fitzgerald made his first home in Nebraska at Plattsmouth, where he owns a very large amount of property. Since becoming a resident of this State, Mr. Fitzgerald, besides his work in Nebraska, was associated with S. Mallory esq., C. E., of Chariton, Iowa, and Martin Flynn esq., of Des Moines, Iowa, in the construction of the Cincinnati Southern road through Tennessee; also in building the Denver, Memphis & Atlantic railway, in association with the Fitzgerald & Mallory Construction Company. The latest enterprise of our active town-man is the construction of the St. Louis & Canada railroad in Michigan and Indiana.

Mr. Fitzgerald has very extensive landed property in Nebraska. The man who as a boy looked with tear-filled eyes upon the few fields from which he and his father were evicted, is to-day the owner of two of the largest and best managed farms in America, embracing 8,000 acres of unsurpassed fertility at Greenwood, and 6,000 equally as good in Gage county, in this State. In addition, he has several farms in Wisconsin and other states.

His investments in commercial lines are many and extensive. He owns the large West Lincoln Brick and Tile Works, and also has a controlling interest in the Rapid Transit company, of which he is President. He is also President of the First National Banks of Plattsmouth and Greenwood, and of the Nebraska Stock Yards Company, and a Director of the First National and Union Savings Banks of Lincoln. Mr. Fitzgerald is also largely interested in mercantile investments, and has stores in different parts of the State.

His first experience with Lincoln was Colonel Tom Hyde's invitation to the hospitality of a shanty, and his first bed in the same shanty was a buffalo robe on the ground, damp with recent rains. To-day his magnificent residence and beautifully laid out grounds crown Mount Emerald, the finest elevation in the city, and here he loves to extend the genuine hospitality typical of the Geraldine.

His splendid wholesale business block at the corner of Seventh and P is rapidly approaching completion, and it is but the precursor of other stately edifices with which Mr. Fitzgerald's enterprise will embellish the city he has chosen for his home, and which owes so much to his untiring energy.

Although the most liberal and tolerant of men, Mr. Fitzgerald is a strict Roman Catholic, and a munificent contributor to his church. The Convent of the Holy Child Jesus is the gift of Mr. Fitzgerald to the nuns of that order, and his subscriptions in aid of the Catholic Church of Lincoln have been generous and constant. Some three years ago he gave a large sum to help in the construction of St. Patrick's Church in Rome, and Pope Leo XIII, in recognition of his generosity, sent him a valuable gold medal.

The Geraldine race, kin with the Gherardini of Florence, and boasting its descent from Eneas, the Trojan hero, has been conspicuous for its heroic fidelity to the fate and fortunes of the Irish nation. Its blood has poured out on every battlefield for Irish liberty, its sons

have perished with stoicism in the dungeon, and looked scorn from the scaffold. The castles of the Geraldines stud the river banks and mountain glens of Munster, and few are the tales of fairy lore and weird romance in which some Fitzgerald does not play a conspicuous rôle. With the blood of this fiery clan in his veins, it is but natural that Mr. Fitzgerald should be ardently attached to the cause of Ireland. From boyhood to the present moment he has supported every movement consecrated to Irish liberty, and there has hardly been an Irish convention which he has not attended. Unambitious for office, with no personal views, but influenced by an earnest desire to see his country enjoy the liberty so many of his race had died for, his time, and his purse, and his quiet word of sound advice, were ever at the service of Ireland. The qualities of the man could hardly escape recognition, and in 1886 he was chosen President of the Irish National League of America. His period of office has been a troubled one, great events having transpired during his administration; but he has filled the position with honor to himself and to the Irish cause. His cool, conservative policy, his strong determination to keep the league free from political entanglements and from alliances that could in any way compromise the action of Parnell and his colleagues, has merited and received the warm approbation not only of the Irish leaders, but of the best friends of Ireland in America. To everything that can add to the welfare of the Irish cause, and to the benefit of his race, John Fitzgerald has been conspicuously generous.

Mr. Fitzgerald is, in American politics, a strong Democrat, and a warm supporter of his party, but has invariably refused to accept any political honors. From men of all shades of religious and political belief Mr. Fitzgerald receives the respect due to his strict integrity and his boundless energy.

Fortunate in his business, he is equally blessed in his domestic life. Mrs. Fitzgerald is a most estimable lady, and as remarkable for her kind, unostentatious benevolence, as her husband is for his more active qualities. Their family consists of four children, and since their marriage no cloud has darkened the summer of their lives.

John P. Sutton was born in Ireland in 1845, and came to this country in 1865. Mr. Sutton entered the army and was Post Sergeant Major of Fort Bridger, Wyoming, in 1866, and subsequently of Fort

Sedgwick, Colorado, in 1868. When discharged he was First Sergeant of H Company, Eighteenth Infantry. Mr. Sutton was recommended by his superior officers to apply for a commission, but the great reduction of the army at that time, and the prospect of continued peace, gave small encouragement to a young officer's hopes of advancement; so Sergeant Sutton abandoned his military career after receiving the highest commendations from Col. Carrington, Lieut. Col. Mills, Major A. S. Burt, and other officers. His family had emigrated from Ireland to Canada in 1864, and his father filled a responsible position in the

HON. JOHN P. SUTTON.

Union Bank of Lower Canada, in Quebec. Mr. Sutton rejoined his family with the intention of remaining only a short time, but smitten by the charms of a young Irish-Canadian lady, he married and settled down in Canada. He always considered himself an American citizen, and carefully eschewed all participation in Canadian politics. He was for several years accountant for Ross & Co., one of the greatest mercantile houses in Canada. Owing to his independence of all political parties, and his advocacy of the Irish cause, he was very popular with his countrymen in Quebec, and was President of the Quebec branch of the league while he remained in that city. In 1885 he moved to Chicago, and while there was asked to return to Canada and stir up the Irishmen of the Dominion to active support of the cause. His efforts were rewarded with a large measure of success. In January, 1886, he accepted the Secretaryship of the Irish National League during Mr. Egan's administration, but resigned in May of the same year to assume the position of Assistant Treasurer of the Fitzgerald & Mallory Construction Co., offered him by John Fitzgerald, who was General Manager and Treasurer of the company. At the Irish League convention of 1886, Mr. Sutton was unanimously reëlected Secretary of the league, and returned to Lincoln in October of the same year, and has since resided here. Mr. and Mrs. Sutton have a family of four children.

Hon. Patrick Egan, now Minister Plenipotentiary from the United States to the Republic of Chili, South America, was born at Ballymahon county, Longford, Ireland, August 31, 1841. At the age of fourteen he entered the office of an extensive grain and milling firm in Dublin, and before he was twenty had been promoted to the post of chief bookkeeper and confidential man. Later he was elected managing director of this, as a stock company, it being the most extensive one in Ireland. He was, at the same time, senior partner in the most extensive bakery establishment in the county. He had been an industrious learner before going into business, and all this time took evening lessons of various instructors, and particularly of a brilliant young Episcopal minister of Dublin named Porte.

His extensive and close connection with the business interests of the country brought him face to face with the terrible system of landlord oppression and tyranny which was impoverishing the country and decimating the people, and as far back as 1863 he became an active worker in the ranks of the advanced national party, taking his full share of all the labors and risks of the movement which brought about the attempted insurrection of 1867. In 1871, with Isaac Butt and others, Mr. Egan took an active part in founding the Home Rule League, and as one of the council of that body helped to spread the good work throughout the country.

For ten years prior to the formation of the Land League, in 1879, Patrick Egan was regarded as if not the ablest at least one of the most important factors in the national movement in Ireland.

All this time he was the close friend and confidant of the brilliant Isaac Butt, founder of the Home Rule movement; of John Martin, Professor Galbraith, Charles Stuart Parnell, and men of equal eminence.

When the Land League was formed, in October, 1879, Patrick Egan was unanimously chosen one of its three trustees and its acting Treasurer, and in December of that year he relinquished the management of his large business entirely to his partners and threw himself into the work of the Land League relief fund, in which he labored almost night and day for months, distributing relief to the victims of landlord extortion, besides performing much labor for the general amelioration of the agricultural, financial, and commercial, condition of the Irish people. Near the close of 1880, he, with twelve others, including Parnell, Dillon, Bigger, Sexton, Sullivan, Sheridan, and Harris, were singled out by the government for prosecution for alleged conspiracy. After a costly trial of sixteen days the jury stood ten for acquittal and two for conviction. The government did not dare arraign them again, but brought in a bill to suspend the *habeas corpus* act, and to permit the arrest of any one obnoxious to the government, intending to proscribe all members of the league.

Messrs. Parnell, Dillon, Davitt, and other patriotic leaders, persuaded Mr. Egan to go to Paris to prevent the government from confiscating the league funds. He took up his residence in Paris in February, 1881, and remained until the close of 1882. Much of this time the entire management and responsibility for the policy and acts of the league fell upon him, because the other members of the executive committee were in English prisons. But he performed the work to the satisfaction of his colleagues, handling large sums of money and accounting for every cent, and so profitably investing it as to turn over to the league $826,000 in returns. For these three years he gave his time to the league without a cent of compensation.

During the struggle from 1880 to 1882 Mr. Egan was frequently pressed to stand for parliament, in fact, was twice unanimously nominated, once for Queen's county and again for county Meath, but he declined because he could not take the oath of allegiance to England required by the government.

Learning that the English government was conspiring to arrest himself and colleague, and make him the victim of a pretended trial, he quietly removed to Holland, and then came to the United States and became a citizen of Lincoln, Neb. Here he settled down to his accustomed grain business, but never lagged for a moment in his activity in defense of the cause of Ireland.

He was one of three upon whose call was held the great Irish convention of April, 1883, at Philadelphia, at which the Land League was dissolved and the present Irish National League of America was founded, and at the next convention of the league, held in Boston, in

HON. PATRICK EGAN.

1884, he was elected President, which office he held for two years. During his term of office the league in America was eminently successful. It sent to Ireland about $350,000, besides doing much to solidify the Irish element in this country. Under the rules of the league the President is entitled to a salary of $3,000 per year, but Mr. Egan returned, as a donation to the league fund, his two years' salary of $6,000.

He was, all this time, an active and useful citizen of city, State, and nation. He espoused the principles of the Republican party, especially with reference to the revenue policy of this country, regarding the free-trade theories as certain to produce the same calamities to the people of this nation as British free trade has brought upon Ireland. In May, 1888, he was elected delegate-at-large to the National Republican Convention by a vote of 594 to 67, and was a conspicuous figure in that convention, declining the chairmanship in favor of Hon. John M. Thurston.

But, perhaps, Mr. Egan's most brilliant achievement remains to be told. The English Government and London *Times* had entered into a conspiracy to destroy Charles Stuart Parnell, and through him the cause of Ireland, by arraigning him before a prejudiced court on a false charge, based on letters forged by a man named Piggott, who had sold the forgeries to the *Times* for money. By a systematic comparison of Piggott's known writing and language with the forgeries, as well as by means of facts already known in part to Mr. Egan, he was enabled to weave such a demonstration of the forgeries that, at a critical moment in the trial, when the Tories almost felt sure of victory, Piggott was suddenly confronted with Mr. Egan's overwhelming proofs of his villainy. He confessed his iniquity, fled to Europe, and destroyed himself. Of course the case against Mr. Parnell fell to the ground, amid the derision of the world. This culmination came about the first of the present year.

He is the father of fourteen children, nine of whom are living, one daughter being married and a resident of Dublin. One of his children was born in France, one in America, and the others in Ireland. His residence in Lincoln has been at 1447 Q street.

CHAPTER XXI.

THE BANKS OF THE CITY AND HER OTHER FINANCIAL INSTITUTIONS—LINCOLN AS A SOLID FINANCIAL CENTER OF THE STATE.

The first bank of Lincoln was established in June, 1868, by James Sweet and N. C. Brock. Preceding chapters give a record of this bank and the gentlemen who conducted it, it being one of the most important and prominent of the early banking institutions of the State. This enterprise was not long allowed to occupy the field alone.

The First National Bank of Lincoln, southeast corner O and Tenth streets, established and chartered February 24, 1871, is the successor, so to speak, of a private bank founded a short time previously by Judge Amasa Cobb and J. F. Sudduth, Judge Cobb being President, and Mr. Sudduth Cashier. Among the early stockholders of the First National bank can be named Robert D. Silvers, E. E. Brown, A. L. Palmer, John Cadman, J. N. Eckman, W. R. Field, Chester Schoolcraft, Prof. J. G. Miller, George W. Cobb, and W. P. Phillips. Judge Cobb was the first President of the bank after its incorporation, and J. F. Sudduth the first Cashier. In 1874 Messrs. John Fitzgerald and John R. Clark bought an interest in the bank, and soon after this Mr. Fitzgerald was made President, and Mr. Clark Cashier, Mr. Sudduth being made Vice President, which place he held to the time of his death, which occurred in 1880. No change was made in the officers of the bank from that time until June, 1889, when Mr. Clark was made President, D. D. Muir Cashier, and C. S. Lippincott Assistant Cashier. Mr. Muir had previously been Assistant Cashier for a number of years. Since 1880 the management of the bank has been almost entirely in the hands of Mr. Clark, and to his financial ability, and careful management is the success of the institution chiefly due. As a matter of history, and showing the growth of business of the bank, a comparison of some figures from 1872, with the report of its condition on July 12, 1889, will be of especial interest.

21

In 1872 the loans and discounts amounted to $87,177.63; U. S. bonds, $50,000; together with other items making up total resources of $252,969.97. The liabilities at that time were: Capital stock, $50,000; surplus fund, $10,000; circulation, $45,000; deposits, $123,-865.76; and other items making the balance.

On June 12, 1889, the official statement of the bank shows as follows: Resources — Loans and discounts, $920,906.50; U. S. bonds, $50,000.00; real estate, $76,510.52; expenses and taxes, $2,221.69; cash and sight exchange, $345,153.39; total, $1,394,792.00.

RESIDENCE OF J. D. MACFARLAND.

Liabilities — Capital stock, $200,000; surplus and profits, $72,-382.10; circulation, $45,000; deposits, $1,077,409.90; total, $1,394,-792.00.

The present directors are John R. Clark, John Fitzgerald, J. D. McFarland, and D. D. Muir.

The State National Bank, of Lincoln, is one of the oldest and most prosperous financial institutions of Nebraska. It was founded in

1872, by the Richards Brothers, and was purchased by Messrs. E. E. Brown, K. K. Hayden, and others, in 1885, and reorganized. Since the second organization it has made constant progress in its business and in public favor. This will be perceived to be manifest when the fact is stated that in four years past it has doubled its capital, and more than doubled its business, notwithstanding the organization of five new banks in the city during that period. The confidence of the public in this excellent institution is exhibited in the very large aggregate sum of deposits its official statements now show. In this proof of public favor it has no superior in the State, all things considered.

The success of the State National Bank doubtless rests upon the able business ability of its officers and directors, and their high character as citizens. It is only necessary to refer to the names of these gentlemen to demonstrate that they are a very strong company, considered in the light of long business experience in this community and State, unquestioned integrity, and their peculiar fitness for conducting the extensive financial affairs of the bank.

Hon. E. E. Brown, President of the bank, has been identified with the city and its progress almost from the time Lincoln was founded: He was Mayor of the city in 1872, and was for years recognized as the most able attorney, and scarcely excelled in legal acquirements in the State. He was always distinguished for his very thorough business habits, his prudence and sagacity in business, and his financial success. He discontinued his law practice when he accepted the Presidency and a large share of the responsibility in the management of the bank, in order to give its affairs the more perfect attention.

Hon. J. J. Imhoff is the Vice President of the State National Bank, and also one of the directors. Mr. Imhoff was a successful merchant and capitalist of Nebraska City before Lincoln was platted, in 1867, and was one of the leading founders of the city. He built up the Capital Hotel property from a value of $5,000 to a value of $115,000 in fifteen years. He is one of the largest, most successful, and enterprising capitalists of Lincoln, and one of the city's most useful and respected citizens.

Hon. G. M. Lambertson, for eight years United States District Attorney for Nebraska, now serving his second term as the City Attorney for Lincoln, and one of the most able lawyers and business men of the city, is also a director in this strong financial institution. Mr.

Lambertson's personal integrity is too well established in Lincoln to require more than a mention.

Another director, and also the Cashier of this bank is Mr. K. K. Hayden, who is one of the most thorough business men in Nebraska. Mr. Hayden has built himself into his present honorable and responsible position by his unyielding courage, his tireless application to every detail of all business entrusted to his charge, and his inflexible adherence to strict business methods at all times. His personal career has been admirable as well as remarkable. He was born on a planta-

STATE NATIONAL BANK BUILDING.

tion in St. Mary's county, Maryland, in 1855, and was the child of luxury and the pet of his own slaves until the war totally ruined the family fortune and brought young Hayden to absolute poverty. After the war he sold papers on the streets of Baltimore, and earned his way by hard experience in other occupations. He came to Omaha in 1866, and in 1870 secured a position as bell boy in the First National Bank of Omaha, at a salary of $15 per month. Within five years, or when twenty years old, he was teller in that bank, and remained with the First National for eleven years. He then accepted the position of

Assistant Cashier in the Nebraska National Bank of the same city, and held this position until he was appointed National Bank Examiner, by President Cleveland, in 1885, his district being Nebraska and Kansas.

His duties made him acquainted with the business prospects of Lincoln, and the merits of the State National Bank of this city, and he resigned his office as Bank Inspector, to accept the position of Cashier of this bank, a position he has held ever since. It is easy, therefore, to understand why the State National Bank is popular, and commands the respect of business men, with such thorough business men as the gentlemen named, with all their special training, on guard over the details of its business.

The other directors of the bank, Messrs. Geo. McMillan, E. Finney, and H. L. Smith, though not so familiar to the people of Lincoln as some of the gentlemen named, are of scarcely less merit in financial or business standing, and their equal in personal integrity. Mr. C. E. Waite is the Assistant Cashier, and is a man who attends strictly to business, and has also had considerable banking experience, having resigned the cashiership of the First National Bank, Humboldt, Neb., to accept his present position with the State National Bank.

No financial institution of Lincoln has shown a more constant growth than the Nebraska Savings Bank, now located at the southeast corner of O and Thirteenth streets, and no other bank in the city is more progressive in adopting methods that contribute to the interests and advantage of the people of the city and surrounding country. This bank was organized on July 20, 1886, and its deposits have grown from less than $2,000 on August 1, 1886, to about $85,000 on the same date in 1889. It does a general banking business.

The management of the bank seeks to encourage habits of frugality and success among the people, and to this end has adopted a savings-bank department for the public schools of the city, similar to the system so successful in Europe and some of the Eastern States. In this course the Nebraska Savings Bank was in advance of all other banks in this State. The principle of this system is to open accounts with the school children and receive deposits of ten cents or more, upon which interest is paid at the rate of five per cent per annum, compounded semi-annually. This education in economy is carried on systematically, by visiting the schools and seeing all the pupils, a growing number of whom are becoming regular depositors, thus inculcating fixed habits of saving and business, in a manner never to be eradicated during life, and which will be of great value to the pupils when they have grown to manhood and womanhood. The schools have regular deposit days, and 1,500 children have opened accounts and deposited the large sum of $8,000, of which about $4,000 stands to their credit at this date. This feature of banking has the hearty approval of leading educators and the progressive public.

The officers of the bank are: J. G. Southwick, President; Rev. E. M. Lewis, Vice President; L. C. Humphrey, Cashier; W. E. Taylor, Assistant Cashier. Directors.—C. C. White, Merchant Miller, Crete, Neb.; J. G. Southwick, Banker, Bennett, Neb.; James Kilburn, Capitalist, Lincoln; J. L. Miles, Banker, Omaha; George E. Bigelow, Real Estate Broker, Lincoln; D. L. Brace, Real Estate Broker, Lincoln; L. G. M. Baldwin, President Baldwin Investment Company, Lincoln; C. T. Brown, Grain Dealer, Lincoln; L. C. Humphrey.

The Capital National Bank, located on the southeast corner of O and Eleventh streets, is one of the most carefully-managed and successful banks in the city. It has a capital stock of $300,000. Of this bank C. W. Mosher is President; H. J. Walsh, Vice President; R. C. Outcalt, Cashier; and J. W. Maxwell, Assistant Cashier.

The American Exchange Bank was incorporated on December 1, 1888, and began business at the southeast corner of N and Eleventh streets, with a capital stock of $100,000. It is a carefully-managed institution and transacts a general banking business. Its officers are: I. M. Raymond, President; Lewis Gregory, Vice President; S. H. Burnham, Cashier; and D. E. Wing, Assistant Cashier.

The Lincoln Savings Bank Safe and Deposit Company was established on January 1, 1889, at the southeast corner of P and Eleventh streets, with a capital of $250,000. Its specialty is the safe-deposit vault, built of twenty-seven tons of steel, containing 1,000 safes for customers. This vault is both fire and burglar proof, and is the only one of its kind in the city. The officers of this bank are: Henry E. Lewis, President and Manager; A. P. S. Stewart, Vice President; John H.

McClay, Treasurer; and R. Welch, Teller. The Directors are: A. P. S. Stewart, H. J. Walsh, Henry E. Lewis, John B. Wright, W. H. McCreery, Fred Williams, H. P. Lau, Wm. McLaughlin, and John H. McCleary.

A solid and well-conducted institution of the city is the Lincoln National Bank, located in the Richards Block, on the northeast corner

THE RICHARDS BLOCK.

of Eleventh and O streets. It transacts all forms of a banking business, and its prosperity grows steadily from year to year. It was organized in August of 1882. Its present capital is $100,000, and its surplus is $35,000. Its officers now are: Nathan S. Harwood, President; R. E. Moore, Vice President; C. T. Boggs, Cashier; and Frank M. Cook, Assistant Cashier.

The Union Savings Bank, at 141 South Tenth street, was incorporated under the laws of the State April 26, 1886, and has been very successful. Its capital stock is $200,000, and the liabilities of the stockholders are $400,000. Its deposits amount to $180,000. Its officers are: R. E. Moore, President; E. E. Brown, Vice President; C. H. Imhoff, Cashier; and the Board of Directors—John Fitzgerald, C. E. Yates, R. E. Moore, E. E. Brown, T. E. Calvert, J. J. Imhoff, John R. Clark, K. K. Hayden, and J. McConniff.

One of the oldest existing financial institutions in Lincoln is the Lancaster County Bank, located at 117 South Tenth street. It was organized about nineteen years ago, now enjoys a large business, and is in a sound condition, its capital being $50,000 and its surplus $17,000. Its present officers are: W. J. Lamb, President; W. A. Green, Vice President; and E. B. Green, Cashier.

A prominent financial institution of Lincoln is the German National Bank, located in the Burr Block, at Twelfth and O streets. It was established on December 10, 1886, and has steadily grown in public favor. It has a paid-in capital of $100,000, and a surplus of $20,000, and transacts a general banking business, making a specialty of foreign collections. Its officers are: Herman H. Schaberg, President; C. C. Munson, Vice President; Joseph Boehmer, Cashier; and O. J. Wilcox, Assistant Cashier. The Directors are: Messrs. Herman H. Schaberg, C. C. Munson, Joseph Boehmer, C. E. Montgomery, Alex. Halter, F. A. Boehmer, B. J. Brotherton, Walter J. Harris, and J. A. Hudelson.

The Lincoln Loan and Trust Company is located in the basement of the Richards Block. It was organized in 1884, and is officered as follows: N. S. Harwood, President; W. G. Houtz, Vice President; C. T. Boggs, Treasurer; and Joseph Kelly, Manager. The Directors are: J. E. Houtz, John H. Ames, and W. R. Kelly.

The Capital Loan and Investment Company is located on the sixth floor of the Burr Block. It was organized May 1, 1889, makes a specialty of building loans, and has a growing business. It has a corps of officers as follows: J. T. Englehardt, President; W. W. W. Jones, Vice President; A. J. Millikin, Treasurer; H. F. Albers, Secretary; and S. B. Pound, Attorney.

The Baldwin Investment Company, at 106 South Thirteenth street, is a new and popular financial concern, incorporated on June 1, 1889. It was organized for the purpose of buying and selling commercial paper and other negotiable securities, including real estate mortgages. It has an authorized capital of $100,000, and a paid-in capital of $50,000. Its business is conducted with great prudence, the management having adopted the plan of loaning only on "two-name" paper, running not longer than eight months. In all cases they require written statements as to financial condition from the makers of paper, who must also have good commercial rating and a reputation for prompt paying. This plan carried out will insure to the company first-class securities to offer to its Eastern correspondents. The Board of Directors, who pass upon all loans, have had years of experience in loaning in Lincoln, and are competent judges as to the quality of paper offered. Its real estate loans are all made on not to exceed forty per cent of a conservative valuation, with insurance policy assigned with mortgages, or additional security, making this class of investments perfectly safe. The company invests its own funds in all paper offered for sale and guarantees payment at maturity. Its business has been very successful to date, it being large and growing constantly. Its officers are: Le Grand M. Baldwin, President; L. C. Humphrey, Vice President; and A. H. Humphrey, Secretary and Treasurer.

The Security Investment Company is located in rooms 1, 2 and 3, on the second floor of the Richards Block, corner of O and Eleventh streets. It was organized February 1, 1886, and has since been very prosperous, now having over $5,000,000 loaned in Nebraska. It also buys municipal bonds. Its officers are: R. E. Moore, President; John Moore, Vice President; T. W. Moore, Secretary and Treasurer. Its capital is $100,000.

The Clark & Leonard Investment Company, with offices in the First National Bank building, at Tenth and O streets, was organized October 1, 1886, and is one of the excellent institutions of the kind in Lincoln. It does a large business in mortgage loans, bonds, and other securities, having a capital of $200,000. Its officers are: Wm. M. Clark, President; J. W. McDonald, Secretary; and Wm. M. Leonard, Treasurer.

One of the most prosperous financial institutions in the city, probably because one of the most carefully managed, is the Farmers & Merchants Insurance Company. As its name indicates its risks are mainly confined to the property of prudent merchants and good farmers, and for that reason its financial condition continues to improve from year to year.

It was organized on July 2, 1885. According to law it made to the Auditor of State its first annual statement on December 31, 1885, as follows:

ASSETS.

First mortgage loans and accrued interest	$19,506.54
Bills receivable and accrued interest	13,558.41
Office Furniture and all other property	777.98
Cash in bank and company's office	23,488.54
Cash premiums in course of collection	1,028.35
Stockholders' secured notes	50,000.00
Total	$108,359.82

LIABILITIES.

Stock	$100,000.00
Reserve for reinsurance, per law	7,604.14
Liabilities	641.25
Net Surplus	114.43
	$108,359.82

The business of the Company steadily progressed, and in a manner most favorable to the success of the management of the company's affairs, as the exhibit of its condition reported to the State Auditor, under oath, on December 31, 1888, will show, when compared with the like statement of December 31, 1885:

ASSETS.

First mortgage loans and accrued interest	$65,263.90
Premium bills received and accrued interest	77,354.82
Bills received and interest secured by chattel mortgages	1,905.04
Cash in bank and company's office	24,133.63
Cash premiums in course of collection	9,405.61
Office furniture and other property	1,279.06
Stockholder's secured notes	50,000.00
Total	$229,342.06

LIABILITIES.

Capital stock	$100,000.00
Reserve for reinsurance required by law	97,846.15
Liabilities	1,846.15
Surplus	29,684.52
Total	$229,342.06

Or recapitulating the statements of the four years, we have the following very flattering exhibit:

	Premiums Received.	Losses.
1885	$21,903.47	$704.84
1886	76,001.25	6,740.85
1887	95,972.68	16,183.75
1888	108,153.98	20,068.25
Totals	$302,031.38	$43,697.69

Another feature of peculiar merit connected with this company's business policy is that it discards the technical delays in paying losses, which are so aggravating and injurious. It has paid losses within twenty-four hours after the fires occurred, and seldom allows a delay of over three or four days in paying a loss. This reform has won it much popular favor.

The officers for the present year are: D. E. Thompson, President; H. J. Walsh, Vice President; S. J. Alexander, Secretary; C. W. Mosher, Treasurer.

Dun's Commercial Agency is represented by a local office in the First National Bank block, by Frank D. Blish. This office was established in 1882, and is one of the best conducted institutions of the city.

An office of Bradstreet's Commercial Agency was opened in the State National Bank building during the present year, of which H. C. Patterson is the accommodating manager.

CHAPTER XXII.

THE PRESS OF LINCOLN — AS IN OTHER THINGS, SO IN NEWSPAPERS, DOES LINCOLN STAND AT THE FRONT — THE PAPERS THAT HAVE BEEN AND ARE AND THE MEN WHO PUBLISH THEM.

Lincoln has been fortunate in many particulars, and among others in having good newspapers. A good newspaper is a standing advertisement to the outside world that a good town is behind it, and this has been the only advertisement that Lincoln has ever had.

On the 14th of August, 1867, the Commissioners for the location of the seat of government for the State of Nebraska, selected and officially announced Lincoln, up to that time the town of "Lancaster," as the place. On the following day there appeared in the columns of the Nebraska City *Press* a prospectus for the publication of a weekly newspaper at Lincoln, to be called the *Nebraska Commonwealth*, over the signature of C. H. Gere. On the 7th day of September, the first copy of the new paper was printed at the office of the *Press*, there being at that time no accommodations for a newspaper office at the new capital. "C. H. Gere & Co." were the announced publishers.

On November 2d, the second number of the *Commonwealth* was issued at Lincoln, printed in the office of Hon. S. B. Galey, a stone building on the north side of the Government square, W. W. Carder, publisher, and C. H. Gere, editor. It was a seven-column sheet, of dingy appearance, the type being some old primer and nonpareil taken from the used-up material of the Nebraska City *Press*; the press used being the first "Washington" ever brought across the Missouri river into Nebraska territory.

Before the third number was issued (and it came out two weeks later) the *Commonwealth* had moved into an office of its own, a stone building of small dimensions on the corner lot of the Academy of Music block, which was torn down several years ago to make way for improvements. The issues thereafter were regular, except when some accident of transportation prevented the arrival of printing paper in time for the press.

In the May following, Mr. Gere, who had edited the paper from Omaha, removed permanently to Lincoln, and became associated with Mr. Carder in the business management of the paper, and the office was soon after removed to more roomy quarters over Jas. Sweet & Brock's bank, in the corner of what is now termed "Union block." In the spring of '69, the name of the paper was changed to the *Nebraska State Journal*.

In November of that year Mr. Carder was succeeded by Mr. J. Q. Brownlee, and shortly after the office, still in search of more room, was taken across O street, and occupied the second floor of the frame building second door east of the State block.

On the 20th day of July, 1870, the day on which the Burlington & Missouri River Railroad ran its first train into Lincoln, and struck death to the stage line that had been the only means of transportation to the capital of Nebraska, the *Daily State Journal* first saw the light.

A daily edition had prior to this time been worked off on the hand press, during the session of the Legislature in the winter of '69 and '70, but it contained little more than the summary of legislative proceedings, and some local items.

A new Taylor cylinder press had been added to the *Journal* machinery, and after a dozen years of continual faithful service, it gave way to the largest size, two-revolution, Cottrell press, with all modern improvements, including folder.

Still crowded for room, owing to its rapid growth, the *Journal* office in the spring of '71 returned to the State block, took possession of the rooms over Rudolph's grocery house, that had just been extended fifty feet in the rear, making its quarters 25x100, and amply sufficient for its accommodation. Shortly after, Mr. Brownlee disposed of his interest to Hon. H. D. Hathaway, of the Plattsmouth *Herald*, taking an interest in the *Herald* as part payment, and the firm name became Gere & Hathaway.

In the fall of 1872 a separation was made between the newspaper and the job business, and the *State Journal* Company was organized, the members being Messrs. Gere & Hathaway, and Messrs. A. H. Mendenhall and Geo. W. Roberts, of Peoria, Ill., Mr. Mendenhall having long been the foreman of the *Transcript* office, and the latter, the proprietor of a bindery and blank book establishment in that city.

A large addition of material and machinery for book and job printing, bindery, and blank book making, was made to the old job department of the *Journal*, and again more room had to be obtained. The second stories of the five buildings, known as Commercial block, on the southwest corner of Government square, were connected by a common hall, and after some alterations, nearly the whole of the upper half of the block was taken, part for the *State Journal* company, and part for the newspaper, still owned and published by Gere & Hathaway.

STATE JOURNAL BUILDING.

In 1887, Mr. Roberts having sold his interest in the *Journal* company to Mr. John R. Clark, and it having been incorporated under the laws of the State, Messrs. Gere & Hathaway transferred the newspaper to the company.

The officers of the company are: C. H. Gere, President; A. H. Mendenhall, Vice President; John R. Clark, Secretary, and H. D. Hathaway, Treasurer.

The beginning of the year 1882, found the *State Journal* company in the occupancy of their handsome and spacious new building, situated upon the corner of P and Ninth streets. This building is a substantial stone and brick structure, three stories and basement, with a frontage of 75 feet on P street, and 142 feet on Ninth street. The ground was broken in June, 1880, and the various departments ready for occupancy the first of December, 1881.

Prior to this last removal into its own quarters, the company had added a small line of stationery for its jobbing trade. This department has reached such proportions that it now occupies one-third of the building — the part that was for a time rented. Its mechanical and artistic departments have also grown in the same proportions. A dozen steam presses are used for its job and book work. Its bindery is the largest and completest in the west.

To its thoroughly equipped electrotyping and stereotyping department, it has added a very complete engraving and lithographing establishment, which is employed to its full capacity in furnishing Nebraska work to Nebraskans. The two-revolution Cottrell press has been sent to the job-rooms, and the *Journal* has for some time been printed on a Hoe perfecting press, with a capacity of 10,000 double sheets per hour, delivered folded to the hands of the mailers and newsboys.

The volume of the business of the *Journal* Company, in all its departments, reached, in 1882, the first year of its occupancy of its own building, $130,000. For the fiscal year ending July 15, 1889, it amounted to $288,306.31. It paid for labor during those twelve months an aggregate of $105,176.53, a fraction over $2,000 per week. Its freight bills for the year amounted to $7,318.79.

The history of the democratic press of Lincoln is a varied one. Democratic newspapers have had a precarious existence, and have changed names and owners frequently. In 1867 the Nebraska *Statesman* was founded by Augustus Harvey as a weekly. It was sold within eighteen months to Randall & Smails, who changed it from a weekly to an evening daily. Owing to Randall's mismanagement, the concern broke financially, and the material went into the Fremont *Tribune* office. About 1878 General Vifquain founded the *State Democrat*, which also changed hands frequently. Among the prominent Democrats who have had control of the paper may be mentioned Hon. Albert Watkins, Hon. A. J. Sawyer, and Hon. J. W. Barnhart. Changes continued to occur until August 1, 1886, when the property passed into the hands of J. D. Calhoun, who successfully conducted the paper for twenty-three months. On July 1, 1888, Mr. Calhoun sold out to the "*Call* Publishing Company," which changed its politics. In the following August, Messrs. J. A. Emmons and Sol. Oppenheimer purchased an outfit and established the *Weekly State Democrat*, which is yet in publication and enjoys a good circulation and fair patronage. Mr. Oppenheimer soon sold his interest to Capt. Emmons, who is now the editor, the publishers being the *Democrat* Publishing Company. The *Democrat* is ably edited, and is earnest in its support of party principles and in pushing Lincoln to the front.

On July 1, 1888, was issued the first number of the Lincoln *Daily Call*, as an evening paper, by the "*Call* Publishing Company." Of this company H. M. Bushnell is President, Sam D. Cox Secretary, Treasurer, and Business Manager, and Al. Fairbrother, Managing Editor. Under the management of these three gentlemen the *Call* has grown rapidly in circulation and influence. It is Republican in politics, although free to criticise where criticism is thought to be needed.

Few business enterprises of the city have grown more rapidly than the Lincoln *News* plant. Beginning as a very small job office, in 1880, by Mr. E. B. Hyde, it has now expanded into a large printing house, including an excellent book bindery, facilities for stereotyping, and two newspaper and a number of job presses. The *Daily News* was first published on the 26th of October, 1881, as a four column folio, the day of President Garfield's funeral, by Mr. T. H. Hyde, who actively joined his son, E. B. Hyde, in the business at that time, and has been the main factor in the enterprise ever since. The paper was started to contribute to the business interests of the job department. The winter of 1881-2 was one of commercial activity, and the *News* prospered, so that early in the spring of 1882 the daily was enlarged to a five-column folio, and advanced to a six-column folio late in the fall of that year. The *News* continued to grow, and in 1885 Mr. Walter Hoge became interested in the business, and the firm became Hyde, Hoge & Hyde. The pressure of patronage required another enlargement of the *News* in 1887, when it became a seven-column folio. About the first of the year 1888 a stock company was formed called the "*Lincoln News* Company," and it so continues to the present time, with Messrs. Thomas H. Hyde and E. B. Hyde as the leading stockholders. The daily was again enlarged in the fall of 1888 to an eight-column folio. Mr. Hoge retired from the company during the summer of 1888. Mr. Harry Dobbins became connected with the editorial department in 1888, and he and Mr. T. H. Hyde do the main editorial work, Mr. Hyde being managing editor. Mr. E. B. Hyde is manager of the mechanical and business departments.

The *News* Company now occupies three floors of the brick building at 121-3 North Tenth street. The daily is steadily increasing its circulation and business, and the weekly *News* has a large circulation among the people of the county. Altogether the *News* establishment is the largest printing house, except that of the *Journal*, in the South Platte section of Nebraska.

The first German newspaper published in the city of Lincoln was called the *Staats-Zeitung*, and was owned and edited by Dr. F. Renner, now of Nebraska City. The doctor, a well educated man and strong Republican, started the *Staats-Zeitung* in 1871, and made a strong fight for General Grant's reëlection in 1872. The *Staats-Zeitung* was afterward moved to Nebraska City, where it is now published by Mr. Bentler.

The Germans of the city of Lincoln, feeling the necessity of having an organ in their own language, contributed, in the year 1880, a large sum of money, and guaranteed a good patronage, to Peter Karberg, who was known as an old and experienced newspaper man in Dubuque. He moved to Lincoln in the month of May, 1880, and published the first number of his *Nebraska Staats-Anzeiger* on June 1st, 1880. Karberg's experience and energy soon made the *Staats-Anzeiger* one of the best and most influential German papers in the State. The early death of Mr. Karberg, on July 2, 1884, made the sale of his paper necessary, and Mr. Henry Brügmann became the successor of Mr. Karberg. Financial troubles caused the foreclosure and sale of the *Staats-Anzeiger* in October, 1887. The creditors bought the material, and after disposing of the job department formerly connected with the paper, sold it to Schaal & Esser, who now continue its publication. The *Anzeiger* was a strong advocate of Republican principles under its first two proprietors, who themselves were strong party

22

men. The present publishers are Democrats, and the paper has no avowed policy.

The Lincoln *Freie Presse* is the youngest, but the most successful, German paper, not only in the city of Lincoln, but in the whole State of Nebraska. Its publisher and editor, Major J. D. Kluetsch, is one of the best-known Germans of our State. Being one of the oldest citizens of our city, Mr. Kluetsch knows the wants of our German population, and publishes just such a paper as is demanded and needed. The Lincoln *Freie Presse*, a seven-column, eight page weekly, was first published on September 1st, 1884, by G. Z. Bluedhorn, who sold it on February 15, 1886, to its present owner, Mr. J. D. Kluetsch. It has now the largest circulation of any German paper in the State. Its circulation is unlimited among the German residents of this and adjoining States, and it accordingly enjoys a very large advertising patronage. Independent in politics, tolerant in religious matters, and fearless, though true, in matters pertaining to the welfare of our city and State, the *Freie Presse* has done more than any other German paper to build up the State of Nebraska and city of Lincoln. The history of Lincoln, written by the *Freie Presse* in the German language, in a series of twenty-eight able articles, has advertised our city all over the United States, and also abroad, and Mr. Kluetsch and his paper have been highly commended for the enterprise shown by these articles. John D. Kluetsch, editor and publisher of this paper, was born on the 22d day of March, 1833, in a town called Uelmen, near Coblentz, on the river Rhine, in the kingdom of Prussia. After passing the primary schools of his town, he studied at the gymnasiums at Recklinghausen, in Westphalia, and at Coblentz and Trier, in the province of Rhenish Prussia. The gymnasium at Trier, (no doubt the oldest city in Western Europe, and at one time the residence of Constantine the Great,) was always considered one of the best schools in Germany. After graduating, Mr. Kluetsch visited the University of Bonn, and the Academy of Forestry at Eisenach, the city in which Martin Luther was held as a prisoner, and where he translated the Bible. Having finished his studies, Mr. Kluetsch entered the Prussian Army as a one year volunteer in the Eighth Prussian Sharpshooters' Battallion, at Wetzlar, near Giessen, the well-known German university. After this we find Mr. Kluetsch at the city of Cologne, where he remained in the government's employ, with the exception of a few months during the Franco-Austrian war, in 1859, when he joined the Prussian army again, until he emigrated to this country, in May, 1861, shortly after the breaking out of the rebellion. Mr. Kluetsch enlisted as a private in the Eighty-second Illinois Volunteers, and received many promotions for his bravery and good behavior. He served on the staffs of Generals O. O. Howard and Carl Schurz, and took part in some of the hardest-fought battles of our last war; for instance, Fredericksburg, Chancellorsville, Gettysburg, Mission Ridge, and Lookout Mountain. After leaving the army, Mr. Kluetsch moved to Chicago, where he held a number of positions in the postal service, and in the recorder's office as map clerk. He was elected collector of taxes for West Chicago in 1870, and reëlected in 1871, and moved to Lincoln on the 1st of May, 1872. Here he followed several vocations, until the 15th day of February, 1886, when he purchased the Lincoln *Freie Presse*, of which paper he is the sole owner.

The *Hausbesucher* (Home Visitor) is another German paper published in this city by Rev. Chr. Bruegger, pastor of the German Methodist Church, corner of Fifteenth and M streets, under the auspices of this church. It was founded by Rev. Karl Harris, the former pastor, on June 1, 1881. Its circulation is largely among the members of the above church, and reaches about 300 copies.

The *Capital City Courier* was started with an office desk, but now has one of the finest and most complete newspaper and job printing establishments in the State. The *Courier* was established by its present proprietor, Mr. L. Wessel jr., December 9, 1885. By successive enlargements the *Courier* grew from a four to a six-column folio. At the end of six months it blossomed out as a full-fledged newspaper, and charged a subscription price. For the State Fair, of 1887, the proprietor published an edition of 10,000 copies, each eight pages of six columns, and the paper has continued that size ever since. It is one of that class of journals known in the West as "society papers," but it also has full and carefully edited departments devoted to the drama, literature, sport, fashions, humor, music, religion, woman, home architecture, and correspondence, besides chatty comments on politics and other current events.

In connection with the paper a department for the prosecution of the artistic in printing and publishing is maintained. The offices are on Twelfth street, in the new Burr block, where two store-rooms are occupied, one for the *Courier* and business department and the other for the composing and press-rooms.

Believing that there was an opening in the city for a first-class distinctive Sunday morning paper, the *Sunday Morning Globe* was brought into existence, in April, 1889, the publishers and editors being W. L. Hunter, late of Illinois, and J. C. Seacrest, who had been for two years identified with the newspaper business of the city. The *Globe* is an eight-page, six-column paper, independent in politics, and devoted especially to the interests of society, secret fraternities, sports, and city events touching the interests of the masses. It aims to be a people's paper. The business is done in the name of the *Globe* Publishing Company. The office of the company is located in the Windsor block. The daily *Globe* was started September 28, 1889.

The first agricultural paper published in Lincoln, the *Nebraska Farmer*, was established in 1872, by General J. C. McBride and J. C. Clarkson, now of Chicago. At the time this publication was established, the farming and live-stock interests of Nebraska amounted to very little; they were too young to support a paper published in their interest. But the main reason for the establishment of the paper was to promote, by its influence, the success of certain land deals in the State in connection with a railway project of that early day. In 1880, however, the farming and live-stock interests of the State had grown to larger proportions, making the field of an agricultural paper broader and more lucrative. In that year General McBride purchased his partner's interest in the journal and conducted it alone for some time, when he sold an interest in the paper to O. M. Druse. Soon after this transaction General McBride was appointed postmaster, and the entire paper became the property of Mr. Druse. At this time the *Farmer* was a monthly publication. In January, 1887, L. L. Siler, of Lawrence, Kas., and H. E. Heath, of Kansas City, purchased the paper of Mr. Druse, who had been running it for some time as a semi-monthly.

The new firm soon changed it to a weekly publication. In January, 1888, Mr. Siler sold his three-fifths interest to his partner, H.

E. Heath, who in the following spring took his brother, H. A. Heath, a practical farmer from Western Nebraska, into partnership, since which time the firm has remained unchanged. The *Nebraska Farmer* is recognized as the leading farm journal published in the West. It is ably edited, and has a large force of contributors and correspondents, made up of men who have practical knowledge of the things about which they write. It has an extensive circulation through Nebraska, Kansas, Colorado, and other Western States.

In the fall of 1886, Colonel H. S. Reed and Ex-Governor Robert W. Furnas established a monthly journal called *Western Resources*, the first number of which was issued in January, 1887. In the fall of 1887 Colonel Reed purchased the interest of Governor Furnas, and continued to conduct the paper as a monthly until January 1, 1889, when the form of the paper was changed, as was also the time of publication. It is now issued three times per month, viz: on the 10th, 20th, and 30th.

At the time *Western Resources* was established it was made a general farm paper, but when Colonel Reed became sole proprietor he changed policy and made the paper exclusively a live-stock journal, devoted to the live-stock interests of the State. Since the paper has been conducted on this line of policy, more live-stock organizations have been formed in the State than ever before, for which Colonel Reed is mainly responsible. *Western Resources* is without a peer in its line in the West, and is acknowledged to occupy second place among the live stock journals of the entire country. Its circulation is about 10,000 copies, and it is the official organ of the following associations, which shows that it is appreciated by the men in whose interest it is published: Nebraska Draft Horse Breeders' Association; Trotting Horse Breeders' Association; Hereford Breeders' Association; Imported Stock Breeders' Association, and the Association of Expert Judges of Swine.

The *Nebraska State Laborer* was established in August, 1888, by the organized workingmen of this city, and is published under the auspices of their principal organization, the Central Trades and Labor Union. It earnestly champions the cause of the workingmen, and ably advocates all measures which tend to ameliorate the condition of the laboring masses and elevate them to a higher plane of usefulness and enjoyment. It has grown rapidly in popular favor, and is exercising a wide influence among that class to whose interest it is devoted. It is edited by B. S. Littlefield, a former well-known teacher in Lillibridge & Roose's business college.

There are at this time twenty-six periodicals published in Lincoln. Besides those referred to at greater length, may be mentioned, more or less in detail, the following additional publications: The *Nebraska Methodist*, published at Wesleyan University, in the interest of that institution and Nebraska Methodism generally; the *Hesperian* is the organ of the students of the State University; the *Proscenium* is a theatrical sheet, issued in the interests of Funke's Opera House; the *Congregational News*, by Rev. H. A. French, is a journal devoted to the interests of the Congregational Church; the *Lincoln Monthly*, by Messrs. Lillibridge & Roose, represents the interests of the Lincoln Business College; the *New Republic* is the organ of the Prohibition party in the State, of which Hon. W. H. Hardy is now the editor; the *Western Workman*, by Professor F. F. Roose, is the Western organ of the Ancient Order of United Workmen; the Lincoln *Journal of Commerce*, is a monthly price current, published in the interests of the city jobbing trade, and for other business purposes; the Nebraska Railway *Gazetteer*, by Professor F. F. Roose, is a monthly periodical devoted to western railway affairs; the *Daily Stock Dealer* is a daily published by Mr. Walter Hoge for the benefit of the Lincoln Stock Yards, Packing and Provision Company, and the stock dealers of this vicinity; the *Home News* is a little folio in the interests of the Home for the Friendless; the *Farmers' Alliance* is a monthly, designed to represent the association of farmers by that name; the Lincoln *Newspaper Union* is the trade journal of the Lincoln newspaper ready-print supply and publishing house, managed by Mr. Frank Rohm; this house also prints the Nebraska State *Capital*, a story paper; *Modern Bookkeeping*, by Lillibridge & Roose, is published in the interests of accountants and students.

The Cherrier Directory Publishing Company, of which A. B. Cherrier and N. Hall are the members, has for two years past published city directories which are better arranged, more convenient of reference, and more complete, than any directory before published.

CHAPTER XXIII.

INCARCERATION OF THE CITY COUNCIL—A MEMORABLE OCCURRENCE IN THE CITY'S HISTORY—A SKETCH OF THE PROCEEDINGS, AND A LEGAL HISTORY OF THE CASE.

In the fall of 1887, the Mayor and eleven members of the City Council were imprisoned in the county jail of Douglas county for alleged contempt of the Circuit Court of the United States, District of Nebraska. The following is a brief statement of the facts which occasioned this extraordinary action on the part of the Federal Court:

Sometime in the month of August certain parties, gamblers in the city of Lincoln, preferred charges in writing with the Council, against Albert F. Parsons, Police Judge, alleging that he had been guilty of malfeasance in office, in that he had not accounted for moneys collected by him as fines as required by law. These charges were the result of a warfare made upon the gambling fraternity of the city by the newly-elected Mayor, A. J. Sawyer, and the Marshal and police appointed by him. In compliance with the request of the persons making the charges, a committee of the Council was appointed to investigate the charges. The committee met, and after hearing much testimony pro and con, reported to the Council that in their opinion the charges were true, and that the Police Judge had not paid over to the Treasurer all the money by him received, and recommended that his office be declared vacant, and that a successor be appointed by the Mayor. The ordinance then in force relating to removal of city officers not providing for trial by a committee of less than the whole of the Council, it was amended, and the committee's report again filed.

While the resolution declaring the office vacant was pending, Mr. Parsons appeared with his attorney, Mr. L. C. Burr, and requested that action be delayed until a certain day, when the evidence could be read and counsel heard before the whole Council, stating that if this was done they would be satisfied with the action of the Council in the premises. Their request was acceded to, and a day fixed as desired.

Before that day arrived, however, Mr. Parsons had obtained from Judge Brewer, of the United States Circuit Court, an order restraining the Mayor and Council from taking further action in the premises until he could hear and determine the matter. After careful consideration, and after taking advice of counsel, the Mayor and Council became satisfied that the restraining order was made without authority of law, and was of no binding force or effect. They accordingly disregarded it, and proceeded to declare the office of Police Judge vacant, and the Mayor appointed and the Council confirmed Mr. H. J. Whitmore as Police Judge to fill the vacancy.

The action of the city officials was at once brought to the attention of the court, and an order entered, requiring the Mayor and Council to appear and show cause why they should not be punished for contempt.

At the appointed time the parties appeared and presented their reasons for violating the injunction, and averred that the court was without jurisdiction to issue the same, and that consequently they were under no obligations to obey it. Judge Brewer, however, held that his order was properly issued, and adjudged the defendants guilty of contempt, and sentenced Mayor Sawyer, and Councilmen Briscoe, Burks, Cooper, Pace, and Dean, to pay a fine of fifty dollars each, and Councilmen Billingsley, Graham, Hovey, Ensign, Fraas, and Dailey, to pay a fine of six hundred dollars each. One and all declared their intention to suffer imprisonment rather than pay the fine imposed, and they were accordingly taken in charge by the United States Marshal, and confined in the Douglas county jail.

Their attorney, Hon. G. M. Lambertson, had in the meantime prepared the proper papers for an application to the Supreme Court of the United States for a writ of *habeas corpus*, and took the first train for the city of Washington and made his application in person to Justice Miller. The writ was immediately issued as prayed, and after a week of imprisonment, the Lincoln city government was once more at liberty. The application for a writ of *habeas corpus* was most elaborately argued in the Supreme Court, and great interest was manifested in the case by the legal fraternity and public generally. January 12, 1888, the decision of the Supreme Court was announced, and with but two exceptions, the judges united in declaring the imprisonment unlawful, and ordering the release of the prisoners. The legal aspect of the case was as follows:

It was contended by the petitioners that the Circuit Court of the United States, sitting as a court of equity, had no jurisdiction and authority to make the order under which they were held by the Marshal.

On this point the court said: "The office and jurisdiction of a court of equity, unless enlarged by express statute, are limited to the protection of rights of property. It has no jurisdiction over the prosecution, the punishment, or the pardon, of crimes or misdemeanors, or over the appointment and removal of public officers, or to sustain a bill in equity to restrain or relieve against proceedings for the punishment of offenses, or for the removal of public officers, is to invade the domain of the courts of common law, or of the executive and administrative department of the Government."

The court then reviewed the petition of Mr. Parsons upon which the restraining order was granted. The matters of law stated in that bill as grounds for the intervention of the Circuit Court were that the amended ordinance was an *ex-post-facto* law, and that all the proceedings of the City Council and its committee, as well as both ordinances, were illegal and void, and in conflict with and in violation of those articles of the Constitution of the United States which provide that no person shall be deprived of life, liberty, or property, without due process of law; that in all criminal prosecutions the accused shall enjoy the right to a speedy and public trial by an impartial jury of the State and district where the crime shall have been committed, and to have compulsory process for obtaining witnesses in his favor, and that no State shall pass any *ex-post-facto* law, or deprive any person of life, liberty, or property, without due process of law, or deny to any person within its jurisdiction the equal protection of the laws. The court held that the articles which provide that no person shall be deprived of life, liberty, or property, without due process of law, and to secure to the accused in criminal prosecutions trial by jury, and compulsory process for his witnesses, apply to the United States only, and not to laws or proceedings under the authority of a State, and that the provision which prohibits any State to pass *ex-post-facto* laws applies only to legislation concerning crime; that if the ordinances and proceedings of the Council were in the nature of civil as distinguished from criminal proceedings, the only possible ground for the interposition of the courts of the United States in any form was that Parsons, if removed from office, would be deprived by the State, of life, liberty, or property, without due process of law, or has been denied the equal protection of the laws. For this a remedy could be found in the courts of the State, by proper proceedings, and the equity courts were powerless to interfere. But that whether the proceedings of the Council were to be regarded as in their nature criminal or civil, judicial or merely administrative, they related to a subject which the Circuit Court of the United States, sitting in equity, has no jurisdiction or power over, and can neither try and determine for itself, nor restrain by injunction, the tribunals and officers of the State and city from trying and determining; that the court being without jurisdiction to entertain the bill for an injunction, all its proceedings in the exercise of the jurisdiction which it assumed are null and void; that it had no power to make the restraining order; that the adjudication that the defendants were guilty of contempt in disregarding that order was equally void; and that their detention by the Marshal under that adjudication was without authority of law, and they should be discharged.

The termination of this proceeding in the manner above indicated, completely vindicating the action of the Council, was greeted by the citizens of Lincoln with great rejoicing, and the released councilmen were the heroes of the hour.

CHAPTER XXIV.

THE TARTARRAX PAGEANT—THE ORIGINATOR OF THE IDEA—THE PARADE—THE PURPOSE TO MAKE THE TARTARRAX PARADE AN ANNUAL OCCURRENCE.

Mr. Robert McReynolds, manager of Funke's Opera House, is a man of large ideality, and possesses a high appreciation of the romantic, poetic, and spectacular. He has seen the world, and has an eye to what will please the people. He is not afraid to do and dare, and take reasonable chances on winning success. He was one of the pioneer adventurers into the Black Hills, and went there as early as February, 1876. During the closing months of that year he explored Mexico, visited Cuba, and meditated on the poetic deeds of Christopher Columbus while standing by his tomb in the cathedral of Santo Domingo, in Havana. During 1878 and 1879 he traveled over the battle-scarred Southern States, and wrote what he saw for the press. When the great gold excitement was taking thousands to Leadville, he assisted in leading the van. He is the author of several novels that have been published in book form, and his newspaper "fairy tale," which resurrected Brigham Young, the late president and priest of the Salt Lake "Saints," and found him hidden away near Lincoln, was one of the most successful canards published in recent years. He settled down to business in 1880, in this city, and it so happened that during recent months that he read the tale of mythological heroism displayed by the Spanish general, Coronado, who traveled from Mexico to Nebraska to see whether King Tartarrax really did live in golden splendor in the Land of the Quivera, as related in another chapter of this book.

When it was proposed during April and May to celebrate the Fourth of July this year, the city seemed to think it ought to be done. Lincoln had not attempted a worthy observance of the day for a number of years. Various plans were proposed, to the end that something unique and entertaining might be produced. Mr. McReynolds suggested to several of his friends of the city press that the story of King Tartarrax might be adopted, in some way, to produce at least a fine spectacular parade and effect. He could see, in his mind, how great a pageant the Court of Tartarrax and the armored cavaliers of Coronado would make. There would be the glitter, the pomp, the richly-colored uniforms, the panoplied knights, the arms and banners of the time; and all this was Nebraska's own tradition, peculiar to herself. It was practically fitting, and, it seemed to him, a "drawing card."

ROBT. McREYNOLDS, ORIGINATOR OF THE TARTARRAX PAGEANT.

He explained his scheme to R. L. Rowe, among others, then with the *State Journal*, who, in writing about it afterward, found it necessary to reconcile the fact that, while many had fallen in with the Tartarrax plan of celebration, the labor organizations of the city had decided to have a symbolic display of the industries and business of the city. He proposed that the Tartarrax representation and the trades display be united on the plan of exhibiting Nebraska in the semi-barbaric days of the weird Spanish invasion, under the rule of kings, and Nebraska in 1889, under the prosperity and laws of the Republic.

This scheme of unification was adopted and substantially carried out. To encourage the people to make the pageant as great a success as possible, he also urged, in the paper, that the Tartarrax and Trades Display be used as the foundation for an annual carnival, similar to that of the Veiled Prophet, in St. Louis, and Mardi Gras, in New Orleans, that the nation might become more familiar with Nebraska and Lincoln, through the interesting combination of the poetic past and the patriotic and realistic present. This possibility was also kept in view in the preparation of the Tartarrax and Industrial Pageant, and it is not improbable that Tartarrax will come to be a great National attraction during the next five or six years, more interesting than the Veiled Prophet or Mardi Gras, because more appropriate to the institutions of our country, and more heroic and poetic.

On the 17th of May Mr. McReynolds appeared before the city Board of Trade, which convened in the county court room, on the third floor of the building on the corner of Eleventh and M streets. He proposed to the board that it give official sanction and encouragement to a grand Fourth of July celebration movement, indicating briefly the nature of the proposed exposition. The board hesitated a little, as it was making a vigorous effort to raise $10,000 by subscription to advertise the city, and feared that a second call for money might imperil the success of the main subscription. But Messrs. Thomas Lowrey, M. Ackerman, and others, pressed the matter and said the board would be asked for no money. The use of its name was all that was solicited. The matter was finally disposed of by the appointment of a committee of five to report to the board, at an early meeting, on the feasibility of attempting a celebration of the kind projected. This committee was composed of Messrs. M. Ackerman, J. J. Butler, C. J. Ernst, A. D. Kitchen, and Robert McReynolds.

A week later, May 24th, this committee reported to the board at the same place, and unanimously agreed "that a grand celebration of the Fourth of July be heartily recommended by the Lincoln Board of Trade." This report was adopted by the board, and a committee of ten was named to represent the board in the preparation of the display, said committee being strictly instructed to incur no financial liability in the name of the board. The committee selected was as follows: Robert McReynolds, Chairman; M. Ackerman, C. J. Ernst, Frank Perkins, Phelps Paine, C. C. Munson, H. Woltemade, J. J. Butler, T. F. Lasch, J. C. Seacrest.

Later in the evening, a committee representing the Central Trades Union of the city, appeared before the board, and announced, through its chairman, Mr. George A. Fox, that the workingmen had decided upon a celebration in the city, and asked the board's coöperation. Mr. E. E. Brown moved that the board committee be instructed to coöperate with all other committees in arranging for a Fourth of July celebration. This was unanimously agreed to. On the evening of June 3d, these committees met on the stage of Funke's Opera House, organized by electing Robert McReynolds chairman of the joint committee, appointed subcommittees to take charge of the various features of the celebration, such as finance, decorations, the press, advertising, and so on.

Then the work went on with energy. Such a pageant was an experiment in Lincoln, and it was hard work to devise plans new to all, get the people interested, and come up to the requirements of the advertisements that had to be put out at once. But here the peculiar ability of Robert McReynolds was best displayed. He planned, encouraged, and pushed the scheme with constant energy. He sent out printed matter in the form of edicts and commissions from King Tartarrax, to his faithful subjects, and commissions from Coronado to his faithful cavaliers, commanding them to appear and aid in the pageant. These productions were in illuminated colors, with oriental and cabalistic embellishments, and were wonderfully unique. After much zealous labor, in which Robert McReynolds was the inspiring presence, and M. Ackerman, T. F. Lasch, G. A. Fox, and J. H. Kramer, distinguished themselves for tireless, energetic assistance, the great anniversary day came, bright and salubrious. Early in the day every window, and many house tops, from O and Twenty-seventh streets to Eighth, and for several blocks in all directions from O and Tenth, on the line of the procession, were filled with eager faces. Every foot of sidewalk on the route was occupied, and the side streets were filled with vehicles loaded with persons, full of patriotic interest.

It had been arranged that when the parade was ready to begin, a couple of messengers should ride swiftly and deliver to Lieutenant C. P. Walter, commander of the State University artillery, on the uni-

VIEW OF THE TARTARIAN PARADE.

versity campus, orders to fire the national salute, which was to be the signal to the great procession to start, and to the people that it was in motion. Harry Bartruff and William McClay, two bold young men, were each mounted on a "runaway" horse, and stood just at the head of the parade, at Twenty-fourth and O streets. The street was clear of street-cars, vehicles, and people, the entire length. The army of spectators were earnestly expectant. The king, Mr. Richard O'Neill, in fine costume of gold, silk, velvet, brass armor, and crown, gave the signal that all was ready. Marshal W. W. Carder, and the city police, all mounted, dressed into position, ready for the boom of the cannon and command, "Forward." The head of the column was at once on the alert.

Then the two heralds were given the word to "go." Their racers fairly sprang into the air, and were off like the wind. It had been the intention of the riders to make the start on the dead run, then move more slowly from Nineteenth to Fifteenth streets, and then make another swift dash the remainder of the distance. But one horse took the bit in his teeth and made a dead race of it all the way to the postoffice; in fact made a race of it without regard to his rider. The other horse, of course, kept up as best he could. This spectacle electrified the great concourse of people, and many declared it one of the most picturesque and inspiring sights of the day. The heralds started at 11:56½ o'clock A. M., and the first boom of the cannon resounded over the city just as the clock in Temple hall began to strike for noon. Then the great procession began to slowly move westward on O street; and it was a pageant which probably never was approached in beauty, magnitude, and complexity of display, west of the Missouri river, certainly not in Nebraska or outside of San Francisco, if even there. The column filled the street, in many parts, to its full width, for a continuous distance of over thirty blocks, or two and one-half miles. The horsemen and footmen were in the varicolored costumes of medieval Spain, or of modern Turks, and other nations, and all were decked in more or less gold and silver ornaments. Many wore some sort of brilliant armor, crested helmets, and other striking imitations of antique costumes and heraldry. Bright spears and battle axes, gorgeous banners, plumes, and glittering shields, were numerous. The head of the procession represented the Tartarrax scheme. The main portion of the display was for the arts, trades, resources, and principles of the modern republic.

After the police, mounted, in uniform, and wearing light colored helmet caps, came Gordon's drum corps, fantastically costumed, led by Marshals L. S. Gillick and A. T. Cameron. Then followed the king's herald, splendidly mounted, and dressed like a Turkish pasha. The king's buglers, sounding the king's coming, were in Spanish dress. Then followed King Tartarrax, Mr. Richard O'Neill, mounted on a white horse, costumed in red velvet, with rich trimmings. He wore a long gray beard and gray hair, a crown of gold studded with brilliant jewels. Following him were fifty mounted cavaliers in knightly costumes. The king and his guard were Knights of Pythias. Next came the University Cadet Band, musicians to the queen of Tartarrax. The queen, Miss Nellie Graves, robed in purple and scarlet satin, followed, riding in a gorgeously decked chariot, surrounded by her court, all clad in rich and appropriate costumes. Following were two other large display chariots, filled with members of the queen's court. These were mainly Odd Fellows and Daughters of Rebekah. Mr. A. H. Weir was the queen's minister. Curtice & Thiers's Military Band were musicians to General Coronado. Mr. T. Lowrey followed the queen, costumed like a Spanish officer of three hundred and fifty years ago. Mr. E. W. Hunt, chief of the staff, rode at the general's left, and his richly armed and warlike staff came next in brilliant array. Then came the Omaha Wheel Club, other wheelmen, and the Lincoln Wheelmen, the latter rigged out in show attire of red, white, and blue, and their wheels bright with flags and bunting. A phalanx of colored spearmen, in striking dress of knightly cut, marched ahead of the open barouches conveying Mayor Graham, Ex-Mayor Sawyer, Hon. G. M. Lambertson, and R. H. Oakley, president of the Board of Trade, and other citizens.

Then came the industrial and merchants' parade, making a highly creditable display. After the line of march had been completed, the exercises at the capitol grounds came next in order, where Tartarrax welcomed his visitors, Coronado, and ambassadors from the courts of Mexico and other Southern States, and was presented with the keys of the city by his honor the Mayor.

The Tartarrax parade proved to be a wonderful success, and if in future years the idea is reproduced and made more elaborate in its production, the pageant of 1889 will be looked back to as the starting point of one distinguishing feature about Lincoln which will make her name a household word throughout the country.

CHAPTER XXV.

Lancaster Pioneers—The Formation of the Old Settlers' Association—The Membership of the Association on August 1, 1889.

The great men and women of this nation have generally been pioneers, or the descendants of pioneers. Abraham Lincoln, General U. S. Grant, Andrew Jackson, James A. Garfield, and Benjamin Harrison, are examples of pioneer manhood. It takes a man or woman who has the constancy and courage of heroes to go to a wild and unsubdued region and battle with nature, Indians, poverty, years of hard labor, and deny themselves the luxuries of organized society, for the purpose of earning a home and competence for their declining years. The pioneers are among the heroes of progress and civilization, to whom society will ever be indebted.

Their hardships develop a spirit of fraternity among them, and when the conflicts of the wilderness are over, they take delight in forming associations to commemorate the deeds done in conquering the wilderness and creating a new State. They recount the history of the past, smile at early hardships, recall situations of terror and distress with grim humor, and sing "Auld Lang Syne" with a zest and brotherly warmth that is the very spirit of eloquence.

The time is now ripe for an Old Settlers' Association in Lincoln and Lancaster county, and such an association is now in existence, probably for a long life, to gratify the pioneers, and to record their history while engaged in the work of erecting this splendid commonwealth on the site of the coyote's den, and making way for the flying palace car in place of the Indian trail of 1860.

An attempt was made to organize a permanent association in 1882, but the time did not seem ripe, and it was a failure. Twenty-five old settlers then met, on July 4th, and drafted a constitution and signed it, and elected officers.

The signers at that convention were the following well-known gentlemen:

- Levi Snell.
- M. G. Bohanan.
- F. H. Bohanan.
- Stewart McConiga.
- T. P. Kennard.
- Louis Helmer.
- S. B. Galey.
- J. W. Prey.
- E. T. Hudson.
- Sam McClay.
- J. L. Porter.
- Wm. Mills.
- A. G. Hastings.
- T. M. Ganter.
- J. M. Young.
- John McManigal.
- D. Banghart.
- C. H. Gere.
- J. O. Young.
- R. R. Tingley.
- H. G. Jessup.
- W. W. Carder.
- L. H. Robbins.
- O. N. Humphrey.
- Austin Humphrey.

The officers elected were as follows: President, J. W. Prey; Vice President, E. T. Hudson; Secretary, Austin Humphrey; Treasurer, N. C. Brock. The meeting of July 4th adjourned to meet July 15th, but only four persons were present at that time, and an adjournment was taken to September; but the organization never had another meeting.

But the attempt to organize an association the present year has been very successful, owing very largely to the untiring and enthusiastic efforts of Mr. M. G. Bohanan, who has kept it constantly before the minds of the pioneers, and by personal solicitation has secured nearly four hundred names for membership in the association. The meeting for organization took place at the council chamber, at the northwest corner of Q and Tenth streets, on April 23, 1889. Mr. A. J. Sawyer was called to the chair, and Mr. J. P. Hebard was chosen Secretary. A committee was appointed to draft a constitution for the association, the same to be reported at a future meeting. This committee consisted of Messrs. A. W. Field, Levi Snell, S. C. Elliott, N. S. Harwood, M. Tower, and A. J. Sawyer. A committee for each township in the county was selected, whose duty it would be to augment the membership, and generally promote the interests of the association. It was agreed that eligibility to membership should be based on a residence in the county dating as early as 1875.

The next meeting was held at Bohanan's hall, on the southwest corner of Tenth and N streets, on May 11, 1889. Captain L. W. Billingsley was called to the chair and Mr. J. P. Hebard was continued as secretary. Nearly one hundred of the pioneers were present, and a complete organization was effected.

Mr. A. J. Sawyer, for the committee appointed to draft a constitution for the association, reported a set of by-laws and rules for the government of the organization, which were adopted. The basis of membership was made a fifteen years' residence in the county, so that the continuance of the association may be perpetual. It was also arranged that a general rally at Cushman park should take place on June 19, 1889. Various committees were named to prepare the programme for that occasion.

Most of the old settlers present signed the constitution. The committee appointed to nominate permanent officers for the association recommended the following persons for the positions specified:

PRESIDENT—Mr. L. W. Billingsley.

VICE PRESIDENTS — Oak Precinct, J. S. Hermance; Denton Precinct, E. T. Hudson; Little Salt Precinct, Mat. Maule; Yankee Hill Precinct, Ans. Williams; West Oak Precinct, L. B. McFarland; Centerville Precinct, D. E. Prey; Highland Precinct, Nicholas Bahl; Elk Precinct, J. W. Smith; Buda Precinct, H. C. Roller; Grant Precinct, J. S. Umangst; South Pass Precinct, Phil Burling; Lancaster Precinct, Phil Hacker; Waverly Precinct, J. P. Loder; Stevens Creek Precinct, J. H. Wilcox; Olive Branch Precinct, Henry Holman; North Bluff Precinct, John Dee; Middle Creek Precinct, J. W. Castor; Panama Precinct, O. N. Hazleton; Nemaha Precinct, Wm. Roggencamp; Mill Precinct, John Dale; Stockton Precinct, Charles Retzliff; Saltillo Precinct, W. E. Keys; Garfield Precinct, Ed. Garfield; Lincoln, First Ward, Patrick Hayden; Second Ward, F. H. Bohanan; Third Ward, Amasa Cobb; Fourth Ward, C. M. Parker; Fifth Ward, H. T. Davis; Sixth Ward, W. W. Carder.

SECRETARY— Mr. J. P. Hebard.

TREASURER — Mr. J. W. Prey.

EXECUTIVE COMMITTEE — Messrs. Levi Snell, M. G. Bohanan, and J. V. Wolf.

The meeting adjourned to meet on June the 8th to complete the arrangements preliminary to the rally at the park on June 19th.

The picnic was a great success, the day was beautiful, and the old settlers assembled by hundreds from all parts of the county. The number of pioneers present were estimated at 600, and with their children and friends, perhaps had an aggregate attendance of fifteen hundred people.

The exercises began at 11 o'clock with prayer by Rev. H. T. Davis. Then the principal address of the day was delivered by Mr. C. H. Gere. This was made up of historical reminiscences of the principal events in the founding of the city, and settling the county, between the years 1867 to 1871 inclusive. After singing "Auld Lang Syne" Mr. J. V. Wolf, the association poet, read a set of rhymed collections.

Judge S. B. Pound spoke on "Lincoln, Law, and Groceries," referring to the years of 1866 to 1868, when he was engaged in both occupations without great inconvenience to himself. Colonel J. E. Philpott followed with some remarks on "The Missouri as a Highway to Nebraska in 1867," detailing some river experiences of the very early days, and the importance of the river routes in reaching the interior of the great west.

After further vocal music, Mr. Stewart McConiga detailed how the settlers rushed in for claims at "The United States Land Office Twenty Years Ago," at which he was the Register. Mr. A. J. Sawyer recounted the years of trial during which the grasshoppers scourged this region, the period being from 1874 to 1876. Rev. H. T. Davis related some entertaining reminiscences of the early churches.

Then followed a "basket dinner" and social among the pioneers. After dinner, the feature which first attracted attention was the exhibition of a Lancaster county pony twenty-six years old. The animal was then and there declared a member of the Old Settlers' Association and was decorated with a badge. The horse was the property of S. W. McKesson. It was ridden across the sight of Lincoln before the town was laid out, by John C. Fremont. McKesson, who was on hand, explained the circumstance fully. The pony was nimble enough to clamber up into the speakers' stand, a feat which not many horses can be induced to attempt.

Colonel George B. Skinner told about having been auctioneer for the lot sales of 1869. He received $1,500 for five days' work, and when he took the money said to T. P. Kennard that he would not give that roll of bills for the whole town and the whole county of Lancaster. But he has radically changed his mind since. Mr. John S. Gregory then told of the early days on the Salt Basin and the village of Lancaster, in a racy and entertaining manner. Mr. Levi Snell recalled some reminiscences of the State lot sales. Elder E. T. Hudson closed the programme with some stories of the very early settlements. Then the old settlers were photographed in a body, and the first Congress of the Old Settlers adjourned. The meeting was just such a wholesome, happy, affair as affords joy to the heart of a pioneer.

Not all present on this occasion have joined the association, but the record of those who have is a valuable part of the history of this county and city, and is therefore appended in full.

Here is the Old Settlers' Association, as its roster appeared in July, 1889, the native State and year of coming to this county being also given:

ROLL OF OLD SETTLERS.

A. S. Godfrey, Massachusetts, '70.
Louie Meyer, Austria, '70.
E. E. Brown, New York, '70.
C. B. Beach, Ohio, '69.
A. B. Beach, Ohio, '70.
W. H. Dobson, Ontario, '72.
B. Cox, Virginia, '72.
Mrs. E. B. Cox, Ohio, '72.
John Schuller, Austria, '74.
S. B. Hohmann, Pennsylvania, '69.
S. Peckham, England, '74.
James B. Hale, Indiana, '66.
J. W. Smith, Indiana, '73.
John Y. Ellenburg, Germany, '73.
R. J. Williams, Pennsylvania, '68.
J. H. Painter, Pennsylvania, '73.
Dr. A. K. Painter, Pennsylvania, '74.
J. N. T. Jones, Kentucky, '69.
Adelia Boyd, Sweden, '70.
A. H. Wilson, New York, '66.
W. Flanigan, Canada, '71.
M. V. Radford, Illinois, '70.
N. G. Franklin, Ohio '71.
H. E. George, Illinois, '70.
E. Duling, Ohio, '79.
Luther Batten, Wisconsin, '70.
H. L. Andrews, Wisconsin, '71.
O. M. Druse, New York, '71.
P. Hayden, Ireland, '70.
H. Wittman, Germany, '73.
H. Malberts, Germany, '65.
D. L. Peckham, Michigan, '67.
J. L. Porter, Virginia, '66.
L. N. Haskin, New York, '63.
James Gilmore, Indiana, '72.
Wm. Frohn, Germany, '70.
W. W. W. Jones, Illinois, '74.
A. E. Hargreaves, England, '72.
J. W. Castor, Ohio, '73.
Charles Hichewick, '67.
Robert Pickel, Illinois, '67.
J. K. Honeywell, New York, '68.

H. Schultz, Germany, '66.
George A. Mayer, Germany, '63.
F. S. Wittstruck, Germany, '65.
J. C. Clarke, Vermont, '71.
Ed. Bingham, England, '67.
J. P. Walton, Ohio, '71.
C. C. Pace, Kentucky, '74.
Mrs. M. P. Husted, Michigan, '67.
W. J. Turner, Ohio, '69.
W. E. G. Caldwell, New Hampshire '70.
W. J. Cooper, New York, '69.
John Currie, Pennsylvania, '72.
Chris Fossler, Germany, '69.
M. Bowden, Ireland, '68.
R. S. Browne, England, '79.
W. C. Burke, Ohio, 68.
Fred Schmidt, Iowa, '70.
H. H. Blodgett, New York, '69.
J. S. Lefferdink, Holland, '71.
H. Heffner, Germany, '69.
G. M. Blodgett, New York, '69.
J. H. Myer, Hanover, '69.
Fred Funke, Germany, '74.
D. L. Graham, Ohio, '70.
George Sexton, Ohio, '75.
J. Farmer, New Jersey, '70.
Thomas Morrissey, Ireland, '69.
J. A. Morrissey, Tennessee, '66.
J. D. Klentsch, Prussia, '72.
C. G. Bullock, New York, '73.
E. G. Bohanan, Illinois, '75.
W. R. Horn, Illinois, '70.
Thomas C. Mawe, England, '72.
H. S. Gordon, Massachusetts, '74.
C. A. Tucker, Nebraska, '71.
A. Chandler, Pennsylvania, '69.
A. C. Ricketts, Ohio, '72.
W. B. Hargreaves, England, '70.
J. D. Johnson, Sweden, '70.
A. Keens, England, '72.
W. L. Gorton, New York '70.
I. N. Leonard, Ohio, '70.

OLD SETTLERS' ASSOCIATION. 351

H. Oehlchlager, Germany, '74.
F. Claus, Germany, '69.
Thomas Price, Ireland, '69.
George W. Prey, Wisconsin, '56.
Wm. Charlton, Iowa, '73.
H. F. Mitchell, Ohio, '73.
H. F. Warner, Iowa, '64.
A. G. Warner, Iowa, '64.
J. S. Howard, Ohio, '72.
Adna Dobson, Wisconsin, '72.
T. R. Prey, Massachusetts, '56.
L. H. Meyer, Iowa, '68.
W. H. Meyer, Iowa, '72.
Henry Bartells, Germany, '73.
Silas Sprague, Ohio, '68.
M. Oppenheimer, Germany, '68.
Joseph Oppenheimer, Missouri, '70.
John Thompson, 71.
Robert M. Manley, Ohio, '68.
Robert Mitchell, England, '71.
J. H. Kellum, Massachusetts, '71.
Cornelius Moran, Lincoln, Neb., '61.
M. G. Bohanan, Illinois, '68.
E. T. Roberts, New York, '73.
H. D. Hathaway, Ohio, '72.
George Sherrer, Germany, '72.
Maurice Dee, Nebraska, '60.
N. D. Smith, Ohio, '71.
E. R. Sizer, Illinois, '74.
A. W. Field, Illinois, '63.
N. C. Abbott, New York, '71.
T. C. Kern, Indiana, '72.
Wm. Roggenkamp, Friezen, '60.
H. W. Hardy, New York, '71.
J. A. Bailey, Ohio, '68.
Timothy Kelley, Ireland, '69.
Ed. A. Church, England, '68.
J. B. Trickey, Illinois, '70.
Mark Howe, Ohio, '70.
R. H. Corner, England, '73.
H. H. Grimes, Ohio, '74.
W. E. Wittman, Indiana, '70.
W. J. Marshall, Vermont, '70.
C. H. Foxworthy, Indiana, '74.
J. H. Foxworthy, Indiana, '73.
M. Shay, Ireland, '59.
Ellen Shay, Ireland, '59.
E. B. Hyde, Illinois, '69.

Eddie I. Bohanan, Nebraska, '71.
Isaac Whited, Ohio, '71.
J. F. Schultz, Germany, '67.
C. C. Morse, Vermont, '72.
A. C. Munson, Nebraska, '71.
Mat Maule, ——, '71.
D. C. Brown, Missouri, '72.
R. W. Kent, Illinois, '73.
W. H. Schmale, Germany, '67.
C. A. Porter, Iowa, '66.
H. Perkins, Indiana, '69.
M. B. Donahue, Iowa, '68.
M. Cobb, Wisconsin, '71.
Harry Abbott, England, '71.
J. A. Snyder, Indiana, '62.
Wm. Bohanan, Illinois, '69.
C. F. Retzliff, Germany, '58.
E. L. English, Illinois, '70.
A. G. Kellum, Massachusetts, '71.
Henry Alberts, Germany, '65.
H. H. Schaberg, Wisconsin, '70.
T. E. Longstreet, New York, '70.
A. W. Stutheit, Iowa, '66.
S. C. Blasier, New York, '68.
John Lundgreen, ——, '73.
L. B. McFarland, Ohio, '74.
G. A. Spencer, New York, '71.
C. G. Beams, Ohio, '74.
Sam McClay, Ohio, '67.
James Burcham, Ohio, '68.
John Fisher, Pennsylvania, '69.
Phil Bohanan, Nebraska, '71.
E. Warnes, England, '62.
J. C. McNair, Maryland.
George A. Nandichle, New Jersey, '69.
J. J. Robinson, New York, '71.
G. E. Cox, Nova Scotia, '71.
T. D. Moulton, Illinois, '75.
L. N. Fuller, Massachusetts, '70.
E. S. Reed, New York, '72.
W. M. Oyler, Missouri, '75.
Jacob North, England, '72.
Wm. McClain, Indiana, '65.
A. M. Davis, Indiana, '67.
H. J. Walsh, Ireland, '69.
John Schmidt, Bavaria, '71.
Eli Bates, Ohio, '74.
J. R. Bing, Ohio, '72.

C. M. Leighton, Maine, '68.
Dennis Merriman, Ireland, '68.
W. H. Boyer, Ohio, '68.
Wm. Hopkins, Delaware, '71.
Chris Rocke, Atlantic Ocean, '70.
C. E. Hedges, Illinois, '73.
J. F. Bishop, Indiana, '70.
J. W. Hedges, New York, '73.
J. W. Rees, Ohio, 70.
A. H. Masterman, West Indies, '71.
Adam Bax, Germany, '68.
W. W. Wilson, Pennsylvania, '71.
John Reed, Wisconsin, '71.
W. E. Keys, Ohio, '63.
Eleanor G. Keys, Canada, '63.
J. J. Butler, Newfoundland, '69.
W. F. Little, Pennsylvania, '72.
J. S. Gregory, first permanent settler, Vermont, '62.
C. O. Strickland, Illinois, '69.
John Michael, Pennsylvania, '56.
W. L. Wilcox, West Virginia, '70.
I. M. Raymond, New York, '71.
O. P. Davis, Ohio, '73.
W. H. Goodrich, New York, '70.
R. P. R. Millar, Missouri, '84.
M. D. Henry, Ohio, '67.
W. E. Field, Massachusetts, '74.
C. H. Hobmann, '69.
T. J. Dickson, Scotland, '71.
A. L. Frost, Iowa, '68.
C. C. Munson, Connecticut, '70.
H. Gardner, England, '73.
J. R. Clark, Ohio, '71.
J. H. North, England, '73.
F. A. Hovey, New York, '69.
G. F. Hodges, Iowa, '67.
S. K. Hale, Ohio, '75.
Nels Westover, Canada, '70.
C. H. Castor, Ohio, '73.
J. H. Bullock, New York, '73.
H. Vanderpool, New York, '72.
W. E. Hardy, New York, '71.
W. G. Bohanan, Illinois, '69.
T. H. Hyde, Vermont, '68.
W. G. Roberts, New York, '73.
J. F. Cadman, Illinois, '59.
G. R. Wolf, Prussia, '73.

L. P. Fisher, New York, '70.
C. J. Heffly, Pennsylvania, '67.
M. L. Hiltner, Pennsylvania, '69.
R. Schneider, Switzerland, '71.
A. G. Barnes, Ohio, '74.
E. A. Morgan, New York, '70.
A. G. Hastings, Connecticut, '69.
J. P. Loder, Ohio, '57.
Robt. McCartney, Illinois, '69.
J. M. Meyers, Ohio, '69.
J. M. Tiger, New Jersey, '67.
Oscar Lau, Pennsylvania, '67.
Hiram Polly, New York, '74.
W. J. Harris, Ohio, '65.
A. S. Williams, Massachusetts, '68.
Henry Townson, England, '74.
W. D. Gulick, New Hampshire, '72.
J. E. Philpott, Indiana, '67.
J. H. White, England, '69.
L. B. Treeman, New York, '73.
B. F. McCall, New York, '66.
J. Wheeler, Ohio, '68.
P. O'Shea, Canada West, '71.
Gottlieb Meyer, Germany, '73.
D. D. Helweg, Germany, '73.
James Kane, Ireland, '71.
J. H. Ames, Vermont, '69.
E. C. Ames, Nebraska, '75.
Kate Martin, Ireland, '67.
W. J. Lamb, New York, '68.
C. C. Burr, Illinois, '68.
M. W. Sargent, New York, '71.
W. C. Davis, Indiana, '70.
W. T. Scott, England, '72.
J. N. Larsh, Indiana, '70.
D. E. Prey, New York, '56.
Wm. Krueger, Iowa, '69.
V. A. Markle, Canada, '68.
R. R. Tingley, New Jersey, '68.
Laurena Tingley, New York, '68.
Jackson Johnson, Tennessee, '69.
F. R. Denton, Ohio, '67.
W. M. Seeley, Illinois, '73.
S. G. Owen, Ohio, '70.
Thos. Carr, Ireland, '74.
W. C. Spencer, Vermont, '69.
Frank Chaffee, Ohio, '73.
A. N. Burd, Pennsylvania, '65.

OLD SETTLERS' ASSOCIATION. 353

Cyrus Carter, Ohio, '65.
George Wornholz, Germany, '68.
S. W. Gettier, Pennsylvania, '69.
S. J. Douglass, New York, '75.
John Thompson, England, '71.
F. C. Zehrung, Iowa, '74.
Palmer Way, Pennsylvania, '68.
G. M. Lambertson, Indiana, '74.
J. D. Macfarland, Pennsylvania, '71.
M. F. McWilliams, Ohio '69.
R. Wallingford, Ohio, '58.
Jerome Shamp, Ohio, '66.
J. D. Monell, New York, '68.
D. E. Bomgardner, Pennsylvania, '70.
W. C. Rohde, Germany, '74.
L. Barr, Europe, '74.
O. N. Humphrey, Ohio, '69.
John Sheedy, Ireland, '70.
T. J. Noonan, Missouri, '70.
J. J. Lichty, Pennsylvania, '73.
S. P. Ritchy, Kentucky, '71.
G. H. Simmons, England, '74.
C. D. Jewett, New York, '71.
H. W. Keel, Germany, '66.
P. H. Sudduth, Ohio, '66.
Amasa Cobb, Illinois, '69.
G. S. Foxworthy, Indiana, '74.
S. B. Pound, New York, '61.
P. E. Beardsley, New York, '71.
Nellie M. Beardsley, Iowa, '71.
J. P. Beardsley, Nebraska, '74.
W. A. Doggett, Massachusetts, '75.
G. W. Lee, Illinois, '71.
L. Stewart, Pennsylvania, '68.
G. B. Skinner, Connecticut, '70.
L. C. Pace, Virginia, '75.
H. C. Meadows, West Virginia, '70.
W. W. Webster, Ohio, '69.
L. H. Robbins, Illinois, '69.
T. W. Lowrey, Illinois, '71.
F. W. Krone, Germany, '69.
H. A. Poston, Virginia, '75.
J. A. Wallingford, Ohio, '54.
David May, France, '69.
C. F. Damrow, Indiana, '68.
Geo. Leavitt, England, '70.
L. J. Bumstead, Connecticut, '71.
D. N. Syford, Pennsylvania, '74.

M. L. Trester, Indiana, '69.
J. O. Carter, Ohio, '72.
J. H. Harley, Nova Scotia, '71.
J. H. Barrett, Vermont, '70.
Jacob Rocke, Germany, '69.
W. S. Latta, Pennsylvania, '73.
J. C. McBride, Ohio, '74.
D. B. Howard, Indiana, '74.
W. M. Leonard, Illinois, '74.
M. B. Cheney, New York, '69.
O. C. Bell, Indiana, '72.
J. J. Deck, Wisconsin, '68.
W. C. Griffith, Pennsylvania, '69.
T. M. Marquett, Ohio, '74.
F. M. Hall, Illinois, '76.
A. J. Guthridge, Ohio, '68.
Lewis Gregory, Connecticut, '75.
W. A. Cadman, Illinois, '59.
E. Hallett, Massachusetts, '71.
H. J. Byam, New York, '70.
J. R. Webster, New York, '69.
D. G. Courtney, New York, '74.
S. M. Melick, New Jersey, '70.
J. H. McMurtry, Indiana, '71.
C. E. Loomis, New York, '71.
W. E. Stewart, Indiana, '60.
T. H. McGahey, Pennsylvania, '72.
J. J. Imhoff, Pennsylvania, '72.
Eugene Woerner, Germany, '71.
H. A. Ensign, Iowa, '70.
A. D. Baker, Ohio, '74.
M. E. Chevront, Virginia, '72.
E. P. Childe, New York, '75.
J. P. Lyons, New York, '74.
Wm. Brokelmeyer, Germany, '74.
J. T. Beach, Ohio, '68.
B. Ringer, Ohio, '68.
A. Bolar, Ohio, '68.
Carl Funke, Germany, '68.
C. Wisner, Holland, '68.
Charles Philpott, Nebraska, '75.
H. D. Pierson, Indiana, '68.
Ed. Franklin, Ohio, '72.
John Franklin, Ohio, '72.
Flora Frost Snell, Iowa, '68.
Mrs. C. Paine, England, '73.
S. C. F. McKesson, Illinois, '67.
S. W. McKesson, Pennsylvania, '67.

E. Eisler, Germany, '73.
Almon Tower, Minnesota, '68.
— Waltemade, Germany, '71.
John Gieser, Germany, '69.
Mrs. E. C. Martin, England, '71.
S. W. Knight, Ohio, '74.
H. C. Foster, Pennsylvania, '69.
John Burke, Ireland, '70.
D. W. Huff, Michigan, '70.
Wm. Hogan, Illinois, '70.
Theo. Benninghoff, Pennsylvania, '69.
T. J. Crawford, Ohio, '66.
W. T. Shuckman, Pennsylvania, '70.
Wm. Wilson, Massachusetts, '71.
B. H. Hollister, New York, '73.
A. Ward, Maryland, '69.
James Brown, Kentucky, '72.
George Bosselman, Germany, '72.
Mary G. Cochran, Ohio, '67.
E. P. Beecher, New York, '69.
Wm. Wilson, England, '78.
G. H. Exley, England, '71.
J. Burkendorf, Missouri, '72.
Zack Hammel, Ohio, '71.
L. Leavitt, Ohio, '71.
Howard W. Caldwell, Ohio, '74.
Allen Barber, Rhode Island, '73.
D. A. Gilbert, New York, '72.
Mrs. H. A. Tuttle, Massachusetts, '71.
Mrs. A. C. Clark, Illinois, '71.
George C. Spencer, England, '71.
E. E. Gillespie, Nebraska, '69.
Charles F. Joers, Germany, '74.
Manuil Davey, Illinois, '64.
A. Hitchcock, Canada, '70.
Mrs. Duke Beal, New York, '75.
Anthony Gregg, New York, '71.
C. W. Pierce, New York, '71.
C. S. Cadwallader, Ohio, '66.
W. J. Weller, Ohio, '69.
W. L. Hermance, Nebraska, '74.
C. C. Waldo, New York, '75.
Isaac Oppenheimer, Germany, '70.
Rev. D. Kinney, Ohio, '71.
Henry Veith, Germany, '69.
Mrs. H. Veith, Germany, '72.
Katie Veith, Lincoln, '74.
Henry Veith jr. Lincoln, '72.

Mrs. J. C. Johnston, New York, '75.
John F. Wittstruck, Illinois, '70.
H. H. Leavitt, Missouri, '74.
Oren Snyder, Wisconsin, '62.
Major Moore, North Carolina, '74.
John G. Stine, New Jersey, '68.
George Seifert, Germany, '72.
Pat McGerr, Ireland, '69.
R. J. Campbell, Ohio, '72.
Sam Arbuckle, Illinois, '75.
Celestine Theibeaut, France, '71.
G. H. Butler, England, '71.
R. H. Oakey, New York, '70.
Andrew Bayless, Tennessee, '72.
W. P. Phillips, Ohio, '71.
N. S. Harwood, Michigan, '71.
P. J. Grant, Ireland, '69.
Charles W. Woodward, Iowa, '74.
J. F. Egger, Switzerland, '71.
Wm. B. Harlow, New York, '72.
Mrs. Jennie May, New York, '67.
H. T. Davis, Ohio, '67.
G. H. Augdin, West Virginia, '75.
J. P. Munson, Kentucky, '66.
John Naderhoff, Illinois, '70.
James Giles, England, '69.
E. S. Hudson, England, '69.
Solomon Kirk, Tennessee, '57.
W. E. Bates, Michigan, '74.
John Lemke, Wisconsin, '59.
S. Westerfield, Missouri, '72.
G. W. Pleasant, North Carolina, '74.
John Gesler, Iowa, '68.
Joel N. Converse, Ohio, '70.
S. J. Dobson, ———, '71.
M. W. Griswold, New York, '69.
Herman M. Reeves, New York, '70.
Dr. W. Queen '60.
W. J. Knowlton, '69.
Henry Waterman, '70.
Wm. Robertson, '71.
Myron Tower, '68.
W. W. Carder, '67.
Thomas Hornby, '74.
W. Smith, '70.
A. L. Pound, '66.
G. C. Hickox, '72.
J. J. Hunt, '69.

P. H. Cooper '65.
John Hermance, '72.
L. W. Billingsley, '69.
N. Carpenter, '69.
F. H. Bohanan, '68.
D. A. Cline, '70.
T. R. Burling, '68.
John W. Crist, '71.
Isaac Johnson, '71.
W. W. English, '71.
M. D. Tiffany, '70.
Wm. M. McLaughlin, '68.
John Morrison, '69.
J. L. McConnell, '58.
C. Rellar, '69.
John Dee, '56.
Thomas Maloy, '67.

Michael Noonan, '69.
H. H. Wilson, '73.
J. P. Hebard, Connecticut, '69.
E. W. Rykert, '67.
Levi Snell, '69.
John W. Prey, '56.
E. G. Clements, '69.
Alexander Buchanan.
C. H. Gere.
George Gardner.
L. J. Byer.
W. W. Holmes.
Louis Heimer.
D. J. Hunt.
J. A. Leonard.
J. F. Ereeson.
Ira J. Hunt.

As an interesting addendum to the foregoing roster of the old settlers, Mr. T. H. Hyde, editor and founder of the Lincoln *Daily News*, on June 20, 1889, printed a list of the business and professional men of the city who were engaged here prior to 1875, and still so continue. This list is as follows:

Rev. H. T. Davis, first Methodist minister.
L. K. Holmes, manufacturer of brick.
J. B. & E. L. Trickey, watchmakers and jewelers.
Leopold Barr, same.
Bohanan Brothers, meat market, livery, and sale stables, hacks, omnibusses, etc.
Wm. Hyatt and Frank Rawlins, same.
W. H. Brown, W. J. Turner, J. H. Harley, druggists.
W. N. Rehlaender, pharmacist.
J. & D. Newman, dry goods.
Fred Schmidt, dry goods and general merchandise.
L. H. Robbins, M. D.
James Ledwith, grocer.
Wm. D. Gulick, baker and grocer.
Henry Veith, baker and grocer.
Wm. Harlow, baker and dealer in fancy groceries.
Charles Spicer, baker.

J. A. Bailey, house painter and decorator.
Humphrey Brothers, farm implements and hardware.
Raymond Brothers, wholesale grocers.
A. S. Godfrey, C. C. Munson, lumber.
J. W. Hedges, founder.
State Journal, C. H. Gere, editor; H. D. Hathaway, business manager; A. H. Mendenhall, superintendent mechanical department.
H. W. Hardy, furniture.
A. E. Hargreaves, retail grocer in 1875 to wholesale in 1878.
E. G. Clements, photography.
S. H. King, dental surgeon.
F. H. Hohmann & Sons, music, musical instruments and teaching.
A. M. Davis, carpets, rugs, mattings, curtains, etc.
P. H. Cooper, ice.
A. C. Zeimer, passenger and ticket agent B. & M.

D. L. Peckham, L. J. Byer, Sam McCord, carpenters and contractors.
J. J. Butler, architect and builder.
J. P. Lantz, J. F. Lansing, real estate and insurance.
J. H. McMurtry, same.
J. H. Woodworth, saddlery manufacturer.
S. C. Elliott, crockery, glassware, etc.
J. E. Philpott, S. B. Pound, C. C. Burr, S. J. Tuttle, Harwood & Ames, J. H. Foxworthy, T. M. Marquett, L. W. Billingsley T. F. Barnes, W. J. Lamb, attorneys.
R. L. Smith, machinist.
David May, A. Hurlbut, clothiers.
John Morrison, John McWhinnie, and C. F. Damrow, merchant tailors.
T. W. Lowrey, grain elevator, flouring mills.
R. C. Manley, fruit, cigars, etc.
Louie Meyer, dry goods.
E. T. Roberts, undertaker.
Geo. Seifert and George E. Fischer, harness and saddlery.
J. A. Buckstaff, lumber.
Joseph Whittman, harness.

This list will be exceedingly small in ten years from this time, but the work of the old settlers will live on in the generations to come, when not a man now on the roster shall live to answer at roll call.

CHAPTER XXVI.

LINCOLN AS A BUSINESS CENTER.—THE GROWTH OF HER BUSINESS INTERESTS FROM SMALL BEGINNINGS—MENTION OF SOME OF THE MEN WHO HAVE BUILT UP THE CITY.

From the wild prairie hamlet of 1867, possessing less than fifty people, Lincoln has grown to a city of over 50,000 people in just twenty-two years. From an insignificant settlement in a wilderness, without trade or developed resources, there has been built up here a property worth not less than $50,000,000, the State Capitol building, the State Penitentiary, the Asylum for the Insane, the State University, the Wesleyan University, the Christian University, which will open this fall, and city school property valued at $500,000. Out of the prairie sod has grown the educational center of the Northwest, the political center of the State, and the most remarkable radial railway center west of the Missouri river, comprising four great systems, twelve diverging lines, reaching 1,000 towns, whose trade represents 154,000 square miles of territory.

Here now are operated seventy factories, eighty wholesale houses, eleven banks. The city possesses thirty-eight churches, twenty-six schools, thirteen temperance societies, five public libraries, twenty-six newspapers and periodicals, and nearly two hundred moral, social, fraternal, charitable, and similar organizations. The State Fair has been located at Lincoln for five years. The city possesses strong companies for supplying illumination by gas, the arc, and also incandescent electric light. It has eight miles of paved streets, twenty miles of sanitary sewers, ten miles of storm-water sewers, and an ample system of water-works. It possesses five street car companies, one of which has a capital of $1,000,000, and they are now operating thirty-one miles of track. Among its great enterprises are the stock-yards and two large packing-houses, three immense paving-brick works, seven building-brick works, a large woolen mill, a paper mill, a cracker factory, two planing mills and wood-working factories, a large tannery, three foundries, and extensive stone-cutting works. Lincoln is a division station on every railroad system entering here, and it seems probable that the great Rock Island railroad system will be added to her railway advantages in the near future.

The city is supplied with the Western Union and Pacific Mutual Telegraph companies, who employ forty operators, and have through wires to all cities. Its telephone service includes over 600 local instruments and direct connection with sixty towns in Nebraska and sixty-six in Iowa. Its express service comprises the combined facilities of

RESIDENCE OF FRANK SHELDON.

four great companies, with arrangements to bill direct over 70,000 miles of road without transfer, with a constantly and rapidly increasing business. It also possesses an organized message service under the name of Lincoln District Telegraph Company. This was organized on May 21, 1887, and possesses a very strong support in its board of stockholders, who are: G. W. Holdrege, J. D. Macfarland, C. E. Yates, J. McConniff, C. Thompson, E. E. Brown, John R. Clark, R. H. Oakley, George W. Bonnell, J. J. Dickey, L. H. Korty, and Charles G. Burton. Mr. Burton is Secretary and Manager. This company's office is at the southwest corner of O and Tenth streets. It furnishes messengers and hacks at all hours, day and night; delivers trunks, and distributes advertising matter and invitations, and provides night watchmen.

The internal improvements made in the city in 1888 reached the grand aggregate of $3,287,418, including the erection of 1,000 residences at a cost of over a million dollars. The jobbing business advanced over twenty-five per cent during the past year. Over 600 traveling men now reside here. The growth of the city for 1889 is more solid and extensive than ever before, many costly brick blocks, residences, and other improvements, being in process of construction, including a county court-house to cost $200,000, a new city well and pumping station, and two new houses for fire companies, with additional costly fire apparatus.

But while the city has grown so rapidly, it has been the result, mainly, of the efforts of those men who from the early days evinced their faith in the city and in its future development by their acts, and who, through months and years of depression, disappointment, and discouragement, never lost their nerve, but kept the future always in view, and spoke words of encouragement to those who were hesitating whether to make Lincoln their home. These men — most of them, at least — have been amply rewarded for their faith, and mention of a few of them will not be out of place in a work dealing with the founding and growth of the city.

Hon. Isaac M. Raymond, senior member of the firm of Raymond Brothers & Co., wholesale grocers, is one of the most able and successful business men of Lincoln, and one whose work is closely identified with the city's progress for eighteen years.

His father was the Rev. H. A. Raymond, pastor of the Dutch Reformed Church at Niskayuna, N. Y., and was a graduate of both Yale College and Rutger's Theological Seminary, New Jersey. He continued as pastor of the church at Niskayuna for sixteen years, where he was very highly esteemed, both personally and as an able minister, declining, in the meantime, frequent calls to city churches at a higher salary. Here seven of his nine children were born.

The mother of I. M. Raymond was born in Passaic county, New

Jersey. She was a woman of positive views and earnest character, and sought to impress the value of correct principles upon her children.

I. M. Raymond was born at Niskayuna, Schenectady county, New York, on the 3d of May, 1842. He received a common-school education, and then spent one term in the Jonesville Academy, Saratoga county, New York, and a term at the Chittenango Polytechnic Institute, and at this date closed his seventeenth year. He then taught

HON. I. M. RAYMOND.

two terms of country school in Schoharie county, devoting about a year to this employment. He then removed to Waterloo, Iowa, where he worked on a farm for six months, and then obtained a clerkship in the grocery store of his elder brothers, at Waterloo. He worked hard from 1861 to 1865 in this position, and then went to Waverly, Iowa, and took the management of a grocery store there, owned by his brothers. While in Waverly he held his first political office, being a member of the city council. He managed the store at Waverly until November, 1871, and then removed to Lincoln, Nebraska, and established the wholesale grocery house of Raymond Bros. & Co., of which he has ever since been the able manager, and which has been remarkably successful.

In 1886 he was elected a member of the House of the Twentieth Session of the Nebraska Legislature, and was the author of the Primary Election Law, now in operation, a very important and satisfactory measure, as it is in accordance with the very fundamental principles of republican government, allowing all the people to nominate candidates, instead of a few schemers.

In 1887 it became a very practical question whether the jobbing trade of Lincoln, or any interior point in Nebraska, could long survive the fatal effects of the discriminations in freights, founded upon the Missouri river, where rates were adjusted at the expense of Nebraska, without regard to the length of haul. This condition of freight charges threatened to put a stop to the commercial growth of Lincoln, and to require Nebraska generally to pay a ruinous tribute to the Missouri river railway combination that would continue to sap the prosperity of the State, as it had done for many years.

Mr. Raymond began to agitate the necessity of the people of Lincoln rising and making a most determined resistance to these oppressive discriminations, and finally wrote a strong letter, explaining to the people in clear and forcible terms how dangerous it would be to longer continue to suffer the unfair freight tariffs to retard and even threaten the life of the city's commerce. This letter was published in the daily papers of Lincoln, and led up to the reorganization of what had become a totally dormant Board of Trade, and later to the organization of a Freight Bureau in connection with the Board of Trade, designed to study the problem of railway freight charges, and devise such plans as would afford substantial relief.

In this great contest Mr. Raymond was the main inspiration and directing force, and so skillfully, wisely, and courageously, was the cause pressed that the roads finally decided that it would be wise policy for them to yield, and place Lincoln on the same freight-tariff footing as the Missouri river towns. This was the first positive fracture made in the great Missouri river pool, one of the most powerful combinations of capital that ever existed on this continent. The value to the public of the equitable economic principles of the concessions secured by the Lincoln Board of Trade, not only for Nebraska but the entire

West, cannot well be over-estimated. And the splendid results following that contest may be attributed to I. M. Raymond more than to any other man; in fact, without his aid it is doubtful if success would have crowned the contest.

As a result of the great service he had rendered the public, he was nominated for the State Senate in 1888 almost without opposition, and elected by a large majority. He proved a very useful member of the Legislature, his eminent business ability being recognized in his appointment to the chairmanship of the Committee on Finance, Ways, and Means, in the Senate, the most important committee in the gift of that body. He introduced and secured the passage of Raymond's Banking Bill, a measure which thoroughly and judiciously placed necessary restrictions upon bankers of the State, in the interest of a higher public credit, and for a better defense of depositors. This was one of the most important and valuable measures enacted by the twenty-first session of the Legislature.

Mr. Raymond is a business man of a high order of ability. He has managed the large wholesale grocery business of Raymond Bros. & Co. with eminent success, and that house is one of the most prosperous in the State. In 1882 Mr. Raymond assisted to organize the Exchange National Bank of Hastings, of which he was made president and still continues to hold that position. During the spring of 1889 he became one of the incorporators of the American Exchange National Bank, of Lincoln, of which he was also made President, and to the affairs of which he gives a considerable share of his personal attention. He is also one of the directors of the Lincoln Stock Yards, and a member of the Lincoln Packing and Provision Company. In fact, he is an enterprising and valuable citizen of the city and State, always ready to contribute to the success of really important and deserving public enterprises.

Among the business men of Lincoln there are none more thoroughly representative of the growth and possibilities of the great West than A. E. Hargreaves, the head of the extensive wholesale house of Hargreaves Bros. He is a thoroughly representative Lincoln man as well, having begun his business career in Lincoln when the city was in its infancy, and kept pace with its advancement, growing from a poorly-paid clerk to the head of a firm doing a million dollars' worth of business annually, while Lincoln has developed from a hamlet to a magnificent city of more than fifty thousand people.

Mr. Hargreaves was born in the world's metropolis, London, in 1853. His father, Abraham Hargreaves, was a contractor, and his mother's maiden name was Elizabeth Hingworth.

As he entered commercial life when only eleven years old, his education was confined to the instruction received at an early age in the common schools. But his business education was thorough, and when he left England, in 1872, to seek his fortune in the new world, he knew more about the details of business than many men of twice his age. At this time Nebraska was being extensively advertised in England by the Land Commissioners of the B. & M. railroad, and with others Mr. Hargreaves sailed from England direct for Lincoln.

The journey was an uneventful one, and on August 12, 1872, Mr. Hargreaves found himself at Pacific Junction. That his business career in Nebraska was begun at the bottom of the ladder is evidenced by his statement that at Pacific Junction he found himself in that condition which is designated in the Western vernacular by the expressive word, "strapped," and he was compelled to negotiate a loan of five dollars before he was able to continue his journey to Lincoln. Upon his arrival at Lincoln he was greatly discouraged. The town was a mere hamlet; there was little business of any kind, and remunerative employment was an unknown boon. If he had had the means at this time he would have returned to England. Not having the means, however, with which to get away, he made the most of the circumstances, and secured a job at the fair grounds as a sort of general roustabout.

After working in various capacities on a salary for several years, Mr. Hargreaves decided to go into business for himself, and in 1875 opened up a peanut stand on the south side of O street, between Eleventh and Twelfth streets. He was still anxious to go back to England at that time, but a kind fortune, disguised in the habiliments of poverty, prevented. Careful and industrious, he found his business increasing from year to year. In 1876 he moved into the next block west, when he added books and stationery to his business.

The fruit and confectionery business was evidently the one for which he had a peculiar adaptation, and the one which furnished the widest field. This grew so rapidly that in 1879 he decided to go into the wholesale trade, and selling out his book and stationery business to Clason & Fletcher, erected a two-story building at 1028 P street, and established a wholesale fruit and confectionery house. As the development of the country tributary to Lincoln brought the demand, fancy groceries were added to the trade, and the firm rapidly became one of the best known in the State.

The business increased so rapidly that the firm found it imperative upon them to find more commodious quarters and better facilities for doing business. Accordingly in 1886 they bought the large three-

A. E. HARGREAVES.

story-and-basement building at the corner of Eighth and O streets. The abundant room and ample track facilities here gave opportunity for extending the business indefinitely. A straight line of staple and fancy groceries was put in, and a jobbing business in these goods was built up scarcely second to any in the city. The fruit department was continued under the management of Mr. W. B. Hargreaves, Mr. Hargreaves's younger brother, who was given an interest in the business in 1882. The house is still one of the largest fruit-jobbing houses in the State. In 1888 a department for the exclusive handling of tea and cigars was established, and the tea department is undoubtedly the largest west of Chicago. The business of the firm in 1889 will amount to $1,000,000.

In 1878, Mr. Hargreaves was married to Miss Jennie Blair, of this city, and now has a family of three children. Always at the front in matters of public enterprise, liberal in the treatment of his employés, prompt, and courteous in all his business relations, it is safe to say that Mr. Hargreaves's present popularity and prosperity are but the beginning of what his business career will develop in the future.

Joseph J. Imhoff is one of the most prominent and successful business men of Lincoln, a representative of our best citizenship. He was born in Somerset county, Pennsylvania, on May 8, 1835. His father was Mr. Joseph Imhoff, and his mother Mrs. Catherine Heffley-Imhoff, who were born and spent their lives in that section of the Keystone State. They were descended from German parentage, and inherited the sturdy, industrious, and upright characteristics of their race. Joseph Imhoff was engaged in managing a hotel in Somerset, Somerset county, Pennsylvania, for thirty-eight years, and also in farming, in both of which pursuits he was successful. His son, Joseph J. Imhoff, was the sixth of eight children, and spent his childhood and youthful years among the hills of his native country, acquiring a common-school education, until the age of fourteen, when he began his mercantile experience as a clerk in a store of general merchandise. After devoting three years to this work, he turned his attention to mechanical pursuits, learned the carpenter's trade, and followed it for five years.

Then he decided to go westward, and removed to Urbana, Illinois, where he continued to follow for two years more the vocation of carpenter and builder. He then decided to seek a new and growing country, and located in Omaha, in 1856. Soon afterward he settled in Dakota county, and engaged in the business of carpenter and builder for a couple of years, building thirty-seven houses during that time. He then took up his residence in Nebraska City, where he engaged again in the mercantile business. While here the movement for the location of the State Capital at Lincoln was developed, and Mr. Imhoff became one of the original syndicate of fifteen who came from Nebraska City, and stayed the uncertain fortunes of the venture by assisting to bid off the lots at the appraised value, when the first sale was made on the 17th to the 22d of September, 1867. Had it not been for the courage of these men, it is very doubtful whether the capital would have been located at Lincoln. Ex-Governor Reed, now of Utah, was one of the syndicate at the sale, and remarked that "the people must be d——d fools to invest their money in the wild prairie lots; for himself he would not give $500 for the whole town site." Mr. Reed relented, however, and invested $750 in three lots before leaving town.

In 1872, Mr. Imhoff removed to Lincoln, and for a year was occupied with handling general merchandise, and in a general trading and real estate business, which was lively at that time. In September, 1873, he bought the "Douglas House," and changed the name to "The Commercial Hotel," which he conducted with great success for thirteen years. He made it the leading hotel in Lincoln, the political head-quarters of Nebraska, and the best-known hostelry in the State. He enlarged it from a small affair, until it acquired its present proportions of 108x150 feet, and three stories high. He then sold it for $80,000.

Mr. Imhoff has been a promoter, organizer, and manager, of many of the most important enterprises of the city, and has been one of its most liberal benefactors. He is always cheerful in contributing largely to any really meritorious project for the public welfare. He has ever been willing to assist in founding and building up enterprises of importance to Lincoln. He was one of the organizers of the Union Savings Bank, and is yet a principal stockholder and director. He was mainly instrumental in the establishment of the Union Stock Yards, was at one time Vice President of the company, and is still a stockholder. He was a moving spirit in the organization of the Lincoln Driving Park Association, and was its first President. He finally bought the park, expended $7,500 in improving it, and then sold it for $75,000. He was one of the incorporators of the Lincoln Street Railway Company, the first line in the city, and continued President of the company until its sale to the city corporation. When the Rapid Transit Street Railway Company was organized, Mr. Imhoff also became a leading contributor to its capital, and was made President of the company. He assisted to help form the Lincoln

RESIDENCE OF J. J. IMHOFF.

Electric Light Company, whose capital is $100,000, and has continued its executive officer from the first. These facts will give some idea of the energy and activity of Mr. Imhoff's business life.

Among the benevolent objects for the city's good, in which he has been a principal helper, may be mentioned the erection of the city churches, especially St. Paul Church, of which he is a prominent member, as is Mrs. Imhoff, the Wesleyan University, and the new Young Men's Christian Association building. His good acts are legion, of which these are among the largest and best known. It may be doubted whether any man has done more for the commercial, financial, charitable, and social good of Lincoln than Mr. Joseph J. Imhoff.

On November 5, 1862, Mr. J. J. Imhoff was married to Miss Mary E. Rector, daughter of Mr. and Mrs. Sanford S. Rector, of Nebraska City. Mrs. Imhoff was born in Pickaway county, Ohio, and her parents still reside in Nebraska City. She is one of the most active and useful workers in the Christian enterprises of the city, and their beautiful home at the southeast corner of J and Twelfth streets is one of the most elegant, and at the same time most hospitable, in the city. The children of Mr. and Mrs. Imhoff are four, namely: Mr. Charles H. Imhoff, Cashier of the Union Savings Bank; Mr. Joseph B. Imhoff, Superintendent of the Lincoln Electric Light Company, and Misses Ono May and Hattie J. Imhoff, residing at home.

Mr. Louie Meyer is one of Lincoln's most energetic, successful, and able business men and financiers. From a small beginning, sixteen years ago, he has worked his way steadily upward, in the face of obstacles and discouragements, until he is now at the head of the extensive wholesale and retail business in general merchandising, which he conducts at numbers 108 and 110 North Tenth street, east of Government Square, under the firm name of L. Meyer & Co. Mr. Meyer is one of the typical men of success in the city, and has kept pace with its growth from village days to its arrival at a city greatness.

Mr. Meyer was born August 12, 1853, near Carlsbad, Austria. His father, Dr. David Meyer, was then a physician of prominence in that locality, and since has acquired celebrity owing to his fifty-five years of practice, and to the fact of his being the oldest member of his profession residing in the empire of Austria. His mother, Mary Becker-Meyer, was a lady of refinement and pleasing social disposition, highly esteemed by the people of her acquaintance. Mr. Meyer is the fifth of the eight children of Dr. and Mrs. Mary Meyer.

Louie Meyer attended the schools of his native country from the age of five years to that of fourteen, and was industrious and ready in acquiring learning. After having received a good, practical education, he entered a store in the town of Carlsbad, and spent a year as a clerk, learning the business. Then, feeling that there were greater opportunities in the United States than in his native land, for a young man of courage and energy, he resolved to come to America. Therefore, he sailed for the shores of his adopted land in the summer of 1870. He landed at New York and proceeded to Des Moines, Iowa, where he spent four or five months with relatives.

Having heard of the fair prospects of Lincoln, he came to what was then a very youthful and struggling capital, in January, 1871, and engaged with the merchants, Rich & Oppenheimer, as a clerk. He performed his duties faithfully for four years and became a skillful salesman, thoroughly educated in his line of business.

Feeling that he understood the lay of the land, and having some capital, he decided to engage in business on his own account, and therefore opened a grocery store in 1874, when about twenty-one years old. He pushed his business during the succeeding three years, and his trade was growing steadily and surely; but the flames devoured his stock and store in March, 1877.

His characteristic energy and resolution was here manifested in a signal degree. Though seriously crippled in his finances by the misfortune he had just passed through, he did not hesitate a moment, but immediately began to rebuild his business and his fortune, and has never ceased to push his affairs from that date to the present time with all the vim of his young manhood. The rewards of his patience, perseverance, and skill, are now manifest in the extensive and growing business of L. Meyer & Co., and the esteem of his fellow citizens is also fully and unreservedly shown in various ways. He added dry goods in 1880 and now does an extensive jobbing as well as retail business.

For two years Mr. Meyer served as treasurer of the Board of Trade of Lincoln, a very difficult position to fill successfully, and it is safe to say that he would have been elected again had he not declined to serve. His management of the affairs of this office was able, and his energy in working for the public welfare was not excelled, if equaled, by any other man in the city.

In fact, Mr. Meyer is recognized as one of the most able financiers and safe business men of this city, and ranks among Lincoln's foremost citizens in any important public enterprise. This is manifested in various ways, one of which is his active connection with the work of the Board of Trade, already referred to. Another was his election to the City Council, in April, 1888, from his ward, the Fifth. Mayor Graham has placed Mr. Meyer at the head of the Finance Committee of the City Council, probably the most difficult place to fill in the city government, owing to the constant requirements for new expenditures and enlarged credits, growing out of the rapid development of this young and expanding metropolis. Mr. Meyer has proven equal to the severe tests of his ability, and his recommendations always receive respectful attention and consideration. Mr. Meyer was married to Miss Anna Gunarson, of this city, a lady of many high qualities of mind and heart, on October 2, 1879. Three children cheer their home, including one son, Max Meyer, and two daughters, Pauline and Leah Meyer. They are among the most bright and excellent young people of the city.

Mr. Meyer and Mrs. Meyer rank among the leading people of Lincoln's social circles, and justly have the respect of the entire city.

In January, 1887, Hon. H. T. Clarke, who was then and had for years been one of the most prominent and enterprising business men of Omaha, one of the branches of business in which he was engaged being wholesale drugs, concluded that Lincoln offered better advantages for the wholesale trade, and consequently changed his place of business in that line to this city.

For the accommodation of this business Mr. Clarke erected, at the corner of Eighth and P streets, a magnificent four-story brick and stone building, 100 by 150 feet, in which a heavy stock of drugs was placed, and business commenced. The firm of the H. T. Clarke Drug Company is composed of the following gentlemen: Hon. H. T. Clarke, John C. Clarke, W. E. Clarke, W. C. Mills, and Charles J. Daubach, all gentlemen of business experience and ability. Ever since the opening of this house its business has been steadily growing,

THE CLARKE DRUG HOUSE.

until now it amounts to more than a half million per year. It is one of the institutions of which Lincoln is proud.

Among the early business men should be mentioned Pflug Bros., Martin and Jacob, who were merchants here in 1868 and for several years later. They were active workers for the good of the city.

The work of Elder J. M. Young, W. T. Donovan, Milton Langdon, Seth P. Galey, and John Cadman, has been referred to elsewhere.

No man deserves more credit for good work in building up the moral and social interests of the city than Elder Henry T. Davis, now pastor of Trinity M. E. church, and who has been in the ministry in this county longer than any other man now here. His brother, Mr. A. M. Davis, now conducting a wholesale and retail carpet house at 1112 O street, has for many years aided to push the interests of the city forward. Mrs. A. M. Davis has also been and still is a leader in the cause of charity and humanity.

Messrs. Austin and Oliver N. Humphrey, of the Humphrey Bros. Hardware Company, have been leading builders up of the city for twenty years. Dr. H. G. Gilbert established a drug and hardware store at 101 North Ninth street late in 1867, under the firm name of Hawley, Gilbert & Co. In the spring of 1869 Humphrey Bros. bought the hardware interest of Mr. Hawley, and in the fall of that year bought out Dr. Gilbert, since which time it has been Humphrey Bros., and the Humphrey Hardware Company, the latter company having been incorporated in 1881, when C. J. Heffley became a member. The elegant four-story brick block at 101 and 103 North Ninth street, and their large wholesale and retail implement and hardware trade, attests their success. They are ever ready to aid public enterprises, Mr. Austin Humphrey being a prominent officer in the State Agricultural Society and a member of the city Board of Public Works. Mrs. O. N. Humphrey is a prominent worker in the charities and social progress of the city.

Bohanan Brothers, M. G. and F. H., have been active builders of the city from pioneer days, having been leading business men since 1868. They have conducted their meat market at 937 O street since that date, and their livery barn at 221 South Tenth street for many years. Their brick block, on the southwest corner of Tenth and N, is one of the largest in the city. It was built in 1887, and forms only a part of their possessions.

T. P. Kennard and John Gillespie helped found the city, and have ever been active in building it up, Mr. Kennard now being a director in the city Board of Trade.

Few men have done more to build the city than J. J. Butler, who erected the first brick block in Lincoln, and who has built more blocks than any other man in the place, with one or two exceptions. He now owns two brick blocks, and has commenced the erection of a third. He is a prominent member of the Irish National League, having been president of the Lincoln Branch.

Fred Funke, builder of the Funke Opera House, James Ledwith, proprietor of the Ledwith Block at P and Eleventh, and J. L. McConnell, have contributed to the material prosperity of the city.

W. H. B. Stout is one of the largest building contractors of the State, and has handled very extensive business interests during the past seventeen years. He was elected a member of the State Legislature in 1868, from Blair, took the contract to build the State Penitentiary in 1870, in connection with J. M. Jamison, and removed to Lincoln in 1871. In 1877 he became the lessee of the State Penitentiary for six years. He built the Burlington passenger depot, the county jail, and the present State Capitol, completing the latter on the first of the present year. He has been interested in other large building contracts, and is now engaged in making paving brick and laying the same on the streets of Lincoln, Stout & Buckstaff having contracts for several districts. Probably no man has done more for Lincoln than W. H. B. Stout.

Gran. Ensign is a pioneer business man, having been in the livery and transfer business here since 1869, and been very successful. His interests have grown from a small shed back of the Atwood House on Ninth street, to the large brick structure at 215 to 221 South Eleventh.

Raymond Bros. & Co., wholesale grocers, established in Lincoln in 1872, and have been among our leading business men ever since. The firm consists of I. M. and A. S. Raymond, and G. H. Clark. They have done more to push Lincoln trade into new territory, and protect Lincoln's interests against railroad discriminations, than any other firm. They are now leading capitalists of the city, and prominent in pushing its interests. Their large house at O and Eighth, does an immense jobbing trade.

In this connection should be mentioned Plummer, Perry & Co., wholesale grocers, at 109-113 North Ninth street. This firm is composed of Eli Plummer, R. A. Perry, and John Fitzgerald, and is very popular and successful. The gentlemen composing this firm are among the most liberal and enterprising in Lincoln, always ready to contribute aid to the success of the city. Mr. Plummer is a leading member of the Board of Trade.

H. P. Lau & Co., wholesale grocers, in the Clarke Block, on the corner of Eighth and P streets, do a growing wholesale jobbing trade, and deserve an honorable place in the list of our large business houses. Mr. Lau is a leading capitalist of our city.

No jobbing house has been more successful, all things considered, than the wholesale grocery of Hargreaves Bros., on the southwest corner of O and Eighth streets. The firm is composed of A. E. and W. B. Hargreaves, and their business was begun in 1874, with a capital of $28. Now they have a large brick block there, and do an extensive business. They are among the most enterprising of our citizens in protecting the welfare of the city.

J. A. Buckstaff, Secretary and Treasurer of the Badger Lumber Company, is one of the foremost business men of Lincoln. He conducts a large lumber trade, is engaged in manufacturing paving brick, and is connected with extensive paving contracts. He is ever liberal and enterprising in aiding to build the city.

L. W. Billingsley is a pioneer attorney of the city, has built up a large practice, and is now senior member of the law firm of Billingsley & Woodward. His elegant brick block at 210 South Eleventh street is one of the fine structures of the city. He has been prominently connected with the business and growth of the city for twenty years, having served in the City Council repeatedly.

C. E. Montgomery, whose business block adjoins the Billingsley block, at the corner of Eleventh and N streets, is one of our most enterprising citizens. Examples of his help in building up Lincoln are seen in his block just referred to, Odell's restaurant next east, and the elegant livery stable erected at a cost of $16,000 on M street, south side, between Eleventh and Twelfth.

T. H. Hyde, of the Lincoln *News* Company, is a pioneer in the city, and no one loves to lend encouragement to the city's growth better than he.

Messrs. C. H. Gere and H. D. Hathaway, of the *State Journal*, have been closely identified with nearly every important step in the city's development, almost from its location, and deserve great credit for their work in giving Lincoln one of the best newspapers west of Chicago.

Amasa Cobb assisted to found the First National Bank, and has always been an useful citizen. He is now a member of the State Supreme Court.

John R. Clark, President of the First National Bank, and Secretary of the *State Journal* Company, is an useful and enterprising citizen, who has extended a helping hand to nearly all important public enterprises for the benefit of the city.

T. M. Marquett has practiced law in Lancaster and Lincoln for twenty-six years, though for the first few years a resident of Plattsmouth. He has always been a man of broad views in matters of public interest, and has worthily earned a leading position in the city as one of its best, wisest, and most useful citizens, an able lawyer and orator, and a man of great public experience.

John H. Ames, is one of the pioneers, an able lawyer, and a man who has been conspicuous in pushing the city.

N. S. Harwood is a prominent financier, capitalist, and attorney of the city, and a leading citizen.

R. H. Oakley, now President of the Board of Trade, has proven a very strong man in that position, and through his energy, tact, and wisdom, the board is in the best business condition it ever has been in, and its work for the prosperity of the city has been most commendable.

T. W. Lowrey is a very extensive grain dealer, a capitalist, and an enterprising citizen, always ready to help in pushing the city's welfare. He is a prominent member of the Board of Trade.

H. J. Walsh has been identified with the city's business interests from an early day. He built the Academy of Music block, at the southwest corner of O and Eleventh streets, in company with Israel Putnam, in 1873 and 1882. He is prominently connected with the Lincoln Gas Company, and has been, almost from its organization, a leading stockholder. He has been a member of the City Council, and has served on the Board of Trustees of the Asylum for the Blind He was one of the trustees of the city of Lincoln when the corporation was organized, in 1869.

J. Z. Briscoe is one of the most liberal citizens of Lincoln, and one of the most useful men in both business and general progress. The successful founding of the Christian College owes much to his liberality, courage, wisdom, and industry. He gave the institution $25,000. He has been a member of the City Council, and is always a generous and useful worker for the city's interest, both material and moral.

Frank L. Sheldon has helped greatly in building the city, having been a founder of the street railway service. He erected during 1887-8 the elegant block on the southwest corner of N and Eleventh, the block adjoining the Windsor Hotel on the south, and his elegant residence at Fourteenth and R streets. He ranks among our most enterprising business men.

W. W. Wilson has from the beginning been a faithful worker for the good of the capital city. He, with W. H. B. Stout and T. F. Barnes, built the City Block, on the northwest corner of N and Eleventh streets.

T. F. Barnes, builder of the Windsor Hotel, is a man of nerve, such as it takes to found a city. His energy is witnessed in the brick walls of more than one block.

John R. Webster's enterprise is to some degree witnessed in the Webster Block, north of Temple Hall, on South Eleventh. He has been an industrious builder of the city for many years.

J. H. McMurtry has had few if any superiors as an energetic, courageous citizen in developing the progress of Lincoln, where he has lived for seventeen years. He has ever been ready with means, counsel, and labor, to advertise the city's merits, push home enterprise, and has not feared to cast his fortunes with the city. He erected the brick block where the county offices and court rooms now are, on the west side of South Eleventh, near M. His faith in and work for Lincoln has been rewarded in the development of extensive property interests within and without the limits of the place.

C. C. and L. C. Burr have erected a splendid monument to their industry and business courage in the magnificent Burr Block, at the northeast corner of O and Twelfth streets. Architecturally this is, perhaps, the handsomest building in Nebraska, being six stories in height exclusive of the basement, of rustic-stone finish, and beautifully designed in every detail.

S. B. Pound was one of the very earliest merchants on the site of this city, and he became one of its earliest attorneys, and until recently was a very popular District Judge. He has ever been a respected and excellent citizen since the foundation of the city.

J. R. and L. C. Richards are among the city's leading capitalists, and their prominence as builders of the city is marked by the elegant block which bears their name at the northeast corner of O and Eleventh streets.

A. D. Kitchen is a prominent contributor to the city's growth, being now engaged in building two or three fine brick blocks on O street, between Fifteenth and Sixteenth. He has lent a helping hand in developing Lincoln in many other respects.

J. C. McBride has been a courageous and energetic citizen in the city's interests for years, having been liberal with means and ready with other assistance and encouragement. He has been postmaster of the city, twice a member of the Legislature, and prominently identified with the work of the Board of Trade. He has a fine brick block at the northeast corner of P and Twelfth streets.

Dr. Latta is now completing an elegant block of red sand-stone at 129 South Eleventh. When done it will be one of the finest in the city. It is in room four of this block that this history of Lincoln was written.

John Zehrung has been an active citizen, his brick block at 1213 and 1219 O street being an evidence of his substantial work as a builder of the city.

O. P. Mason and C. O. Whedon are a firm of attorneys about as widely known as any in Nebraska. Judge Mason was on the supreme bench in 1866, and was a distinguished Secretary of the State Board of Transportation, previous to the present year, for two years. C. O. Whedon was a member of the House of the State Legislature during the Sixteenth, Seventeenth, and Eighteenth sessions, and has held various public positions in the city. Both men have been active and influential citizens throughout much of the city's history.

A genuinely earnest builder of the financial, moral, and intellectual features of the city's prosperity, is C. C. Munson. He is a worker with purse, hand, and heart, for the general good. He is building up a large wholesale lumber and lime trade, is helping to erect the Christian University, is a director in the German National Bank, and an active worker in the Board of Trade.

Prominent, earnest, and valuable, workers for the city's development, in the present Board of Trade, are: Joseph Boehmer, C. J. Ernst, Mason Gregg, M. L. Trester, A. H. Weir, C. T. Brown, C. A. Atkinson, and C. W. Mosher.

C. H. Hutchins has erected two fine brick blocks in the past two years, one on Ninth near N, and the other on O near Fifteenth.

Dr. W. G. Houtz has proven himself a valuable and enterprising citizen and builder of the city.

W. R. Kelley, John Doolittle, Hon. E. P. Roggen, A. Hurlbut, H. H. Dean, John Burks, J. H. Harley, and John J. Gillilan, have all shown enterprise and energy, and have done good service as city builders.

J. E. Utt, who, as the very able Secretary of the Board of Trade during 1887-8 was mainly instrumental in securing equitable freight tariffs for Lincoln from Pacific Coast points, rendered the city and State a great and lasting service. He is now interested in the paper mill located in the southwest part of the city.

John Morrison, who was the earliest tailor in the city, except Christian F. Damrow, having been here since 1869, is still doing a good business at 121 North Eleventh. He is one of the popular pioneers.

Few men have had more genuine success than H. H. Schaberg. Beginning as a blacksmith, with his industry and persistent attention to business, in a little shop on the southeast corner of Eleventh and P streets, in 1869, he has hammered his way up to the possession of the brick block on that corner, the presidency of the German National Bank, and a place among the large capitalists of the city. His success shows what men can do in Lincoln who work and use their opportunities.

John B. Wright has been a citizen of Lincoln for fourteen years, having originally come from Rochester, New York, where he was born in 1847. He is one of the largest dealers in grain in this city or State, being interested in forty-two different elevators in Nebraska and Kansas. He makes a specialty of handling flax seed. He has enlarged and improved his big elevator at M and Eighth streets this season, preparatory to opening the immense fall business he will have to manage. He has ever been an active citizen of Lincoln. He was elected Mayor of the city both in 1880 and 1881, and was a member of the House of the State Legislature of the Nineteenth session in

1883. He is now a leading member of the Board of Trade, and did good work in placing the board upon the excellent working basis on which it now stands.

H. W. Hardy, now editor of the *New Republic*, has been twice Mayor of the city, but is most distinguished as the Lincoln William Lloyd Garrison, fighting in favor of temperance, morals, and the improvement of the social welfare of men. He is an uncompromising warrior for the principles of purity and progress, and is the best known character in Nebraska in that work, except alone the late John B. Finch.

Elder P. W. Howe, Chaplain of the State penitentiary and City Missionary, is the executive officer of the City Relief and aid Society, an organization designed to help and protect the weak, needy, and helpless, especially women and children. He is doing a noble work, having followed this line of benevolent service for nine years in New York city, and nearly as many in Lincoln.

Albert Watkins, for nearly four years past, has been postmaster of Lincoln, and a public-spirited citizen. General Victor Vifquain, having founded the *Daily State Democrat* in 1879, Mr. Watkins bought it in 1882 and continued its editor until appointed postmaster, in November, 1885, though Mr. Vifquain bought an interest in 1884. The paper passed into the hands of J. D. Calhoun in August of 1886, who conducted it successfully for two years.

Palmer Way was probably the first tinner of Lincoln, and one of the first hardware men. He has been a business man of the city for twenty-two years.

R. C. Outcalt, cashier of the Capital National Bank, is the oldest banker of Lincoln, Nelson C. Brock excepted. He first entered the bank of Sweet & Brock, in 1870, and has been continuously connected with the banking business in the city ever since. He is one of the best posted financiers of Lincoln.

Hundreds of other men might be named, whose influence and wealth have, for varying periods of years, been used toward making Lincoln what she is to-day; but enough have been given to show that Lincoln's growth has been, in part at least, the result of the faith in her future held by her citizens. Future years will undoubtedly show a continuation of the wonderful progress made by the city in the past twenty-two years. Such, at least, are the signs of the times.

ERRATUM — On page 151, under cut of Sweet's Block, read "Northeast corner of O and Tenth."

LINDELL·HOTEL,

THE MOST SELECT HOTEL IN THE CITY.

A. L. HOOVER & SON, PROPRIETORS.

Corner 13th & M Streets,   LINCOLN, NEBRASKA.

Take 13th Street Car Line from B. & M. Depot, and 10th Street Line from M. P. & F. E. & M. V. Depot

JOHN MORRISON,
MERCHANT TAILOR,

121 North Eleventh Street,   LINCOLN, NEBRASKA.

THE FINEST LINE OF

FOREIGN AND DOMESTIC SUITINGS ALWAYS ON HAND.

SATISFACTION GUARANTEED.

J. B. TRICKEY & CO.

IMPORTERS OF

DIAMONDS.

WHOLESALE AND RETAIL DEALERS IN

All American Watches, Jewelry, Clocks, Solid Silver Ware, Etc.

1035 O STREET, LINCOLN, NEB.

S. J. ODELL.
DINING HALL

1121 N Street.

*The Best Appointed and Most Popular Dining Hall in the West.
Elegant Service and Seasonable Menu.*

Terms for Table Board, $4.50 per Week.   Single Meals, 25 Cents.

J. M. MARKELL & SON,

JEWELERS.

Watches, Clocks, Jewelry, Diamonds, Etc.

FINE WORK A SPECIALTY.

Zehrung Block, 143 South 12th St.   LINCOLN, NEB.

P. J. KENNEDY,

No. 135 North Twelfth Street.

ABSOLUTELY PURE, UNADULTERATED

WINES, WHISKEYS, AND BRANDIES,

FOR FAMILY MEDICINAL USE.

ALL GOODS GUARANTEED AS REPRESENTED.

ALL THE BEST BRANDS OF RYE AND BOURBON.

FINCH'S GOLDEN WEDDING RYE A SPECIALTY.

Genuine Cognac Brandy, and Imported Ports and Sherries.

CARR
SOAP
WORKS

LINCOLN, NEBRASKA.

MANUFACTURER OF

LAUNDRY, BATH, AND TOILET SOAP.

✦ HOTEL SOAP ✦

(ANY SIZE)

Made to Order with Name of House Imprinted on each Cake.

G. B. SKINNER

Owner of SKINNER'S BARN.

Livery, Feed, and Boarding Stables.

DEALER IN FANCY HORSES.

Turns out the Most Stylish Single or Double Rigs in the West. The Prices are made so Reasonable that it is cheaper to hire of Skinner than to keep a Rig of your own.

JAMES C. KIER.
THE HATTER AND FURNISHER.
AGENCY FOR
KNOX WORLD RENOWNED HATS.

Cor. O and 11th Streets.   LINCOLN, NEBRASKA.

N. S. HARWOOD.   JOHN H. AMES.   W. R. KELLEY.

HARWOOD, AMES & KELLEY,
ATTORNEYS AT LAW

Attorneys and Directors of Lincoln National Bank.
145 SOUTH 11TH ST., LINCOLN, NEB.

FARMERS AND MERCHANTS INSURANCE CO.,
LINCOLN, NEB.
FARM AND RESIDENCE PROPERTY A SPECIALTY.

CAPITAL, $100,000.00.   ASSETS, JAN. 1, 1889, $229,342.06.
SURPLUS, AS REGARDS POLICY HOLDERS, $227,500.67.

Elite Studio

226 South Eleventh Street, Lincoln, Neb.   Ground Floor.
T. W. TOWNSEND, Prop.
Photographs, Crayons, and Bromides, finished in the Latest Style of Art.

Fremont, Elkhorn and Missouri Valley
Railroad
—IN—

NEBRASKA,

THE BLACK HILLS

—AND—

CENTRAL WYOMING.

IN CONNECTION WITH THE

Chicago & Northwestern, and the Chicago, St. Paul, Minneapolis & Omaha R. R.

IS THE

Direct Passenger and Fast Freight Line

BETWEEN

Lincoln, Omaha, Hastings,

The Black Hills and Central Wyoming,

—AND—

Chicago, St. Paul, Milwaukee, Minneapolis,

AND ALL POINTS

North, East and West

H. G. BURT,   K. C. MOREHOUSE,   J. R. BUCHANAN,
Gen'l Manager.   G. F. Agent.   Gen'l Pass. Agent.

OMAHA, NEB.

THE PIONEER LINE,

—AND—

NEBRASKA'S

FAVORITE ROUTE,

——OFFERING——

THE BEST LOCAL SERVICE,

—AND RUNNING—

Pullman Palace Sleepers,
Free Reclining Chair Cars,
Pullman Dining Cars,
And Modern Day Coaches.

❧ THE DIRECT LINE TO DENVER ❦

——AND——

ALL COLORADO, KANSAS, WYOMING, UTAH, IDAHO, OREGON, CALIFORNIA, WASHINGTON, AND PUGET SOUND POINTS.

QUICK TIME.
UNEQUALED ACCOMMODATIONS.   MAGNIFICENT SCENERY.

For Rates, Pamphlets, and other information, apply to

E. B. SLOSSON, City Ticket Agent,

1044 O Street, LINCOLN, NEB.

THOS. L. KIMBALL,   C. S. MELLEN,   E. L. LOMAX,
General Manager.   Traffic Manager.   Gen'l Pass. Agent.

OMAHA, NEB.

www.ingramcontent.com/pod-product-compliance
Lightning Source LLC
Chambersburg PA
CBHW031413230426
43668CB00007B/297